SOCIAL STUDIES
Growth of Our Nation

myWorld INTERACTIVE

5

SAVVAS
LEARNING COMPANY

Savvas would like to extend a special thank you to all of the teachers who helped guide the development of this program. We gratefully acknowledge your efforts to realize the possibilities of elementary Social Studies teaching and learning. Together, we will prepare students for college, careers, and civic life.

ISBN-13: 978-0-328-98725-2

ISBN-10:   0-328-98725-5

7 20

Program Authors

Dr. Linda B. Bennett
Faculty, Social Studies Education
College of Education
University of Missouri
Columbia, MO

Dr. James B. Kracht
Professor Emeritus
Departments of Geography and
  Teaching, Learning, and Culture
Texas A&M University
College Station, TX

Reviewers and Consultants

Program Consultants

ELL Consultant
Jim Cummins Ph.D.

Professor Emeritus,
Department of
  Curriculum, Teaching,
  and Learning
University of Toronto
Toronto, Canada

**Differentiated Instruction
Consultant**

Kathy Tuchman Glass
President of Glass
  Educational Consulting
Woodside, CA

Reading Consultant
Elfrieda H. Hiebert Ph.D.

Founder, President and
  CEO, TextProject, Inc.
University of California
  Santa Cruz

Inquiry and C3 Consultant

Dr. Kathy Swan
Professor of Curriculum
  and Instruction
University of Kentucky
Lexington, KY

Academic Reviewers

Paul Apodaca, Ph.D.

Associate Professor,
  American Studies
Chapman University
Orange, CA

Warren J. Blumenfeld, Ed.D.

Former Associate
  Professor, Iowa State
  University, School
  of Education
South Hadley, MA

Dr. Albert M. Camarillo

Professor of History,
  Emeritus
Stanford University
Palo Alto, CA

Dr. Shirley A. James Hanshaw

Professor, Department
  of English
Mississippi State
  University
Mississippi State, MS

Xiaojian Zhao

Professor, Department
  of Asian American
  Studies
University of California,
  Santa Barbara
Santa Barbara, CA

Teacher Reviewers

Mercedes Kirk
First grade teacher
Folsom Cordova USD
Folsom, CA

Julie Martire
Teacher, Grade 5
Flocktown Elementary School
Long Valley, NJ

Kristy H. Spears
K-5 Reading Specialist
Pleasant Knoll Elementary School
Fort Mill, SC

Kristin Sullens
Teacher, Grade 4
Chula Vista ESD
San Diego, CA

Program Partner

Campaign for the Civic Mission of Schools is a coalition of
over 70 national civic learning, education, civic engagement,
and business groups committed to improving the quality and
quantity of civic learning in American schools.

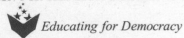
CAMPAIGN FOR THE CIVIC MISSION OF SCHOOLS
Educating for Democracy

🌐 Geography Skills Handbook

✏️ Writing Workshop

🔍 Using Primary and Secondary Sources

Chapter 9 Civil War and Reconstruction

GO ONLINE FOR DIGITAL RESOURCES

 eTEXT

 VIDEO

- **Field Trip Video**
  Gettysburg National Battlefield: Fighting for a Cause
- **Digital Skill Practice**
  Make Decisions
  Classify and Categorize

🔊 AUDIO

Rap About It! lyrics and music

👆 INTERACTIVITY

- **Big Question Activity**
  What is worth fighting for?
- **Quest Interactivities**
  Quest Kick Off
  Quest Connections
  Quest Findings
- **Lesson Interactivities**
  Lesson Introduction
  Key Ideas
  Lesson Review

🎮 GAMES

Vocabulary Practice

☑ ASSESSMENT

Lesson Quizzes and Chapter Tests

The BIG Question What is worth fighting for?

GO ONLINE FOR
DIGITAL RESOURCES

  eTEXT

▶ VIDEO

- **Field Trip Video**
Hometead National
Monument: A
Tribute to American
Pioneers
- **Digital Skill
Practice**
Interpret Graphs
Predict
Consequences

  AUDIO

Rap About It! lyrics
and music

👆 INTERACTIVITY

- **Big Question
Activity**
How did different
groups experience
the growth of the
nation?
- **Quest
Interactivities**
Quest Kick Off
Quest Connections
Quest Findings
- **Lesson
Interactivities**
Lesson Introduction
Key Ideas
Lesson Review

🎮 GAMES

Vocabulary Practice

  ASSESSMENT

Lesson Quizzes and
Chapter Tests

vi

The **BIG** Question How did different groups experience the growth of the nation?

Chapter 11 Industry and Immigration

GO ONLINE FOR DIGITAL RESOURCES

 eTEXT

▶ VIDEO

- **Field Trip Video**
  Ellis Island: A Doorway to America
- **Digital Skill Practice**
  Predict Consequences
  Give an Effective Presentation

 AUDIO

Rap About It! lyrics and music

👆 INTERACTIVITY

- **Big Question Activity**
  What are the costs and benefits of growth?
- **Quest Interactivities**
  Quest Kick Off
  Quest Connections
  Quest Findings
- **Lesson Interactivities**
  Lesson Introduction
  Key Ideas
  Lesson Review

🎮 GAMES

Vocabulary Practice

☑ ASSESSMENT

Lesson Quizzes and Chapter Tests

The BIG Question What are the costs and benefits of growth?

Chapter 12 Struggle for Reform

GO ONLINE FOR DIGITAL RESOURCES

 eTEXT

 VIDEO

- **Field Trip Video**
  Reformers Work for Change
- **Digital Skill Practice**
  Solve Problems
  Use Primary and Secondary Sources

🔊 AUDIO

Rap About It! lyrics and music

👆 INTERACTIVITY

- **Big Question Activity**
  When does change become necessary?
- **Quest Interactivities**
  Quest Kick Off
  Quest Connections
  Quest Findings
- **Lesson Interactivities**
  Lesson Introduction
  Key Ideas
  Lesson Review

🎮 GAMES

Vocabulary Practice

 ASSESSMENT

Lesson Quizzes and Chapter Tests

The BIG Question: When does change become necessary?

Chapter 13 Good Times and Hardships

GO ONLINE FOR DIGITAL RESOURCES

 eTEXT

VIDEO

- **Field Trip Video** Warm Springs, Georgia: FDR's Little White House
- **Digital Skill Practice** Using Primary and Secondary Sources Generate New Ideas

 AUDIO

Rap About It! lyrics and music

 INTERACTIVITY

- **Big Question Activity** How do people respond to good times and bad times?
- **Quest Interactivities** Quest Kick Off Quest Connections Quest Findings
- **Lesson Interactivities** Lesson Introduction Key Ideas Lesson Review

GAMES

Vocabulary Practice

ASSESSMENT

Lesson Quizzes and Chapter Tests

The BIG Question How do people respond to good times and bad times?

Chapter 14 World War II

GO ONLINE FOR DIGITAL RESOURCES

 eTEXT

▶ VIDEO

- **Field Trip Video** World War II: Those Who Were There
- **Digital Skill Practice** Analyze Images Draw Conclusions

🔊 AUDIO

Rap About It! lyrics and music

 INTERACTIVITY

- **Big Question Activity** What is worth fighting for?
- **Quest Interactivities** Quest Kick Off Quest Connections Quest Findings
- **Lesson Interactivities** Lesson Introduction Key Ideas Lesson Review

🎮 GAMES

Vocabulary Practice

☑ ASSESSMENT

Lesson Quizzes and Chapter Tests

The **BIG** Question What is worth fighting for?

GO ONLINE FOR
DIGITAL RESOURCES

 eTEXT

▶ **VIDEO**

- **Field Trip Video**
  Kennedy Space
  Center: Exploring
  Space

- **Digital Skill
  Practice**
  Identify Bias

◀)) **AUDIO**

Rap About It! lyrics
and music

 INTERACTIVITY

- **Big Question
  Activity**
  What are the
  responsibilities of
  power?

- **Quest
  Interactivities**
  Quest Kick Off
  Quest Connections
  Quest Findings

- **Lesson
  Interactivities**
  Lesson Introduction
  Key Ideas
  Lesson Review

🎮 **GAMES**

Vocabulary Practice

☑ **ASSESSMENT**

Lesson Quizzes and
Chapter Tests

The **BIG** Question **What are the responsibilities of power?**

GO ONLINE FOR
DIGITAL RESOURCES

📖 eTEXT

▶ VIDEO

- **Field Trip Video**
National Voting
Rights Museum
Making a Difference
- **Digital Skill
Practice**
Work in Cooperative
Teams

🔊 AUDIO

Rap About It! lyrics
and music

👆 INTERACTIVITY

- **Big Question
Activity**
When does change
become necessary?
- **Quest
Interactivities**
Quest Kick Off
Quest Connections
Quest Findings
- **Lesson
Interactivities**
Lesson Introduction
Key Ideas
Lesson Review

🎮 GAMES

Vocabulary Practice

✅ ASSESSMENT

Lesson Quizzes and
Chapter Tests

The **BIG** Question When does change become necessary?

Chapter 17 Our Nation and the World Today

GO ONLINE FOR DIGITAL RESOURCES

 eTEXT

 VIDEO

- **Field Trip Video**
  New York City: A Memorial to 9/11
- **Digital Skill Practice**
  Evaluate Media Content

🔊 AUDIO

Rap About It! Lyrics and music

👆 INTERACTIVITY

- **Big Question Activity**
  What goals should we set for our nation?
- **Quest Activities**
  Quest Kick Off
  Quest Connections
  Quest Findings
- **Lesson Interactivities**
  Lesson Introduction
  Key Ideas
  Lesson Review

 GAMES

Vocabulary Practice

✅ ASSESSMENT

Lesson Quizzes and Chapter Tests

The BIG Question What goals should we set for our nation?

Quests

Ask questions, explore sources, and cite evidence to support your view!

Maps

Where did this happen? Find out on these maps in your text.

Maps continued

Maps continued

Graphs and Charts

Find these charts, graphs, and tables in your text. They will help you pull it together.

Graphs and Charts continued

Primary Sources

Read the primary sources to hear voices from the time.

Primary Sources continued

Primary Sources continued

People to Know

Read about the people who made history.

Citizenship

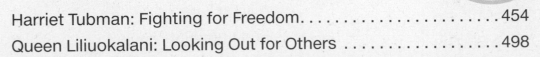

People to Know continued

Biographies Online

Abigail Adams

John Adams

Samuel Adams

Elsie Allen

James Armistead

Benedict Arnold

Clara Barton

Delilah Beasley

James Beckwourth

Chaz Bono

William Bradford

Sergey Brin

Jerry Brown

Edmund Burke

Juan Rodriguez Cabrillo

Tani Gorre Cantil-Sakauye

Christopher "Kit" Carson

César Chávez

Louise Clappe

Thomas Clifford

Christopher Columbus

Hernán Cortés

Juan Crespi

Charles Crocker

Hallie M. Daggett

Juan Bautista de Anza

Pedro Menéndez de Avilés

Samuel de Champlain

Gaspar de Portolá

Antonio Lopez de Santa Anna

María Angustias de la Guerra

Bartolomeu Dias

John Dickinson

Walt Disney

Frederick Douglass

Ralph Waldo Emerson

William Fargo

First Lady Pat Nixon

Wong Chin Foo

People to Know continued

Benjamin Franklin

John C. Fremont

Eric Garcetti

John Gast

Nathan Hale

Alexander Hamilton

John Hancock

Kamala D. Harris

Mary Ludwig Hays

Patrick Henry

Mark Hopkins

Henry Hudson

Dolores Huerta

Collis P. Huntington

Anne Hutchinson

Daniel Inouye

Joseph James

Thomas Jefferson

Hiram Johnson

Billie Jean King

Dr. Martin Luther King Jr.

King Charles III

King George III

Dorothea Lange

Lewis and Clark

Abraham Lincoln

Henry Wadsworth Longfellow

Lord Dunmore

Ferdinand Magellan

Wilma Mankiller

James Wilson Marshall

John Marshall

Biddy Mason

Louis B. Mayer

Sylvia Mendez

Metacom

Harvey Milk

James Monroe

Samuel Morse

John Muir

Nicolás José

Thomas Paine

Charley Parkhurst

William Penn

William Pitt

James K. Polk

Prince Henry the Navigator

Edmund Randolph

Ronald Reagan

Paul Revere

Sally Ride

Jackie Robinson

Eleanor Roosevelt

Sarah Royce

Bernarda Ruiz

Sacagawea

Haym Salomon

Deborah Sampson

José Julio Sarria

Dalip Singh Saund

Junípero Serra

Roger Sherman

People to Know continued

Sir Francis Drake

John Drake Sloat

Jedediah Smith

John Smith

Leland Stanford

John Steinbeck

Levi Strauss

John A. Sutter

Mary Tape

Archie Thompson

Tisquantum

Harriet Tubman

Mariano Guadalupe Vallejo

Earl Warren

Mercy Otis Warren

George Washington

Henry Wells

Phillis Wheatley

Narcissa Whitman

Roger Williams

Sarah Winnemucca

John Winthrop

Jerry Yang

Skills

Practice key skills in these skills lessons.

Literacy Skills

Critical Thinking Skills

Map and Graph Skills

Skills Online

Analyze Cause and Effect

Analyze Costs and Benefits

Analyze Images

Ask and Answer Questions

Classify and Categorize

Compare and Contrast

Compare Viewpoints

Conduct Research

Create Charts

Deliver an Effective Presentation

Distinguish Fact and Opinion

Distinguish Fact From Fiction

Draw Conclusions

Draw Inferences

Evaluate Media Content

Generalize

Generate New Ideas

Identify Bias

Identify Main Idea and Details

Interpret Cultural Data on Maps

Skills continued

Interpret Economic Data on Maps

Interpret Graphs

Interpret Physical Maps

Interpret Timelines

Make Decisions

Predict Consequences

Resolve Conflict

Sequence

Solve Problems

Summarize

Use and Interpret Evidence

Use Latitude and Longitude

Use Primary and Secondary Sources

Use the Internet Safely

Work in Cooperative Teams

Welcome to Your Book!

**Your Worktext is made up of chapters and lessons.
Each lesson starts with pages like this.**

Look for these
words as you read.

Words with yellow highlight are important social
studies words. The sentence with the word will
help you understand what the word means.

Christopher Columbus was a man who made bold
plans. He was from the Genoa region of Italy. Columbus
wanted to find a new route to Asia by sailing west across the
Atlantic Ocean. Columbus had a lot of courage but not much
money for the voyage. He had to find someone to pay for this
dangerous trip.

Lesson 2 — Explorers for Spain

INTERACTIVITY
Participate in a class discussion to preview the content of this lesson.

Unlock The BIG Question
I will know why Spain sent explorers to new lands.

INTERACTIVITY
Explore the key ideas of this lesson.

Vocabulary

patron
conquistador
expedition
empire
colony
epidemic

Academic Vocabulary

organized
demolish

JumPstart Activity

With a partner, discuss reasons why you would travel
to a new place. What risks are involved? Make a list of
the reasons and risks, and then choose one example
of each to act out for the class.

Columbus and his crew set sail from Spain in 1492,
hoping to discover a new route to Asia.

Christopher Columbus

Columbus asked Portugal's king to pay for his voyage.
The king turned down Columbus's request. Columbus did
not give up. He decided to ask Spain's rulers. Columbus told
them that he would bring Christianity to the people of Asia,
and he would bring back riches for Spain. It took several
requests, but King Ferdinand and Queen Isabella finally
agreed to become Columbus's patrons. A **patron** gives
money to support another person or cause.

The Spanish rulers hoped to earn money from the gold
and spices that Columbus expected to trade for in Asia. They
needed money to pay for a war that Spain had recently
fought. Spain was a Catholic country. Ferdinand and
Isabella had just restored Christianity to their lands after
the *Reconquista*. During the *Reconquista* ("reconquering"),
the Spanish had pushed Muslims out of the southern part of
the Iberian Peninsula after a struggle that lasted more than
700 years.

Columbus sailed from Spain with about 90 men on three
different ships. The crew started off very hopeful and excited
for their new journey, but after five weeks at sea, they
became tired and weak. After traveling close to 4,500 miles,
they spotted land and reached shore on October 12, 1492.
Wanting to document the discovery, Columbus wrote:

Primary Source

The crew . . . saw signs of land, and a small branch
covered with berries. Everyone breathed afresh and
rejoiced at these signs.

-Christopher Columbus, *Journal of the
First Voyage of Christopher Columbus,* 1492

1. ✓ Reading Check
Turn and talk with a
partner about why you
think Columbus wrote
that "everyone breathed
afresh and rejoiced."
Ask your partner
other questions about
Columbus's journal.

Reading Checks will help you make
sure you understood what you read.

Your Turn!

Flip through your book with a partner.

1. Find the start of another lesson.
   What do you see on the page?

This book will give you a lot of chances to figure things out. Then you can show what you have figured out and give your reasons.

The Quest Kick Off will tell you the goal of the Quest.

Watch for Quest Connections all through the chapter.

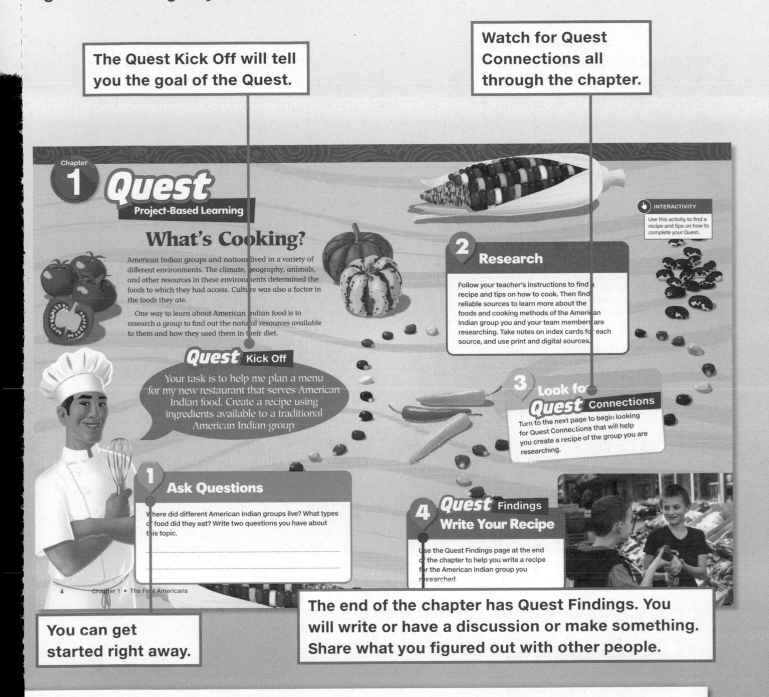

Chapter 1

Quest
Project-Based Learning

What's Cooking?

American Indian groups and nations lived in a variety of different environments. The climate, geography, animals, and other resources in these environments determined the foods to which they had access. Culture was also a factor in the foods they ate.

One way to learn about American Indian food is to research a group to find out the natural resources available to them and how they used them in their diet.

Quest Kick Off

Your task is to help me plan a menu for my new restaurant that serves American Indian food. Create a recipe using ingredients available to a traditional American Indian group

INTERACTIVITY
Use this activity to find a recipe and tips on how to complete your Quest.

2 Research

Follow your teacher's instructions to find a recipe and tips on how to cook. Then find reliable sources to learn more about the foods and cooking methods of the American Indian group you and your team members are researching. Take notes on index cards for each source, and use print and digital sources.

3 Look for Quest Connections

Turn to the next page to begin looking for Quest Connections that will help you create a recipe of the group you are researching.

1 Ask Questions

Where did different American Indian groups live? What types of food did they eat? Write two questions you have about this topic.

4 Quest Findings
Write Your Recipe

Use the Quest Findings page at the end of the chapter to help you write a recipe for the American Indian group you researched.

4 Chapter 1 • The First Americans

You can get started right away.

The end of the chapter has Quest Findings. You will write or have a discussion or make something. Share what you figured out with other people.

2. Find two words with yellow highlight. What page are they on?

3. Find another Reading Check. What does it ask you to do?

4. Find another Quest. What is it called?

Learn to use important skills.

> **Read the explanation. Look at all the text and pictures.**

> **Practice the skill. You'll be ready to use it whenever you need it.**

Map and Graph Skills

Interpret Cultural Data on Maps

▶ VIDEO
Watch a video about interpreting cultural data on maps.

Many different American Indian cultural groups lived in the Americas before Europeans arrived in the late 1400s. They all had their own culture, or way of life.

When you examine data on maps, you look at the map key, or legend, to help you understand what you see. Colors, shading, and symbols on a map help you to interpret, or understand, the information that it shows.

What does the legend tell you on this map? _____

_____

Look at the geographic features on the map. These also can help you interpret information. For example, what can you interpret about American Indian groups that lived on the coasts or near lakes? You could determine that living near water affected their way of life. It likely influenced other resources they used in their environment to survive.

American Indian Cultural Groups

LEGEND
Woodlands
Plains
Northwest
Southwest

Your Turn!

1. Locate and circle these American Indian cultural groups on the map. Then choose one group that lived near a body of water and one that did not. Write about how their environment affected the way they lived. Think about how their environment affected their relations with other American Indian groups.

• Pueblo	• Navajo	• Lakota (Sioux)
• Iroquois	• Creek	• Chinook
• Huron	• Hopi	• Nez Perce
• Crow	• Algonquin	• Pawnee

_____

_____

_____

_____

_____

_____

2. In which regions did the cultural groups listed in question 1 live? Complete the chart.

Woodlands			
Great Plains			
Pacific Northwest			
Southwest			

Your Turn!

Work with a partner.

1. Find another skill lesson. What skill will you learn? Talk about another time you might need that skill.

Every chapter has primary source pages. You can read or look at these sources to learn right from people who were there.

Find out what this source is about and who made it.

These questions help you think about the source.

Primary Source

Benjamin Franklin's Final Speech

At the end of the Constitutional Convention, the framers were deeply divided. Some felt that the Constitution should list basic rights. Others believed this was unnecessary.

Benjamin Franklin, while admitting that the Constitution was not perfect, felt that it was as close to perfect as a group of men with varied opinions could create. In this excerpt, Franklin speaks about the strengths of the Constitution.

Vocabulary Support

a well-managed government will always benefit its people

when the people have become so willingly dishonest and unlawful that they require a broken government

sentiments, *n.*, feelings or attitude

despotism, *n.*, system of government where the ruler has unlimited power and the people do not have rights

incapable, *adj.*, unable to achieve something

Benjamin Franklin

Primary Source

"In these Sentiments, Sir, I agree to this Constitution, with all its Faults, if they are such; because I think a General Government necessary for us, and there is no Form of Government but what may be a Blessing to the People if well administered; and I believe farther that this is likely to be well administered for a Course of Years, and can only end in Despotism as other Forms have done before it, when the People shall become so corrupted as to need Despotic Government, being incapable of any other."

–Benjamin Franklin, final speech at the Constitutional Convention, September 17, 1787

Fun Fact

Benjamin Franklin invented a glass musical instrument called an armonica that was used by Beethoven and Mozart.

This is the source.

Close Reading

1. **Identify** and circle the words in the document that describe Benjamin Franklin's overall feelings about government.

2. **Describe** how Franklin feels about the plan for government outlined in the Constitution.

_____

_____

_____

_____

_____

_____

Wrap It Up

Does the Constitution, as it was planned at the end of the Constitutional Convention, provide enough protection of citizens' individual rights? Support your answer with information from the chapter. Use one quotation from the primary source.

_____

_____

_____

_____

_____

_____

_____

_____

_____

Pull it all together.

2. Find another primary source lesson in your book. What is the source about?

Geography Skills Handbook

Five Themes of Geography

Geography is the study of Earth. Your study of geography can be guided by five themes: Location, Place, Human/Environment Interaction, Movement, and Region. These themes help you understand the wide variety of places found on Earth. Each theme reveals something different about a place.

1. ☑ **Reading Check** **Identify** and use the compass rose to list two states that are north of Colorado.

_____

_____

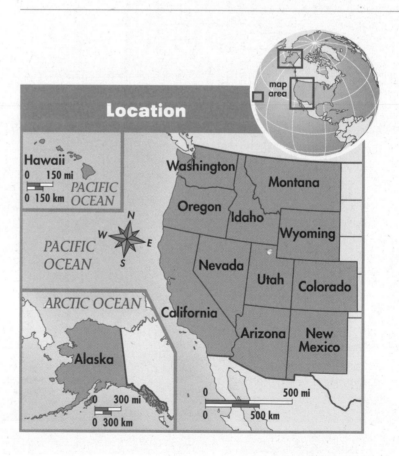

Where can Washington be found within the West region?

A **region** is an area that shares physical or human characteristics. Washington is located in the northern and western part of the West region. It is next to the Pacific Ocean.

| **Place** | **Human/Environment Interaction** |

How is this area different from others?

The United States includes a variety of landforms and bodies of water. A landform is a natural feature of the Earth. Many people enjoy time at beaches and coastal areas such as this beach in Georgia.

How have people changed the place?

In the 1800s, people built canals to connect cities to rivers or lakes. Canals changed the land and made it easier to move people and goods. The Indiana Central Canal helped Indianapolis, Indiana, grow. Today, canals may be used to enjoy the outdoors.

| **Movement** | **Region** |

How has movement changed a region?

Movement describes how and why people move from one place to another. The highways around New York City are often clogged with cars and trucks. People drive cars to get to work, school, and other places. Trucks deliver food and other goods from one place to another.

What else is special about a region?

California's redwood trees can grow to over 320 feet tall. They are the tallest trees on Earth and are found near the coast in northern California. The climate in northern California is cool and wet. **Climate** is the usual weather pattern in a place over a period of time.

2. ☑ **Reading Check** **Discuss with a partner** the place where you live. **Describe** each of the themes of geography in your discussion.

Using Maps and Globes

People use globes and maps to learn about the world. A **globe** is a model of Earth, so it is shaped like a sphere. It is useful for looking at the entire world. A globe shows the continents and the oceans as they really are.

Flat maps, such as those in this text, offer a different view of Earth. Flat maps of Earth are less accurate than globes because they need to stretch out some parts of the world to make them flat. This is called distortion. Still, there are advantages to flat maps. Flat maps fold or can be mounted to walls. They are also useful for looking at smaller areas such as a single country, state, or city.

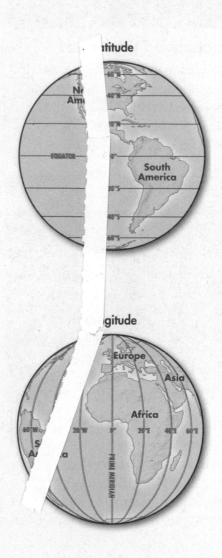

The **equator** is the imaginary line that extends around the center of Earth. It is marked as 0 degrees latitude. **Latitude** lines are evenly spaced and extend around the globe both north and south of the equator. **Longitude** lines are evenly spaced lines that extend north and south between the North Pole and the South Pole. The **prime meridian** is the line of longitude marked as 0 degrees. Other lines of longitude are measured in degrees east or west of the prime meridian. Longitude and latitude are used to tell a place's absolute location. The **absolute location** is the exact location of a place, and it does not change. For example, Los Angeles is 34 degrees north of the equator and 118 degrees west of the prime meridian. The absolute location of Los Angeles is written as 34° N, 118° W.

The equator divides Earth into northern and southern hemispheres. The prime meridian and the 180-degree line opposite it, divide Earth into eastern and western hemispheres. Each **hemisphere** is half of the sphere.

Relative location describes where a place is in relation to another place. For example, you might say that the library is across from the police station. A city may grow based on its relative location to a river or trade route.

3. ☑ **Reading Check** Look at a map of New York. Use the lines of latitude and longitude to **determine** the absolute location of Syracuse. _____

Different kinds of maps give different kinds of information. Political maps show information such as the location of state capitals and other cities. Look at the political map of the United States and find each of these map tools.

Title: The title tells you what the map shows.

Map legend: The map legend defines the symbols used on the map.

Symbol: A symbol is a mark or color that represents something.

Scale: The scale on the map shows distance. There are three scales on this map. Think about why that is so.

Compass rose: A compass rose shows directions on a map.

Vocabulary

globe
equator
latitude
longitude
prime meridian
absolute location
hemisphere
relative location

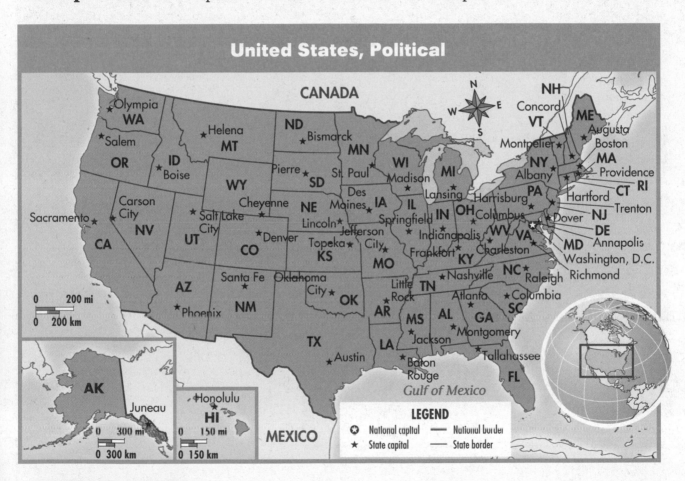

United States, Political

4. ☑ **Reading Check** **Locate** the states that share a border with Mexico. Circle these on the map.

5. ☑ **Reading Check** Work with a partner. **Ask** each other questions about the location of the 50 states and the names of their capitals.

Physical Maps

A **physical map** shows information such as landforms and bodies of water. A **landform** is a physical feature such as a mountain, desert, or valley. Bodies of water can include rivers, lakes, and oceans.

A physical map also shows the **relief** of an area. Relief shows high and low places by using different colors and shading. The elevation or height of the land above sea level is shown in color on the map. Shading is used to show landforms, such as mountain peaks. A **plain** is an open area of flat land.

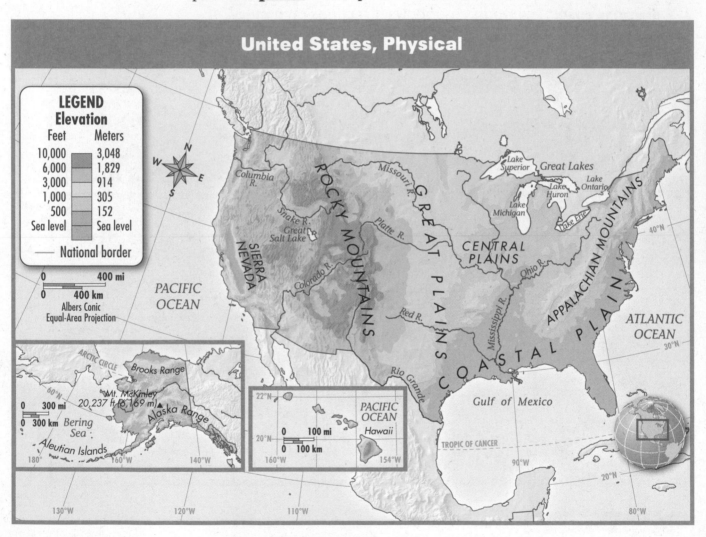

United States, Physical

LEGEND
Elevation

Feet		Meters
10,000		3,048
6,000		1,829
3,000		914
1,000		305
500		152
Sea level		Sea level

—— National border

0   400 mi
0   400 km
Albers Conic
Equal-Area Projection

6. ☑ **Reading Check** What mountain range shown on the map would people have to cross when traveling from the Great Plains to California?

Elevation Maps

Elevation is the distance or height of land above sea level. An **elevation map** allows you to compare and contrast the elevations of different areas. For example, you can compare the elevation of a mountain range to the elevation of a valley or plain. This map uses different colors to show changes in elevation in the state of New York.

Vocabulary

physical map
landform
relief
plain
elevation
elevation map

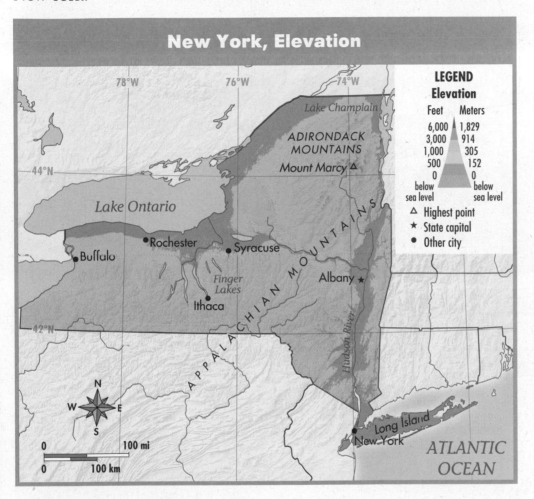

New York, Elevation

LEGEND
Elevation

Feet	Meters
6,000	1,829
3,000	914
1,000	305
500	152
0	0
below sea level	below sea level

△ Highest point
★ State capital
● Other city

Lake Champlain

ADIRONDACK MOUNTAINS

Mount Marcy △

Lake Ontario

Rochester   Syracuse

Buffalo

Finger Lakes

Ithaca

Albany ★

APPALACHIAN MOUNTAINS

Hudson River

Long Island

New York

ATLANTIC OCEAN

N W E S

0   100 mi
0   100 km

7. ☑ **Reading Check** **Identify** which landform in New York has the highest elevation. Then **identify** an area of the state that has one of the lowest elevations.

_____

_____

Human and Physical Characteristics of Regions

A **regions map** shows areas that share similar physical or human characteristics. Regions may result from patterns of human activity, such as population or economic activity. They might be areas that share similar physical characteristics, such as vegetation, landforms, or climate. The map below shows five regions of the United States.

Regions of the United States

8. ☑ **Reading Check** **Identify** which states are in the same region as Utah. Circle them on the map.

9. ☑ **Reading Check** Make a list of the physical and human characteristics that make your state unique.

_____

_____

_____

Historical Maps

A **historical map** shows a particular time from the past. It is important when studying a historical map to notice the date or dates on the map. Historical maps can help you understand how places have changed over time.

This map shows the United States in 1850. During this time, the United States had expanded from the East Coast to the West Coast. Notice that the map also shows free and slave states. The balance between states that allowed slavery and those that did not, divided the U.S. Congress.

Vocabulary

regions map
historical map

United States, 1850

10. ☑ **Reading Check** **Summarize** the location of the slave states and the location of the free states.

_____

_____

_____

_____

_____

Special-Purpose Maps

A special-purpose map gives information related to a certain theme. For example, a drought map, like the maps of California on this page, shows if there is a drought and how severe it is. A **drought** is a long period of low rainfall. In a drought, plants and animals can suffer. People may have to take extra steps to save water. Drought maps change over time as rainfall increases and decreases. The two maps below show how drought levels have changed between the years 2006 and 2016.

A map of drought conditions in 2017 would look very different from drought shown on the 2016 map. In the winter of 2017, unusually large amounts of rainfall in parts of California caused flooding and mudslides. Dams overflowed as rain filled lakes and reservoirs.

11. ☑ **Reading Check** What was the level of drought for Bakersfield in 2006? What was it in 2016? Were there any changes?

_____

_____

_____

_____

Drought Conditions, 2006

LEGEND
- Abnormally dry
- Moderate drought
- Severe drought
- Extreme drought
- Exceptional drought

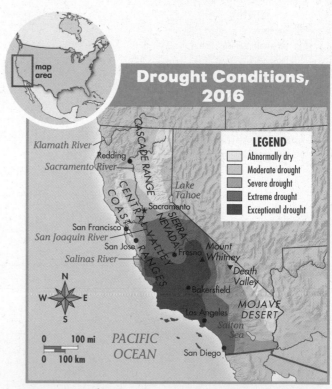

Drought Conditions, 2016

LEGEND
- Abnormally dry
- Moderate drought
- Severe drought
- Extreme drought
- Exceptional drought

Some special-purpose maps are related to current events. **Current events** are events that are in the news. The outcome of a current event such as an election can more easily be seen on a map such as the one below. The map legend helps you know what the colors represent.

Vocabulary

drought
current events

2016 Presidential Election Res____s

LEGEND
Voted for Hillary Clin____
Voted for Donald Tru____

12. ☑ **Reading Check** **Summarize** what is shown o____ ____e election map.

_____

_____

_____

_____

Keys to Good Writing

Good writers follow five steps when they write.

Plan	• Think about how to write about a topic. • Find details about the topic. • Take notes from sources. • Write down your sources. • Plan how to use the details.
Draft	• Write down all of your ideas. • Think about which ideas go together. • Put ideas that go together in groups. • Write a sentence for the introduction and write a sentence for the conclusion.
Revise	• Review what you wrote. • Check that your ideas and organization make sense. • Add time-order words and transitions (words and phrases such as *because* or *for example*). • List any more sources that you used.
Edit	• Check for correct grammar, spelling, and punctuation. • Make a final copy.
Share	• Use technology to print or publish your work. • Make sure that you list all of your sources.

1. ☑ **Reading Check** **Sequence** How might completing these steps out of order affect your writing?

_____

_____

There are three main writing genres—opinion, informative, and narrative. They all have a different purpose for writing.

Opinion Writing

When you write an opinion piece, you are sharing your point of view on a topic. Your goal should be to make your viewpoint clear and to support it with evidence, or facts. Read the steps and sample sentences below to see how to write effective opinion pieces.

Christopher Columbus

1	**Introduce the topic.** *Christopher Columbus landed in the Americas in 1492 after thinking he had reached Asia.*
2	**State your opinion.** *I think Christopher Columbus made a good decision when he chose to leave Spain in search of a western route to Asia.*
3	**Support your opinion with reasons and evidence.** *The trade routes on land were long and dangerous. Columbus sailed across the Atlantic Ocean in 1492 in search of a shorter and faster route to Asia.*
4	**Make sure that your ideas are clear, organized, and written in a logical way to support your purpose.**
5	**Support your opinion statement with a conclusion.** *Columbus did not find the western route to Asia he had hoped for. Yet he made history by being one of the first Europeans to land in the Americas.*

2. **Reading Check** **Analyze** Answer this question with a partner: Why must you use evidence to support a point of view in opinion writing?

Informative Writing

Informative writing is also called explanatory writing, because you are writing to explain a topic to your reader. Reliable sources are important to use in this kind of writing. Make sure to avoid plagiarism. This means using someone else's words without giving that person credit. Take notes on your sources, including what they say and where you found them. Keep in mind that your reader may know nothing about the topic. Try to be clear and thorough in your writing. Read the steps and sample sentences below.

Pilgrims' landing of the *Mayflower*

1	**Introduce the topic.**
	The 13 British colonies were started for different reasons.
2	**Develop the topic with facts, details, definitions, and concrete details.**
	The 13 British colonies were set up in North America between the early 1600s and the early 1700s. A colony is a settlement that is far away from the country that rules it.
3	**Support your writing with a quotation if possible.**
	Some colonies were founded so that people could worship freely. As William Penn explained, "No people can be truly happy . . . if abridged [shortened] of the freedom of their conscience [inner voice]."
4	**Use precise language and content words.**
	In contrast, other colonies were founded for economic reasons. John Rolfe discovered that tobacco grew well in Virginia's soil and it soon became a cash crop for the colony.
5	**Write a conclusion that supports your introduction.**
	Britain's 13 colonies were settled for religious, economic, and political reasons.

3. ☑ **Reading Check** **Infer** Discuss with a partner why it is important to use facts and details from reliable sources.

Using Primary and Secondary Sources

Vocabulary

primary source
autobiography
artifact
secondary source
biography

Primary Sources

Have you ever used a journal or diary to write down something you witnessed? Perhaps you saw an exciting sporting event or went on a trip with your family. If you wrote about those events or took pictures, then you have created a primary source based on events in your life. Read to find out what a primary source is and how historians use primary sources.

A **primary source** is one made or written by a person who witnessed an event. Primary sources help us learn about events or historical periods from people who lived during that time. Primary sources can be written, visual, or oral (spoken).

A historical document, like the United States Constitution, is an example of a written primary source. Letters, journals, and photographs are also primary sources. An **autobiography** is an account of a person's life written by that person. Because it is a firsthand, eyewitness account, an autobiography is a primary source.

Visual primary sources include artwork, maps, and architecture, which show us what people, places, and buildings look like now and in the past. An artifact is another visual primary source. **Artifacts** are objects made and used by people, like a soldier's uniform from the American Revolution. Oral primary sources include speeches, interviews, and recordings of events.

1. **Reading Check** If you have visited a museum, you have seen artifacts. **Identify** an artifact you saw at a museum.

_____

_____

_____

This uniform is a primary source. It is an artifact from the American Revolution.

Secondary Sources

Have you ever written a research report for school? If you have, you very likely used primary and secondary sources. A **secondary source** is material that was written or created by someone who did not witness or experience an event firsthand. A **biography** is a book about a person's life written by someone else. For example, if a historian today writes a biography on Abraham Lincoln, it is a secondary source since the writer was not present during Lincoln's life.

Secondary sources are important because they often analyze events, sometimes long after they have taken place. Some secondary sources offer readers new ideas or facts about people and events. This textbook is a secondary source. Encyclopedias, online or in print, are also secondary sources. Most reference materials, such as dictionaries and instruction manuals, are secondary sources. Books and magazine articles that were not written firsthand are secondary sources.

Like primary sources, secondary sources can be oral or visual. A radio program about Martin Luther King, Jr., or a historical film about the American Revolution are secondary sources. A painting created today showing a battle during the American Revolution is also a secondary source. Charts and graphs that interpret information are secondary sources because they are made from original data after events occur.

Encyclopedias are secondary sources.

2. ☑ **Reading Check** **Describe** the difference between primary and secondary sources.

_____

_____

_____

_____

_____

How to Interpret Primary Sources

One way to interpret, or understand, a primary source is to study the material or object, think about it, and then answer questions. It can also be helpful to compare and contrast primary sources that are about the same subject or event.

The next document is a primary source because it was written by Hernán Cortés, a Spanish explorer who defeated the Aztec empire and claimed a vast area in what is today Mexico for Spain. Moctezuma is the Aztec emperor.

Hernán Cortés

Primary Source

...the inhabitants of this province would often caution [warn] me not to trust these vassals [servants] of Moctezuma for they were traitors, . . . and they warned me as true friends, and as persons who had long known those men, to beware of them.

–Hernán Cortés to King Charles V of Spain, *Second Letter*, 1520

3. ☑**Reading Check** Why do you think Cortés wrote this letter? If Cortés had written a letter to a friend how might it be different than one he wrote to the king?

_____

_____

_____

_____

_____

4. **Apply** Explain why this document is a primary source and not a secondary source.

_____

_____

_____

The next document is also a primary source. Bernal Díaz del Castillo, a soldier who was with Cortés during the conquest of Mexico, wrote an account of the event. Díaz del Castillo's account is considered the most complete description of these events that exists. Unlike the letters of Cortés, the book by Díaz was not written until 1568 when Díaz was 72 years old.

Primary Source

They replied that they were the tax collectors of the great Moctezuma and . . . they now demanded twenty men and women to sacrifice to their god, Huitzilopochtli, so that he would give them victory over us, for they said that Moctezuma had declared that he intended to capture us and make us slaves.

–Bernal Díaz del Castillo,
The True History of the Conquest of New Spain, 1576

5. **Reading Check** **Compare** and **contrast** the similarities and differences between the authors' writings.

_____

_____

_____

_____

_____

_____

_____

_____

_____

_____

_____

How to Interpret Secondary Sources

Your textbook has information about the Lewis and Clark expedition, but the information was not written by someone who was there in real time, like Cortés. This makes it a secondary source. The authors did not see or live through the events that are described. They learned their information by reading other people's writings or looking at other primary sources, like photographs, diaries, and artifacts. You can answer questions to interpret secondary sources just as you did with primary sources. Read the passage below from your textbook and answer the question that follows.

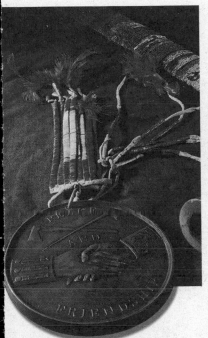

Lewis and Clark took along medals like this one to present to American Indian leaders along their route. The medal is a primary source.

Soon after the Louisiana Purchase, Jefferson finalized plans for an expedition to explore the new lands. He asked Meriwether Lewis to lead the expedition. Lewis had worked as Jefferson's secretary. He was also an explorer and frontiersman.

Lewis asked a fellow frontiersman William Clark to go with him. Together, they put together the Corps of Discovery, a group of capable men who would take the nearly two-year journey to the Pacific Ocean. Jefferson was hoping that they would find a water route that would link the Mississippi with the Pacific Ocean. Such a route would provide access to the western part of the United States. Jefferson also wanted Lewis and Clark to learn about the American Indians who lived in the west, as well as bring back information about the land itself.

6. ☑ **Reading Check** **Compare** the Cortés letter on the previous page to the textbook excerpt. How do they differ?

_____

_____

_____

_____

_____

Civil War and Reconstruction

GO ONLINE FOR
DIGITAL RESOURCES

- ▶ VIDEO
- 👆 INTERACTIVITY
- 🔊 AUDIO
- 🎮 GAMES
- ☑ ASSESSMENT
- 📖 eTEXT

The BIG Question

What is worth fighting for?

▶ VIDEO

Jumpstart Activity

👆 INTERACTIVITY

Work in small groups and discuss ideas for a recess activity for your entire class. After each group presents ideas to the class vote for the activity you like best. Was your group's activity chosen? Did the winning activity interest all your classmates?

_____

_____

_____

_____

_____

Rap About It! ♫

 AUDIO

Fighting for Freedom and Union

Preview the chapter **vocabulary** as you sing the rap:

Division between the North and South grew when
New free and slave states joined the **Union**.
After Lincoln's election, Southern states would secede
And leave the Union to form the **Confederacy**.

At Ft. Sumter shots fired in the early morning mist,
The Civil War had begun, both sides ran to **enlist**.
No one guessed at the time, that the war would last long;
Battles at Bull Run, Gettysburg, Antietam, and more.

During the war, Lincoln issued a **proclamation**,
It set some enslaved free, that's called **emancipation**.
It didn't end slavery but it changed the war,
African Americans joined and gave the Union their all.

Where did the Civil War start?

The Civil War began on April 21, 1861, when the South's Confederate Army fired on Fort Sumter. Locate Fort Sumter on the map.

Fort Sumter

TODAY
You can tour Fort Sumter National Monument in South Carolina.

What happened and When?

Read the timeline to find out about the events that took place before and after the Civil War.

1850

1855

186

1850
Congress passed the Compromise of 1850.

1854
The Kansas-Nebraska Act splits the Nebraska Territory.

Who will you meet?

Abraham Lincoln
The sixteenth president of the United States led the nation during the Civil War

Sojourner Truth
A former enslaved African American activist who collected supplies for African American regiments during the Civil War

Jefferson Davis
The president of the Confederate States during the Civil War

Clara Barton
A hospital nurse during the Civil War and founder of the American Red Cross

 INTERACTIVITY

Complete the interactive digital activity.

1865

1870

1861
The Civil War begins.

1863
The Battle of Gettysburg is fought.

1865
The Civil War ends.

1868
Fourteenth Amendment passed.

TODAY
You can visit the Civil War battle sites in many states.

Sing Along!

Music during the Civil War played an important role for both the soldiers and their families. While in camp and the hospital, soldiers would sing ballads, funny songs, patriotic songs, and sentimental songs that inspired feelings of pride, home, or loved ones.

One way to inspire or entertain people is to write a song. A song is a group of words or a poem that is set to music.

Quest Kick Off

As a new soldier in the army, your mission is to write a song for soldiers that provides comfort, entertainment, or shows patriotism.

1 Ask Questions

How do you want the words and music of your song to make the soldiers feel? What kind of song do you think soldiers would like? Write three ideas for a song.

....

....

....

2 Research

Follow your teacher's instructions to find songs that were popular among soldiers during the Civil War. Read the lyrics of several songs. How do the songs make you feel?

INTERACTIVITY

Complete the interactivity to learn more about music during the Civil War.

....

....

....

....

....

3 Look for Quest Connections

Begin looking for Quest Connections that will help you write your song.

4 Quest Findings
Write Your Song

Use the Quest Findings page at the end of the chapter to help you write your song.

Struggles Over Slavery

INTERACTIVITY

Participate in a class discussion to preview the content of this lesson.

Vocabulary

plantation
Union
states' rights
compromise
Underground Railroad
abolitionist
secession
Confederacy

Academic Vocabulary

obtain
according

Unlock
The **BIG** Question

I will know the causes of the Civil War.

JumpStart Activity

You want to go to the movies and your friend wants to go on a hike. How do you decide what to do? Share your ideas of how to compromise. With a classmate, act out one idea.

Proud Union soldiers march by the White House as President Lincoln looks looks on.

The song "The Battle Cry of Freedom" was popular during the U.S. Civil War.

INTERACTIVITY

Explore the key ideas of this lesson.

Primary Source

"Yes, we'll rally round the flag, boys, we'll rally once again, Shouting the battle cry of Freedom."

—George F. Root, 1862

Both sides were fighting for freedom but disagreed about what *freedom* meant. Their fight was the bloodiest in U.S. history. What divided our nation so deeply? Read on to find out.

The North and South Grow Apart

Much of the South is low and level with rich soil. The climate is warm and sunny for much of the year. Many people lived on big farms called **plantations**. The economy was primarily based on agriculture, supplying raw goods to the North. Many of the farmworkers were enslaved African Americans and the Southern economy depended upon their work.

The geography of the North is very different. It has hills, mountains, and lakes. The climate is cold and snowy in the winter. Northeastern resources include coal for making steel and fueling factory machines. In the 1800s, the Industrial Revolution changed life in the North. Many people moved to urban areas to work in factories. Factories used raw materials from the South, such as cotton, to produce finished products.

The Southern port of New Orleans was important to both regions. To meet the demand for manufactured products, goods were shipped from the North down the Mississippi River to New Orleans. Differences in geography and industrialization shaped the culture and economy of the North and South and divided the two regions. This was called sectionalism, and many feared it would lead to a civil war.

Quest Connection

Read the words to the "Battle Cry of Freedom" What do you think the word *freedom* in the song means? What did freedom mean to the North? What did it mean to the South?

INTERACTIVITY

Learn more about the music of the Civil War.

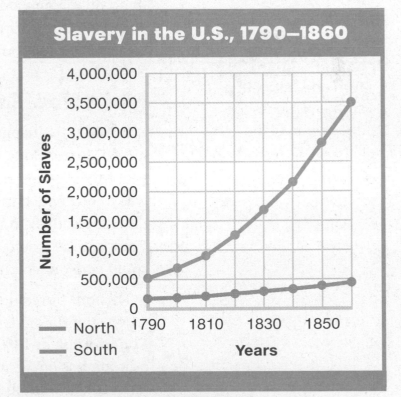

Slavery in the U.S., 1790–1860

Source: University of Virginia Library

Tough Compromises

Academic Vocabulary

obtain • *v.*, to get or acquire
according • *prep.*, in agreement

After the American Revolution, the United States **obtained** the region called the Northwest Territory. This was the area we call the Midwest, and it doubled the country. Congress passed a law called the Northwest Ordinance of 1787. It outlined how new states could be formed. Once admitted to the **Union**, or the United States, a new state would have the same rights as other states.

Slavery was prohibited in this territory, and this ban sparked arguments. Many wanted the same number of slave states, where slavery was allowed, and free states, where it was illegal. They feared that if there were more representatives in Congress for either side, it might threaten **states' rights**, the rights of states to make their own local laws.

In 1819, Missouri asked to join the Union as a slave state. That would upset the balance in Congress. A compromise was worked out. A **compromise** occurs when each side gives in a little to reach an agreement. A law known as the Missouri Compromise was passed in 1820.

According to the Missouri Compromise, Missouri could be a slave state and Maine would join the Union as a free state. In addition, an imaginary line, called the Mason-Dixon line, was used. States north of the line would be free states. States south of the line could allow slavery if they wished.

1. ☑ **Reading Check**
Turn and talk with a partner. Discuss the three parts of the Missouri Compromise.

More New States

In 1845, the Republic of Texas was annexed (united or joined) to the United States. Part of the republic became the state of Texas, a slave state. The rest of the territory was to be divided into four new states. Of the other four new states, those north of the line set by the Missouri Compromise would be free. But those south of the line could vote on whether to allow slavery.

Tensions flared again in 1849 when California applied to join the Union as a free state. The solution was the Compromise of 1850. To satisfy the North, California was admitted as a free state. To satisfy the South, the North agreed to the Fugitive Slave Law.

A fugitive is someone who escapes and runs away. The Fugitive Slave Law said that escaped enslaved African Americans must be returned to their owners, even if they had reached a free state. Congress hoped that this law would keep the country united.

In 1854, Nebraska was split into the Nebraska Territory and Kansas Territory. Under the Kansas-Nebraska Act, the people of each territory could vote to decide if they would allow slavery.

"Bleeding Kansas"

A majority vote would decide whether Kansas would be free or allow slavery. Both sides rushed to Kansas to vote. When the votes were counted, the proslavery side had won. The Kansas Territory would allow slavery.

Northerners demanded that the vote be thrown out. Southerners argued that the vote should stand. Most people who lived in Kansas wanted peace. People clashed all over the Kansas Territory. By 1856, this violence had earned the territory the sad name "Bleeding Kansas."

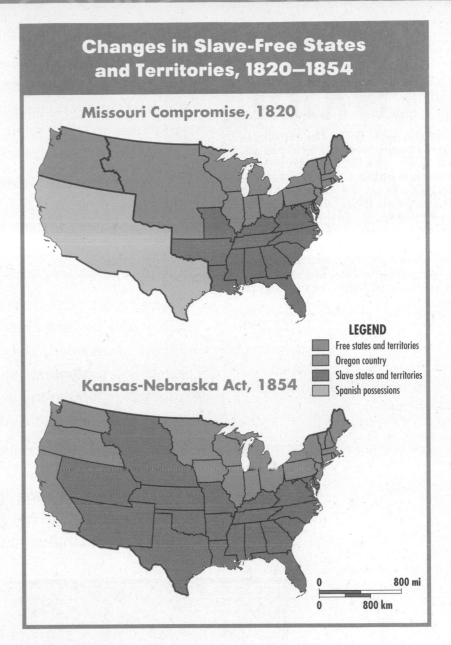

Changes in Slave-Free States and Territories, 1820–1854

Missouri Compromise, 1820

Kansas-Nebraska Act, 1854

LEGEND
Free states and territories
Oregon country
Slave states and territories
Spanish possessions

0   800 mi
0   800 km

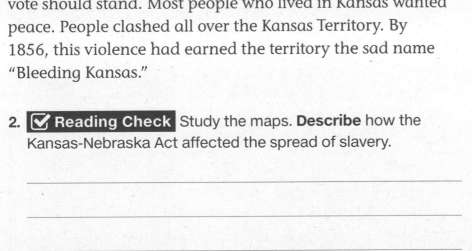

2. ☑ Reading Check Study the maps. **Describe** how the Kansas-Nebraska Act affected the spread of slavery.

_____

_____

_____

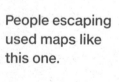

$100 REWARD.

Ranaway from the subscriber's farm, near Washington, on the 11th of October, negro woman SOPHIA GORDON, about 24 years of age, rather small in size, of copper color, is tolerably good looking, has a low and soft manner of speech. She is believed to be among associates formed in Washington where she has been often hired.

I will give the above reward, no matter where taken and secured in jail so that I get her again.
GEORGE W. YOUNG.

November 16th, 1858.

H. Polkinhorn's Steam Job Printing Office, D street, bet 6th & 7th sts., Washington, D.C.

reward flyer for escaped enslaved African American woman

Escape to Freedom

The Fugitive Slave Law said the escaped enslaved African Americans had to be returned to their owners, even if they were in a free state. This did not stop thousands of slaves from trying to escape to freedom, however. The fugitives usually followed different routes on the Underground Railroad.

The **Underground Railroad** was not an actual train. It was an organized, secret system to help enslaved African Americans escape, mostly to the North or to Canada. The "stations" on the Underground Railroad were the houses, churches, and other places the fugitives hid and rested.

Many people helped the escaping African Americans. These people became known as "conductors." Harriet Tubman, an escaped slave, was one of the most famous conductors. At great personal risk, Tubman made many trips south to lead more people to freedom. Tubman's route was one of three major routes that went through New Jersey.

Because the Underground Railroad was secret, no one knows how many enslaved African Americans escaped— probably only a few thousand each year between 1840 and 1860. This seems like a lot of people, but in the 1860s, nearly 4 million people in the United States were enslaved.

People escaping used maps like this one.

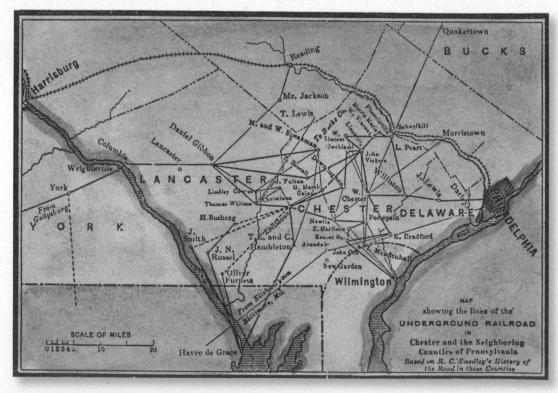

Starting Down the Road to War

The North and South became further divided. In Boston, William Lloyd Garrison published a newspaper called *The Liberator*. Frederick Douglass, an African American who had escaped from slavery, published an antislavery newspaper called *The North Star*. Garrison and Douglass were **abolitionists**, people who wanted to abolish, or get rid of, slavery. In the South, writers and speakers argued for states' rights and the freedom to keep their way of life.

Women played a big role in fighting slavery. Sojourner Truth was an African American woman who had been enslaved in New York, but she was freed when New York outlawed slavery. In 1843, she joined the abolition movement. Harriet Beecher Stowe published a novel called *Uncle Tom's Cabin*. This book described the cruelties of slavery and convinced many people to oppose it.

Anger Grows

One event that made people angry was the case of an enslaved man named Dred Scott from Missouri. Scott's owner had taken him to two free states, Illinois and Wisconsin, before returning to Missouri. When Scott's owner died, Scott claimed he was free because he had lived in free states. In 1857, the Supreme Court ruled that Scott had no rights because African Americans were not citizens.

Then, in 1859, abolitionist John Brown attacked Harper's Ferry, Virginia. Brown had fought in Bleeding Kansas. Now he wanted to attack slavery supporters in Virginia, but he needed weapons. He decided to steal weapons the army had stored at Harper's Ferry. Brown and 21 other men raided Harper's Ferry on October 16, but soldiers stopped them. Brown was caught, tried, and hanged. John Brown's raid did not succeed, but it showed that the fight over slavery was getting fiercer.

4. ☑ **Reading Check** **Explain** how John Brown's raid might have been a sign that war was unavoidable.

_____

_____

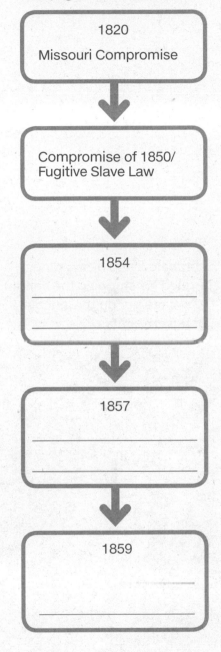

3. ☑ **Reading Check**
Sequence Fill in the missing items to **show the sequence** of events leading to the Civil War.

1820
Missouri Compromise

⬇

Compromise of 1850/
Fugitive Slave Law

⬇

1854
_____
_____

⬇

1857
_____
_____

⬇

1859
_____
_____

The Election of 1860

Abraham Lincoln wanted to keep slavery from spreading to new territories and states. "I hate it because of the monstrous injustice," he said in 1854. The Republican Party in Illinois chose Lincoln to run for the U.S. Senate in 1858. Lincoln's opponent, Democratic senator Stephen Douglas disagreed. He believed that each state had the right to decide whether or not to allow slavery. Douglas won that election, but Lincoln's arguments in a series of famous debates with Douglas made him a leader of the new Republican Party.

The 1860 presidential election had four major candidates. The Democratic Party had split in two. The Northern Democrats chose Stephen Douglas. The Southern Democrats chose John Breckenridge. The Republicans chose Abraham Lincoln. The Constitutional Union Party chose John Bell.

The election reflected the sharp divide between the North and South. Lincoln won, but he did not win any electoral votes in the Southern states because voters there worried that he would end slavery if elected.

While running for the U.S. Senate in 1858, Lincoln had said:

Abraham Lincoln, standing, argued for stopping the spread of slavery during the Lincoln-Douglas debates.

Primary Source

"'A house divided against itself cannot stand.' I believe this government cannot endure permanently half slave and half free. I do not expect the Union to be dissolved . . . but I do expect it will cease to be divided. It will become all one thing, or all the other."

—Abraham Lincoln's acceptance speech to Illinois Republican Party, June 16, 1858

This was a frightening prediction. Soon, Lincoln and his fellow Americans would find out if the Union could survive.

5. ✅ **Reading Check** **Analyze** what the 1860 election showed about what was going on in the country.

_____

_____

_____

The South Breaks Away

Even before the election, some Southern leaders had talked about **secession**, or separating, from the Union. Many Southerners wanted their own country. After Lincoln's election, South Carolina became the first to secede.

By March 1861, Alabama, Florida, Mississippi, Georgia, Louisiana, and Texas had also seceded. These states formed their own government, called the Confederate States of America, also known as the **Confederacy**. *Confederacy*, like *Union*, means "joined together."

The Confederate leaders wrote a constitution and elected Jefferson Davis as president. They seized forts across the South.

States that remained loyal to the U.S. government were still called the Union. A civil war now seemed certain. The word *civil* refers to citizens, so a civil war is a war among citizens of the same country.

Confederate president
Jefferson Davis

INTERACTIVITY

Check your understanding of the key ideas of this lesson.

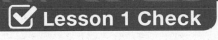
Lesson 1 Check

6. **Describe** one of the differences that made the Missouri Compromise necessary.

_____

_____

7. Write a sentence from the viewpoint of presidential candidate Abraham Lincoln **describing** what he would be willing to fight for.

_____

_____

8. **Quest Connections** **Identify** the words in the song "Battle Cry of Freedom" that would serve to excite people and strengthen their feelings of patriotism.

_____

_____

Critical Thinking Skills

Make Decisions

 VIDEO

Watch a video about making decisions.

Suppose you lived in the United States in the 1860s. Think about the decisions the president had to make as Northern and Southern states grew more divided. How did Congress create the compromises that kept the free and slave states balanced? How did people go about making these life-changing decisions?

Making decisions is a process. By following these steps in order, you can increase your chances of making the right decision.

1. **Identify the situation that requires a decision.** To make a good decision, you must first recognize the problem or question you face. Identify your goal and the outcome you want.

2. **Think of options.** Gather information about how to solve the problem or answer the questions. These are your options.

3. **Predict outcomes.** Focus on each of your options. Ask yourself: What might happen if I choose this option? What are the possible good and bad outcomes?

4. **Take action.** Choose the option that has the greatest chance of meeting your goals. By choosing the option you think is best, you have made your decision.

Once you have made a decision, you can act on it. Develop a plan to carry out the option you chose. Keep your mind open, however. You should be willing to change your decision if the action you take does not work out as well as you hoped.

You make a decision each time you choose which food to buy.

Read the sections in your book titled "Tough Compromises," "More New States," and "'Bleeding Kansas'" in Lesson 1. The country faced a lot of very hard decisions that had to be made to keep the country together. What were the issues? How would you have made a decision? Use the decision-making process to help you decide what you might do.

1. What is the issue or situation that requires a decision?

_____

_____

_____

2. What are the options?

_____

_____

_____

3. What are consequences of each option?

_____

_____

_____

_____

_____

4. What option is best?

_____

_____

_____

INTERACTIVITY

Participate in a class discussion to preview the content of this lesson.

Unlock The BIG Question

I will know the strategies and key battles in the first years of the Civil War.

Vocabulary

enlist
blockade

Academic Vocabulary

overwhelm
horrific

JumpStart Activity

Move into small groups. Each group suggests an activity for the class to do. One group decides what to do. How do the other groups feel about not having a choice?

Most leaders of the Confederacy expected the secession to be peaceful. They believed deciding to secede was one of a state's rights. They didn't think their actions would lead to a long, bloody war. They were very wrong.

Confederate forces fired on Fort Sumter on April 12, 1861. This event touched off the Civil War.

The First Shots

A Union force controlled Fort Sumter in South Carolina. It was in a Confederate state, so Confederate president Jefferson Davis thought the Union force should surrender the fort. He sent South Carolina's governor to ask the Union soldiers to leave the fort, but they refused.

On April 8, 1861, the governor learned that Lincoln was sending a ship to resupply the fort. Jefferson Davis sent soldiers to help the governor.

On April 11, the Confederates again asked the Union soldiers to leave. Again, they refused. At 4:30 A.M. on April 12, Confederate forces began to fire on the fort. The next day, with no supplies left, the Union force surrendered the fort to the Confederates. No one had been killed, but the Civil War had begun.

The Civil War Begins

Lincoln responded to the attack on Fort Sumter by raising an army. Virginia, Arkansas, Tennessee, and North Carolina joined the Confederacy. The Confederacy now had 11 states; the Union consisted of 23. Men on both sides eagerly enlisted. To **enlist** is to join the military. After all, it was an important cause. The North wanted to preserve the unity of the United States as a whole. The North also didn't want to lose access to the Mississippi River. The South was fighting for states' rights and a way of life.

The First Battle of Bull Run

At first, it seemed that the war *would* be over soon—and the Confederates would win. Lincoln sent 35,000 troops against the Confederate capital in Richmond, Virginia. On July 21, 1861, they met Confederate troops at a stream called Bull Run. The Union soldiers did well at first. But the Confederates stood their ground, inspired by a general named Thomas Jackson. "There stands Jackson like a stone wall," declared another Confederate general. His actions earned the general the nickname "Stonewall" Jackson. When Southern reinforcements arrived, the **overwhelmed** Union soldiers fled.

INTERACTIVITY

Explore the key ideas of this lesson.

Quest Connection

Music was often used to stir up patriotic feelings. Underline words and phrases that you might use to write a song.

INTERACTIVITY

Learn more about music during the Civil War by going online.

Academic Vocabulary

overwhelm • *adj.*, beat; vanquish

Lincoln Versus Davis

Abraham Lincoln, the president of the Union, and Jefferson Davis, the president of the Confederacy, were both skilled leaders. Both were born in Kentucky, but Davis had moved to Mississippi and Lincoln had moved to Illinois. Lincoln was trained as a lawyer. Davis, a West Point graduate, became an army officer. Both served in Washington, D.C.

Lincoln and Davis faced different challenges as the war began. The South had fewer resources than the North, but it had better military leaders and stronger reasons to fight.

The two men were different in their wartime strategies, too. Lincoln sought advice from General Winfield Scott, a Mexican War veteran.

1. ☑ **Reading Check** **Compare and Contrast** Complete the chart to **compare** the Union and the Confederacy.

This painting of Abraham Lincoln is based on a photograph taken by Matthew Brady just before Lincoln became president.

The Union and the Confederacy

	United States of America	Confederate States of America
President		
Strategy		
Strengths	• Produced 90% of the country's weapons, cloth, shoes, and iron • Produced most of the country's food • Had more railroads and roads • Had more people	• Had more experienced hunters and soldiers • Had a history of producing great military leaders • Believed they were fighting for freedom • Were fighting for—and on—their own land
Challenges	• Didn't have many war veterans • Didn't have as many talented military leaders	• Lacked big manufacturing centers • Had fewer railroads

Scott planned a three-part strategy. First, the Union would form a naval blockade of the coasts. A **blockade** is a barrier of troops or ships to keep people and supplies from moving in and out of an area. Under a blockade, the South would not be able to ship cotton to European countries and wouldn't have money to pay for the war.

Second, Scott planned to take control of the Mississippi River, which would cut the Confederacy in half. Third, Scott planned to attack the Confederacy from the east and west. He called his strategy the Anaconda Plan because it would squeeze the Confederacy like an anaconda, a huge snake.

Davis had his own strategy. First, he planned to defend Confederate land until the North gave up. Southerners believed that Union troops would quit fighting because they weren't defending their own land. Second, Davis believed the British would help because they needed Southern cotton. Davis was wrong. Britain offered no help to either side.

General Scott's plan was to wrap around the South and "squeeze" it, like a giant snake.

New Tools of War

Wars often result in the invention of new tools and technologies. During the Civil War, guns were improved. The new guns could shoot farther and more accurately. Both Union and Confederate soldiers used early versions of the hand grenade. The Confederacy built a submarine, a ship that could travel underwater.

The Confederates created another new weapon: the ironclad. It was a ship covered, or clad, in iron, so cannonballs simply bounced off it. To make the ironclad, the Confederates covered an old Union ship, the *Merrimack*, with iron plates. They named it the *Virginia*. The *Virginia* successfully sank several Union ships. The Union built its own ironclad, the *Monitor*, which fought the *Virginia*. Since both ships were ironclads, they were unable to cause serious damage to each other.

2. ☑ **Reading Check**
Turn and talk with a partner about what made the *Monitor* and the *Virginia* special.

Brilliant Confederate Generals

While the Union had far greater resources than the Confederacy, the South had brilliant generals, especially Thomas "Stonewall" Jackson and Robert E. Lee. These generals often outsmarted Union forces many times larger than their own.

In 1862, Union general George McClellan hoped to capture the Confederate capital of Richmond, Virginia. McClellan planned to sail his troops to a place on the coast of Virginia, to avoid the Confederate army in northern Virginia. At first, it seemed as though McClellan's plan would work. However, Stonewall Jackson was fighting so successfully in Virginia's Shenandoah Valley that extra Union troops had to be sent there. There was no help for McClellan. Robert E. Lee then badly defeated McClellan's forces at Richmond. Some people feared that the Confederates would now move on Washington, D.C.

With each Confederate success, there was more pressure on Lincoln. Northerners had expected a swift, easy victory. It was beginning to look like the war might be long, and people began to question Lincoln's decision to fight.

General Robert E. Lee commanded the Confederate army of northern Virginia.

The Battle of Fredericksburg in Virginia, in December 1862, was a huge Confederate victory.

The Battle of Antietam

The Union needed a victory. It got one on September 17, 1862, at the Battle of Antietam (an TEET um). This battle was the single bloodiest day in the war. In the end, about 23,000 men lay dead or wounded, evenly divided between North and South. This **horrific** battle led Lincoln to make a decision that would change the war and the country.

Academic Vocabulary

horrific • *adj.*, having the power to horrify; frightening or shocking

3. ☑ **Reading Check** **Turn** and **talk** with a partner. Discuss the reasons why a Northern victory was so important.

INTERACTIVITY

Check your understanding of the key ideas of this lesson.

☑ Lesson 2 Check

4. **Main Idea and Details** Fill in this chart. **Identify** the purpose, or main idea, of the Anaconda Plan. Then fill in details to show how the plan would work.

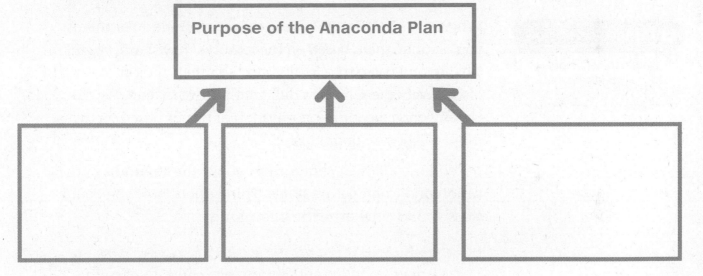

Purpose of the Anaconda Plan

5. **Describe** why Davis was willing to fight.

_____

_____

6. **Understand the** Quest **Connections** Why did many Civil War songs appeal to people's feelings of patriotism?

_____

_____

_____

Classify and Categorize

I liked reading about the strengths of the Union and Confederate states.

I liked it too. What was your favorite part? Can you classify and categorize the information for me?

VIDEO

Watch a video about classify and categorize.

When you **classify** and **categorize** information or things, you arrange them based on the features they share. We might classify and categorize books based on their subject. We might also classify them on how difficult they are to read. We can classify and categorize information or things based on two or more categories, or groups.

Read the following paragraph about the strengths of the Union and Confederate states. Think about how you could classify and categorize the information.

There are lots of different factors that can influence the outcome of battles and a war. The Union and Confederacy had different strengths during the Civil War. The Union states had a large population and lots of railroads and roads. They produced most of the country's food, weapons, cloth, shoes, and iron. In contrast, the Confederate states had experienced hunters and soldiers and a history of producing great military leaders. Also, they were fighting on their own land and believed they were fighting for freedom.

Your Turn!

1. What are the strengths of the Union states? What are the strengths of the Confederate states? Fill in the graphic organizer to classify and categorize the strengths of each country.

Strengths of the Union and the Confederacy

United States of America	Confederate States of America
_____	_____
_____	_____
_____	_____
_____	_____
_____	_____
_____	_____

2. Read the section titled "Lincoln Versus Davis" in Lesson 2. Write several facts about President Lincoln and President Davis that would help you classify and categorize the two different presidents. On a separate piece of paper, write a paragraph summarizing the facts about the two leaders.

_____

_____

_____

_____

_____

_____

Life During the Civil War

 INTERACTIVITY

Participate in a class discussion to preview the content of this lesson.

Vocabulary

proclamation
emancipation
Juneteenth

Academic Vocabulary

prove
exhibit

African American soldiers of the 107th United States Colored Troops

Unlock
The BIG Question

I will know the importance of the Emancipation Proclamation and the roles of different groups in the Civil War.

JumpStart Activity

In a small group, list items that soldiers might like from home. Discuss how the items would help the spirits of the soldiers. Share your group's list with your class.

The U.S. Civil War did not start as a war to end slavery. President Lincoln just wanted to keep the country together. By 1862, however, Lincoln's thinking had changed. He said, "Slavery must die that the nation might live."

The Emancipation Proclamation

Some of Lincoln's advisors said ending slavery would divide the North and unite the South. They were right. But Lincoln was determined. On January 1, 1863, he issued a **proclamation**, or official announcement. It called for the **emancipation**, or setting free, of enslaved African Americans. Lincoln's Emancipation Proclamation freed enslaved African Americans in states at war with the Union.

The proclamation did not end slavery in the border states, slave states that stayed loyal to the Union. These were Delaware, Kentucky, Maryland, Missouri, and West Virginia. It freed enslaved African Americans in the Confederacy, but only those areas controlled by the Union benefited. As a result, most African Americans remained enslaved.

When the Civil War ended, General Gordon Granger was sent to the state of Texas. On June 19, 1865, he read to the people of Galveston, "The people of Texas are informed that . . . all slaves are free." African Americans in Texas celebrated this day as their day of freedom. The tradition of celebrating on this day is now known as **Juneteenth**.

INTERACTIVITY

Explore the key ideas of this lesson.

A Diverse Army

African American abolitionist Frederick Douglass supported Lincoln and encouraged other African Americans to help the Union. Large numbers of them responded by joining the Union army. By the end of the war, about 179,000 African American men had served as soldiers in the Union army.

Many recent immigrants also enlisted. Many German, Irish, British, and Canadian soldiers joined in the fight.

About 20,000 American Indians served in either the Confederate or Union armies. General Ely S. Parker, a Seneca, wrote the surrender document that General Robert E. Lee signed at the end of the war. Parker later told how, during the surrender, Lee said to him, "I am glad to see a real American here." Parker replied to the general, "We are all Americans."

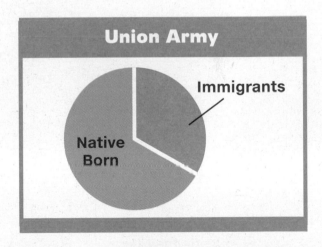

Circle graph showing the breakdown of the Union Army

There were songs written about boredom, marching, and even food. Circle two or three words or phrases that you might use in your song.

Academic Vocabulary

prove • *v.*, find out something is difficult, a problem

👆 **INTERACTIVITY**

Find out more about how to use the soldiers' experiences to compose your song.

A Soldier's Life

The average age of a Civil War soldier was 25. However, boys as young as 12 went into battle as drummer boys. For young soldiers and old, life on the Civil War battlefields was dirty, dangerous, and difficult.

Battles were horrible, but long, boring waits between battles were hard, too. Most battles were in the South, where summers were very hot. Soldiers almost always traveled on foot and might march up to 25 miles a day. The supplies in their backpacks weighed as much as 50 pounds. Marching **proved** even more difficult for Confederate soldiers. The Union blockade kept supplies from reaching the Southerners, so soldiers could not replace worn-out shoes. They often marched and fought in bare feet.

Food was a problem, too. It was rarely fresh. The armies supplied beef and pork. Both were preserved so they did not spoil. Fresh pork had been salted to become "salt pork." Beef was pickled, or preserved in water and spices. In addition, the troops had beans and biscuits. These biscuits were tough flour-and-water biscuits called "hardtack." To survive, troops raided local farms to steal fresh fruits and vegetables.

1. ✓ **Reading Check** For most soldiers, life was very different in the army. **Turn and talk** with a partner to discuss what you would have found to be the most difficult part of being a soldier during the Civil War.

Union soldiers sitting outside their tent

Sick and Wounded

In the mid-1800s, the idea that germs caused disease was a new and untested theory. Most doctors had not heard of it. Many doctors never washed their hands or medical instruments.

A wounded soldier who made it to a hospital might be put in a bed in which someone had just died of fever—without the sheets being changed. Infections were common, and disease spread quickly. There were few medicines and no antibiotics. Twice as many soldiers died of disease as died of gunshot wounds.

Caring for the Soldiers

At this time, there were almost no nursing schools in the United States. Most nurses learned as they worked. One nurse described a field hospital this way:

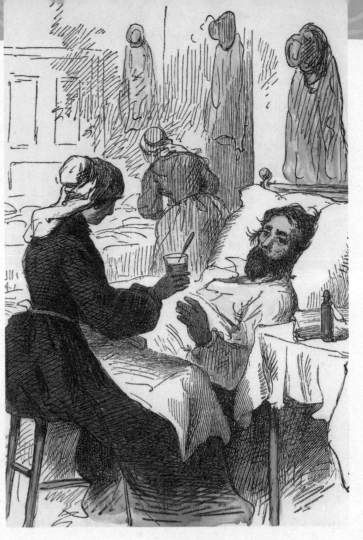

Civil War nurse cares for a wounded soldier

Primary Source

"... just across the lawn there are some of the worst cases & the sight & sounds we have to encounter daily are most distressing. I am mightily afraid we shall have some sort of infectious fever here for it is impossible to keep the place clean & there is a bad smell everywhere."

Clara Barton was the most famous of the volunteer nurses. She went out to where the soldiers were. Barton said her place was "anywhere between the bullet and the battlefield." At the Battle of Antietam, as the cannons boomed, she held the operating table steady for the surgeon. She became known as "the Angel of the Battlefield." After the war, in 1881, she founded the American Red Cross.

Hundreds of women helped on both sides. Juliet Opie Hopkins from Alabama cared for Confederate soldiers. In 1861 she sold all her property and gave the money to the Confederacy to establish hospitals. Hopkins was shot twice while rescuing wounded men on the battlefield.

2. ☑ Reading Check
Identify two things you might do to help nurse soldiers.

_____

_____

_____

_____

Word Wise

Compound Words Some words are made up of two words you may already know, such as *bookshelf* or *snowstorm*. If you are not sure of the meaning of the word, think about the two words that make up the word. Think about the meaning of *battle* and *field* to help you understand the meaning of *battlefield*.

On the Home Front

Most women did not work on the battlefield, they stayed home and took care of their families. They filled the jobs that had been held by men. They ran stores and planted crops.

Women in the South often had to move their families and belongings, as homes and towns were destroyed. They also had to deal with shortages of supplies caused by the North's blockade. Prices increased sharply. The average Southern family's monthly food bill rose from $6.65 just before the war to $68 by 1863. Almost no one could afford food. In April of that year, hundreds of women in Richmond, Virginia, rioted to protest the rise in prices. Women in other Southern cities rioted over the price of bread, too.

When they could, women hid their livestock as the armies came through. Hungry soldiers would kill and eat all the chickens and pigs. Of course, the army would take any other food they could find, too. Often, after an army had passed through, the civilians were left starving. This was the case when the Union army marched through the South.

Women also hid possessions from the enemy soldiers. These included items that had been in their families for generations.

People in the North read about the war. Many sent husbands or sons to fight. In the South, families struggled with the direct effects of the war's destruction.

A family prepares to flee the approaching army

3. ☑ **Reading Check**

Identify three things you would take with you if you had to escape before an enemy army came.

_____

_____

Women in Wartime

Women on both sides contributed to the war effort. In addition to being nurses on the battlefield or keeping farms and family businesses running, they sewed clothing and made bandages. They sold personal possessions to raise money and sent food to the armies.

Some women traveled with their soldier husbands and sons, cooking for them, nursing them, and helping them. A few women even became soldiers. Frances Clalin, for example, disguised herself as a man so that she could fight in the Union army.

Sojourner Truth, a former enslaved African American, had worked for abolition before the war and would work for women's rights after the war. During the war, she gathered supplies for African American regiments. A popular speaker, she often told stories of her life as an enslaved African American.

Sojourner Truth told of her own life as she worked to end slavery.

Primary Source

I have borne thirteen children, and seen most all sold off to slavery, and when I cried out with my mother's grief, none but Jesus heard me!

—Sojourner Truth

Some women became spies. Documents and even weapons could be hidden under the large hoop skirts they wore.

Belle Boyd, nicknamed "La Belle Rebelle," was one of the most famous female Confederate spies. Union soldiers arrested her six times, but she kept spying for the Confederates. After one arrest, Boyd communicated to a Confederate by hiding messages inside rubber balls and throwing them between the bars of her cell windows!

Bringing the War Home

New technology changed the way the war was fought, but it also changed the way people at home experienced the war. People still got news from the battlefield through the "old" technology of soldiers' letters and newspapers.

For the first time, people back home also got to see something of what these soldiers were living through. A new technology, photography, made this possible. The Civil War was the first war to be "taken home" in images. Mathew Brady thought it was important to photograph the war.

People still learn from Brady's photographs showing the details of war. He took pictures of soldiers posing, resting, and cooking. Brady and other photographers also took photos of field hospitals, weapons, and dead bodies on the battlefield. Their photos appeared in newspapers and special **exhibits**.

Academic Vocabulary

exhibit • *n.*, collection of items put out so that people can see them

4. ☑ **Reading Check** **Describe** what caption you would write if you were the photographer of this photograph.

_____

_____

This photograph by Mathew Brady shows wounded soldiers resting between battles beneath a tree.

Camera technology was not well developed at the time. Cameras were large and heavy. All the preparation and developing had to be done in the dark, so the photographers used a "darkroom" wagon. Photographs at that time were taken on specially treated glass plates. The glass plates had to be handled carefully as the wagon bumped through the countryside and across battlefields. Some people claim that as a result of all the letters home and all the photographs, civilians knew more about the Civil War than about any war before.

Mathew Brady spent his own money, buying equipment and hiring assistants, to capture the war in photographs.

INTERACTIVITY

Check your understanding of the key ideas of this lesson.

☑ Lesson 3 Check

5. **Sequence Organize** these events in the correct sequence: Emancipation Proclamation, Juneteenth holiday created, First Battle of Bull Run, Clara Barton starts the Red Cross, Battle of Antietam.

_____

_____

_____

6. Write a letter from the point of view of a Confederate or Union soldier **describing** his experiences to his family. Use an additional sheet of paper if needed.

_____

_____

_____

_____

_____

7. **Understand the** *Quest* Connections Why would soldiers like songs for marching?

_____

_____

_____

The Emancipation Proclamation

President Lincoln reading the Emancipation Proclamation to his Cabinet.

When the Civil War began, President Lincoln was careful to make the war about preserving the Union. He did not support slavery and would have liked to abolish it but Lincoln feared that by ending slavery, he would lose support for the war.

As African Americans joined the Union Army, Lincoln decided to take action. He told a member of his cabinet, that "emancipation had become a military necessity.... The Administration must set an example."

President Lincoln issued the Emancipation Proclamation on January 1, 1863. It did not free all enslaved African Americans. It freed enslaved African Americans in the areas controlled by the Confederacy and anyone who escaped to a free state. The war was now about freeing enslaved African Americans.

Vocabulary Support

The Confederate states rebelling against the United States

will not stop or interfere

thenceforward, *adv.*, going forward from that time or place

thereof, *adv.*, of the thing that is said or mentioned

"...all persons held as slaves within any State or designated part of a State, the people whereof shall then be in rebellion against the United States, shall be then, thenceforward, and forever free; and the Executive Government of the United States, including the military and naval authority thereof, will recognize and maintain the freedom of such persons, and will do no act or acts to repress such persons, or any of them, in any efforts they may make for their actual freedom."

—Emancipation Proclamation

Close Reading

1. **Identify** and circle the organizations or groups that will not interfere with the freedom of enslaved African Americans and their efforts to gain freedom.

2. **Explain** what the Emancipation Proclamation states about the people who are enslaved African Americans and what it means in relationship to the Fugitive Slave Act. In your own words, explain how you think enslaved African Americans would feel when they heard this.

_____

_____

_____

_____

_____

_____

_____

Wrap It Up

Describe how the Emancipation Proclamation is different from other compromises and laws that had been created up to this point. What does it say about a different belief in the Union?

_____

_____

_____

_____

_____

_____

_____

Lesson 4 — The War Ends

INTERACTIVITY

Participate in a class discussion to preview the content of this lesson.

Vocabulary

siege
total war
assassinate

Academic Vocabulary

style
strategy

Unlock The BIG Question

I will know the people, battles, and events that led to the end of the Civil War.

JumPstart Activity

In a small group, list several actions you can take to help restore peace between two friends who have been arguing.

People were eager to see the Civil War end, and both sides became more aggressive. In July 1863, for the first time, Lee led his forces north of the Mason-Dixon line. This line had come to represent the division between free and slave states. The Confederates marched toward Gettysburg, Pennsylvania.

Civil War Battlefields

LEGEND
- Union states
- Confederate states
- Border states
- ★ Major battlefield
- ☆ Other battlefield

IA, MI, NY, MA, CT, IN, OH, PA, Gettysburg, MD, NJ, Antietam, DE, MO, IL, Shenandoah Valley, The Wilderness, Bull Run, Fredericksburg, WV, VA, Cold Harbor, KY, Appomattox Court-House, Peninsular Campaign, Richmond, Prairie Grove, TN, NC, Memphis, Shiloh, AR, Chickamauga, MS, AL, Atlanta, SC, ATLANTIC OCEAN, Vicksburg, Fort Sumter, Red River Campaign, GA, Baton Rouge, LA, Mobile Bay, FL

N W E S

0 — 200 mi
0 — 200 km

Union Victory at Gettysburg

The Battle of Gettysburg was one of the most important battles of the war. It lasted three brutal days and was a turning point in the war.

General George Meade led the Union troops. On July 1, 1863, after a successful Confederate attack, Union soldiers retreated. However, the weary Confederates were unable to follow and gain the victory.

On July 2, fresh Union troops arrived. The Confederates attacked again, but this time the Union troops held their ground. The fighting was fierce.

On July 3, the Confederate forces fired more than 150 cannons. Northern cannons roared back. Commanded by General George Pickett, thousands of Confederate troops attacked. But "Pickett's Charge," as it was called, was a disaster. By the time it ended, more than 5,000 Confederate soldiers lay dead or wounded. The Union had won.

The Battle of Gettysburg was a key victory for the Union, but it came at a steep cost. More than 23,000 Union soldiers and 28,000 Confederate soldiers were dead or wounded.

INTERACTIVITY

Explore the key ideas of this lesson.

Union Victory at Vicksburg

The Confederates had turned back all previous Union attacks at Vicksburg, Mississippi. But controlling Vicksburg meant controlling the Mississippi River, so the Union wanted to take Vicksburg.

Union general Ulysses S. Grant attacked Vicksburg again and again, from the east and then, crossing the river, from the south. But direct attack continued to fail. So Grant laid siege.

A **siege** is a military blockade designed to make a city surrender. The siege lasted 48 days. People in Vicksburg dug caves into the hillside to escape fire from Union cannons. Confederate soldiers and civilians faced starvation. Vicksburg surrendered on July 4, 1863. The tide had finally turned in favor of the Union.

President Lincoln visits Union Army soldiers and officers in Antietam, Maryland battlefield, October 1862.

Grant and Lee		
	Ulysses S. Grant	**Robert E. Lee**
Birthplace	Ohio	Virginia
Education	U.S. Military Academy at West Point	U.S. Military Academy at West Point
Prior military service	Mexican-American War	Mexican-American War
Military rank	General	General
Side	North	South

Ulysses S. Grant

Robert E. Lee

Grant Versus Lee

President Lincoln once said of Ulysses S. Grant, "I can't spare this man. He fights." In March of 1864, Lincoln promoted Grant and gave him control over the entire Union army. Grant was famous for his aggressive fighting **style** and for being relentless.

Academic Vocabulary

style • *n.*, a distinctive, particular, or characteristic of acting or way of moving

strategy • *n.*, a thought-out plan to accomplish a goal over a long time

Robert E. Lee, the chief commander of the Confederate troops, faced a terrible decision when the Civil War broke out. Lee loved the United States and was an officer in the U.S. Army. However, he felt tied to Virginia. He resigned from the Union army and sided with the South.

As a general, Lee was famous for his brilliant military tactics. He was skilled, smart, and daring on the battlefield. He was also known as a gentleman. He was a soldier with refined manners. He used **strategy** rather than brute force. He inspired his troops, because they respected him so much.

Grant and Lee were alike in many ways. Both had received their military training at the U.S. Military Academy at West Point. Both had served in the Mexican-American War. Both were brilliant military leaders.

1. ☑ **Reading Check** **Turn** and **talk** with a partner about how Lee and Grant's military approaches were similar and different.

Sherman in Georgia

Union general William Tecumseh Sherman played a major role in ending the war. Sherman's idea was that war should be as horrible as possible, so the enemy would stop fighting. He didn't just attack military targets; he worked to destroy the South economically, so it could no longer support an army. Sherman's approach came to be known as **total war**.

Leading 100,000 Union troops, Sherman began his invasion of Georgia in May 1864. He headed first for Atlanta. Confederate troops tried to stop Sherman's advance but were driven back by the huge number of Union soldiers.

Sherman began a siege of the city of Atlanta. By September 2, Sherman's forces controlled the city. They destroyed Atlanta's railroad center to disrupt the South's transportation system.

Sherman ordered everyone to leave and then burned much of the city. Union soldiers also took all the food and supplies they could find. Atlanta could no longer offer help to the Confederate army.

From Atlanta, Sherman headed for Savannah on the coast. With 62,000 soldiers, he cut a path of destruction across Georgia. This campaign came to be called "Sherman's March to the Sea." Union troops destroyed everything that might help the South keep fighting. Sherman gave his soldiers only bread to force them to raid villages for food.

Confederate soldiers continued to follow and fight Sherman's forces. They couldn't win, but they reduced the amount of damage done by the Union forces.

On December 21, 1864, Savannah fell without a fight. Union soldiers had caused $100 million worth of damage in their march across Georgia. They then turned north, marching into South Carolina, causing even more destruction in the state where the war began.

Word Wise

Homophones Two or more words that sound the same but have different meanings are homophones. *Role* and *roll* are homophones. Using the wrong word in your writing can make it very confusing for your reader.

Sherman's army left a path of destruction across Georgia as they marched to the sea.

The Road to Appomattox

Union forces were closing in on Lee's army in Virginia. On April 2, 1865, General Lee sent a message to Jefferson Davis that the Confederates should leave Richmond, Virginia. The next day, Union troops entered the city. The Union had captured the capital of the Confederacy! When President Lincoln arrived to tour Richmond, the city's former enslaved African Americans cheered him.

Exhausted and starving, Lee's army of 55,000 men tried to escape west. Grant's force of about 113,000 soldiers trapped them. Grant met Lee in one last battle near the village of Appomattox Court House, Virginia, and once again defeated the weary Confederates. The end had come. The Civil War was over.

On April 9, 1865, General Grant and General Lee met at a farmhouse at Appomattox to discuss the terms of surrender. Among the many Union officers who witnessed the surrender was Ely S. Parker. A Seneca lawyer and Union officer, he had helped write up the terms of surrender.

2. **☑ Reading Check**
Identify Generals Lee and Grant in the painting by labeling them.
Turn and talk with a partner about what the posture of each general suggests.

Grant wanted the healing of the nation to start right away. He didn't take Confederate soldiers prisoner. Instead, he allowed Lee's soldiers to go free. In addition, the Union allowed the Southerners to keep their personal weapons and any horses they had. Grant also offered to give Lee's men food from Union supplies. Lee accepted. As Lee returned to his men, the Union soldiers cheered and fired their rifles, to celebrate their victory over the South. Grant silenced them, saying, "The war is over; the rebels are our countrymen again."

The Cost of the Civil War

The Civil War was the most destructive war in our history. The human costs were very high. About 620,000 people died. Families were torn apart, as some members sided with the Union and others with the Confederacy. The governments of both sides spent billions to fight the war. After the Civil War, many people were in mourning. Eventually a national holiday called Memorial Day was created. It honors all of our nation's fallen soldiers.

Other economic costs were shattering as well. Towns, farms, and industries in the South were ruined. Factories in the North that had relied on Southern cotton were in trouble. However, the economy of the South suffered far greater losses, particularly because the slaves on whom the economy depended were now freed.

Children sitting near ruined buildings in Charleston, South Carolina.

In spite of the destruction, Lincoln still hoped for the healing of the nation. After news of the Confederate surrender reached Washington, D.C., Lincoln appeared before a crowd and asked a band to play "Dixie," one of the battle songs of the Confederacy. "I have always thought 'Dixie' one of the best tunes I ever heard," he told the crowd.

President Lincoln delivering the Gettysburg Address.

The Gettysburg Address

In 1863, thousands of Americans had been killed at Gettysburg, so the battlefield was made into a national cemetery to honor them. On November 19, 1863, about 15,000 people gathered for the ceremony to establish the cemetery. At this event, President Lincoln gave what has become one of America's most famous speeches.

Lincoln's speech, now known as the Gettysburg Address, began with the words "Four score and seven years ago our fathers brought forth upon this continent a new nation." (A score is 20.) Lincoln was reminding people that it had been 87 years since the Declaration of Independence. The fight was about preserving the nation and about self-government.

In the address, Lincoln also praised the soldiers who had given their lives to keep the dream of America alive. It reminded Americans that there was still more work to be done, but also why the work was important.

Primary Source

3. ✔ Reading Check
Underline the words in this excerpt that **describe** democracy.

"We here highly resolve that these dead shall not have died in vain, that this nation under God shall have a new birth of freedom, and that government of the people, by the people, for the people shall not perish from the earth."

—Abraham Lincoln, from the Gettysburg Address

A Terrible Loss for the Nation

Friday evening, April 14, 1865, President Lincoln and his wife, Mary, attended a play at Ford's Theater. During the play, President Lincoln was shot! He died a few hours later, on the morning of April 15.

Lincoln was **assassinated**, or murdered for political reasons, by John Wilkes Booth, a 26-year-old actor who supported the Confederacy. Booth escaped from the theater. But federal troops found him later in a Virginia barn. He refused to surrender. The soldiers shot and killed him. Booth had not worked alone, and Lincoln was not the only target. The whole group of plotters was captured, tried, and hanged.

A funeral train took Lincoln's body to his hometown of Springfield, Illinois, to be buried. It was a tragic loss for the nation. But, before he died, Lincoln had achieved his goal. He had saved the Union.

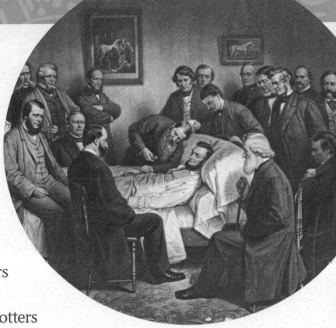

Doctors surround President Lincoln after he is shot.

INTERACTIVITY

Check your understanding of the key ideas of this lesson.

☑ Lesson 4 Check

4. **Main Idea and Details** List three supporting details for the Main Idea: The war turned in the Union's favor. Then explain to a partner how the details support the main idea.

_____

_____

5. **Explain** why Union leaders like General Grant and President Lincoln did not want to punish the South.

_____

_____

_____

6. List at least three major actions that Lincoln is remembered for.

_____

_____

5 Reconstruction

INTERACTIVITY

Participate in a class discussion to preview the content of this lesson.

Unlock The BIG Question

I will know the different plans for Reconstruction and the effects of new amendments to the Constitution.

Vocabulary

Reconstruction
amendment
impeachment
carpetbaggers
segregation
black codes
sharecropping

Academic Vocabulary

enforce
create

JumpStart Activity

In a group of two to three classmates, act out how people on different sides of an argument might react when they meet on the street or playground. Can one person help to make you friends again?

After President Lincoln's assassination, Vice President Andrew Johnson became president. Johnson wanted to carry out Lincoln's plan for **Reconstruction**, the rebuilding and healing of the country. However, Johnson lacked Lincoln's skill at dealing with people. He and Congress fought fiercely.

Like much of the South, Richmond, Virginia, had been destroyed during the Civil War.

Lincoln's plan was to pardon Southerners who swore loyalty to the United States and promised to obey the country's laws. They would also welcome states back into the Union if they outlawed slavery and asked to be let back in. Congress thought these plans were too gentle and felt that the South should be punished for having seceded. However, Congress did want to help newly freed African Americans, called freedmen.

INTERACTIVITY

Explore the key ideas of this lesson.

Congress and Reconstruction

The Republicans who controlled Congress did not trust Johnson. He was a Southerner and had been a Democrat before becoming Lincoln's vice president. Members of Congress began developing a new plan of Reconstruction. They passed the Civil Rights Act of 1866 to grant freedmen full legal equality. Congress then passed several Reconstruction Acts between 1867 and 1868.

The Acts divided the former Confederate states into military districts. The president sent federal troops to the South to keep order and **enforce** emancipation of enslaved African Americans. The Acts required Southern states to write new state constitutions giving African American men the right to vote. The Acts prevented former Confederate leaders from voting or holding elected office. Congress also passed three new amendments to the Constitution. An **amendment** is a change or addition. You will read about these amendments later in this lesson.

Academic Vocabulary

enforce • v., to make people obey a law or rule

Johnson argued that the Reconstruction Acts were against the law because they had been passed without the Southern states being represented in Congress. He said passing laws with half the country unrepresented was unconstitutional. Johnson used his veto power to try to stop Congress. However, Congress was able to override Johnson's vetoes.

Angry about Johnson's attempts to block their laws, the Republicans in Congress tried to impeach Johnson. **Impeachment** is the bringing of charges of wrongdoing against an elected official by the House of Representatives. If an impeached president is found guilty in a Senate trial, he can be removed from office. In May 1868, the Senate found Johnson not guilty. However, Johnson's ability to lead the nation had been seriously weakened.

Rebuilding the South

Reconstruction had many successes. The Freedmen's Bureau had been **created** by President Lincoln to help freed slaves and refugees of the war. The Freedmen's Bureau built schools and hospitals. It hired African American and white teachers from the South and North. New leaders raised taxes to help rebuild roads and railroads and to establish a free education system. Many industries were expanded to provide more jobs.

For the first time, African Americans became elected officials. In Mississippi, two African Americans were elected to the U.S. Senate. In 1870, Hiram R. Revels won the Senate seat that Jefferson Davis once held. In 1874, Blanche K. Bruce was also elected to the Senate. Twenty other African Americans were elected to the House of Representatives.

1. ☑ **Reading Check**
Turn and talk with a partner. **Explain** why education is important for freedom.

Some Southerners resented the new state governments that had been forced on them. Others disliked the Northerners who moved South to start businesses. Because they often carried their possessions in cloth suitcases called carpetbags, these newcomers were called "**carpetbaggers**." Some carpetbaggers came to help, but many came to take advantage of the South's ruined condition. Southerners who supported Reconstruction were given the insulting nickname "scalawags."

People also disliked the new taxes. Many Southerners had a hard time paying these taxes because they were trying to rebuild their farms and homes.

Schools were opened to teach young African Americans to read and write.

Reconstruction also had some failures and segregation was one of these. **Segregation** is the separation of people, usually by race. Schools, hospitals, theaters, railroad cars, even whole towns were segregated.

Right after the war, some Southern states passed **black codes**. These laws denied African American men the right to vote. It kept them from owning guns or taking certain types of jobs. The Civil Rights Act was designed to protect African Americans from these codes.

New Amendments

Ending slavery was one of the first steps in Reconstruction—and the most important. The Emancipation Proclamation had not ended all slavery. The Republicans in Congress now wanted slavery to be illegal everywhere in the United States.

Congress passed the Thirteenth Amendment on January 31, 1865. It abolished slavery. The Fourteenth Amendment was approved in July 1868. It guaranteed equality under the law for all citizens—and it gave Congress the power to enforce this guarantee. It also ruled that important Confederate leaders could not be elected to political office.

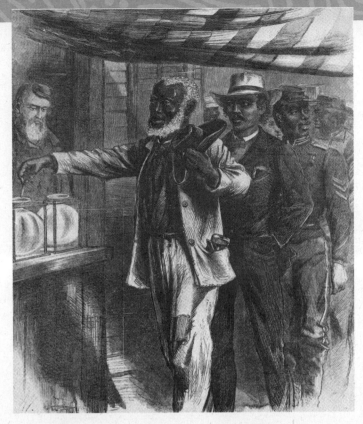

African American men voting

The Fifteenth Amendment, passed by Congress in 1869 and approved by the states in February 1870, gave all male citizens the right to vote without regard to race. It was a big step forward for formerly enslaved African Americans.

Before being allowed back into the Union, former Confederate states had to accept all three amendments. Eventually, all did. By July 15, 1870, all the former Confederate states had been allowed back into the Union.

2. 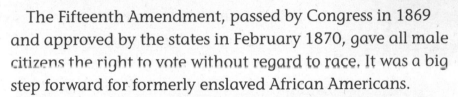 **Reading Check** **Summarize** Use your own words to **describe** how each of these amendments extended rights for U.S. citizens.

13th Amendment	14th Amendment	15th Amendment
ended slavery		

After Reconstruction

After Reconstruction, the South remained poor. Rebuilding was slow. Poverty was widespread. African Americans lost much of the political power they had gained.

Sharecroppers picking cotton after the Civil War.

Many African Americans and poor whites in the South became trapped in a system called sharecropping. **Sharecropping** is a system in which someone who owns land lets someone else "rent" the land to farm it. The renter, or tenant farmer, pays rent with a share of the crops he or she raises. The renter then uses the rest of the crops to feed the family or sell for income.

Sharecropping often kept people in debt. Landowners would charge high interest on money tenant farmers borrowed for seeds and tools. It was often impossible to pay off the debt.

3. ☑ **Reading Check** **Analyze** the picture. What can you infer about the life of a sharecropper?

_____

_____

Negative Reaction

During Reconstruction, some white Southerners objected to rights for African Americans. A few formed a group called the Ku Klux Klan. This group used terror to restore white control. They burned African American schools and homes. They attacked African Americans who tried to vote. They also lynched, or killed, many African Americans. Lynching is when someone is put to death by a mob who has no legal authority.

In 1877, the federal government withdrew the last federal troops from the South. White Southern Democrats regained power in state governments. They passed new laws known as Jim Crow laws that reinforced segregation. Other laws kept African Americans from voting. Some states charged a poll tax, or payment, to vote.

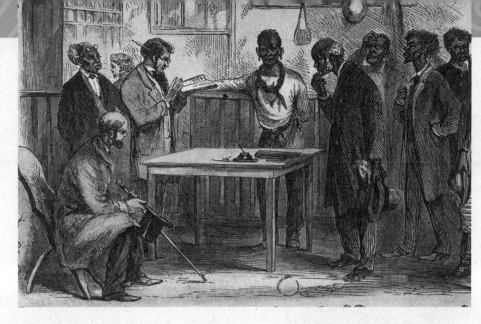

Some states required African Americans to take a reading test before they could vote. Under slavery, many had not been allowed to learn to read or write, and so they failed the test.

A "grandfather clause" was added to some state constitutions. It said that men could vote only if their father or grandfather had voted before 1867. This "grandfather clause" kept most African Americans from voting, because they had not gained the right to vote until 1870. It would be a long time before most African Americans enjoyed the civil rights they should have as citizens.

In some areas, tests or other means were created to prevent African Americans from voting.

 **INTERACTIVITY**

Check your understanding of the key ideas of this lesson.

☑ Lesson 5 Check

4. **Explain** how the struggles of freed African Americans changed after the end of the Civil War and how the amendments that were added to the Constitution helped them.

_____

_____

_____

_____

5. As a result of the war, you are now freed from slavery. In a letter to a friend, **describe** how things have changed for you because of the war.

_____

_____

6. **Identify** three effects the Civil War had on the Constitution.

_____

_____

Quality:
Courage

Harriet Tubman (about 1820–1913)
Fighting for Freedom

Around 1820, Harriet Tubman (born Araminta Ross) was born into slavery in Maryland. Harriet served others and endured harsh living conditions and frequent physical beatings. In her early teens, Harriet courageously stood up for a fieldworker and was forcefully struck on the head; she never fully recovered from this injury.

In 1844 Harriet married John Tubman, a free African American. Fearing she would be sold away, Tubman began her escape to Canada in 1849. She changed her name to Harriet so that her identity would be kept a secret. On her way, she settled in Pennsylvania and met members of the Philadelphia Anti-Slavery Society. She learned all about the Underground Railroad.

After her escape, Tubman worked hard to save money so she could lead rescue missions. In 1851 she returned to Maryland. Over the next six years Tubman put her life at risk and successfully conducted about 300 African Americans to freedom in the North including members of her family. John Brown, a leading abolitionist, described Tubman as, "one of the bravest persons on this continent."

During the Civil War, Tubman served the Union as a scout, a nurse, and even a spy. She was unfairly paid for her wartime service and had to support herself by selling homemade baked goods. After the war, Tubman made a living giving antislavery speeches.

Find Out More

1. Why do you think Harriet Tubman risked her life and freedom to help others?

_____

_____

_____

2. Harriet Tubman was a courageous woman who took great risks to bring people to freedom. Work with a partner to find out about other African Americans who helped the enslaved, such as Harriet Jacobs, Nat Turner, Denmark Vesey, and Gabriel Prosser.

Visual Review

Use these graphics to review some of the key terms and ideas from this chapter.

Union and Confederate Forces and Casualties

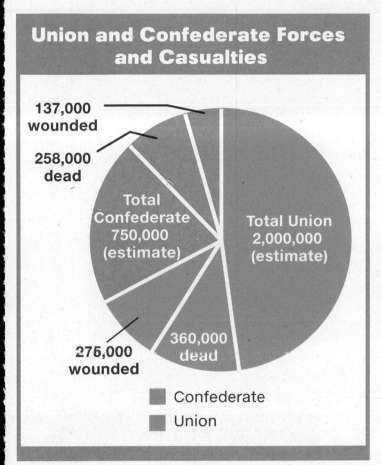

137,000 wounded

258,000 dead

Total Confederate 750,000 (estimate)

Total Union 2,000,000 (estimate)

275,000 wounded

360,000 dead

■ Confederate
■ Union

Source: Navy Department Library War Casualty Statistics

States with 15 or More Civil War Battles

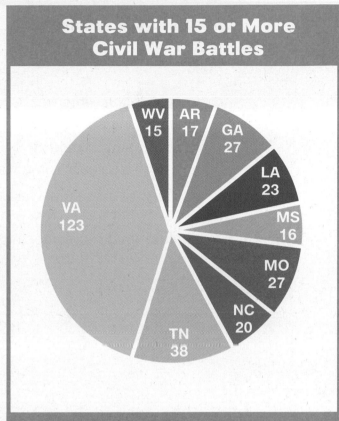

WV 15

AR 17

GA 27

LA 23

MS 16

MO 27

NC 20

TN 38

VA 123

Source: National Park Service

Laws and Amendments

1820 – Missouri Compromise

1850 – Compromise of 1850

1854 – Kansas–Nebraska Act

1863 – Emancipation Proclamation

1865 – Thirteenth Amendment

1866 – Civil Rights Act

1867 – First Reconstruction Act

1868 – Fourteenth Amendment

1870 – Fifteenth Amendment

● **GAMES**

Play the vocabulary game.

Vocabulary and Key Ideas

1. What is **segregation**?

_____

2. Complete the sentences. Choose from these words: siege, enlist, amendment, states' rights, compromise.

In an attempt to keep the country united, Congress had to _____ and each side gave something to get something.

At the start of the Civil War Southerners were fighting for _____.

3. **Explain** what sharecropping is and some of the problems it caused.

_____

_____

_____

_____

4. **Analyzing a Map** Look at the map. Why did the Confederate government want to capture Fort Sumter? Why did the Union government want to keep it?

_____

_____

_____

_____

_____

_____

_____

_____

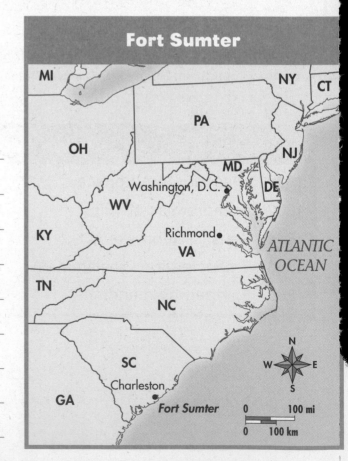

Fort Sumter

Critical Thinking and Writing

5. **Analyze** the economic and geographic differences between the North and the South that helped lead to the feelings of sectionalism.

_____

_____

_____

_____

_____

_____

6. **Interpret** Fill in the circle next to the best answer. Which of the following was part of the Compromise of 1850?

(A) Maine joined the Union as a free state.

(B) The Fugitive Slave Law became a law.

(C) African American men were allowed to vote.

(D) The U.S. Supreme Court declared that African Americans were not citizens.

7. **Analyze** What did the Emancipation Proclamation accomplish? How was it limited?

_____

_____

_____

8. **Revisit the Big Question** Why might many people say the Civil War was worth fighting?

_____

_____

_____

_____

9. **Writing Workshop: Write an Opinion** Imagine you heard President Lincoln deliver the Gettysburg Address. On a separate paper, write a letter to a friend and explain how you felt about the speech and how the audience reacted. Include details from the text to support your opinion.

Analyze Primary Sources

"Times are very hard here every thing is scarce and high ... corn is selling for 10 dollars, bacon 45 cents per pound .... We cannot get a yard of calico for less than one dollar."

—In a letter dated August 23, 1862,
a Virginia woman complaining to her sister about hard times and high prices

10. This letter was written by a woman living in Virginia during the Civil War. During the war the armies often took food from farmers as they passed by. How does this letter help you to understand the hardships that people living in the Southern states experienced?

_____

_____

_____

Make Decisions

11. You are a doctor during the Civil War and the Union army needs doctors. You want to support your country and the soldiers. However, you have patients in your town who need a doctor also. What can you consider as you try to make a good decision?

_____

_____

_____

_____

_____

Quest Findings

👆 INTERACTIVITY

Learn more about Civil War music with an online activity.

Sing Along!

You have read the lessons in this chapter and now you are ready to plan and write your song. Remember that the goals of the song are to offer comfort, to entertain, or to inspire others.

1 Prepare to Write

Organize the information you have learned about the Civil War. Decide what type of song you want to write. Should it be a marching song, a ballad, or a funny song? Choose the type you want to write.

2 Write a Draft

Use your notes and the music you have collected from your Quest Connections to write a draft. Some ideas to consider while you are writing include:

- What is the song about?
- How do you want your audience to feel when they listen to it?
- Is there a chorus in your song? How often should it be used?

3 Write Your Song

Put the words and music together to create your song. Share your song with a partner or another group. Listen to what others say. Is your message getting through?

4 Revise

Make changes to the words and music to improve your song. Did other classmates use different musical styles? How does each style make you feel?

Chapter 10

Expanding West and Overseas

GO ONLINE FOR DIGITAL RESOURCES

- VIDEO
- INTERACTIVITY
- AUDIO
- GAMES
- ASSESSMENT
- eTEXT

The BIG Question

VIDEO

How did different groups experience the growth of the nation?

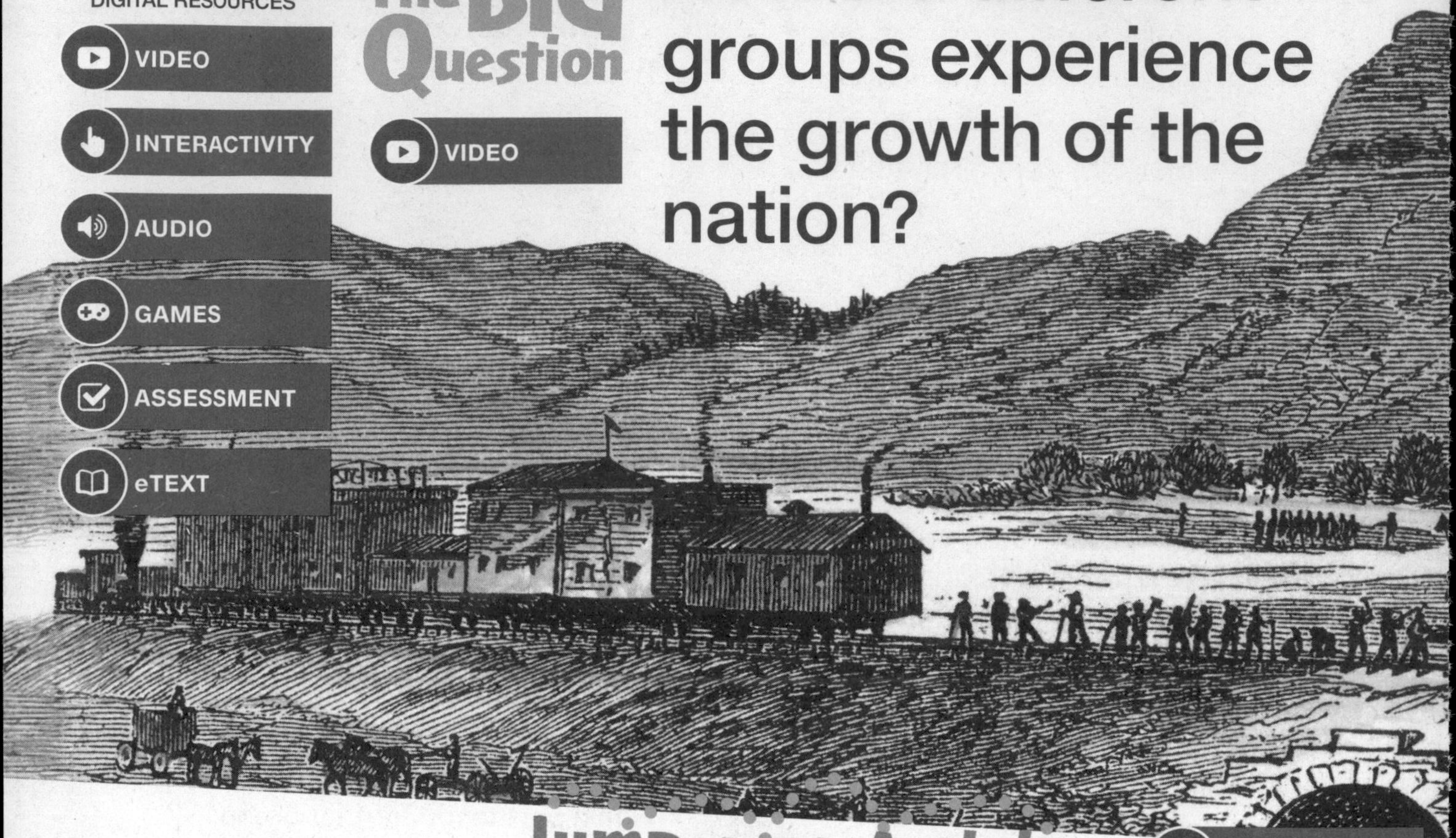

Jumpstart Activity

INTERACTIVITY

Think about people you know who have moved to a new home, county, state, or country. With a partner, create a list of three reasons why people move. Then share the list with another pair of students.

____

____

____

____

____

____

All Aboard!

Preview the chapter **vocabulary** as you sing the rap.

All aboard the train for new land and new gains,
Moving east to west, across the Great Plains.
Farmers, miners, ranchers, **pioneers** of all kinds
There was plenty of land and a **gold rush** to mine.

Bustin' some sod and creating new homes
One hundred sixty acres for our family to roam.
Moving west so fast would create a new enemy,
"But anything west of me was **manifest destiny**."

The government needed land and raw materials to
    follow its course,
This expansion of the country had no time for remorse.
So the American Indian tribes were pushed out
    of the way
Onto Indian **reservations** that still exist to this day.

Annexing so fast, with the wealth it amassed,
New lands and its people would not be surpassed.
Hawaii, Alaska, and the Caribbean too,
Those made the United States that every country knew.

Expanding West and Overseas

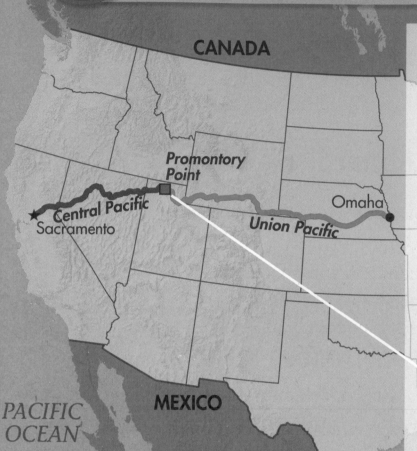

CANADA

Promontory Point

Central Pacific
Sacramento

Union Pacific

Omaha

PACIFIC OCEAN

MEXICO

Where did the transcontinental railroad work begin and end?

The Central Pacific Railroad Company started work near Sacramento, California. The Union Pacific Railroad Company started work in Omaha, Nebraska. They joined together in Promontory, Utah.

The Golden Spike

TODAY
You can visit the Golden Spike National Historic Site at Promontory Summit.

What happened and When?

Read the timeline to find out about the events that helped our nation grow.

1850   **1860**   **1870**   **1880**

1862
President Lincoln signs the Homestead Act of 1862.

1869
Transcontinental railroad links East to West.

Who will you meet?

Nat Love
An African American cowboy from the Old West

Chief Joseph
An American Indian chief of the Nez Perce

Chief Sitting Bull
An American Indian chief of the Sioux

Queen Liliuokalani
Hawaii's first queen and last royal ruler

 INTERACTIVITY

Complete the interactive digital activity.

1890   1900   1910   1920

1890
Battle of Wounded Knee brings Indian Wars to an end.

1898
The Spanish-American War fought.

TODAY
More than one million ships have passed through the Canal.

1914
Panama Canal opens.

Quest
Project-Based Learning

Read All About It!

Many Americans believed in Manifest Destiny, or the idea of expanding across North America. The transcontinental railroad played an important part in the growth of our nation. It linked the East Coast to the West Coast. Many cities grew around the railroad stations, and workers from the East moved west to make new homes. The railroads helped to boost the economy and move goods and products more quickly across the country.

Quest Kick Off

As a young news reporter, your mission is to write an interesting article explaining the impact of the transcontinental railroad on the growth of our nation.

1 Ask Questions

How do you think the railroad helped the growth of the nation? What struggle did the railroad cause? Did everyone have the same opinion about the transcontinental railroad? Write two questions of your own.

2 Research

INTERACTIVITY

Explore how the transcontinental railroad influenced the growth of the nation.

Follow your teacher's instructions to find examples of yellow journalism—newspaper articles that use exaggeration as a way to attract attention. What do the articles have in common?

....

....

....

....

....

....

3 Look for *Quest* Connections

Begin looking for Quest Connections that will help you write your newspaper article.

4 *Quest* Findings
Write Your Article

Use the Quest Findings page at the end of the chapter to help you write your article.

Railroads, Miners, and Ranchers

INTERACTIVITY

Participate in a class discussion to preview the content of this lesson.

Unlock
The BIG
Question

I will know how the expansion of the railroads changed American life.

Vocabulary

pioneer
Manifest Destiny
transcontinental railroad
gold rush
cattle drive

Academic Vocabulary

fiercely
distribute

JumPstart Activity

Work with a partner to make a list of 2–3 technology items that have changed your life and explain how. Then choose one of the ways you listed to act out.

It is 1860. There are crowded cities in the eastern part of the United States. Families came to these cities from Europe to find a better life. Now many people are deciding to migrate to the western plains to find more economic opportunity. It is a long, hard trip, but this journey will be the start of a new life.

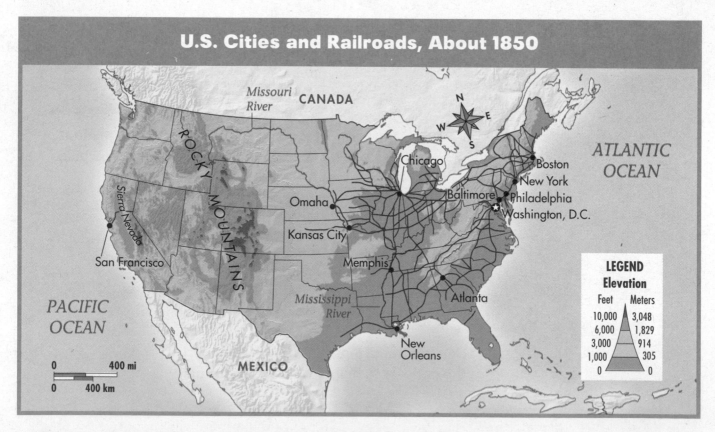

U.S. Cities and Railroads, About 1850

The Movement From East to West

While the eastern cities were crowded, the western United States offered people plenty of space to live and work. The West also had many resources. There was fertile farmland for growing wheat and other crops. The thick forests provided lumber, while the flat plains offered large grassy areas for grazing cattle. Miners could search for rich deposits of minerals, such as gold and silver.

INTERACTIVITY

Explore the key ideas of this lesson.

Getting to the West was not easy, however. Most people went west by stagecoach or wagon, which were slow and dangerous ways to travel.

With so many resources, it's no wonder the federal government encouraged people to move west. These **pioneers**, or early settlers, included farmers, miners, ranchers, and immigrants such as Germans, Irish, and Jewish people from Eastern Europe. In addition, Mormon settlers moved to Salt Lake City, in what is now Utah. Many of these settlers believed in the idea of **Manifest Destiny**. According to this belief, the United States should keep expanding west, across the continent, to the Pacific Ocean.

The pioneers provided an important link between the cities in the East and the open land in the West. In the East, factory workers made goods, such as textiles, to sell to other countries. But these factories needed raw materials, such as lumber and minerals. At the same time, growing cities needed to feed their workers.

The much-needed food, lumber, and other important resources came from the West. But the pioneers soon faced a serious problem. How could they transport goods to the East more quickly? There was no railroad link between the Mississippi River valley and the Pacific coast. That situation was about to change.

1. **☑ Reading Check** **Make Predictions** How would pioneers benefit from a railroad link between the Mississippi River and the Pacific coast?

_____

_____

_____

A National Railroad System

Many people supported building a **transcontinental railroad**, one that stretched across the country. Congress passed the Pacific Railway Act of 1862, which gave the job of building the railroad to two companies. The Union Pacific Railroad Company would build a railroad west from Omaha, Nebraska. The Central Pacific Railroad Company would build a railroad east from Sacramento, California. The government paid the companies with money and land as they went. As a result, each one raced to finish first.

Many of the workers on both railroads were Chinese immigrants. Their skills with gunpowder made blasting tunnels through the mountains possible.

Four years later, workers from both companies completed the first transcontinental railroad. On May 10, 1869, the two lines joined at Promontory Point, Utah. To celebrate the event, a golden railroad spike was hammered into place. At long last, Americans could travel by rail from coast to coast.

Trains like this one linked the Mississippi River valley with the West Coast.

Quest Connection

The American government was heavily involved with the transcontinental railroad. What benefits would a transcontinental rail system have on the nation?

INTERACTIVITY

Explore how the government encouraged settling the West.

Mining in the West

The 1849 **gold rush** attracted people to California who wanted to find gold and become rich. Ten years later, more gold was discovered throughout the West. Miners also discovered silver, zinc, copper, and lead.

Sometimes miners' tools were very simple. Some miners shook a tin pan filled with soil and water. With luck, heavier pieces of gold sank to the bottom. New technology also provided tools that improved miners' work. Miners used large amounts of water to separate gold from the soil. Machines, such as the water wheel, could deliver water up to the stream bank where miners shoveled soil. No matter what process was used, mining was difficult and often dangerous.

Some miners did become rich. Most did not. But large-scale mining damaged the land. For example, drilling created rock dust. Dumping this rock dust into rivers polluted the water and ruined towns and farms.

Often miners and farmers disagreed about the effects of mining on the land. Farmers were worried because certain types of mining destroyed the soil. Mining released poisonous gases into the air. To remove gold, miners used a metal called mercury. Too much mercury poisoned streams and rivers.

Some miners used a water wheel in their search for gold.

2. ✓ **Reading Check** **Explain** how the water wheel helped improve the work of gold miners.

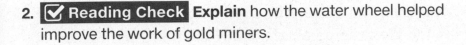

_____

_____

Cowboys and Ranchers

Cattle raised in the West provided beef for people living in the growing eastern cities. At the end of the Civil War, millions of cattle grazed freely across the open Texas plains. The land was better suited for ranching than for farming. But there was one problem. How could ranchers get their cattle to market?

In 1867, the Kansas Pacific Railroad helped solve this problem. The company built a rail line to Abilene, Kansas. After that, cowboys guided huge herds of cattle to Kansas. Then they sold the cattle to buyers from the East, who shipped the herds on the railroad to meat-packing plants in Chicago and eastern cities.

Word Wise

Prefix When you see an unfamiliar word, try using prefixes to figure out the meaning. For example, you will see the word _disagreed_ in the third paragraph on this page. At the beginning of the word you see the prefix, _dis-_, which means _not_. It changes the meaning of the word _agree_ to _not agree_.

fiercely • *adv.*, in a violent manner

By the 1880s, waves of settlers pushed farther west across the plains, setting up farms. Meanwhile, the new Santa Fe Railroad helped ranches expand farther west. Soon farmers and ranchers were competing **fiercely** for land in the Southwest.

The Impact of the Railroads

The growing railroad system changed the economy across America. Raw materials from the West now shipped more quickly to factories and ports in the East. Cowboys no longer guided cattle to market along dusty trails. Now these **cattle drives** ended at railroad towns, where the cattle were carried by train to Chicago and to the coasts. At the same time, railroads carried products made in eastern factories to cities and towns in the West.

Cowboys could move cattle quickly by using cattle cars on the railroads.

Of course, the many new railroads carried people, too. For the first time, passengers could travel by train across the country. Bad weather could no longer slow their trips. Travelers and business people were eager to move by train. After 1869 at least one train from the East and one train from the West ran across the entire country each week.

Academic Vocabulary

distribute • *v.*, to divide out

Train travel helped the West to develop more quickly. Cities and towns were **distributed** along the train lines. More and more Americans lived west of the Mississippi, and more states joined the Union. By 1900 only three western territories remained—Oklahoma, Arizona, and New Mexico.

3. **☑ Reading Check**
By 1920, westward expansion had given Americans access to many resources. In the map legend, **identify** and circle five resources made accessible to the East by the railroads.

Resources of the United States by 1920

LEGEND

🐂 Cattle   ✕ Mixed farming
🦫 Copper
🌱 Corn   🐑 Sheep
🐚 Cotton   🐟 Silver
🍶 Dairy   ➖ Timber
🍞 Gold   🌾 Wheat
🔨 Lead   ⚒ Zinc

Every month new settlers traveled west by rail to build new lives. At the same time, railroads helped other industries develop too. These included the lumber and mining industries.

4. ☑ **Reading Check** **Identify** and list three ways the railroad impacted American life.

_____

_____

_____

_____

☑ Lesson 1 Check

👆 **INTERACTIVITY**

Check your understanding of the key ideas of this lesson.

5. **Cause and Effect Identify** ways in which the rapid growth of technological developments, such as the transcontinental railroad, affected the economy of the United States.

_____

_____

_____

6. **Draw Conclusions** If you were a settler moving into the West, what geographic features would you look for to find the best economic opportunities?

_____

_____

_____

7. **Understand the** _Quest_ **Connections** Explain the effects the transcontinental railroad had on the economic growth and development in the United States during the 19th century.

_____

_____

_____

Compare Line and Bar Graphs

Graphs show information in a visual way. They help you to better understand facts in what you read, including in your social studies book. Reading a graph helps you to analyze complex information quickly.

Line graphs show how something has changed over time. The line graph to the right shows the total number of miles of railroad tracks in the United States. It presents this information over a period of time, from 1860 to 1910. It helps you see how railroads changed in the United States during this period. Each section of the line shows a change between years.

Bar graphs help you compare the different sizes or amounts of something by analyzing the size of each bar. Look at the bar graph to the right. It shows the miles of railroad track in different parts of the United States in one year, 1870. The numbers on the left side of the graph show the number of miles of track. The labels on the bottom of the graph show different regions of the country. Each bar represents a different region.

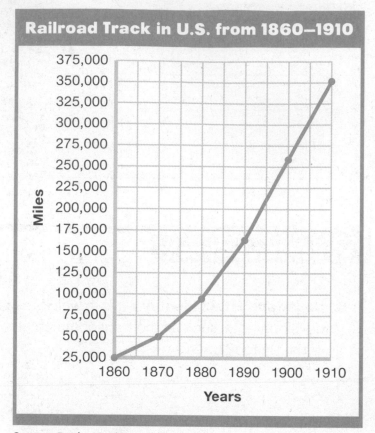

Railroad Track in U.S. from 1860–1910

Source: Davis, Hughes, McDougal, *American Economic History*

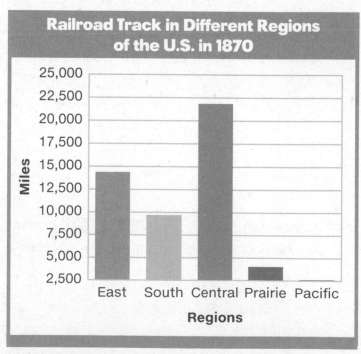

Railroad Track in Different Regions of the U.S. in 1870

Source: *Historical Statistics*, Series Q 32

Your Turn!

1. Between 1860 and 1880, about how many miles of railroad track were built in the United States? _____

VIDEO

Watch a video about interpreting graphs.

2. Between 1880 and 1900, about how many miles of railroad track were built in the United States? _____

3. Suppose that you wanted to travel by rail in the United States. Could you travel to more places in 1890 or 1860? Explain.

_____

_____

_____

4. Study the line graph. What is one generalization you can make about the data in this graph?

_____

_____

_____

5. Now look at the bar graph.

   • What part of the country had the highest number of railroad miles in 1870? _____

   • What part of the country had the lowest number of railroad miles in 1870? _____

6. **Apply** Suppose you made a graph recording the number of people who moved west between 1860 and 1910. Which type of graph would help you more easily find the year with the greatest number of new settlers? Explain your answer.

_____

_____

_____

_____

👆 **INTERACTIVITY**

Participate in a class discussion to preview the content of this lesson.

Unlock The BIG Question

I will know what it was like to be a homesteader in the West during the nineteenth century.

Vocabulary

Homestead Act
homesteader
drought
irrigation
dry farming
sodbuster

Academic Vocabulary

productive
appeal

Jumpstart Activity

Life on the homestead was not easy. Look at the picture on this page. What can you hypothesize about life on a homestead?

A pioneer family stood alone on the Great Plains, looking at miles of flat, empty, wind-swept grassland that stretched far into the distance. They were eager to begin living their dream. What would their future be like?

Homesteaders led difficult lives on the prairie. They had to fight many odds including limited supplies and difficult weather conditions.

160 Acres!

To encourage settlers to move west to the Great Plains and to areas beyond, President Abraham Lincoln signed the **Homestead Act** of 1862. Under this law, new settlers received 160 acres of land for a small fee—$18.00. **Homesteaders** also had to build a home on their land within six months. After living there for five years, the land would be theirs.

The federal government hoped the settlers would turn the West into **productive** farmland. The land offered in the Homestead Act **appealed** to Americans and immigrants alike. Immigrants from Sweden, Norway, Denmark, Germany, and Russia brought their languages, customs, and traditions to their new homes.

Homesteading was hard work. Prairie land was flat and open, with few trees, and the thick grass could grow six feet tall. In the summer it was blazing hot. Fierce rain, windstorms, and swarms of grasshoppers could destroy crops. Often, severe **droughts** meant long periods without rain. During the winter, blizzards sometimes trapped people under the deep snow. The freezing cold killed many farm animals.

These hardy pioneers built their homes near hills to protect them from the strong prairie winds. It was also important to live near a railroad. Farmers wanted an easy way to transport their crops and cattle to market.

Adapting to the Environment

Settlers learned to adapt, or change, so that they could live in their new homes. For example, farther west, the land became much dryer, and many kinds of wheat did not grow well there. But immigrants from Russia brought a new kind of winter wheat that could grow better in dry land.

Farmers modified their environment, too. Some tapped into the underground supply of water and used irrigation. **Irrigation** directs water from a source to a place that needs it. In one system, pumps gathered water into a pond. Then the water ran through irrigation ditches to the fields.

INTERACTIVITY

Explore the key ideas of this lesson.

Academic Vocabulary

productive • *adj.* able to produce a large amount of something

appeal • *v.*, to be interesting or attractive to someone

1. ☑ **Reading Check**
List two challenges homesteaders faced while living on the prairie.

_____

_____

_____

_____

Other homesteaders used a farming method called **dry farming**. With this method, farmers conserved moisture in the soil during dry weather.

The settlers on the prairie were called **sodbusters** because they had to cut through the thickly rooted grass, or sod, to build their homes and plant crops. Cutting sod bricks was hard work, and building a sod house could take many weeks. Often, settlers built a small, dark shelter into the side of a hill to live in while they built their houses. Sometimes, as the family did in the photo, they built their home right around the original shelter.

To build a sod house, settlers cut the sod into bricks. It took 3,000 sod bricks to build a small house. To make the roof, settlers used cedar poles to hold up bundles of mud, grass, and more sod.

Sod houses were not very clean and they were a bit damp. But sod is an excellent insulation. Sod homes were cool in the summer and warm in the winter. Since they were made from dirt, they were even fireproof.

Settlers built their sod houses against hills for protection from the weather.

Many homesteaders adapted the land to their own needs. But some could not adapt. Harsh weather, accidents, and sickness were serious problems. Living on the Great Plains could be very lonely, especially during the winter. Some homesteaders gave up and went home, while others moved on to the growing cities on the West Coast.

Farming on the Great Plains

Sometimes farmers adapted to their new life by using natural resources. Other times, they used new technology. Inventors built new kinds of machines to help settlers farm their land and keep their crops safe.

Iron plows used in the East didn't work very well in the Midwest. The rich soil stuck to the bottom of the plow. To solve this problem, in 1837 John Deere built a stronger plow made of steel. Another inventor, James Oliver, made a new kind of iron plow in 1869. This plow was less expensive and was long lasting. Best of all, farmers could use it in any kind of soil. Another important farm machine, the mechanical reaper, was invented by Cyrus McCormick in 1831. Large horses pulled the reaper across the fields. Now farmers could harvest crops much faster.

Farmers on the Great Plains faced yet another problem. How could they protect their crops from animals or keep their animals from wandering away? Farmers needed strong fences, but there were few trees or large stones available. To solve this problem, Joseph Glidden invented barbed wire in 1873. Farmers now had a way of enclosing their fields. They could also fence in their cattle.

Farmers used barbed wire as a way to keep things in and out of their fields.

2. **☑ Reading Check** **Identify** and list two inventions that solved problems faced by farmers on the Great Plains.

_____

_____

"From Sea to Shining Sea"

Wave after wave of homesteaders pushed across the land toward the Pacific Ocean. By 1900 they had filed claims to own 80 million acres of land. The population of the western United States grew by almost 30 percent. Between 1861 and 1907, seven western territories became states: Kansas (1861), Nebraska (1867), Colorado (1876), North Dakota (1889), South Dakota (1889), Montana (1889), and Oklahoma (1907).

To encourage further settlement, the federal government offered free land in Oklahoma in 1889. People from all across the country traveled there by railroad and wagon. On the morning of April 22, an excited crowd of settlers waited for the signal. At noon, soldiers fired pistols in the air. Then thousands of men and women surged forward to claim their free homesteads.

The Oklahoma land rushes beginning in 1889 helped close the western frontier. By 1890 the United States no longer had a frontier. A new stage in United States history was beginning.

3. ☑ **Reading Check** **Describe** how settlers modified the environment of the United States between 1850 and 1890.

_____

_____

_____

_____

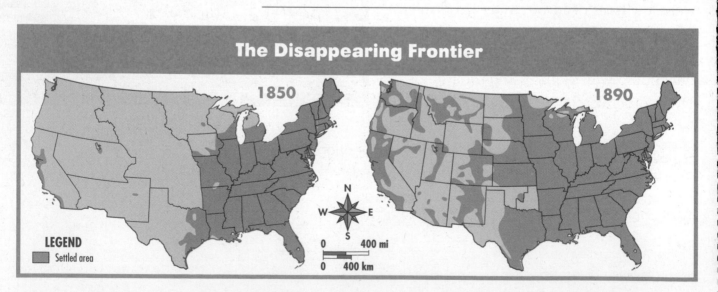

The Disappearing Frontier

1850

1890

LEGEND
Settled area

N W E S

0   400 mi

0   400 km

This painting, entitled American Progress, was painted by John Gast in 1872. The painting has come to symbolize the American belief in Manifest Destiny.

INTERACTIVITY

Check your understanding of the key ideas of this lesson.

☑ Lesson 2 Check

4. **Make Generalizations Analyze** the role of immigrants and pioneers in the growth of the United States.

_____

_____

_____

5. **Describe** one of the challenges farmers faced on the Great Plains and how they were able to resolve it.

_____

_____

_____

6. **Identify** the accomplishments of John Deere and **explain** how his invention mechanizing agriculture changed American life.

_____

_____

_____

Make Predictions

Predicting involves making a guess about what will happen in the future. When you **make predictions**, you analyze the information by combining reading clues with past experiences. Then you try to figure out what might happen next. For example, the title of Lesson 2 is *Sodbusters and Homesteaders*. The pictures throughout the lesson are clues to what the lesson is about. Past experience tells you that people who settled the West had lots of challenges. You might predict that the lesson will be about challenges faced by early settlers.

Make predictions before, during, and after reading.

- Making predictions before reading accesses what you already know about the topic.

- Making predictions during reading lets you make connections between what you already know and new information. Predicting helps you set expectations about what you will read next.

- Making predictions after reading connects and extends what you have learned to a larger setting.

Here is an example of a prediction you might make during reading.

Making Predictions

1 - Clues
The Homestead Act offered settlers 160 acres of land for $18.

3 - Prediction
Many people will move west to own cheap land.

2 - Experience or Prior Knowledge
People like to get something valuable for a low price.

Read and analyze the following passage to complete the Making Predictions graphic organizer.

▶ VIDEO

Watch a video about predicting consequences.

The Homestead Act drove many settlers to the Great Plains and beyond. They were not the first to settle the West. American Indian tribes had lived on these lands for centuries, but they did not believe they owned the land. They shared the resources and used only what they needed. Settlers wanted to own the land and change it. As more settlers moved into these territories, tensions increased.

Complete the graphic organizer below with clues and experience or prior knowledge you can use to make a prediction about what might happen as the number of settlers moving west increases.

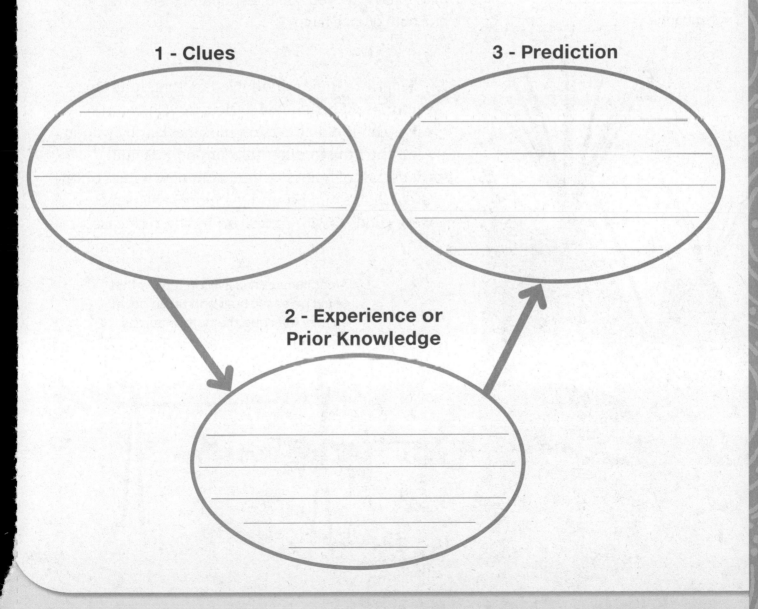

1 - Clues

3 - Prediction

2 - Experience or Prior Knowledge

American Indians Struggle to Survive

 INTERACTIVITY

Participate in a class discussion to preview the content of this lesson.

Vocabulary

tepee
reservation

Academic Vocabulary

exchange
stage

Unlock The BIG Question

I will know why there were conflicts between settlers and American Indians in the West.

JumpStart Activity

Imagine you and your friends want to build a club house. You find the perfect spot, but another group of friends already built a club house there. Make a list of two to three ways you could respond. Is there a way to make both groups happy?

American Indians had lived on their lands for centuries. At first, a few settlers traveled onto American Indian lands on horseback or by wagon. After the transcontinental railroad was built, thousands of homesteaders built new homes on the Great Plains and beyond. As more settlers moved west, conflicts with American Indians increased.

American Indians lived in tepees that could be easily built and taken down as they followed the buffalo across the plains.

Who Owns the Land?

American Indians and settlers viewed land ownership differently. Lakota Sioux Chief Crazy Horse said, "One does not sell the land people walk on." American Indians did not believe they owned the land. Instead, they respected the natural world and used its resources to provide for their families. For example, American Indians living on the Great Plains hunted and gathered food. Their homes, called **tepees**, were constructed of wood poles, bark, and animal skins.

Unlike the American Indians, settlers wanted to own their land. The United States government said that after living in their new homes for five years, the land belonged to the settlers.

The End of the Buffalo

For centuries, American Indians on the Great Plains had depended on buffalo for food, clothing, and shelter. No part of a buffalo went to waste. Even the horns became spoons and bowls. The Plains Indians hunted buffalo without destroying the large herds. In 1865, around 15 million buffalo still roamed the West.

When the new settlers arrived, they killed millions of buffalo for their meat and their hides. Eastern hunters shot many buffalo for sport and sold the hides.

By 1889, fewer than 1,000 buffalo were left in the United States. The destruction of this precious resource angered American Indians and hurt their way of life. It also deepened the conflict between the two groups.

1. **☑ Reading Check** This buffalo hide shows the importance of buffalo to the Plains Indians. **Make Predictions** How do you think life would change for the Plains Indians as a result of the decline of the buffalo?

_____

_____

_____

INTERACTIVITY

Explore the key ideas of this lesson.

Quest Connection

In about 20 years, the buffalo population went from 15 million to 1,000. What role did the transcontinental railroad play in this population decline?

INTERACTIVITY

Explore how the transcontinental railroad affected American Indians.

A Growing Conflict

In the early 1800s, American Indians' rights to large areas of land were unchallenged. American Indians did what they could to live peacefully with the settlers. Then, in 1828, gold was discovered on Cherokee land in Georgia. Suddenly, this American Indian land was very valuable. How could settlers take possession of it?

The Indian Removal Act forced thousands of American Indians to relocate from their homes.

Academic Vocabulary

exchange • *n.*, the act of giving or taking something for something else of equal value

In 1830, Congress passed the Indian Removal Act. Under this law, the United States government gave American Indians unsettled prairie land. This would become new Indian Territory. American Indian groups living east of the Mississippi River, like the Cherokee, were forced to give up their own, more valuable land in **exchange**.

No one asked the American Indians what they thought about this exchange. Some groups fought the new law in court, but they were not successful. Others refused to leave and tried to defend their land.

Between 1830 and 1840, United States troops forced 100,000 American Indians from their homes. Most walked 800 miles to Indian Territory in present-day Oklahoma. More than 4,000 people died on the journey, which is called the Trail of Tears.

2. ☑ **Reading Check** **Analyze** and explain the effects of limited resources, such as fertile land and gold, on the growth of the United States.

_____

_____

_____

The Reservation System

After the end of the Civil War, the United States government began to pay close attention to western settlement. Leaders wanted American Indians to relocate to areas of land called **reservations**. To move there, American Indian groups had to give up their own land. In exchange, the government said it would pay them in cash, livestock, and supplies. But the government was not always true to its word, and reservation land was usually different from traditional lands. A reservation was often much smaller. Also, it was far away from the group's original home. It might also have completely different resources.

American Indians from the plains found life on reservations very different from their old ways. For centuries they had followed herds of buffalo. Now they had to stay in one place. Trying to raise crops on the reservation was difficult because the land was often not suitable for farming.

Also, American Indians did not have many legal rights on a reservation. Their children could be taken away and sent to boarding schools. If someone suspected they weren't loyal to the government, they could be arrested. United States soldiers kept American Indians on the reservations with military force that eventually led to war.

The Carlisle Indian Boarding School was one of several schools that pushed American Indian children into adopting the American culture and denying their own heritage.

3. ☑ Reading Check **Generalize** Based on the text and your knowledge of pioneer settlements, what generalization can you make about the location of reservations?

_____

_____

_____

Thirty Years of War

From the end of the Civil War to the 1890s, battles raged between American Indians and the United States Army. In 1864, Army troops attacked Cheyenne (shye-AN) people living in Sandy Creek, Colorado. Soldiers killed about 400 Cheyenne.

The Sioux (soo) believe that the Black Hills of Dakota are sacred, or spiritually important. When gold was found in the Black Hills, miners rushed there. The result was war.

In 1876, Colonel George Custer led his soldiers against a band of Sioux led by Chief Sitting Bull. The battle took place at the Little Big Horn River in Montana Territory. At the Battle of the Little Big Horn, Colonel Custer and more than 200 of his soldiers were killed. The battle was an important victory for American Indians. But soon the United States government sent many more troops to the West to fight.

In 1855, the United States had created a large reservation for the Nez Perce (nez purs) people that included most of the tribe's land in Oregon. But when gold was discovered there, the government wanted to take away most of the new reservation.

This painting shows the Battle of the Little Big Horn.

In 1877, United States soldiers attacked the Nez Perce leader Chief Joseph and a small group of warriors. The Nez Perce War began. For the next five months, soldiers chased Chief Joseph and his people 700 miles as they fled to Canada. But Chief Joseph did not want his people to continue to suffer. With great sadness he finally surrendered, saying, "I will fight no more forever."

4. ☑ **Reading Check** **Analyze** the negative consequences of gold mining in the Black Hills.

_____

_____

Other American Indian Leaders

Sitting Bull had become the principal Sioux chief in 1867. He helped his people by extending their hunting grounds to the west. At the Battle of the Little Big Horn, Sitting Bull led his warriors to victory. After the battle, he and his followers escaped to Canada, but he later returned to the United States. In December 1890, Sitting Bull was killed when reservation police tried to arrest him.

Another Sioux leader, Crazy Horse, had been fighting to preserve his people's way of life since he was a teenager. He fought at the Battle of the Little Big Horn and spent the next winter attacking and being chased by soldiers during the Great Sioux War. In 1877, he surrendered and was killed by a soldier who claimed Crazy Horse was trying to escape.

The great Apache leader Geronimo (juh-RAHN-ih-moh) was born in Mexico in 1820. In the early 1870s, he and his warriors successfully fought the Army. The last **stage** of the Apache Wars began in April 1886. More than 5,000 soldiers tracked Geronimo and his followers to their camp in northern Mexico. Geronimo surrendered in September. He died in 1909.

Word Wise

Context Clues When you see an unfamiliar word, try using context clues to figure out its meaning. Rereading the sentence to understand the text will help you determine what the meaning of the unfamiliar word might be. For example, you will see the word *preserve* on this page. Use the context to determine what the word *preserve* means.

Academic Vocabulary

stage • *n.*, a period or step in an activity or process

5. ✓ **Reading Check** Fill in this chart to **identify** American Indian leaders from these two pages.

American Indian Leaders

Leader	Group	Actions	Date
Sitting Bull	**Sioux**	**Battle of Little Big Horn**	**1876**
Crazy Horse	_____	_____	_____
Chief Joseph	_____	_____	_____
Geronimo	_____	_____	_____

The Armed Conflict Ends

On December 29, 1890, soldiers attacked a group of Sioux warriors and their families at Wounded Knee, South Dakota. At the time, the warriors were trying to give up their weapons, but United States soldiers killed more than 150 of them, including women, children, and the elderly. The battle at Wounded Knee brought the wars between American Indians and the United States government to a sad and bloody end.

By 1900, most American Indians lived on reservations in the West. Reservation life remained difficult. It changed American Indian cultures and weakened their traditions.

A Sioux family living on a reservation

The United States government passed a new law in 1885. Under this law, each American Indian family received 160 acres of land to farm. After 25 years of living on these acres, the land owners would become United States citizens.

6. ☑ **Reading Check** Study the image of the Sioux family. **Identify** and circle three items that show traditional American Indian culture. **Explain** the challenges American Indians faced in maintaining their culture on reservations.

_____

_____

_____

_____

_____

_____

_____

Many American Indian leaders opposed the law. They believed that it would destroy their cultures by attempting to make them more like white people. Also, the law opened up even more American Indian land to white settlers.

Sadly, the leaders were right. American Indians faced many problems trying to become farmers. By 1900, the size of reservation land was reduced further due to new settlement. The traditional cultures of American Indians were badly damaged.

This monument stands on the site of the battle at Wounded Knee.

INTERACTIVITY

Check your understanding of the key ideas of this lesson.

☑ Lesson 3 Check

7. **Draw Conclusions Identify** the opportunities offered to American Indians in the 1885 law.

_____

_____

_____

_____

8. **Analyze** the effects of limited resources on migration in the United States during the nineteenth century.

_____

_____

_____

_____

9. **Understand the** *Quest* **Connections Explain** why American Indian groups fought so hard against the settling of the West and the transcontinental railroad.

_____

_____

_____

_____

"I Will Fight No More Forever"

Chief Joseph's "I Will Fight No More Forever" speech was given as he surrendered after a four month retreat towards Canada. The Nez Perce had been ordered to move to a reservation in Idaho, and Chief Joseph and his people resisted the order. He traveled with his people through Oregon, Washington, Idaho, and Montana fighting against the U.S. Army along the way.

   He traveled with 700 to 800 of his people, but only 200 were soldiers. After more than three months of running, many of his people had died and the survivers were exhausted. He surrendered in October of 1877, delivering these words to U.S. Army General Nelson A. Miles.

Primary Source

Vocabulary Support

the names of chiefs who have been killed

the decision is not for him to make

an expression for his sadness from the heavy loss

Portrait of Chief Joseph

. . . I am tired of fighting. Our Chiefs are killed; Looking Glass is dead, Ta Hool Hool Shute is dead. The old men are all dead. It is the young men who say yes or no. He who led on the young men is dead. It is cold, and we have no blankets; the little children are freezing to death. My people, some of them, have run away to the hills, and have no blankets, no food. No one knows where they are—perhaps freezing to death. I want to have time to look for my children, and see how many of them I can find. Maybe I shall find them among the dead. Hear me, my Chiefs! I am tired; my heart is sick and sad. From where the sun now stands I will fight no more forever.

   – Chief Joseph, "I Will Fight No More Forever," 1877

Close Reading

1. **Identify** and **circle** the sentence that tells us of what Chief Joseph is tired. Highlight details that describe why he is tired.
2. **Describe** why Chief Joseph says "I will fight no more forever." Why did he decide to stop fighting for his people?

_____

_____

_____

_____

_____

_____

_____

Wrap It Up

What other American Indian groups were fighting the U.S. Army at this time? How were their fights alike and different? Support your answer with information from the chapter.

_____

_____

_____

_____

_____

_____

_____

Vocabulary

raw material
Monroe Doctrine
yellow journalism
isthmus
annex

Academic Vocabulary

interfere
imply

Unlock The BIG Question

I will know that, in the late 1800s, the United States became a major world power.

Jumpstart Activity

Work with a partner. Write a headline that a newspaper might be able to use to describe the United States in today's world. It can be about the American economy, government, or overseas interests.

At the end of the nineteenth century, American factories were producing more and better goods and shipping them around the world. The United States was becoming a major economic power. Now it was ready to become a world political power, too.

American industrialization spurred an increase in foreign trade. This helped make the United States a major economic and political power.

U.S. Foreign Trade, 1870–1910

Value of Foreign Trade in billions of dollars

Years

Source: U.S. Department of Commerce

Becoming an Economic Power

Between 1880 and 1900, the number of American factories doubled. The United States was rich in **raw materials**, or natural products used in manufacturing. These included lumber, silver, gold, and oil. New technology helped to create better and cheaper products. New inventions, such as the electric light bulb, the telephone, and the automobile, helped create new industries.

Every region in the country was part of the economic boom. Eastern cities like Pittsburgh, Pennsylvania, were still important manufacturing centers. Chicago, Illinois, was now a major meat-packing center. Throughout the Midwest, factories made farm equipment and lumber products. Across the South, cotton and lumber production expanded.

The United States exported large amounts of grain, minerals, and manufactured goods. By 1890, the United States was one of the most powerful economic powers in the world. Now it needed new markets for its goods.

INTERACTIVITY

Explore the key ideas of this lesson.

1. ✅ **Reading Check**
Identify and underline two reasons the United States became an economic powerhouse.

United States Trades Around the World

The United States wanted to trade with Japan. But Japanese ports were closed to foreigners and had been for centuries. How could a trade partnership begin?

In July 1853, Commodore Matthew Perry led four United States battleships to Japan. Most Japanese had never seen ships like these. The steamships' size and power impressed them. In March 1854 the Japanese government agreed to trade with the United States. In 1899, European countries agreed to let America share in their trade with China.

The United States wanted to show the world its powerful navy. In 1907, President Theodore Roosevelt sent 16 huge, white battleships around the world. For the next two years, the "Great White Fleet" toured 20 ports on six continents.

The "Great White Fleet" showed the world the power of the U.S. Navy as well as the United States as a nation.

The Spanish-American War

In the 1890s, the United States became involved in Latin America, the region that includes Mexico and Central and South America. In 1823, President James Monroe had warned European countries not to **interfere** with nations in the Western Hemisphere. This policy was known as the **Monroe Doctrine**.

By 1890, Spain still controlled Puerto Rico and Cuba, two Caribbean islands. When the Cuban people revolted, Spanish soldiers killed or imprisoned many of them. Spain's actions in Cuba angered many Americans. Americans living in Cuba worried about their safety.

President William McKinley sent the battleship USS *Maine* to Cuba in January 1898. On the night of February 15, an explosion ripped through the ship. More than 250 American sailors died. No one knew who or what had caused the blast, but American newspapers **implied** that Spain had sunk the ship. This type of false or exaggerated reporting is called **yellow journalism**.

Based on these news stories, Americans were outraged at Spain. In April, Congress declared war on Spain. American battleships sailed to the Philippine Islands, which were controlled by Spain. On May 1, 1898, the American Navy destroyed the Spanish fleet in the Battle of Manila Bay.

Academic Vocabulary

interfere • *v.*, to become involved in the affairs of others

imply • *v.*, to strongly suggest

Quest Connection

Work with your group to research other examples of yellow journalism. What do they all have in common?

INTERACTIVITY

Learn more about yellow journalism.

An artist's interpretation of the USS *Maine* explosion

2. ☑ **Reading Check** The USS *Maine* was sent to Cuba to protect Americans living there. **Explain** how the press influenced the Spanish-American War.

_____

_____

_____

_____

_____

_____

An American force also invaded Cuba. A young lieutenant colonel named Theodore Roosevelt led a group of volunteers called the Rough Riders. They and other American troops fought their way across Cuba. By August 12, the Spanish-American War was over. Spain and the United States signed a peace treaty giving the Philippines, Puerto Rico, and Guam to the United States. The United States was becoming an important world power.

Building the Panama Canal

In 1900, sailing from the Atlantic to the Pacific coast of the United States took months. Ships had to travel around the southern tip of South America. The journey was 12,000 miles long. Americans wanted a faster way to move people and goods from the Atlantic to the Pacific.

To solve the problem, engineers built a canal across the Isthmus of Panama. An **isthmus** is a narrow strip of land connecting two landmasses. The 51-mile Isthmus of Panama connects North and South America. The isthmus belonged to Colombia, in South America. When Panama declared its independence from Colombia, the United States supported Panama. In return, the new nation agreed to a treaty that created the Panama Canal Zone. The United States paid Panama $10 million for the rights to the zone.

More than 40,000 people worked to build the canal. The Panama Canal opened in 1914. The voyage between New York and San Francisco was now 8,000 miles shorter.

3. ☑ **Reading Check**
Make Predictions What effect would the Panama Canal have on the price of goods shipped from one coast to the other? Explain.

_____

_____

_____

_____

_____

_____

The Panama Canal

San Francisco

New York

NORTH AMERICA

ATLANTIC OCEAN

New York to San Francisco through the Panama Canal

Panama Canal

PANAMA

New York to San Francisco before the Panama Canal

N E W S

SOUTH AMERICA

PACIFIC OCEAN

0   1,000 mi

0   1,000 km

Alaska and Hawaii

In 1866, Russia offered to sell its territory of Alaska to the United States. This huge region is twice the size of modern Texas. The price was $7.2 million in gold, or about two cents per acre. United States Secretary of State William Seward worked out the treaty with Russia. On April 9, 1867, the Senate approved the agreement.

Most Americans didn't think Alaska was much of a bargain. Newspapers called it "Seward's Icebox" or "Seward's Folly." Then gold was discovered along the Klondike River near Alaska in 1896. Americans suddenly began to see its value.

At the end of the nineteenth century, the United States still wanted to expand. For more than 50 years, Americans had been investing in the Hawaiian Islands in the Pacific Ocean. American-owned sugar cane and pineapple plantations were there. The Hawaiian king signed a trade agreement with the United States in 1875. But the next ruler of Hawaii didn't like foreign control of the islands. Her name was Queen Liliuokalani (lih LEE oo oh kah LAH nee). In 1891, she became the first woman to rule Hawaii.

In 1893, American and European businessmen and the United States Marines took control. Sanford Dole, an American planter, became the new president of Hawaii. The American planters pushed for Hawaii to be **annexed**, or added to the United States. Then the Spanish-American War started. During the war, battleships used an American naval base in Hawaii. This was another way in which the Hawaiian Islands could benefit the United States. On July 7, 1898, President William McKinley annexed Hawaii.

Queen Liliuokalani was the last ruler of Hawaii before it became the 50th state.

4. 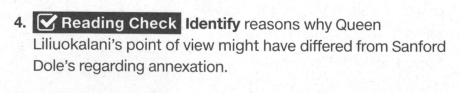 **Reading Check** **Identify** reasons why Queen Liliuokalani's point of view might have differed from Sanford Dole's regarding annexation.

_____

_____

_____

5. ☑ **Reading Check** Write two newspaper headlines. In the box on the left, write a headline about the United States acquiring Alaska in 1867. In the box on the right, write a headline about the United States annexing Hawaii in 1898.

Daily Moose	*Island Times*

☑ **Lesson 4 Check**

INTERACTIVITY

Check your understanding of the key ideas of this lesson.

6. **Cause and Effect Identify** one economic effect of the Spanish-American War.

_____

_____

7. **Explain** how American ideas about progress and expansion affected the economic growth of the United States.

_____

_____

8. **Understand the** *Quest* **Connections** Do you think the Spanish-American War would have started without the interference of the press? Explain your reasoning.

_____

_____

_____

Quality: Leadership

Queen Liliuokalani (1838–1917)
Looking Out for Others

In 1838, Queen Liliuokalani was born into a royal Hawaiian family. Her birth name was Lydia Kamakaeha. Since she had attended the Royal School, she as well as her brothers were considered worthy of succeeding to the throne of King Kamehameha IV.

In 1891, upon the deaths of her brothers, she became the first queen of Hawaii. During her brother's reign, Hawaii's monarchy lost power as a result of the increasing control of the islands by the United States. Queen Liliuokalani tried to draft a new constitution in order to restore her monarchy and power to her citizens, but she met resistance from pro-American groups.

On January 16, 1893, a group of U.S. marines landed to protect American interests. The next day, pro-American groups overthrew her monarchy. To prevent war and to protect her people, Queen Liliuokalani surrendered. The revolutionaries eventually took over the islands and created the Republic of Hawaii, with the goal of becoming an American state.

In 1895, she was imprisoned after a rebellion to restore her rule failed. In order to free herself and her supporters from jail, she gave up her throne. As a result, she and her supporters were freed. In 1900, the United States annexed Hawaii, but it didn't become a state until 1959.

Find Out More

1. Would you consider the actions of Queen Liliuokalani to be the acts of a good leader? Why or why not?

_____

_____

_____

2. Queen Liliuokalani had a strong sense of leadership. She dedicated her life to protecting her country's sovereignty. Ask some people you know who they consider a great leader and why.

Use these graphics to review some of the key terms, people, and ideas from this chapter.

THE FIRST TRANSCONTINENTAL RAILROAD

1863–1869

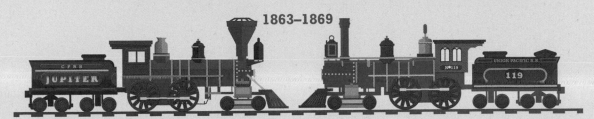

Benefits of the Transcontinental Railroad:

Provided new methods of transportation that were faster and safer:

- replaced wagon trains
- replaced stagecoach lines that transported people and goods from the East Coast to the West Coast
- provided another option to sea journey, which went down around the southern tip of South America back up to the California coast

Central Pacific Facts:

- Laid tracks from Sacramento to Promontory Summit, Utah Territory
- Most of the workers were Chinese immigrants
- Had to blast holes through the Sierra Nevada mountain range

Union Pacific Facts:

- Laid 1,006 miles from Omaha, Nebraska to Promontory Summit, Utah Territory
- Employed a mix of Union veterans, Irish immigrants, Mormons, and others
- Had to work through the Rocky Mountain range

The Golden Spike

The final spike that connected the Central Pacific and Union Pacific was made of gold. Leland Stanford joined the rails on May 10, 1869. Today, the golden spike is on display at the Cantor Arts Museum at Stanford University.

Important Dates

1849 – Gold Rush	1889 – Oklahoma Land Rush
1862 – Homestead Act	1890 – Battle of Wounded Knee
1876 – Battle of the Little Big Horn	1898 – USS *Maine* Explodes

🎮 GAMES

Play the vocabulary game.

Vocabulary and Key Ideas

1. **Define** What is **Manifest Destiny**?

_____

_____

2. Complete the sentences below. Choose from these words: *pioneers, cattle drive, homesteader, droughts, raw materials,* and *annex.*

In an attempt to increase the size of the nation, the federal government encouraged _____ to move west.

Many homesteaders had to deal with extreme hardships, such as fierce rain, windstorms, and severe _____, or long periods without rain.

The United States was rich in _____, which made it easy for the number of American factories to double in the late 1800s.

3. **Explain** what **reservations** are and some of the problems associated with them.

_____

_____

_____

_____

_____

4. **Analyzing a Graph** Look at the graph. What happened to the buffalo population? What may have caused this to happen?

_____

_____

_____

_____

_____

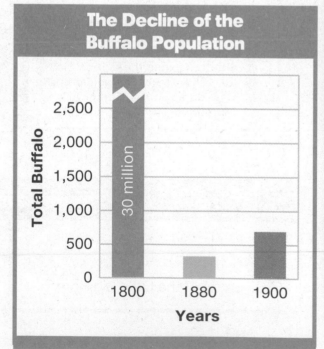

The Decline of the Buffalo Population

Total Buffalo: 2,500 — 2,000 — 1,500 — 1,000 — 500 — 0

30 million

Years: 1800, 1880, 1900

Source: US Fish and Wildlife Service, National Bison Range

Critical Thinking and Writing

5. **Describe** one reason why people from the eastern United States moved west during the 1800s.

_____

_____

_____

6. **Interpret** Who led American Indians to victory at the Battle of the Little Big Horn?

   (A) Chief Joseph

   (B) Sitting Bull

   (C) Geronimo

   (D) Black Horse

7. **Analyze** the effects of limited resources on the treatment of American Indians during the nineteenth century.

_____

_____

_____

_____

_____

_____

8. **Revisit the Big Question** How did different groups experience the growth of the nation?

_____

_____

_____

_____

_____

9. **Writing Workshop: Write an Opinion** During the late 1800s, the United States economy grew quickly. This growth depended in part on the rich resources of the West, but in order to gain access to the resources the American Indians were forced off their lands. On a separate sheet of paper, write two paragraphs explaining your opinion on whether the country could have grown without causing harm to the American Indians and their lands. Include details from the text to support your opinion.

Analyze Primary Sources

"Look at me and look at the earth. It was our father's and should be our children's after us. . . . If the white men take my country, where can I go? I have nowhere to go. I cannot spare it, and I love it very much. Let us alone."

—From a speech by Sitting Bull, 1877

10. During the westward expansion the U.S. army often brutally attacked American Indians and forced them to leave their homes for reservations. How do these words spoken by Sitting Bull help you to understand the hardships that the American Indians experienced?

_____

_____

_____

_____

Make Predictions

11. In what ways do you think the United States and its citizens will benefit from westward expansion and settlement?

_____

_____

_____

_____

Quest Findings

Read All About It!

You have read the lessons in this chapter, and now you are ready to plan and write your article. Remember that the goal of the article is to explain the impact the transcontinental railroad had on the growth of the nation.

 INTERACTIVITY

Use these activities to help you prepare to write your article.

1 Prepare to Write

Think about the different groups of people affected by the transcontinental railroad: farmers, travelers, American Indians, immigrants, railroad employees. Write a list of all the ways the transcontinental railroad impacted each group. Use the list to prepare a message for how the transcontinental railroad impacted the growth of our nation.

2 Write a Draft

Use your notes and the articles you have collected from your Quest Connections to write a draft article. Some ideas to consider while you are writing include:

- Whose point of view are you writing from?
- How did the railroad impact the growing nation from your group's viewpoint?
- How do you want your audience to feel when they read it?
- What catchy title can you use to attract a reader's attention?

3 Write Your Article

Put the words and point of view together to write an article that might have been published in the late 1800s. Share your article with a partner or another group. Listen to what others say. Is your message getting through?

4 Revise

Make changes to the words to make your article stronger. Check to make sure your spelling and grammar are correct.

Industry and Immigration

GO ONLINE FOR
DIGITAL RESOURCES

 VIDEO

 INTERACTIVITY

▶)) AUDIO

GAMES

☑ ASSESSMENT

📖 eTEXT

The **BIG** Question

 VIDEO

What are the costs and benefits of growth?

Jumpstart Activity

 INTERACTIVITY

Imagine that you held a bake sale to raise money for a class trip. Everyone in your class baked one item to sell, and the sale was a great success. Now you want to raise more money, so you decide that everyone will bake three items each for a second sale. With a group, discuss the costs and benefits of growing your bake sale.

_____

_____

_____

_____

Inventing America

Preview the chapter vocabulary as you sing the rap.

The late eighteen hundreds was an exciting time,
Scientists and inventors were just hitting their prime.
Creating goods and services for everyone to try,
Americans were **consumers** that were ready to buy.

Edison made the light bulb, and Ford the **assembly line**,
The Wright brothers flight at Kitty Hawk couldn't have
    come at a better time.
These inventions made things easier, and let us move
    around,
But it made our cities bigger than the little rural towns.

With all the new cities and all the new places,
Big business needed money to invest in all the spaces.
They sold **stock** to **investors** to form a **corporation**,
Which built the roads and rail that created this
    great nation.

Having to leave their homes to build a better life,
Escaping wars, **oppression**, as well as political strife,
Immigrants came to America trying to flee adversity,
They made America a **melting pot** adding to its great
    diversity.

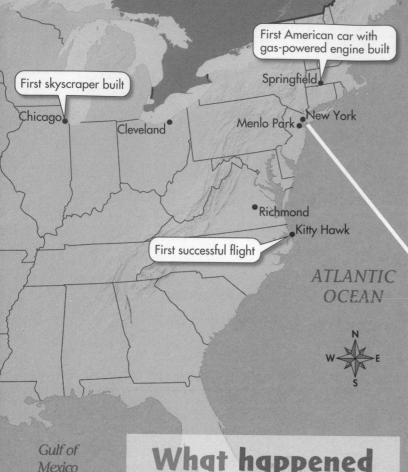

First American car with gas-powered engine built

Springfield

First skyscraper built

Chicago

Cleveland

Menlo Park

New York

Richmond

Kitty Hawk

First successful flight

ATLANTIC OCEAN

N
W E
S

Gulf of Mexico

Where did immigrants arrive when they came to the United States?

Millions of immigrants passed through Ellis Island in New York City on their way to a new life in America.

Ellis Island

TODAY
Ellis Island is a historic landmark and museum that you can visit to learn about some of the immigrants who passed through its doors.

What happened and When?

Read the timeline to find out about several inventions and innovations that developed between the mid-1800s and early 1900s.

| 1860 | 1865 | 1870 | 1875 |

1863
Cleveland, OH: Rockefeller opens his first oil refinery.

1876
Menlo Park, NJ: Edison opens research lab.

Who will you meet?

Thomas Edison
Invented many devices, including the incandescent lightbulb, that are still used today

George Washington Carver
Born into slavery and became a world-renowned scientist and inventor

Andrew Carnegie
Became a wealthy entrepreneur by increasing the supply of steel at a low cost

Henry Ford
Created the assembly line for use in his automobile plants

 INTERACTIVITY

Complete the interactive digital activity.

1880	1885	1890	1895	1900

1887
Richmond, VA:
The first electric streetcar is built.

1893
Springfield, MA:
First gas-powered car is driven.

TODAY
Cars and electricity are used by billions of people.

Quest

Project-Based Learning

Taking a Risk

America is home to some of the most successful entrepreneurs in history. Some of them had to convince other people to take a risk and invest money in their idea. Entrepreneurs still face the task of convincing investors to take that risk.

Quest Kick Off

Your mission is to work with a group to write a business plan. The plan will describe the steps you will take to meet your goal and explain why an investor should take a risk on your team's venture.

1 Ask Questions

What kinds of skills do entrepreneurs need? What personal qualities are important for someone who is trying to start a business?

....

....

....

....

2 Research

Think of a few famous modern-day entrepreneurs. Follow your teacher's instructions to research their ventures or businesses to learn how and why they thrived.

INTERACTIVITY

Use this activity to help you prepare your assignment.

....

....

....

....

....

SPACE FOR RENT

3 Look for *Quest* Connections

Begin looking for Quest Connections that will help you write your plan.

4 *Quest* Findings Write Your Plan

Use the Quest Findings page at the end of the chapter to help you write your plan.

Inventors and Inventions

Vocabulary

consumer
telegraph
investor
profit

Academic Vocabulary

remain
competitor

American cities bustled
with economic activity in
the late 1800s.

Unlock
The BIG
Question

I will know that Americans developed new
inventions that changed life in the United
States and around the world.

JumPstart Activity

Work with a partner to discuss inventions that make
life easier. Choose two products or devices and talk
about how life would be different without them.

The late 1800s was an exciting time. The United States
had become a major economic power. In Chicago, Illinois,
the first skyscrapers were built. More and more Americans
were becoming consumers. A **consumer** is someone who
buys or uses goods and services.

Scientists and inventors were creating things that would
have a huge impact on the country. And consumers were
ready to buy those things.

In 1867 Christopher Sholes invented the first practical typewriter. He also developed the keyboard arrangement we use today. By 1874, typewriters were available in stores. Inventions such as the typewriter quickly became popular. It was among many inventions that changed life during this period.

Some scientists and inventors looked for ways to feed the growing population. African American scientist George Washington Carver got Southerners to grow peanuts and sweet potatoes, and he developed many **uses** for these crops.

INTERACTIVITY

Explore the key ideas of this lesson.

New Ways to Communicate

In the mid-1800s, Samuel Morse had invented the **telegraph**. This device sent little bursts of electricity along wires. Morse developed a code based on short bursts (dots) and longer bursts (dashes). The telegraph used this code, called Morse code, to send messages quickly. Americans used the telegraph system for the first time in May 1844.

During the mid to late 1800s, investors helped develop new inventions. An **investor** is someone who puts money into a business to make a profit. **Profit** is the money an investor earns when the business does well. One investor, Cyrus Field, started a company to lay a telegraph cable across the Atlantic Ocean. It was difficult. But by July 1866, the transatlantic cable made it possible to send telegraph messages to Europe.

Alexander Graham Bell was a teacher. He trained teachers of hearing-impaired students in Boston, Massachusetts. He also worked on a device that would send sound through wires. On March 10, 1876, Bell and his assistant, Thomas Watson, were testing this first telephone. Bell claimed that he called Watson for help using his new machine: "Mr. Watson, come here. I want to see you." This exchange was the first telephone call.

Alexander Graham Bell speaks into one of his telephones.

Edison's Bright Idea

Thomas Alva Edison introduced the world to a lot of new inventions. Edison set up a research laboratory in Menlo Park, New Jersey, in 1876. He worked with a team of young scientists to solve problems. His was the first research lab of its kind. In 1877, Edison invented a machine that could record sounds and play them back. It was called a phonograph, and it made him famous. He was called the Wizard of Menlo Park.

Two years later, Edison made a working light bulb. Inventors had tried for years to make a light bulb that would **remain** bright for more than a few minutes. At first, Edison couldn't find the right material for the filament—the tiny wire inside the bulb that glows when the light is turned on. Finally, he tried a carbon filament. It worked. On December 3, 1879, he showed his light bulb to the investors of the Edison Electric Light Company.

Edison's light bulb was a great success. However, it would only burn for a few days. An African American inventor named Lewis Latimer improved the light bulb so it would burn longer. Edison was so impressed, he asked Latimer to join his team.

Before electric lights, people used candles, kerosene, or oil lamps for light at night. But Edison and Latimer's work made the world brighter.

Edison also gave the world movies. In 1888, Edison and another scientist invented a movie camera. They also invented a device for viewing the movies. Edison never stopped inventing. Working alone or with others, he created 1,093 inventions, a world record.

Academic Vocabulary

remain • *v.*, to continue in a specific condition

1. ☑ **Reading Check**
Examine the timeline. For each date, **identify** the invention and name of the inventor.

American Inventions, 1840–1900

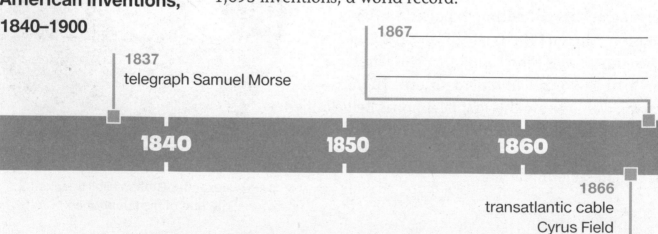

1837
telegraph Samuel Morse

1867 _____

_____

1840   **1850**   **1860**

1866
transatlantic cable
Cyrus Field

The Impact of Electricity

Edison had to find a way of getting electricity into homes and businesses. On September 4, 1882, he opened the first electric power station in the United States at Pearl Street in New York City. Electricity produced there traveled through wires to nearby buildings.

At first, the Pearl Street station served just 59 customers. But Americans wanted electricity. Nikola Tesla, a Serbian immigrant, developed the type of electricity that we use today. In 1884, he sold his invention to George Westinghouse, Edison's biggest **competitor**. Soon, power stations opened in many American cities.

By the 1890s, electric power stations were set up throughout the country. Electricity powered streetlights and electric trolley cars. Inventors created new machines that ran on electric power. Small, private electric companies began to merge into bigger ones. These large companies could create electricity more cheaply. As the cost of electricity dropped, more and more people used it. Our world today would be very different without electricity. Nearly every aspect of our work and daily life is touched in some way be something that is powered by it.

Thomas Edison in his lab

Academic Vocabulary

competitor • *v.*, a rival, someone selling or buying goods in the same market

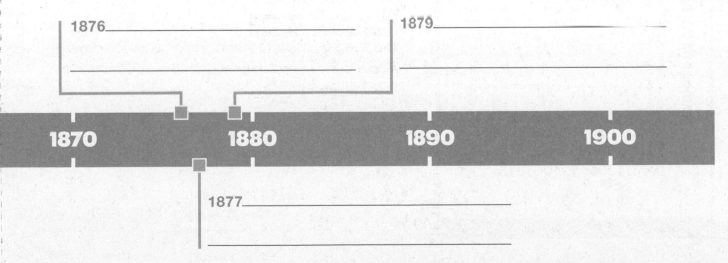

1876 _____

1879 _____

1870   1880   1890   1900

1877 _____

New Ways to Travel

In 1832, people in New York City had a new way to get around. Instead of coaches that bumped along rough streets, they could now ride in streetcars that ran on smooth, steel railroad tracks. Like a coach, a streetcar was pulled by horses, but the tracks made the ride more comfortable and faster. People called this streetcar a horsecar. Riders paid about ten cents for a ride. Horsecars traveled about six to eight miles per hour. Like buses, they made regular stops. They became very popular. By the mid-1880s, more than 400 companies around the nation were carrying 188 million passengers a year over more than 6,000 miles of "street rail" track.

In 1887, Julian Sprague developed a streetcar system in Richmond, Virginia. Sprague's streetcar, or trolley, was half the size of a modern bus. It was powered by electricity. Rides cost only a nickel. An electric streetcar could travel up to 20 miles per hour. Americans liked them better than horsecars. By 1903, there were 30,000 miles of street rail tracks in the United States, and electric trolleys ran on almost all of them.

A streetcar in Detroit, Michigan

In 1886, Charles Duryea saw a gasoline engine at the Ohio State Fair. The engine seemed small enough for a carriage or wagon. That sparked an idea. He and his brother built a car with an engine in their Springfield, Massachusetts, workshop. On September 22, 1893, they drove this early car for the first time. People called the first automobiles, or cars, "horseless carriages."

2. ☑ **Reading Check** **Draw Conclusions Analyze** the line graph. Write a conclusion you can draw about car ownership based on the information in the line graph.

_____

_____

_____

_____

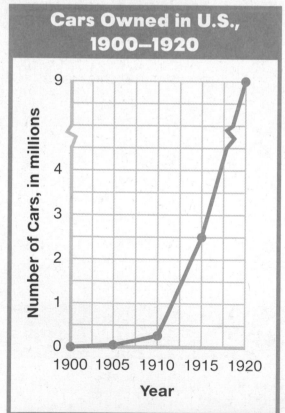

Cars Owned in U.S., 1900–1920

(Line graph: Number of Cars, in millions on the y-axis ranging 0 to 9; Year on the x-axis from 1900 to 1920. Values: 1900 ≈ 0, 1905 ≈ 0, 1910 ≈ 0.3, 1915 ≈ 2.5, 1920 ≈ 9.)

Airplanes and Flight

Using trains and trolleys, people were now traveling more quickly. Soon, two American inventors would take to the skies. Brothers Wilbur and Orville Wright ran a bicycle repair shop in Dayton, Ohio. But they dreamed of building a flying machine.

The Wright brothers working with one of their airplanes

The Wright brothers experimented with kites to learn more about how wings worked. In October 1900, they tested a glider at Kitty Hawk, a small fishing village in North Carolina. A glider has no engine. It just glides, or floats, on the wind. The glider didn't work as well as they hoped, but they didn't give up.

The brothers built a wind tunnel to do experiments. They kept testing and improving their design. The next step was to design a machine with a gasoline engine for power. On December 17, 1903, this new powered machine, *Flyer I*, was ready to be tested.

As five citizens from Kitty Hawk watched with Wilbur, Orville took the controls. *Flyer I* lifted and flew 120 feet. This first airplane flight lasted just 12 seconds. Then Wilbur flew even farther. By the end of the day, both brothers had flown twice. For the first time, humans had flown a powered machine that was heavier than air. The world would never be the same.

The Impact of Inventions

Thousands of miles lie between the West Coast and the East Coast of the United States. So inventions that made distances easier to cross became popular quickly. As people began to talk, drive, or fly over long distances, these inventions changed lives and the economy. Telephones and other communication technologies continue to make your life easier today.

3. ☑ **Reading Check**
Turn and Talk to a partner about the accomplishments of the Wright brothers. Discuss why they were successful.

Quest Connection

Think about the most important inventions of the late 1800s and early 1900s. How did they relate to people's needs at that time?

👆 **INTERACTIVITY**

Take a closer look at these important inventions and their impact on daily life.

Telephone operators at a switchboard in 1925

Telephones linked more and more people. The Bell Telephone Company was formed, and the first investors included Alexander Graham Bell, Bell's wife Mabel, and Thomas Watson, the man who had received the first phone call. Soon, more companies were providing telephone service.

To connect telephones, wires had to be run to a central office. This office was called a telephone exchange. An operator connected calls by putting the two ends of a cord into the correct places on the switchboard. Today, telephone calls are connected automatically. Telephones look much different, too.

The automobile was another invention that changed life in the United States. Americans loved cars and took to the road in increasing numbers. The automobile industry created many new jobs. But there were costs, too. With people moving faster, there were more traffic accidents. Do you think the benefits have been worth the dangers?

Inventions Shrink Distances

Talking	Driving	Flying
<ul><li>In 1877, the Bell Telephone Company was formed.</li><li>In January 1878, the first telephone exchange opened in New Haven, Connecticut.</li><li>In February 1878, an exchange opened in San Francisco, California.</li><li>The telephone dial was invented in the 1890s.</li></ul>	<ul><li>By 1908, more than 200 companies manufactured cars in the United States.</li><li>In 1925, a new word was coined: motel. It was a "motor hotel," or hotel for people on driving vacations.</li><li>In 1936, Duncan Hines published the first guidebooks for people traveling by car.</li></ul>	<ul><li>In the early 1920s, airline companies started.</li><li>By the end of the 1920s, most U.S. cities had airports.</li><li>In 1927, American pilot Charles Lindbergh flew alone across the Atlantic.</li><li>In 1932, Amelia Earhart became the first woman to fly alone across the Atlantic.</li></ul>

Ours is the commencement [start] of a flying age, and I am happy to have popped into existence at a period so interesting.

—Amelia Earhart, 1928

More and more people wanted to fly, too. At first, passenger planes could not fly at night or over high mountains. Engineers soon solved these problems. Designs improved. Metal replaced wood and cloth in airplane construction.

Airplane uses and designs changed quickly. Jet engines were developed, and then rockets. People began to wonder if they might even be able to travel in space one day. On July 20, 1969, just 66 years after the Wright brothers' first flights, two American astronauts walked on the moon.

4. ☑ **Reading Check**
Turn and talk with a partner whether you think it would be harder to live without a car or a telephone.

INTERACTIVITY

Check your understanding of they key ideas in this lesson.

☑ Lesson 1 Check

5. **Summarize** What effect did the telephone have on Americans?

_____

_____

_____

6. **Explain** how technological innovations in communications have benefited your own life.

_____

_____

7. **Understand the** *Quest* Connections What if the airplane had not been invented? Describe the impact of the absence of flight.

_____

_____

_____

_____

Predict Consequences

A consequence is what happens as a result of another event. It is what follows and is caused by an action or event. If you can predict consequences, you can better choose what action to take and get better results.

▶ **VIDEO**

Watch a video about predicting consequences.

You have learned about many inventions. Using those inventions had many consequences. For example, the use of cars led to whole new industries but also to crowded roads. Could these consequences have been predicted?

Predicting consequences can help you better understand what you are reading. These steps can help you predict consequences.

- Think about what is happening.

- Look for clues about what might happen next.

- Think about what you already know about similar actions and their results or consequences.

Today, new inventions using Earth's resources are being developed. Read this article about solar energy. Then answer the questions that follow.

Solar Energy

Every day, Earth receives energy from the sun. This energy is called solar energy. Solar energy cannot be used up, and it does not produce pollution.

The easiest way for people to use solar energy is by collecting the heat. Flat-plate collectors face the sun and heat up. The heat is carried by water or air flowing through the collectors. However, the sun's energy is weak at Earth's surface. So collectors need to be large.

Look at the flat-plate collectors on the roof of the house in the picture. These can heat the water used by one family.

A house with solar panels

Your Turn!

1. **Summarize** two important facts about solar energy that you learned in this article.

   _____

   _____

   _____

2. What is one invention that uses solar energy? What does it do?

   _____

   _____

   _____

3. What do you think is one possible good consequence and one possible bad consequence of using this invention?

   _____

   _____

   _____

4. Think about an invention you use every day that is important to you. **Describe** the consequence of having that invention taken away.

   _____

   _____

   _____

5. Choose an invention or innovation that you learned about in the chapter. What were the consequences of it? How did it impact the economy and American life?

   _____

   _____

   _____

The Impact of Big Business

INTERACTIVITY

Participate in a class discussion to preview the content of this lesson.

Unlock The BIG Question

I will know that the growth of big business had a great impact on life in the United States.

Vocabulary

urbanization
free enterprise system
entrepreneur
corporation
stock
assembly line
refinery
monopoly

Academic Vocabulary

abundant
official

JumpStart Activity

With a group, have a discussion about recent inventions or innovations that make some jobs unnecessary. On the other hand, what kinds of jobs are created by these innovations?

In the late 1800s, new inventions were everywhere. New tools made work easier. Some inventions made farming more efficient, but this meant fewer workers were needed on farms. At the same time, other inventions were creating jobs in cities. To fill these jobs, workers from the farms flooded into the cities. The growth of cities is called **urbanization**.

The economy of the United States is a **free enterprise system**. That means people are free to start their own businesses or do whatever work they want. The time between 1880 and 1900 was important for the development of the free enterprise system. This was a time when a lot of people were starting new businesses. The number of factories and jobs more than doubled.

Carnegie Steel Company

Business Leaders Take Risks

 INTERACTIVITY

Explore the key ideas of this lesson.

It was, and still is, risky to start a business. But if you are successful, there are great rewards. One thing that was needed in the rapidly growing cities was steel. An entrepreneur named Andrew Carnegie was determined to supply it. An **entrepreneur** creates and runs a new business and takes on all the risks of the business.

Carnegie's family was poor, so Carnegie began working at a factory at age 12. But he studied hard and made the most of every opportunity. By the time he was 30 years old, he was a wealthy investor. Then he started to make steel.

Steel had always been expensive, because it was hard to make. Then in 1856 a British engineer named Henry Bessemer perfected a new way to make steel. The Bessemer process produced good steel at a much lower cost. The steel was processed in huge, egg-shaped metal pots, which could be tilted to pour out melted steel.

In the 1870s, Carnegie became the first person in the United States to build steel plants that used the Bessemer process. But Carnegie did not stop there. He kept finding new ways to make steel better, faster, and cheaper. When demand for steel increased, Carnegie was ready to supply it. When a company has enough supplies to meet the demand, the company can make a lot of money. There was a huge demand for steel to build railroads. This demand from new industries helped the economy grow.

Carnegie wanted to keep his costs as low as possible. He bought the iron and coal mines that produced the raw materials for steel. Next, he bought the ships and railroads that transported the raw materials. In 1889, he created the Carnegie Steel Company. He helped turn steel into a major American industry. By 1910, the United States made more steel than any other country in the world. Carnegie was rich, but he remembered what it was like to be poor. He gave much of his money to build schools and libraries, and to help others.

Word Wise

If you come across a vocabulary word that is unfamiliar, look for clues in the text that tell you what the word means. Reread the third paragraph on this page. What do you think the word *perfected* means? What other words in that paragraph give you clues about its meaning?

A painting of workers in a Pennsylvania steel mill

Inventions and Businesses

1. ✓ **Reading Check** Under each photograph, **write** the product to which each businessperson is linked.

Harvey S. Firestone

_____

Henry Ford

_____

William Boeing

_____

Growing cities needed bigger buildings. The strength of steel made bigger buildings possible. In 1885, the first skyscraper was built in Chicago, Illinois. Soon, tall buildings were going up everywhere.

Automobiles were exciting, but they were expensive. Then, in 1903, American entrepreneur Henry Ford started the Ford Motor Company. The Ford Motor Company is a corporation. A **corporation** is a business owned by investors. Investors buy **stock**, a share of the company, to become partial owners.

Henry Ford had a new idea about how to build cars: the assembly line. With an **assembly line**, a product is put together as it moves past a line of workers. Each worker works on a part of the product before it moves to the next worker. So products can be made faster and more cheaply.

In 1908, the Ford Motor Company started to produce one of its most popular cars: the Model T. It was a simple car that many people could afford, and Ford sold millions.

In 1904, the Firestone Tire & Rubber Company, founded by Harvey S. Firestone, started to make tires for cars. Firestone invented a special kind of tire for the Model T, a tire filled with air.

The popularity of the automobile created all kinds of jobs. Workers were needed to build roads, repair engines, and operate gas stations. Others found jobs providing services to tourists traveling by car.

Bigger companies could produce goods at a lower cost, so businesses began to join together. In 1901, banker J.P. Morgan helped create the United States Steel Corporation, which combined the Carnegie Steel Company and several other steel companies.

In 1918, airplanes began to transport mail for the U.S. Post Office. William Boeing's airplane company was chosen to carry mail across the country. The Boeing Airplane Company grew quickly. By 1928, Boeing was one of the largest airplane manufacturers in the world.

Industry and Resources

The country's natural resources also helped the economy grow. Rich farmland produced **abundant** crops, and industries developed to process and package food. Forests produced wood for lumber that was used to build homes for the growing population. Iron ore from Pennsylvania and the Great Lakes region supplied the steel industry. Many cities and state capitals were established near major rivers and bodies of water. This allowed people to travel and trade easily and transport goods by boat. State capitals attracted people to work in politics and public service.

There was one important natural resource that Americans needed more and more: oil. Oil helped machines work. So the more industry grew, the more important oil became. Oil was also used to make gasoline to power cars and airplanes.

On August 27, 1859, a drill struck oil in western Pennsylvania. In 1863, entrepreneur John D. Rockefeller built his first oil refinery near Cleveland, Ohio. A **refinery** turns oil into useful products, such as gasoline. Two years later, this refinery was the largest in the region.

Rockefeller started the Standard Oil Company in 1870. He used his profits to buy other oil refineries. By the early 1880s, Standard Oil controlled almost all the oil business in the country. It also owned most of the pipelines that carried oil to the railroads. Standard Oil became a monopoly. A **monopoly** is a company that has control of an entire industry.

Once people started looking for oil, they found it in other parts of the country. In 1901, oil drillers made an incredible discovery. They struck oil at Spindletop, near Beaumont, Texas. This strike was one of the largest in history. One year later, more than 1,000 oil companies operated in that area.

The area around Spindletop became crowded with oil drills.

Academic Vocabulary

abundant • *adj.*, having plenty of something

**Connection**

How did their skills and experience in the business world help entrepreneurs such as Andrew Carnegie and John D. Rockefeller to succeed?

👆 **INTERACTIVITY**

Learn more about influential entrepreneurs of the late 1800s and early 1900s.

Andrew Carnegie's massive steel mills employed hundreds of workers.

Cities and Businesses

Cities linked to important industries grew quickly. People moved to Cleveland, Ohio, to work in oil refineries. They moved to Pittsburgh, Pennsylvania, to work in steel plants. They moved to Detroit, Michigan, to make automobiles. Workers found jobs in Philadelphia, Baltimore, and New York City. Within the cities, workers made clothing in factories or worked in stores and hotels. Some sold food and clothes to the growing population.

Academic Vocabulary

official • *adj.*, relating to a position of authority and its activities

Every ten years the government makes an **official** count of all Americans. This is called a census. The 1920 census showed that, for the first time, more Americans lived in cities than on farms.

Big cities were connected more and more by railroads, airplanes, and highways. Raw materials moved to the cities, and finished goods moved out of the cities. Different regions relied on one another more and more.

Although it was an exciting time, problems were developing. The tall buildings and new forms of transportation brought crowding and traffic. Growing industries created pollution. Some businesses were dangerous for workers or people living nearby.

2. **☑ Reading Check** **Identify** how the growth of the railroad industry affected the city of Pittsburgh. **Describe** the costs and benefits of industry there.

_____

_____

_____

3. **☑ Reading Check Draw Conclusions** Study the bar graph. **Draw a conclusion** about changes in the United States population between 1860 and 1920.

_____

_____

_____

_____

_____

_____

Urban and Rural Population in the U.S., 1860–1920

☑ Lesson 2 Check

INTERACTIVITY

Check your understanding of the key ideas in this lesson.

4. **Draw Conclusions** Why did people create very big companies?

_____

_____

_____

_____

5. A tire company is almost out of supplies to make their tires. **Describe** the effect that would occur if the demand for tires also increased.

_____

_____

6. **Understand the Quest Connections** How might the experience of an entrepreneur cause an investor to take a risk on the entrepreneur's new business idea?

_____

_____

_____

Henry Ford on His Assembly Line

The first cars were custom built and very expensive to make. Henry Ford wanted to make cars available to everyone. The first step was making them more affordable. The Model T was simple and less expensive, but Ford wanted to bring the price down even more.

To do this, he needed to increase efficiency in his factories. Ford developed a new mass-production method in order to manufacture cars in sufficient numbers to meet his goals. Over the course of five years, Ford perfected this method, called the assembly line. By 1913, Ford was producing cars at a record-breaking rate.

Vocabulary Support

Workers barely had to move to do their job. ••••••

Fewer men were now needed to do the same amount of work. ••••••

principle, *n.*, a basic truth, theory, or general rule

operation, *n.*, the system of carrying out work on a large scale

comparatively, *adv.*, when measured against something else

efficiency, *n.*, the ability to do something without wasting time or materials

"We now have two general principles in all operations— that a man shall never have to take more than one step, if possibly it can be avoided, and that no man need ever stoop over.

. . . In short, the result is this: by the aid of scientific study one man is now able to do somewhat more than four did only a comparatively few years ago. That line established the efficiency of the method and we now use it everywhere. The assembling of the motor, formerly done by one man, is now divided into eighty-four operations—those men do the work that three times their number formerly did."

–Henry Ford, "My Life and Work,"
McClure's Magazine, 1922

Fun Fact

When he was young, Ford used tools that he had made himself to repair the watches of his friends and family.

Close Reading

1. **Identify** and circle how many steps Ford said it took to assemble a car at his factory.
2. **Explain** in your own words how cars were assembled before Henry Ford's assembly line.

_____

_____

_____

_____

Wrap It Up

The assembly line allowed Ford to make cars faster. How do you think that affected the automobile industry? Support your answer with information from the chapter. Use a quote from the primary source.

_____

_____

_____

_____

_____

Workers on an assembly line in a Ford factory

Lesson 3 Immigration

 INTERACTIVITY

Participate in a class discussion to preview the content of this lesson.

Vocabulary

diversity
prejudice
oppression
tenement
labor union
melting pot

Academic Vocabulary

overwhelming
renew

A Chinese immigrant's business in San Francisco, California

Unlock The BIG Question

I will know some of the costs and benefits of being an immigrant.

Jumpstart Activity

What do you think it would be like to go to a brand new country to start a new life? With a small group, role-play a scene where an immigrant is arriving in America. Characters could include the immigrant's family, the first person the family meets after arriving, and a person the newcomer approaches for a job.

Immigrants had always come to the United States in search of freedom and opportunity. But after the Civil War, immigrants started arriving in greater numbers. They came by ship from countries all over the world. The voyage was now easier and faster, thanks to improved transportation.

New Immigrants

 INTERACTIVITY

Explore the key ideas of this lesson.

There were two major waves of immigrants who came to America after the Civil War. The first wave arrived between 1865 and 1890. During that time, about 10 million people moved to the United States. Most of them came from Ireland and countries in northern Europe, such as Germany, Great Britain, Finland, Sweden, and Norway.

The second wave of immigrants to the United States arrived between 1890 and 1920. Most came from eastern and southern European countries. These included countries such as Poland, Russia, Italy, Austria-Hungary, and Greece. They were called the new immigrants.

People came to America from other countries, too. Some moved south from Canada. Others moved north from Latin America. Still others came from Japan and China.

Most of the new immigrants came from cultures that differed from the cultures of previous groups. Some did not come to stay but just wanted to make money and return home. It was not an easy time for many Americans, as they tried to compete with the newcomers for jobs, understand the new cultures, and cope with the overcrowding that the huge number of newcomers created.

More than 15 million of these "new immigrants" arrived in the second wave. Many immigrants arriving from Europe moved into the industrial cities in the East and Midwest. Immigrants coming from Asia landed on the West Coast and often settled there. Wherever they came from, immigrants brought their languages and traditions with them. These new cultures added to the **diversity**, or variety, of American life.

Word Wise

Compound words are two words that are joined together to form a new word. Read the fourth paragraph on this page. What do you think the word *overcrowding* means? Use the word in a sentence.

1. ☑ **Reading Check**
Identify and circle the European countries from which most immigrants to the United States came after 1890.

Europe, 1900

0   400 mi
0   400 km

SWEDEN AND NORWAY   Finland

DENMARK

IRELAND   GREAT BRITAIN

NETHERLANDS

ATLANTIC OCEAN

GERMANY   POLAND

BELGIUM

LUXEMBOURG

SWITZERLAND

FRANCE

AUSTRIA-HUNGARY

ROMANIA

SERBIA

RUSSIA

PORTUGAL   SPAIN

ITALY   MONTENEGRO   ASIA

GREECE

AFRICA

Reasons for Immigration

Immigrants left their homelands for many reasons. Some escaped wars. Many faced prejudice because of their religious or political beliefs. **Prejudice** is unfair negative opinions about a group of people. Some, like Russia's Jews, faced more than prejudice. They faced violence and oppression. **Oppression** is unjust treatment by a government. Often, immigrants came from poor areas. In many countries there were limited resources because there wasn't enough land to farm or food to eat. There were few jobs. For most immigrants, life in their old homelands had been very difficult and offered no hope for improvement.

What did they hope to find in the United States? They wanted a better life. They wanted political and religious freedom. And they wanted to work. America was the land of opportunity. Immigrants wanted to start businesses or find jobs in factories or on farms. Letters from friends and relatives already living in the United States had told them about life in America. They knew their new lives would not be easy, but the United States would offer a new start.

Asian immigrants arriving at Angel Island

2. **✓ Reading Check**

Analyze why people immigrated, then fill in the chart with information from this page.

Why People Immigrated	
Why Immigrants Left Their Homelands	**What Immigrants Hoped to Find in America**
1. They were poor.	
2. They faced war, prejudice, and oppression.	
3. There were no opportunities or resources in their homelands.	

Gaining Entrance

Most immigrants during this period arrived at one of two islands: New York's Ellis Island or San Francisco's Angel Island. In these two places, they would be checked for criminal records or diseases, and then they could enter the country.

Many immigrants had friends or family here already who could help get newcomers settled. Many organizations were formed to provide help in the unfamiliar country. Most immigrants came from small villages. In American cities in 1900, there were electric streetcars, automobiles, and crowds of people. Buildings were incredibly tall. Everywhere, people spoke different languages. The change could be **overwhelming**.

Academic Vocabulary

overwhelming • *adj.*, causing strong emotions; overpowering

A Rough Start

For most immigrants, life in the United States had many benefits. But the sudden population growth had costs. There were more people than there were places to live.

In large cities, many moved into tenements. A **tenement** is a building that has been divided into small apartments. Often, large families shared one small apartment. Some rooms had no windows. There was little fresh air. All the people on one floor might have to share a single sink. With so many people living there, tenements often became dirty and run down.

Most unskilled workers looked for factory jobs. As immigration continued, jobs became harder to find, because there were so many workers. Employers liked immigrant labor because of its low cost. However, many workers who had been born in the United States feared job loss or worried that immigrants brought problems with them. Still, most immigrants did well, and many became very successful.

Some families worked in their tenement apartments to earn money.

Immigrants Make Contributions

Immigrants, such as entrepreneur Andrew Carnegie, helped change American life. They started thousands of small businesses and many large ones.

Jacob Riis was an immigrant from Denmark. In 1873, Riis became a newspaper reporter in New York City. He wrote about and photographed the living conditions of poor immigrants in the tenements. Because of his work, new organizations were started and laws were passed to improve the lives of immigrants.

Samuel Gompers immigrated to America from Great Britain in 1863. In New York City, Gompers made cigars in a factory. Working conditions were poor, so he formed a labor union. A **labor union** is a group of workers who unite to demand better wages and working conditions. Labor unions may also support political candidates who share their views.

George Shima came to the United States from Japan in 1888. He saved enough to buy farmland and raise potatoes. Known as the "Potato King," Shima became an important leader in California's Japanese American community.

That's Entertainment

Stories about America's immigrants began appearing in literature, both in the United States and overseas. Israel Zangwill was a British writer who viewed the United States as a **melting pot**: a place where Europeans could "melt" old ideas and prejudices and be molded into a new people called Americans. His play about Russian immigrants, which he titled *The Melting Pot*, became hugely popular, and the term *melting pot* became part of American language.

California's movie industry was created in large part by immigrants. The founders of all the big studios, including Warner Brothers, Metro-Goldwyn-Mayer, Paramount, and Columbia, and most of the famous directors of the early 1900s, were Jewish people who had immigrated from Russia and eastern Europe.

Irving Berlin came to the United States fleeing anti-Jewish violence in Russia in 1893. As a young boy, he sang on the streets of New York City to help his family earn money. Later he wrote many famous songs for movies and Broadway shows. One of his most famous songs is "God Bless America."

Welcome to a New Land

Immigrants who entered New York Harbor, on the way to Ellis Island, were greeted by a huge statue. The statue is named *Liberty Enlightening the World*, but most people call it the Statue of Liberty. It was a gift from the people of France to the United States. To Americans and the world, it is a symbol of freedom.

This statue of a woman has a torch in her right hand. In her left hand, she holds a tablet. On it is the date July 4, 1776, which is the date of the Declaration of Independence. The Statue of Liberty celebrates the founding ideals of our nation.

The Statue of Liberty stands 305 feet tall, including its base. On the base is a famous poem written by Jewish American poet Emma Lazarus. The poem welcomes those who are poor or who want freedom. Part of the poem is quoted below.

3. ☑ **Reading Check**
Turn and talk with a partner to determine what the last line of the Lazarus poem on the base of the Statue of Liberty means.

An illustration of European immigrants arriving in New York

Give me your tired, your poor,
Your huddled masses yearning to breathe free,
The wretched refuse of your teeming shore,
Send these, the homeless, tempest-tossed to me,
I lift my lamp beside the golden door!

Becoming American

As immigrants learned about American ways, most came to love their new home. Most found the freedom and the opportunities they wanted.

A Polish immigrant named Casimir Cybulski stated, "I wouldn't go [back to Poland] because it's 100 percent better here. The United States you still got everything. It's perfect."

Thousands of immigrants still come to the United States every year. They come for the same reasons they did 100 years ago: freedom and opportunities.

Reaction Against Immigrants

Most immigrants found a new life in the United States. But some found they were not welcome. New immigrants worked for lower wages. The labor unions in particular fought immigration. How could workers ask for better pay or conditions when millions waited to take their jobs? Samuel Gompers worked hard to keep out new immigrants.

Also, many new immigrants were different from other Americans. Some formed their own neighborhoods, such as Chinatown and Little Italy.

At first, Chinese people were welcomed. They were hard workers, and the West needed workers. However, attitudes changed as more and more people competed for jobs and resources. Also, Asian culture was very different from European culture. Some Chinese traditions were hard for other Americans to accept.

In 1882, Congress passed a law to prevent Chinese workers from entering the country for ten years. This was called the Chinese Exclusion Act. The law was **renewed** in 1892 and then made permanent in 1902.

Immigrants celebrating their new American citizenship

Academic Vocabulary

renew • *v.*, to begin again

Many Americans worried that the new immigrants would change America. So in 1924, the United States government passed another law to restrict immigration. It stopped immigration from Asia and tried to reduce immigration from southern and eastern Europe. The new law limited the yearly number of immigrants arriving from each European country.

4. ☑ **Reading Check** **Describe** two reasons people began to want to limit immigration.

_____

_____

_____

INTERACTIVITY

Check your understanding of the key ideas in this lesson.

☑ Lesson 3 Check

5. **Summarize** Summarize life for immigrants in the United States between 1880 and 1920, including the challenges they faced.

_____

_____

_____

6. Suppose that you are a new immigrant to the United States in 1900. What do you think are the costs and benefits to you of moving here?

_____

_____

7. **Analyze** the effects of immigration on the economic growth and development of the United States. **Explain** one positive and one negative effect.

_____

_____

_____

Give an Effective Presentation

Millions of immigrants came through Ellis Island in the late 1800s and early 1900s.

▶ **VIDEO**

Watch a video about delivering effective presentations.

The picture above shows immigrants moving through Ellis Island in the late 1800s. If you gave a presentation about immigration, this image could help you. Paintings and photographs are primary-source visual materials. You can find them on the Internet or in encyclopedias. Graphs and charts are secondary-source visual materials. You can find them in books or online. You can also make them yourself to analyze data for your presentation.

Here are some other keys to an effective presentation:

1. Research your topic and visual aids. Include the main ideas as well as supporting details and ideas in your report. You may also express some ideas based on your experiences.

2. Practice reading your report orally in front of a mirror or in front of a friend or family member. Then practice some more.

3. Know everything you want to say ahead of time. Write key points on notecards. When possible, talk directly to your audience.

4. Speak loudly. Your voice must reach the person farthest away from you. Do not rush. Pause to take a breath between ideas.

Your Turn!

1. Suppose you wanted to give a presentation about immigration to the United States in the late 1800s and early 1900s. Make notes about the kinds of images that you would want to include and why you think each image would make your presentation stronger. Think about the entire immigration experience as you plan your visuals.

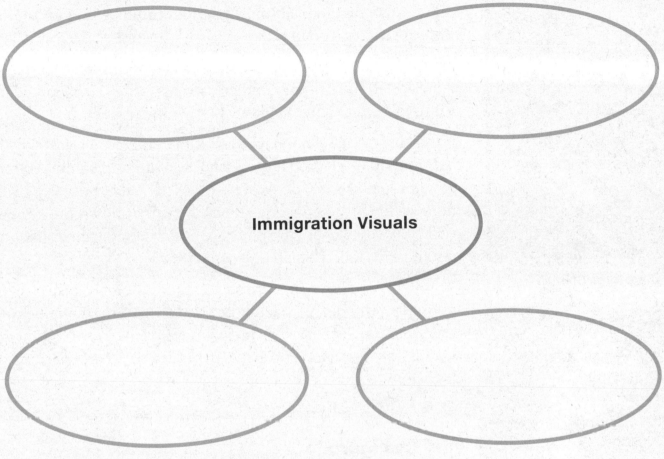

Immigration Visuals

2. What else could you do to make your presentation effective?

_____

_____

_____

3. Reread the information about European and Asian immigrants in Lesson 3. How would you start a presentation about their journey that would grab the attention of your audience?

_____

_____

_____

Quality:
Problem Solving

George Shima

George Shima (1864–1926)
Problem Solving Through Innovation

George Shima, born in Japan with the name Ushijima Seikichi, arrived in California in 1889. One of his first jobs was working as a farm hand in the Sacramento–San Joaquin Delta. Later, he became a potato farmer. His innovative farming ideas produced high-quality potatoes. Shima's potatoes could be sold for more than the average potato.

Shima had found just the right kind of soil for his potatoes, and he perfected the irrigation process on his farms. He irrigated using narrow trenches in every 30 rows of potatoes.

In the early 1900s, Shima met Lee Allan Phillips, a wealthy investor. Phillips leased large amounts of land to Shima. Shima's crews planted 14,000 acres of potatoes. By 1906, he was growing more potatoes than anyone else in the world. He became known across the country as "the potato king." By 1910, Shima began to purchase his land instead of leasing it.

Despite his success, Shima faced discrimination because of his Japanese heritage. As a result, he tried to help resolve issues of discimination. He served as president of the national Japanese Association of America from 1908 through 1925 and became an important leader for Japanese people living in the United States.

Find Out More

1. Identify how George Shima solved problems. Explain the effects of his problem-solving skills.

_____

_____

_____

_____

2. People are challenged by problems every day. Create a series of questions and interview a family member or friend to find out about a challenge they faced and what they did to resolve it.

Visual Review

Use these images and graphic to review some of the key terms, people, and ideas from this chapter.

Samuel Morse invented the telegraph in the mid-1800s. This was a new way of communicating across long distances.

Alexander Graham Bell was a teacher who invented the telephone.

Wilbur and Orville Wright built the first airplane.

Harvey Firestone invented a special kind of tire that was filled with air.

Boeing's airplane company was chosen to transport mail for the U.S. Postal Service.

John D. Rockefeller built his first oil refinery and started the Standard Oil Company.

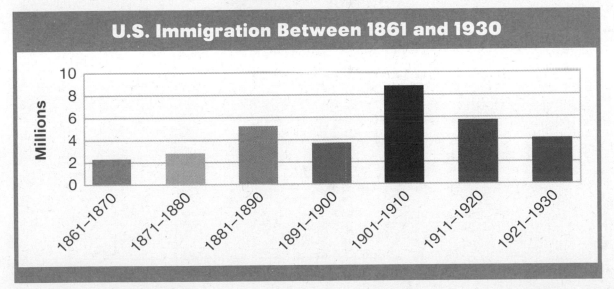

U.S. Immigration Between 1861 and 1930

Millions

10
8
6
4
2
0

1861–1870
1871–1880
1881–1890
1891–1900
1901–1910
1911–1920
1921–1930

Source: Census Bureau, 2016

Chapter 11 ✅ Assessment

 GAMES

Play the vocabulary game.

Vocabulary and Key Ideas

1. **Describe** Write a sentence to describe why each of the following inventions benefited society.

   Telephone

   _____

   Light bulb

   _____

   Airplane

   _____

2. **Explain** How does an invention covered in this chapter affect life today?

   _____

   _____

3. **Define** What is an investor?

   _____

   _____

4. **Define** the free enterprise system and explain how it affected the United States in the late 1800s and early 1900s.

   _____

   _____

   _____

   _____

   _____

Critical Thinking and Writing

5. **Predict Consequences** List three consequences you think would eventually result from the overcrowding of American cities and the worsening of life in tenements.

_____

_____

_____

_____

6. **Draw Conclusions** What invention or innovation discussed in this chapter do you think had the greatest influence on life in the early 1900s? Explain.

_____

_____

_____

_____

_____

7. **Revisit the Big Question** What were the costs and benefits of economic growth in the United States between the late 1800s and early 1900s?

_____

_____

_____

_____

_____

8. **Writer's Workshop: Write a Narrative** On a separate sheet of paper, write a diary entry from the perspective of a young immigrant whose family has just arrived in the United States. Include details about why the family came to America and describe their reaction to living in a large American city.

Analyze Primary Sources

"We are embarked as pioneers upon a new science and industry in which our problems are so new and unusual that it behooves [to be worthwhile to] no one to dismiss any novel [new, different] idea with the statement that 'it can't be done!'"

-William Boeing

9. How does this quote reflect the attitude of the inventors and entrepreneurs that you have learned about in this chapter?

_____

_____

_____

_____

Give an Effective Presentation

10. What kind of visuals and details would you use for a presentation about the economic and cultural impact of immigration on the United States? Use evidence from the chapter.

_____

_____

_____

_____

_____

Quest Findings

Taking a Risk

You've read about successful American entrepreneurs, and now you are ready to plan your own small business or venture. Remember to include all the reasons why your team's idea would appeal to an investor.

 INTERACTIVITY

Use this activity to help you prepare your assignment.

1 Organize Your Ideas

Your team should gather its research and evidence from the Quest Connections to write an outline for its plan. The team should use what it learned about successful businesses to plan its own entrepreneurial success.

3 Create Visual Aids

As a group, create or choose images that will be paired with your plan.

2 Write a Draft

Make sure the team's ideas follow each other in a logical way. Remember to address why your group's idea is a good one. Include examples and details.

4 Present Your Plan

Present your business plan to your class. Ask for feedback about its strengths and weaknesses. Were any of your classmates encouraged to invest in your idea?

12 Struggle for Reform

The BIG Question When does change become necessary?

▶ VIDEO

JumPstart Activity

What if your school library made a rule that allowed only teachers to have the right to borrow books? Work with a partner to write a protest sign explaining why you think this rule is fair or not fair. Write ideas for your signs on the lines. Then hold a protest march in the classroom.

_____

_____

_____

_____

_____

Rap About It!

🔊 AUDIO

Pushing for Progress

Preview the chapter **vocabulary** as you sing the rap.

The workers didn't have a say, to work what day
  or night,
So they decided to have a **strike**, with labor unions'
  might.
Now unions and workers could breathe easy and stay,
Because they now only had to work eight hours a day.

As time moved on the rules were black or white,
African Americans were barred their **civil rights**.
"Separate but Equal" was the law of the land,
With this unfair treatment, they had to take a stand.

During this same time women could not vote,
Their rights were limited and they had little hope.
Suffrage is a right that women should have had,
But it took the Nineteenth Amendment to make
  it ironclad.

12 Struggle for Reform

Women's Rights
Seneca Falls Convention

Seneca Falls

New York

Workers' Rights
Hull House

Chicago

Workers' Rights
Triangle Shirtwaist fire

Women's Rights
Nineteenth Amendment

Nashville

Daytona
Beach

Civil Rights
Bethune-Cookman
College

New Orleans

Civil Rights
Plessy v. Ferguson

Where were the key events of the struggle for reform?

During the Progressive Era, African Americans, workers, and women fought for rights.

A separate waiting area segregated people by race.

TODAY
You can visit the Center for Civil and Human Rights museum in Atlanta, Georgia.

What happened and When?

Read the timeline to see some of the events related to the Progressive Era.

1870

1880

1890

1869
National Woman Suffrage Association founded.

1886
American Federation of Labor founded.

1889
Jane Addams founds Hull House in Chicago.
Today
You can visit Hull House Museum.

1896
The Supreme Court rules in *Plessy* v. *Ferguson*.

Who will you meet?

Theodore Roosevelt
As president, supported laws to protect workers, consumers, and the environment

Ida Wells-Barnett
Supported an end to violence against African Americans by writing articles and giving speeches

Booker T. Washington
Supported the education of African Americans

Susan B. Anthony
Worked for equal rights for women and suffrage for women

 INTERACTIVITY

Complete the interactive digital activity.

1900   **1910**   **1920**

1909
NAACP founded.

1911
Fatal fire rages at the Triangle Shirtwaist Company.

1920
The Nineteenth Amendment gives women the right to vote.

Express Yourself!

The Progressive Era was a time of great change in the late 1800s and early 1900s. Labor leaders fought against terrible working conditions and child labor. African Americans, women, and others protested for equal rights. Immigrants and the poor struggled to succeed.

Your group will create four pages of a graphic novel that shows an issue from the Progressive Era. A graphic novel tells a story through images and words.

Quest Kick Off

Your task is to write four pages of a graphic novel for my publishing company. You will work with a small group of your talented classmates to write and illustrate a graphic novel about one of the important issues or groups from the Progressive Era.

1 Ask Questions

What group or issue do I want to feature in my graphic novel? What type of images should we show? Write at least two questions of your own.

....

....

....

② Use Sources

Follow your teacher's instructions to learn how to use primary and secondary sources in your graphic novel. As you find sources answer these questions.

1. What does the primary or secondary source show or say?

....

....

2. What message does the author or artist want to send?

....

....

INTERACTIVITY

Go online to learn more about the parts of a graphic novel.

③ Look for Quest Connections

Begin looking for Quest Connections that will help you create your novel.

④ Quest Findings
Publish the Graphic Novel

Use the Quest Findings page at the end of the chapter to help you publish your graphic novel.

INTERACTIVITY

Participate in a class discussion to preview the content of this lesson.

Vocabulary

trust
strike
strikebreaker
boycott
Progressive
muckraker
conservation

Academic Vocabulary

challenge
process

This poor area of New York City shows the overcrowded conditions typical of most big cities in the early 1900s.

Unlock
The **BIG** Question

I will know that changes in the American economy led to problems that Progressives tried to solve.

JumpStart Activity

Choose a piece of paper that your teacher will provide. You will either be a worker or a factory owner. Workers will gather together and think of things that they might want from the owners. The group of factory owners will get together and discuss what the workers' requests will cost them. Encourage students to try to compromise.

The United States was changing rapidly in the early 1900s. New inventions were changing people's lives. Across the country, growing industries created jobs that attracted workers to cities. The number of people moving into cities and doing new kinds of jobs caused some problems. However, many groups and individuals worked to help solve the problems.

Industrialization Leads to Challenges

Industrialization was an important issue in the twentieth century. More and more Americans had jobs in factories, but working conditions were often very bad. Workers toiled for ten hours at a time, six days per week. Many factories were unhealthy and even dangerous places to work. Industrialization also led to urbanization. As more workers moved to cities to find jobs, cities became overcrowded. Housing was limited.

INTERACTIVITY

Explore the key ideas of this lesson.

The companies that owned the big factories kept growing. Some of them joined together to form large groups called **trusts**. These trusts could control an industry and drive other companies out of business. As the trusts grew stronger, they had more control over working conditions.

One tragedy showed why new laws were needed to change working conditions. The Triangle Shirtwaist Company in New York City produced clothing. During the day, the main doors were locked to keep workers from stealing. When a fire started on March 25, 1911, workers could not open the doors. Firefighters' ladders could not reach the eighth-floor workshop. Some workers died jumping from windows. Others died when the fire escape collapsed. Most of the 146 who died were young women.

Another problem was child labor. In 1900, almost 2 million children worked in factories and mines. Some were as young as five years old. Others worked on the street, selling newspapers or shining shoes. Few poor children, especially those from other countries, had ever gone to school.

Americans knew that progress had to be made to solve these problems. These ideas would change the economic growth and development of the country.

In the early 1900s, many American children worked in mills, mines, or factories like this one.

The Labor Movement

By the late 1800s, workers demanded shorter workdays, better wages, and better working conditions. Workers began turning to labor unions for help.

One of the first national labor unions, the Knights of Labor, was organized in 1869. It was effective at first, but it attracted radicals, or people with extreme views, so people left the group. In 1886, a new union replaced it. This union was the American Federation of Labor, or AFL.

The founder of the AFL was Samuel Gompers, a Jewish immigrant who wanted better wages and working conditions for members. The new union grouped members by skill. All the carpenters belonged to one craft union. The hat makers belonged to another. By 1904, the AFL had about 2 million members.

Meanwhile, the United Mine Workers relied on the help of Mary Harris "Mother" Jones. In the 1890s, Jones unionized coal miners in Pennsylvania. Later, she worked to end child labor in the Pennsylvania mills.

Starting in 1882, parades were held to honor workers' rights. In 1894, Congress recognized the labor movement by making Labor Day a national holiday.

Unions Demanded Change

Unions wanted more money and better working conditions. However, business owners wanted to keep expenses down to make products affordable. Creating lasting change was a **challenge**. Sometimes union leaders tried to achieve their goals by calling a strike. During a **strike**, workers refuse to work until business owners agree to their demands.

Some strikes turned violent. In July 1892, steelworkers in Homestead, Pennsylvania, went on strike. Thousands of immigrants eagerly replaced the striking workers. These replacements were called **strikebreakers**. The striking workers attacked the replacements. Armed guards were hired to protect the strikebreakers. By the time the strike ended, several people had been killed or injured.

Mary Harris "Mother" Jones

1. ☑ **Reading Check**
Turn and talk with a partner to **describe** the significance of Labor Day becoming a national celebration.

Academic Vocabulary

challenge • *n.*, something difficult

U.S. Union Membership, 1898–1920

Millions of Members

5.0
4.5
4.0
3.5
3.0
2.5
2.0
1.5
1.0
0.5
0

1898 1902 1906 1910 1914 1918

Years

Source: U.S. Department of Commerce, Bureau of the Census

2. ☑ **Reading Check**
Analyze the line graph. **Turn and talk** to a partner, and **explain** what factors might have contributed to an increase in union membership in the early 1900s. Then **circle** the point on the graph when union membership reached 2 million members.

Word Wise

Word Origins During the 1870s, farmers in Ireland faced a crisis. A retired British army captain named Charles Boycott tried to evict some farmers from their land. When people found out, everybody refused to work with him or buy his goods. His crops soon rotted. Soon, Boycott's name was used everywhere to describe a refusal to buy goods.

Another union strategy was the boycott. During a **boycott**, people agree not to buy goods made by a certain company. When the company agrees to change the way it operates, the boycott ends.

As unions became stronger, working conditions improved. Some cities and states passed laws that shortened the workday to eight hours. Another law made employers responsible for helping injured workers. Samuel Gompers supported state laws that helped end child labor.

Solving America's Problems

By the late 1800s, many cities faced overcrowding, big trusts, dangerous factories, and dishonest politicians. Some of the people who tried to find solutions to these problems were called **Progressives**. A group of writers helped spread the Progressives' ideas. These writers were called **muckrakers**, because they uncovered "muck," or shameful conditions in American business and society.

Young boys who work selling newspapers sleep on a warm grate before their early-morning shift.

Quest Connection

Look at the image of the boys. What can you tell about their lives? Think about the image as a document you want to use for your Quest.

INTERACTIVITY

Your graphic novel will be more powerful with good images. Go online to learn how to use images effectively in your graphic novel.

Academic Vocabulary

process • *n.*, system by which something is done

Ida Tarbell showed the danger of trusts in *The History of the Standard Oil Company*, about John D. Rockefeller's oil company. Another muckraker, Upton Sinclair, wrote *The Jungle*. This novel described the horrible conditions in the meatpacking industry. Jacob Riis photographed the terrible living conditions of many immigrants and working people in overcrowded cities. His work was called *How the Other Half Lives*. Muckrakers focused Americans' attention on these issues, and people began to call for change.

3. ☑ **Reading Check Explain** why the books the muckrakers wrote were important.

_____

_____

_____

_____

_____

Roosevelt Takes Action

Theodore Roosevelt became president in 1901. He supported many Progressive ideas. In 1902, Roosevelt used a law, the Sherman Antitrust Act, to break up many big business trusts into smaller companies. President Roosevelt sometimes supported striking workers, too. In 1902, he helped coal miners in the state of Pennsylvania win higher wages and a shorter workday.

In 1906, Roosevelt supported two laws to help make the **process** of making food and medicine safer. The Meat Inspection Act said that inspectors must check meat to make sure it was safe. The Pure Food and Drug Act made companies reveal the ingredients in their products.

Achievements of the Progressive Era

Some Progressives wanted to improve life for immigrants and others who might need some help, especially in the cities. One individual who made great contributions to society was Jane Addams. In Chicago in 1889, she started a settlement house, or center that offers help to needy people. She called it Hull House. It offered English classes and other courses. Working parents could leave their children in a nursery there. Hull House was a great accomplishment. Soon, settlement houses opened all over the country.

Progressives supported other laws to change American life. Many workers now worked eight hours, instead of ten or more. President Woodrow Wilson backed laws to end child labor and to protect workers injured on the job. He also declared strikes and boycotts to be legal. Other laws made homes and workplaces safer. Children now had to attend school. Cities built the first playgrounds in crowded neighborhoods.

As government tried to do more, it became more expensive. Congress passed the Sixteenth Amendment in 1913, so the government could tax people's income, or wages. The money from this tax helped pay for new programs. Under the Seventeenth Amendment, citizens could elect their senators directly. This gave people more political power.

4. ☑ **Reading Check** **Summarize** Complete these statements about changes during the Progressive Era.

   a. Roosevelt used the Sherman Antitrust Act to break up

   _____.

   b. To pay for programs, the government began to tax

   _____.

   c. President Wilson declared _____ to be legal.

   d. Jane Addams opened _____.

   e. The _____ let inspectors check meat.

President Roosevelt (right) visited Yosemite with John Muir (left) in 1903.

Other Progressive Goals

Progressives often helped people who society overlooked. Rebecca D. Lowe, of the Atlanta Women's Club, worked to develop public kindergartens in rural areas of Georgia. She wanted to provide a better education for very young children living in poor areas outside the cities.

Clara Barton was another important reformer. During the Civil War she had been a nurse. Later she worked to get international laws passed that would help the sick and wounded during war. In 1881, she organized the American Red Cross.

Dorothea Dix was another Civil War nurse. For most of her life, she worked to improve the treatment of people who were mentally ill. Their mistreatment in a Massachusetts prison shocked her. After visiting other state prisons, she sent a report to the legislature. Because of this report, the legislature voted to enlarge the state hospital facilities. For the next 40 years, Dorothea Dix worked to make other states build hospitals for the mentally ill.

Progressives also worked for **conservation**, or the protecting and saving of the wilderness. In 1872, the government established Yellowstone, the world's first national park. People like John Muir urged the government to establish Sequoia (sih KWOI uh) and Yosemite (yoh SEM uh tee) National Parks in 1890.

President Roosevelt strongly believed in conservation. He loved the outdoors and worked to protect the country's wilderness areas. In 1905, Roosevelt urged Congress to create the U.S. Forest Service.

National parks are places where people can hike, climb, and enjoy nature. Here a father and daughter scale a mountain in Yosemite.

INTERACTIVITY

Check your understanding of the key ideas of this lesson.

☑ Lesson 1 Check

5. **Cause and Effect** How did the accomplishments of the Progressives affect the lives of workers in the United States?

_____

_____

_____

6. Imagine you are a reporter visiting Hull House for the first time. **Identify** the individual who started Hull House. Write about how this accomplishment contributed to improvements in the lives of people in Chicago.

_____

_____

_____

7. **Understand the** *Quest* **Connections** Choose a picture from this lesson. On a separate sheet of paper, list three details about it. Then decide whether you can use the image in your graphic novel.

Critical Thinking Skills

Solve Problems

The Progressives tried to solve political and social problems in the United States. To **solve a problem**, follow these steps:

- Identify the problem.
- Gather information about possible ways to solve the problem. Then list and consider the options.
- Consider the advantages and disadvantages of each option.
- Identify a solution and evaluate its effectiveness.

This chart identifies a problem that presidents Roosevelt and Wilson tried to solve during the Progressive Era. Read the steps each president followed to find a solution.

Problem

Large groups of companies, called trusts, controlled entire industries. These trusts could drive out competitors.

Possible Solutions

- There was an 1890 law called the Sherman Antitrust Act. It said trusts should not exist.

- A president can encourage Congress to pass new laws to stop bad practices, such as trusts.

- The president, as head of the executive branch, can make sure that laws are put into action.

Solution

President Roosevelt used the Sherman Antitrust Act to break up trusts. President Wilson urged Congress to pass a new law to prevent trusts.

Your Turn!

1. Upton Sinclair wrote a novel about the horrible conditions in Chicago's meatpacking plants. Complete the chart below to show how President Theodore Roosevelt solved the problem.

 VIDEO

Watch a video about solving problems.

Problem:
The conditions in the meatpacking plants were horrible.

Possible Solutions:
- Find a way to make these plants safer.
- Find a way to check up on the plants to see that they are clean and food is safe.
- Let people know what they are eating.

Solution:
_____
_____
_____
_____
_____
_____

2. **Think** about a problem affecting your school or community. **Use** a problem-solution chart to show the steps you would follow to solve it. Include information about why this solution will be effective.

Lesson 2

Unequal Opportunities for African Americans

 INTERACTIVITY

Participate in a class discussion to preview the content of this lesson.

Vocabulary

civil rights
Great Migration

Academic Vocabulary

motivation
advocate

Unlock The BIG Question

I will know that it was necessary to change the unfair treatment of African Americans.

JumpStart Activity

Work with a partner to identify an example of unfair treatment. You may include your own experience, or other events you have seen or heard about. Together, think of some ways to make the situation more fair.

After Reconstruction ended, African Americans faced many difficulties. Harsh laws separated the races in the United States, especially in the South. Even the U.S. Supreme Court did not help to end this unfair treatment. Trying to escape this prejudice, many African Americans moved north to start new lives.

People protest Jim Crow laws.

Jim Crow Laws

Between the end of Reconstruction and the mid-1950s, hundreds of laws made segregation legal. Segregation is the separation of people of different races. These laws were known as Jim Crow laws.

Under Jim Crow laws, white Americans and African Americans led almost completely separate lives. These laws segregated schools, theaters, buses, trains, and other public spaces. Blacks and whites could not sit together in the same restaurants or use the same restrooms. They could not drink at the same water fountains.

In southern states, other laws were passed to keep African Americans from voting. Beginning in 1890, some states required voters to pass a reading test to vote. Because the education of African Americans was often discouraged, many could not pass the test. In other states, African Americans had to pay a voting tax.

Segregation Limits Opportunities

Segregation limited the civil rights of African Americans. **Civil rights** are the rights all citizens should have under the U.S. Constitution. In 1890, Louisiana passed a Jim Crow law that segregated railroad cars. Two years later, Homer Plessy challenged this law by purposely sitting in a railroad car reserved for white people. After his arrest, Plessy sued Louisiana. The case was called *Plessy* v. *Ferguson*.

In 1896, the Supreme Court ruled in this case. Most of the justices thought Plessy was guilty. They said that it was legal to separate the races if the facilities for blacks and whites were equal. This is called the separate but equal principle.

One Supreme Court judge disagreed. John Marshall Harlan said the court's decision was wrong. He wrote that

Many bus and train stations had separate waiting rooms for African Americans.

Primary Source

". . . in the eyes of the law, there is in this country no superior, dominant, ruling class of citizens."

—John Marshall Harlan, Dissenting Statement, 1896

Migrating North

Academic Vocabulary

motivation • *n.*, reason to take an action

Low wages and unfair laws in the South gave many African Americans a **motivation** to leave. Between 1916 and 1970, about 6 million African Americans moved from farming areas in the South to big cities in the North. This movement is known as the **Great Migration**.

The hope of better-paying jobs and better living conditions drew African Americans to New York, Detroit, Cleveland, and Chicago. They read about job opportunities in the *Chicago Defender*. This was an important African American newspaper that encouraged the Great Migration.

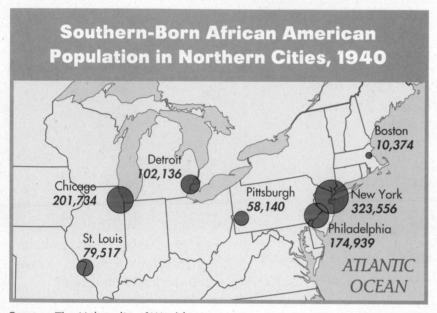

Southern-Born African American Population in Northern Cities, 1940

Boston 10,374
Detroit 102,136
Chicago 201,734
Pittsburgh 58,140
New York 323,556
Philadelphia 174,939
St. Louis 79,517
ATLANTIC OCEAN

Source: The University of Washington

Prejudice was only one of the problems that pushed people out of the South. African Americans working as sharecroppers found it hard to escape poverty. Also, many southern farms failed after insects damaged cotton crops in the 1890s.

African Americans faced prejudice in the North, too. Some northern states had segregated schools, theaters, hotels, and restaurants. Some African Americans lived together in poor neighborhoods. However, many created thriving communities with successful African American businesses. These communities impacted the growth of the economy. Neighborhoods such as Chicago's Bronzeville and New York City's Harlem became vibrant centers of African American arts and culture.

1. ☑ **Reading Check**
Analyze the map. **Circle** the names of the three cities that had the largest population of Southern-born African Americans.

African American Leaders

Booker T. Washington was one of the most famous and respected African American leaders of his time. He had been enslaved as a child and grew up in poverty during Reconstruction. But he was determined to get an education, and he put himself through school.

Washington believed that African Americans needed education before anything else. Useful skills would lead to better jobs. Over time these jobs would help African Americans overcome prejudice. He dedicated his life to creating educational opportunities for African Americans.

W.E.B. Du Bois (doo BOYZ) was another important African American **advocate** for civil rights. His life was very different from Washington's. Du Bois was never enslaved. Born in Massachusetts in 1868, he graduated from Fisk University, an African American college in Tennessee.

Mary McLeod Bethune also believed that education was the best way to achieve racial equality and civil rights. In 1904, she founded a school for African American girls in Daytona Beach, Florida. Later her school became Bethune-Cookman College.

Ida Wells-Barnett was born in Mississippi in 1862. After 1895 she lived in Chicago, where she worked for a newspaper. She also founded the first voting rights club for African American women in Illinois. In her speeches and articles, she supported an end to violence against African Americans. Wells-Barnett once proclaimed,

Academic Vocabulary

advocate • *n.*, person who supports a particular cause

Quest Connection

Read the quote by Ida Wells-Barnett. What do you think "educate public sentiment" means? What other questions can you ask yourself about her words?

Primary Source

"Get yourselves united and educate public sentiment on this subject, and there will certainly be a reaction."

—Ida Wells-Barnett, speech, 1896

INTERACTIVITY

Go online to learn more about how to use primary sources in your graphic novel.

2. ☑ **Reading Check**
Turn and talk with a partner. **Identify** what both Booker T. Washington and Mary McLeod Bethune saw as the key to success, and why.

Mary McLeod Bethune

New Institutions

Robert S. Abbott founded the *Chicago Defender* in 1905. Over time it became one of the most important African American newspapers in America. You have read that the *Defender* played a part in the Great Migration. Later, during World Wars I and II, the newspaper supported equal treatment for African American soldiers.

In 1909, W.E.B. Du Bois joined Ida Wells-Barnett and others to start the National Association for the Advancement of Colored People, or the NAACP. This organization wanted to end prejudice and segregation in housing, schools, jobs, voting, and other areas. Lawyers from the NAACP argued against segregation laws at the Supreme Court. These lawyers, such as future Supreme Court Justice Thurgood Marshall, won the case that ended school segregation in 1954.

Booker T. Washington founded the Tuskegee Institute in 1881. At first, the school taught farming and practical job training to African Americans. For example, students could learn carpentry and printing. In addition, Tuskegee students studied history, science, math, and English. The famous scientist and inventor George Washington Carver did important research at the school. His research helped farmers become more successful.

George Washington Carver (center) was in charge of the agriculture department at the Tuskegee Institute.

A dozen other colleges for African Americans opened, and older colleges began accepting African American students. However, Tuskegee remained a leader in education for African Americans. In 1943, Tuskegee's fourth president helped start the United Negro College Fund to provide scholarships to deserving students. The Institute became Tuskegee University in 1985.

3. ☑ **Reading Check** **Describe** Booker T. Washington's feelings toward education.

_____

_____

_____

☑ **Lesson 2 Check**

 INTERACTIVITY

Check your understanding of the key ideas of this lesson.

4. **Cause and Effect** How did growing industries in the North affect the Great Migration?

_____

_____

_____

5. You are an African American worker who moved to a northern city in 1910. Write a short letter that **describes** your life and what you would like to see change.

_____

_____

_____

6. **Understand the** *Quest* **Connections** Write a question you could ask about Ida Wells-Barnett's words as you plan your graphic novel.

_____

_____

_____

Nat Love's Personal Memoir

Nat Love was born in Tennessee in 1854. At that time, he and his family were enslaved. After the end of the Civil War, when Love was just 15 years old, he left the South to look for a better job.

When Love migrated to the West, he worked as a cowhand. Eventually, he became a railroad worker in Colorado. He was a hard worker, and he soon made up to $40 a month. For the late 1800s, this was a very good wage.

In 1907, Love published a memoir about his life and work. He told the story of his childhood in the South and his first search for work.

Vocabulary Support

After walking everywhere looking for work for two days

the children thought I was very rich

secured, *v.*, found
notwithstanding, *prep.*, in spite of
jubilant, *adj.*, joyful
impart, *v.*, to tell
commence, *v.*, to start

After tramping around the country for two days, I finally secured work with a Mr. Brooks, about six miles from home at one dollar and fifty cents a month. Notwithstanding the smallness of my prospective wages, I was happy and returned home in a jubilant frame of mind, to impart the news to mother. I was to commence the next morning. Mother said it was not much, but better than nothing. I told mother that I thought I could bring some food and clothing home for the children before the month was out. The little ones hearing this, were overjoyed and looked on me as a rich man indeed.

– Nat Love, Personal Memoir, 1907

Fun Fact

In the year 1900, the average American wage was $36.50 per month.

Close Reading

1. **Identify and circle** the two reactions Love's family had when he got his first job.
2. **Infer** why Love's family had different reactions to his job. Why does he describe his own reaction as "jubilant"?

_____

_____

_____

_____

_____

Wrap It Up

Compare Love's description of his first job to his job on the railroad in Colorado. Write a paragraph to describe how Nat Love's career changed over time. Explain how leaving the South affected his career.

_____

_____

_____

_____

_____

_____

_____

_____

_____

Lesson 3 — The Fight for Women's Rights

INTERACTIVITY

Participate in a class discussion to preview the content of this lesson.

Vocabulary

temperance
suffrage
suffragist

Academic Vocabulary

announce
propose

Unlock The BIG Question

I will know that many people worked to gain equal rights, including voting rights, for women.

JumpStart Activity

In small groups, vote to choose where you would like to go this weekend. Discuss how you would feel if one member of your group had not been able to vote.

In the early 1900s the United States was changing, and women wanted to be part of that change. New jobs and better educational opportunities made their lives richer. But women's rights were limited, and they still could not vote.

The first department stores appeared in the 1800s. These large stores offered many job opportunities for women.

Changing Roles for Women

Most married women in the mid- to late-1800s were homemakers. They stayed at home and cared for their husbands and children. Before they married, many women in cities worked as maids or in factories, mills, and workshops. Better-educated women were teachers. Very poor women kept working after they married. Often, they washed and mended clothes. By 1900, about 4 million women worked in jobs other than farming. Few women worked in the same professions as men.

Life was different for women in rural areas. In the country, pioneer women always shared farm or ranch chores with their husbands. Both women and men had to work to survive. Equal work often resulted in equal rights for rural women.

Between 1900 and 1925, job opportunities for women grew quickly. More women were graduating from colleges and universities. Women still cared for families and homes, but better education made other jobs possible.

Women worked in large offices or as telephone operators. They became nurses, professors, librarians, and social workers. A few were lawyers, doctors, and writers. But jobs changed for other reasons, too. Washing machines, vacuum cleaners, and other work-saving devices meant fewer jobs for maids, so former maids began working in department stores.

The changing American way of life created more opportunities for work, but also more need for income. Families now bought cars and telephones. They wanted to live in better homes. More women went to work than ever before, and their income helped pay for these new products. These changing ideas about the equality of opportunities for women affected economic growth in the United States.

INTERACTIVITY

Explore the key ideas of this lesson.

1. ☑ **Reading Check** Describe one way in which life changed for women in the late 1800s.

_____

_____

This is the cover of the program, or plan, for a women's suffrage march in 1913.

Working for More Rights

In the 1800s, many jobs were closed to women. Married women couldn't own property. In the 1800s, the abuse of alcohol was widespread, so often women had problems in the home. Many women (including Susan B. Anthony) joined the temperance movement. **Temperance** was a call for people to reduce or stop drinking alcohol. Many women also worked to end slavery. In time, women realized that they should also gain more rights for themselves.

In July 1848, two women's rights leaders, Lucretia Mott and Elizabeth Cady Stanton, organized a meeting in Seneca Falls, New York, to discuss women's rights. Stanton read a statement based on the Declaration of Independence. It was meant to **announce** that men and women were equal. She declared that,

Primary Source

"[Man] has compelled [woman] to submit to laws, in the formation of which she had no voice."

—Elizabeth Cady Stanton, "Declaration of Rights and Sentiments," 1848

Later the convention voted on 12 statements about women's rights. The ninth one demanded that women have the right to vote. The women's suffrage movement grew stronger. **Suffrage** is the right to vote, and people who worked for women's suffrage were called **suffragists**. In 1851, Susan B. Anthony joined Elizabeth Cady Stanton, and the two led what was called the "woman suffrage" movement for 50 years.

Other women played important roles in this movement. In 1850, Lucy Stone helped organize the first national convention on women's rights. Other women worked at the state level. Lillian Feickert helped to organize the New Jersey League of Women Voters.

Word Wise

Word Origins The term *temperance* first appeared in English around the 14th century A.D. It is from the Latin verb *temperare*, which means "to moderate." At first, *temperance* referred to both eating and drinking. By the late 1800s, however, *temperance* had come to refer specifically to alcohol.

2. ☑ **Reading Check**
Identify four things women were working to change in the 1800s. Underline these reforms on the page.

Academic Vocabulary

announce • *v.*, to make known officially or publicly

Women's Right to Vote

In 1869, Susan B. Anthony and Elizabeth Cady Stanton founded the National Woman Suffrage Association. In that same year Lucy Stone started the American Woman Suffrage Association. Stone wanted state governments to change their constitutions so women could vote in each state. In 1890, the two groups joined, and they worked together for the next 30 years.

These suffragists faced a tough fight. In 1874, the Supreme Court ruled that being a citizen did not automatically give a woman the right to vote. Instead, each state should decide women's political rights.

Women had more rights in the West. As a territory, Wyoming gave suffrage to women in 1869. When it entered the Union in 1890, it was the first state with full suffrage for women. The small town of Argonia, Kansas, elected Susanna Medora Salter mayor in 1887. She was the country's first female mayor. By 1900, women had full voting rights in Utah, Colorado, and Idaho. Other states followed. In 1917, Jeannette Rankin, a reformer and women's rights leader, became the first woman elected to the United States Congress. By 1918, women had the same voting rights as men in 15 states.

3. ☑ **Reading Check**
Identify and fill in the missing events in the timeline.

Timeline of Important Events in Suffragist History

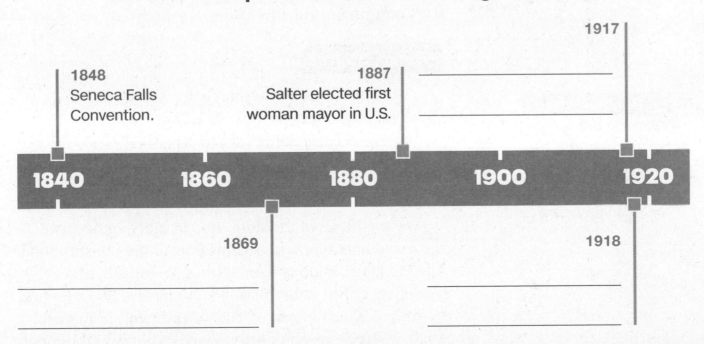

1848
Seneca Falls
Convention.

1887
Salter elected first
woman mayor in U.S.

1917

1840   1860   1880   1900   1920

1869

1918

The Nineteenth Amendment

By the late 1800s, women in a few other countries, such as New Zealand, were beginning to win the right to vote. In 1878, Elizabeth Cady Stanton decided to **propose** a suffragist amendment to the Constitution. It was presented in every Congress.

In 1914, the United States Congress failed again to pass the amendment giving women the vote. Suffragists did not give up. Support for women's suffrage continued to increase around the country and in Congress. After all, women in 15 states were electing representatives to Congress. These elected officials had to listen to women voters now.

Then the United States entered World War I in 1917. Women played an important role in the war. When men went to fight, women took over their jobs at home. Nearly 11,300 women joined a special branch of the U.S. Navy. They did not fight in battles, but they translated documents, studied fingerprints, designed camouflage, and did other important tasks. Some served as nurses in hospitals in France. If women could serve their country during war, why could they not vote?

In 1919, Congress passed the Nineteenth Amendment to the Constitution. The law said:

Primary Source

"The right of citizens to vote shall not be denied or abridged [limited] by the United States or by any state on account of [the] sex [of a person.]"

—United States Constitution, Nineteenth Amendment, 1919

Now two thirds of the states had to ratify, or approve, the amendment for it to become part of the Constitution. The first states to do so were Illinois, Wisconsin, and Michigan. Other states followed. But by law, 36 states had to ratify, or vote in favor of, the amendment. In August 1920, it was Tennessee's turn to vote. What would happen?

Academic Vocabulary

propose • *v.*, to suggest

Women joined the military during World War I.

4. ☑ **Reading Check**
Turn and talk with a partner. **Summarize** the events that led to the passing of the Nineteenth Amendment.

At first, the vote in the Tennessee legislature was tied. Then on August 18, Harry Burn, a young legislator, changed his vote to yes, because his mother told him to. But other legislators still opposed women's suffrage. They delayed official approval of the amendment a little longer. Finally, on August 24, 1920, Tennessee became the thirty-sixth state to ratify the amendment. Two days later it became part of the United States Constitution. Almost 75 years after the Seneca Falls Convention, all American women could finally vote.

In 1920, all American women were finally able to vote.

5. ☑ **Reading Check** This woman is voting for the first time. What would you ask this woman in a newspaper interview?

_____

_____

_____

 INTERACTIVITY

Check your understanding of the key ideas of this lesson.

☑ Lesson 3 Check

6. **Summarize Explain** one way in which changing roles for women in the early 1900s had an impact on the economic development and growth of the United States.

_____

_____

7. You attend a woman suffrage rally. **Describe** the rally and what people there have to say about it.

_____

_____

8. Think of the people you read about in this lesson. List four leaders you would like to know more about.

_____

_____

Interviews and Oral Material

There are many ways we can learn about events or issues in the United States. One way to get information is through oral materials. An **oral material** is something one person says to another. An **interview** is one kind of oral material. In an interview, a journalist asks a person questions that they answer. Journalists often interview people to get information directly from a person who saw or experienced an event. This makes an interview a primary source. Another oral material that is a primary source is a speech. A **speech** is a formal address given to an audience. Many news programs broadcast interviews and speeches. You can listen to interviews and speeches on the radio and the Internet. You can also get information about oral materials using secondary sources, such as news articles.

When you read or listen to oral material, look for key details. Names can help you identify who is speaking. Dates can tell you when an interview happened or a speech was given. These details help you better understand events and issues.

Read the passages below. The first passage is an **interview** between a muckraker and a meatpacking worker:

Muckraker: What kind of hours do you work at the factory?

Worker: I work 12 hours a day. Sometimes more.

Muckraker: Would you change your workday if you could?

Worker: Yes. I'd make it shorter because I'm tired each day.

The next passage is an excerpt from a **speech** given by Theodore Roosevelt in 1912:

Primary Source

"We propose . . . to secure the liberty of the wage workers, of the men and women who toil in industry . . ."

—Theodore Roosevelt, "The Liberty of the People" campaign speech, 1912

Read the two passages below. **Answer** the questions about oral material.

In this passage, a journalist is talking to a child at Hull House:

Journalist: Why are you here at Hull House?

Child: My family needed a place to live.

Journalist: What is life like at Hull House?

Child: Life is better at Hull House. We have a place to live and more food to eat.

In this passage, Theodore Roosevelt is addressing an audience in 1906:

Children at Hull House play table hockey.

Primary Source

At this moment we are passing through a period of great unrest—social, political, and industrial unrest. It is of the utmost importance for our future . . . to secure the betterment of the individual and the nation.

–*Theodore Roosevelt, "The Man with the Muck-rake,"*
April 14, 1906

 VIDEO

Watch a video about using primary and secondary sources.

1. What type of oral material is the first passage? How do you know?

_____

_____

2. What type of oral material is the second passage? How do you know?

_____

_____

_____

3. Use the Internet to find out more about Roosevelt's speech "The Liberty of the People." On a separate piece of paper, write two to three sentences that **describe** why Roosevelt gave the speech. Use primary and secondary sources to support your answer.

Quality:
Determination

W.E.B. Du Bois (1868–1963)
Writing and Speaking Out for Change

W.E.B. Du Bois was born in Massachusetts soon after the end of the Civil War. He obtained an education, and as a young man he was a teacher and a journalist. In 1895, Du Bois became the first African American to receive a doctorate from Harvard University.

Over his lifetime, Du Bois published 21 books on subjects about Africa, the African American community, and the inequalities it suffered. He wrote many articles about the struggle for civil rights. His work made Du Bois a famous and respected author. Du Bois did not always agree with other African American leaders of the time. He had many debates with another well-respected African American leader: Booker T. Washington.

Du Bois was a man of action, and he believed that African Americans must work to change unfair laws. In 1902, Du Bois wrote that

Primary Source

"[Jim Crow laws] cannot be laughed away, nor always successfully stormed at [changed through anger], nor easily abolished [ended] by act of legislature. And yet they cannot be encouraged by being let alone."

—W.E.B. Du Bois, "On the Training of Black Men," 1902

Find Out More

1. Based on Du Bois's quote, what action does he believe African Americans should take to fight against Jim Crow laws?

_____

_____

_____

2. African Americans worked for many years to change unfair laws. Work with a partner to research Jim Crow laws in the South. Report your findings to the class.

Visual Review

Use these graphics to review some of the key terms, people, and ideas from this chapter.

1881
Booker T. Washington founds the Tuskegee Institute.

1906
Upton Sinclair publishes *The Jungle.*

1913
Ida Wells-Barnett founds a club for African American women's suffrage.

| 1870 | 1880 | 1890 | 1900 | 1910 | 1920 |

1874
Mary "Mother" Jones travels the country to support workers' rights.

1917
Jeannette Rankin becomes the first woman elected to the U.S. Congress.

Key Events of the Progressive Era

1848: Lucretia Mott and Elizabeth Cady Stanton organize the **Seneca Falls Convention on women's rights**.

1890: Jacob Riis publishes his photojournalism book, *How the Other Half Lives*.

1896: The Supreme Court rules on ***Plessy v. Ferguson***.

1909: W.E.B. Du Bois, Ida Wells-Barnett, and others found **the NAACP**.

1911: The Triangle Shirtwaist Company fire takes place.

1920: The **Nineteenth Amendment** passes.

GAMES

Play the vocabulary game.

Vocabulary and Key Ideas

1. Who were the **Progressives**?

_____

_____

_____

2. Draw a line to match the definitions to the correct terms.

strikebreakers	a call for people to reduce or stop drinking alcohol
muckrakers	replacements for striking workers
civil rights	the right to vote
temperance	writers who uncovered shameful conditions
suffrage	what all citizens should have under the U.S. Constitution

3. What was the role of a **suffragist**?

_____

_____

Critical Thinking and Writing

4. Analyze reasons for the formation of labor unions. Explain how unions protected the rights of workers.

_____

_____

_____

_____

5. **Interpreting a Bar Graph**

   Analyze the graph. It shows information from the Great Migration.
   Circle the two decades for which the number was highest.

   Describe what happened between 1900 and 1920.

   _____

   _____

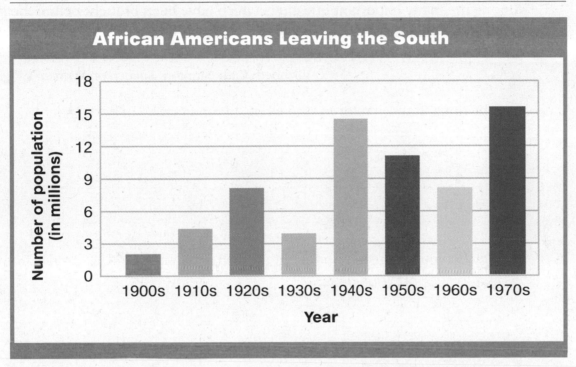

Source: United States Census Bureau

6. **Interpret** Fill In the circle next to the best answer.
   Which of the following was a main goal of the NAACP?

   (A) to form trusts

   (B) to end prejudice and segregation

   (C) to tear down tenement housing

   (D) to work for women's suffrage

7. **Revisit the Big Question** Choose one group that was in need of changes
   during the late 1800s and early 1900s. Explain why changes were needed.
   Use details from the text to support your claim.

   _____

   _____

   _____

8. **Writing Workshop: Write an Opinion** Imagine you are a Progressive during the late 1800s. Write an opinion piece about one of Jacob Riis's photos. On a separate sheet of paper, propose a solution to the problem that the photo shows. Include details from the text to support your opinion.

Analyze Primary Sources

"Among the many important questions which have been brought before the public, there is none that more vitally affects the whole human family than that which is technically termed Woman's rights."

–Elizabeth Cady Stanton, Speech on Women's Rights, 1848

9. Why does Stanton refer to "the whole human family" in her speech?

_____

_____

_____

10. Why do you think Stanton fought for women's suffrage? Use details from the text to support your ideas.

_____

_____

_____

Solve Problems

11. Identify the problem that labor unions had before the founding of the AFL. How did the AFL solve problems for labor unions?

_____

_____

_____

_____

_____

Quest Findings

👆 **INTERACTIVITY**

Use this interactivity to help you publish your graphic novel.

Publish Your Graphic Novel

You have read the lessons in the chapter, and you know more about the Progressive Era. Your group needs to decide on your topic and create your graphic novel. The graphic novel should have text, pictures, and facts.

1 Find Your Sources

Choose primary and secondary sources you want to use. One way to analyze sources is by asking and answering questions.

2 Write Your Draft

Use your sources and your questions to write evidence-based answers to your questions. Use the answers to write your graphic novel. A good graphic novel starts with a story that interests the reader. Think about using a quote from one of your primary sources.

3 Design Your Graphic Novel

How will your pages look? What pictures or images will you use? Have the artistic members of your team use a sheet of paper to sketch the design for each page.

4 Publish Your Graphic Novel

Make changes to your pages using feedback from your group. Correct any grammar or spelling errors. Revise and finish the layout and text.

Good Times and Hardships

GO ONLINE FOR DIGITAL RESOURCES

 VIDEO

 INTERACTIVITY

 AUDIO

 GAMES

 ASSESSMENT

eTEXT

The BIG Question

 VIDEO

How do people respond to good times and bad times?

Lesson 1
World War I

Lesson 2
The Roaring Twenties

Lesson 3
The Great Depression

Lesson 4
The New Deal

Jumpstart Activity   INTERACTIVITY

Identify an event from your life that was very happy or very difficult. Work with a partner to act out how you responded to the event. Describe how you responded to the events in the space provided below. Then share your events and responses with another group of partners.

_____

_____

_____

_____

_____

Good Times and Bad

Preview the chapter **vocabulary** as you sing the rap.

At the end of World War I,

Americans were glad that it was all done.

This was a time of **mass production**,

Which gave way to **mass consumption**.

All this new found wealth created an obsession,

And the economy declined with the **Great Depression**.

Farmers couldn't farm and **consumers** couldn't buy,

There was way less demand and too much supply.

With work all gone and without a meal,

President Roosevelt coined the **New Deal**.

This **New Deal** created jobs with ease,

Like roads and bridges, dams and trees.

chapter 13

Good Times and Hardships

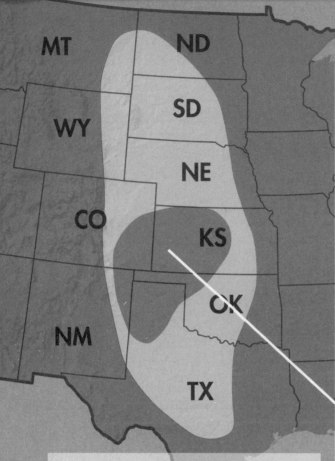

MT
ND
SD
WY
NE
CO
KS
OK
NM
TX

Where did the Great Depression seem to hit the hardest?

A large area of the United States was affected by the Dust Bowl. Many families living in portions of Kansas, Colorado, New Mexico, Oklahoma, and Texas suffered deeply. Thousands abandoned their farms and fled to other states in the midst of the Great Depression.

A dust storm in Kansas

What happened and When?

Read the timeline to learn about some of the good events and difficult events of the early twentieth century.

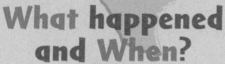

1910	1915	1920	1925

1914–1918
World War I fought.

1920
Prohibition begins and women win the right to vote.

Who will you meet?

Charles Lindbergh An American pilot who was the first person to fly solo across the Atlantic Ocean without stopping

Amelia Earhart An American pilot who was the first female aviator to fly solo across the Atlantic Ocean

F. Scott Fitzgerald An American author who is known for his novels about the Jazz Age, such as *The Great Gatsby*

Zora Neale Hurston An African American novelist of the Harlem Renaissance known for her 1937 novel, *Their Eyes Were Watching God*

 INTERACTIVITY

Complete the interactive digital activity.

1930   1935   1940

1929 The Great Depression begins.

1932 Franklin D. Roosevelt is elected President.

1935 The area plagued by dust storms is called the "Dust Bowl."

TODAY Farming methods now prevent Dust Bowls.

Expressing Change!

People often use art, such as poetry, paintings, collages, and murals, as a way to express their feelings about the world around them. There are many pieces of literature and artwork that reflect the World War I Era, Jazz Age, and Great Depression Era. These pieces stir up mixed emotions in their readers or viewers, but they all express the artist's point of view of the world.

Quest Kick Off

As a young artist, your mission is to create a poem or artwork that expresses the mood from either the World War I Era, Jazz Age, or Great Depression Era.

1 Create a List

Once you have received your assignment, work with your group to select an era to study. Learn about that time and create a list of words that describe the mood, emotions, and mindsets of the era you selected.

....

....

....

....

....

2 Research

Follow your teacher's instructions to research famous poems and art forms from the early 1900s. As you research, think about how the form of artwork you selected represents or illustrates a bigger meaning or a message. Ask yourself: What is this art form telling me about the viewpoint of the artist?

....

....

....

....

INTERACTIVITY

Complete the interactivity to learn more about how art and literature reflect the time in which they were created.

3 Look for *Quest* Connections

Begin looking for Quest Connections that will help you create your poem or artwork.

4 *Quest* Findings
Create Your Piece

Use the Quest Findings page at the end of the chapter to help you write your poem or create your artwork.

INTERACTIVITY

Participate in a class discussion to preview the content of this lesson.

Vocabulary

alliance
Allied Powers
Central Powers
imperialism
militarism
nationalism
isolationism
scarcity

Academic Vocabulary

declaration
honor

Unlock The **BIG** Question

I will know the causes and effects of World War I.

JumpStart Activity

Think of conflicts or wars that you have read about or heard about before. Work with a partner to make a list of reasons why countries decide to go to war with one another. Share your list with another group.

Today, most of the countries of Europe get along fairly well. That was not true in the early 1900s. Quarrels between European nations were common. The actions of some countries led others to fear attack. As a result, it was a time of great tension. In 1914, that tension exploded into warfare. At the time, people called it the Great War. We know it today as the First World War or World War I.

German infantry on the battlefield in 1914

Conflict in Europe

Alliances were a key cause of the war. An **alliance** is an agreement among nations to defend each other. In World War I, the main alliances were the **Allied Powers** and the **Central Powers**. Great Britain, France, and Russia were the Allied Powers. Germany, Austria-Hungary, and the Ottoman Empire were the Central Powers. The members of each alliance were allies. They promised to defend any other member of the alliance who was attacked.

INTERACTIVITY

Explore the key ideas of this lesson.

Another cause of war was imperialism. **Imperialism** is the policy of trying to take control of other lands and peoples. In 1914, both the Allied Powers and the Central Powers were imperialists.

A third cause was militarism. **Militarism** is a policy in which a country builds up its troops and makes plans for war. Even a small crisis can cause such a country to put its war plans into action. This policy was common in Europe, where countries competed for power.

The event that actually triggered the war came about from another cause—nationalism. **Nationalism** is a strong feeling of pride in one's nation or culture. At the time, the empire of Austria-Hungary ruled Serbia. Nationalists in Serbia wanted to unite with Serbs from other countries and separate from the empire. As part of their plan, one Serb nationalist assassinated Archduke Franz Ferdinand, the heir to the Austrian throne, along with his wife, Countess Sophie. The date was June 28, 1914.

The War Begins in Europe

The assassination of the archduke and his wife led Austria-Hungary to make strong demands on Serbia and promise punishment if the demands were not met. Russia then said that it would fight Austria-Hungary if Serbia was attacked. Then Germany declared war on Russia and its ally, France. Great Britain then joined the conflict on the side of its allies, France and Russia.

All of this happened between June 28 and August 4, 1914. World War I had begun.

Archduke Franz Ferdinand of Austria-Hungary and his wife, Countess Sophie

1. ☑ **Reading Check**
World War I started in 1914. The next year, Bulgaria joined the Central Powers and Italy joined the Allied Powers. More changes came later. **Choose** two colors for the legend. Then color in the Central Powers and the Allied Powers to match the legend.

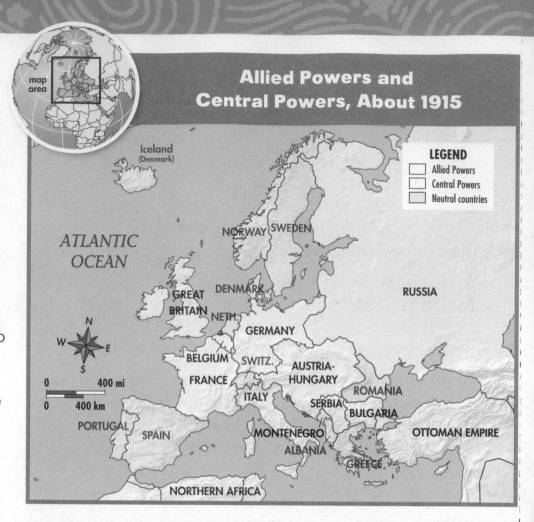

LEGEND
☐ Allied Powers
☐ Central Powers
☐ Neutral countries

The United States Enters the War

At first, Americans wanted to remain neutral in what they saw as a European war. To be neutral is to avoid taking sides. Safe across the Atlantic Ocean, the United States had long followed a policy of **isolationism**. It wanted to stay out of other countries' affairs. This policy reached back as far as the late 1700s when George Washington warned Americans to avoid political ties with other nations.

Two events persuaded Americans to join the Allied Powers. The first was the sinking of a passenger ship, the *Lusitania*, by a German submarine in 1915. One hundred and twenty-eight Americans died. Americans called for war.

The second event was the Zimmermann Note. This coded telegram asked Mexico to join the Central Powers if the United States declared war on Germany. In return, Germany would help Mexico get back territory it had lost to the United States. The note fell into the hands of the British, who decoded it. When it became public, demands for war with Germany grew louder.

Meanwhile, German submarines again attacked and sank several American ships in early 1917. On April 2, United States President Woodrow Wilson called for a **declaration** of war. He said, "The world must be made safe for democracy." On April 6, 1917, Congress declared war on Germany. Within months, the first American troops arrived at the Western front—the battle zone in France. They would help shorten the war.

Academic Vocabulary

declaration • *n.*, the act of making an official statement about something

Trench Warfare

Both sides in the war thought they would win quickly. They were wrong. The war, especially for the soldiers, seemed endless. Territory was won. Then it was lost. Then it was won and lost again—over and over.

In the first few major battles along the borders of France, Germany, and Belgium, armies clashed face to face in the traditional way of fighting. But soon leaders realized that too many soldiers were dying. The armies decided to "dig in." Soldiers on both sides dug trenches. These deep ditches often stretched for miles. Troops ate and slept in the trenches, which offered some shelter from enemy gunfire. However, the trenches were muddy and cold, crowded and unclean. Diseases spread easily.

Battles in trench warfare followed a pattern. The infantry, or foot soldiers, charged up and out of the trenches. Some held a rifle with a long knife attached to the end, called a bayonet. Cannons fired constantly from both sides.

At the beginning of the war, trenches were shallow. But by the end of 1914, a complex system of trenches developed.

Even in the trenches, behind coils of barbed wire, soldiers were not safe. Some of the shells fired at them contained poison gas. Gases such as chlorine caused severe injuries. They choked the throat and burned the eyes. Mustard gas blistered the skin. To survive chemical warfare, soldiers began wearing protective clothing and gas masks.

2. ☑ **Reading Check** **Explain** how technology changed warfare by 1914.

_____

_____

Many battles were fought where neither side won. Often tens of thousands of men died trying to take over a small area. The battle area between the two enemies' trenches became known as a "no-man's land." It was so dangerous that neither side could control it or would try to capture it.

New War Technologies

Poison gas was a horrifying new weapon. But it was not the only new weapon of World War I. German submarines, called U-boats, could sneak below ships and sink them with torpedoes, or underwater bombs. Airplanes had only recently been invented, in 1903. Eleven years later, fighter planes dropped bombs on enemy targets. They could also attack other planes or troops on the ground with machine guns.

The machine gun became the weapon of choice for defending trench positions. It could fire 600 bullets per minute at targets 1,000 yards away. That was enough to stop an attack by soldiers on horseback or on foot.

The British built a vehicle that machine-gun fire could not stop. It could smash through barbed wire and cross muddy ditches without getting stuck. This armored vehicle ran on metal tracks instead of wheels. It was called a tank.

Tanks were able to pass through the trenches and move toward the enemy line.

3. ☑ **Reading Check** **Identify** and write how the submarine and the tank changed traditional warfare in World War I.

_____

_____

_____

_____

_____

On the Home Front

While American soldiers fought in Europe, their families and friends worked at home to support their efforts. More than 3 million men served in the United States armed forces. That opened up job opportunities for many other Americans.

Workers were needed to build weapons and equipment for the troops. Up to half a million African Americans migrated from the South to find jobs with northern businesses. Around 1 million women worked in factories, offices, stores, and hospitals. Thousands more joined the armed forces in noncombat jobs.

The United States shipped tons of food overseas during the war. As a result, food shortages at home were a problem. Officials such as future President Herbert Hoover, then head of the United States Food Administration, urged people to accept "meatless Mondays" and "wheatless Wednesdays."

One solution to the food **scarcity**, or shortage, was a victory garden, also called a war garden. People started growing their own food in their backyards. Some towns set aside areas for community victory gardens.

Posters encouraged Americans, including children, to grow their own food.

Costs of the War

Finally, the Allies, with the help of about 1,500,000 American troops, won a huge battle in northeastern France. On November 11, 1918, the Central Powers surrendered, ending the war.

Around 116,000 Americans died and more than 200,000 were wounded in World War I. Human losses suffered by other countries were far greater. Around 8 million soldiers died in the war. Most died in battle, but many were victims of disease.

Another major cost was financial. The United States spent about $33 billion on the war. Much of that came from Americans' purchase of Liberty Bonds. These small loans to the government would later be repaid with a fee called interest.

4. ☑ **Reading Check** **Identify** List the costs of World War I. Was the war worth these costs?

_____

_____

_____

_____

_____

_____

The Treaty of Versailles

In Allied countries, the day World War I ended, November 11, became a holiday called Armistice Day. An armistice is a cease-fire. November 11 remained Armistice Day in the United States until 1954. Congress then changed the holiday to Veterans Day. On this day each year, we **honor** all Americans who have served in the armed forces.

Academic Vocabulary

honor • v., to show respect and admiration for someone in a public way

The official peace treaty for World War I was signed on June 28, 1919, in Versailles (vair SYE), France. The Treaty of Versailles punished Germany for its role in starting the war. Germany lost about 10 percent of its lands. It had to pay back war costs to the Allied Powers. The treaty also called for creating a League of Nations. The League's member nations would work together for peace.

After the war, Americans wanted a return to isolationism. This feeling prevented the United States Senate from approving the Treaty of Versailles. Also, some Americans did not approve of the harsh treatment of Germany. The United States did not join the League of Nations either. They feared it would force Americans to fight in future foreign wars.

Today, Americans celebrate Veterans Day on November 11, the day World War I ended. On Veterans Day, often in parades such as this, we honor those who corvod in the United States armed forces.

 **INTERACTIVITY**

Check your understanding of the key ideas of this lesson.

 **Lesson 1 Check**

5. **Cause and Effect** Which events **caused** the United States to enter the war?

_____

_____

_____

6. **Draw Conclusions** If you were a soldier fighting in the trenches of World War I, what would you write in your letters home? Write a passage from a letter that **describes** your experiences.

_____

_____

_____

7. **Summarize** how nationalism contributed to World War I.

_____

_____

_____

Documents and Biographies

Often, when we want to locate valid information about the United States, we look in a textbook or an encyclopedia. However, there are many other valid **sources**, or types of information. Two sources are **documents** and **biographies**. A **document** is an official record of an event. Because the information was written when the event took place, it is called a **primary source**. The best way to locate a primary source is through an Internet search. A **biography** is a true story about a person's life. Because it is written after events in the person's life, it is called a **secondary source**. Biographies can be located on the Internet or in a library.

Read the two passages below.

- **An Opinion by a Supreme Court Justice, 1896**

  The white race deems [considers] itself to be the dominant [most powerful] race in this country. . . . But in the view of the Constitution . . . all citizens are equal before the law.

  1. This passage was written by a judge who was explaining his decision in a court case in 1896. It is a **document**.

  2. A person could use this to understand issues in the United States at that time. It is a **primary source**.

- **From "Zora Neale Hurston: A Voice From the South"**

  Zora Neale Hurston was the most successful female African American writer of the first half of the 1900s. During this time, African Americans in the South faced great hardships as a result of discrimination.

  1. This passage describing Hurston was written after Hurston had become famous. It comes from a **biography**.

  2. This passage notes issues during the period in the 20th century in which Hurston worked. It is a **secondary source**.

Your Turn!

Read the two passages below. Answer the questions about documents and biographies.

 VIDEO

Watch a video about using primary and secondary sources.

1. Albert Carpenter was a 19-year-old student from Oklahoma when he enlisted in the United States Army. Carpenter served in France during the final days of World War I. He returned to the United States and married in 1920. A diary of his experience in World War I is found at the Library of Congress. It covers a single month, October 1918.

2. *Wednesday 9* The battle continues . . . A shell just went over my head and killed Lt. Lowery . . . Under heavy fire all day. *Friday 11* 12 A.M. A gas shell came over. Did not get my gas mask on quick enough. Sent to field hospital. Taken about 20 pills. *Saturday 12* My lungs are very sore and throwing up blood. *Monday 14* Still raining, sleep in open all night, nearly froze.

1. Is source 1 a biography or a document? What type of source is it? How can you tell?

_____

_____

2. Is source 2 a biography or a document? What type of source is it? How can you tell?

_____

_____

3. Which source tells you more about the experience of soldiers in World War I? Give an example.

_____

_____

4. Which source would you use to research a report on soldiers from Oklahoma who fought in World War I?

_____

INTERACTIVITY

Participate in a class discussion to preview the content of this lesson.

Vocabulary

consumer

mass production

mass consumption

Jazz Age

Great Migration

migrant worker

Academic Vocabulary

root

prevent

Women celebrate winning the right to vote.

Unlock The BIG Question

I will know that the 1920s was a time of progress and plenty for some, but of hardship for others.

JumpStart Activity

Make a list of all the products you and your family use on a regular basis. Think of appliances in your kitchen, bathrooms, and living rooms. Share your list with a partner. Which ones make your life easier? Why?

When World War I ended in 1918, Americans breathed a sigh of relief. Now their lives could return to normal. Jobs were few, and people's earnings remained low for several years. But by 1921, business was booming and spirits were high. The decade became known as the Roaring Twenties.

New Products

Entrepreneurs and the industries they started led to the growing United States economy. They even produced more goods than consumers wanted, and at a faster rate. **Consumers** are people who buy and use products and services.

The production of cars rose especially fast during the 1920s. Henry Ford developed an assembly line system to build his Model T cars. In this system, a car started as a frame. The frame moved along a line on a track. Workers at each station on the line added parts to the car. Each worker did just one task, over and over. The assembly line allowed Ford to make large numbers of the same car quickly and inexpensively, which made it possible for more Americans to afford to buy one. This process is known as **mass production**.

Other mass-produced products of the time were radios, washing machines, refrigerators, irons, toasters, and hair dryers. The 1920s became a time of **mass consumption**, or the large-scale demand for goods.

Improvements for Women

For women, the 1920s started on a positive note. After decades of struggle by Susan B. Anthony and others, Congress passed the Nineteenth Amendment, giving women the right to vote. In 1920, the amendment officially became part of the United States Constitution. The law was passed partly in reaction to women's work during the war and in other new industries.

After the war, most women returned to working in the home. Many of the mass-produced products that were now available also saved time and effort. These time-saving products made housework much easier.

As the economy grew, wages rose and people had more money to spend. They consumed, or used, more goods and services. That helped raise Americans' standard of living, or financial well-being and comfort. This consumption also encouraged the economy to grow even more.

INTERACTIVITY

Explore the key ideas of this lesson.

Word Wise

Prefixes When you see an unfamiliar word, use the prefix to figure out the meaning. For example, you will see the word *inexpensively* on this page. The prefix *in-*, which means *not*, is at the beginning of the word. You know what the word *expensive* means. Use the prefix to determine the meaning of the word *inexpensively*.

The Culture of the Roaring Twenties

For many Americans, the 1920s "roared" with power and excitement. Traditional ways were cast aside in favor of modern things. It was a time of change.

There is no better symbol of that change than the flapper. Flappers were women who dressed and behaved in a daring manner. They wore shorter skirts, which sometimes rose to the knee. They cut their hair short, in a bobbed style.

The cultural lives of most other Americans also changed. They had more leisure time, so they took longer vacations, attended sporting events, and went to the movies. Silent movies attracted millions of people to buy movie tickets each week. In 1927, the first motion pictures with sound came out. Then movie attendance rose even higher.

At home, families tended to gather around the radio. They could sing along with the latest popular music. They could follow national news, such as the nonstop solo flight of Charles Lindbergh across the Atlantic Ocean in 1927. Many Americans tuned in every night to hear their favorite musical or comedy show. During the day, they might listen to an exciting baseball or football game.

1. ✓ **Reading Check**
Compare Think about how women dressed in the late 1800s. How did the fashions of the 1920s differ? Circle the ways the flapper fashion shown in this picture differed from traditional ways.

Radio and the movies both helped to create a popular culture that everyone shared. Americans across the country listened to the same songs and saw the same movies. They became fans of the same stars. Actors, such as Charlie Chaplin and Mary Pickford, packed movie theaters. Lindbergh and fellow pilot Amelia Earhart were heroes. Baseball player Babe Ruth and the football player Red Grange were also major celebrities.

The Jazz Age

Many musicians also gained fame during the 1920s. The era was also known as the **Jazz Age**. Jazz is a style of music that has **roots** in traditional African American sounds and rhythms. In the 1920s, jazz became widely known and popular. This was the time when jazz music moved out of small clubs and onto the national stage.

Louis Armstrong did much to bring jazz to a wider audience with his creative trumpet playing. Composer George Gershwin mixed jazz and classical music to create a fresh, modern sound. Bands led by Duke Ellington and Fletcher Henderson got people up on their feet and dancing. Popular dances during the Jazz Age included the Charleston and the Lindy Hop. Both involved quick movements and fancy steps. Young people crowded into dance halls to kick and swing to the lively beat.

Writers, too, caught the excitement of the Jazz Age. In his novel *The Great Gatsby*, F. Scott Fitzgerald looked closely at the modern world. He wrote about the parties, the music, and the people—like himself and his wife, Zelda—who had grown rich in the booming economy. But he saw that the culture of the 1920s was breaking from the past in ways that were not always good. Without traditions to rely on, some people felt lost. Ernest Hemingway also wrote about feelings of loss in the postwar world. His novels include *A Farewell to Arms* and *The Sun Also Rises*.

2. ☑ **Reading Check** **Identify** and circle three people mentioned on these two pages. Then, below, list their names and what career they were famous for.

Name	Career
Charlie Chaplin	movie star

The Harlem Renaissance

In the 1920s, an area of New York City called Harlem became a center for the arts. African American writers, musicians, and painters gathered there to share ideas and to examine their world. These artists explored the experiences of African Americans in the past and in the modern age. This time of great creativity became known as the Harlem Renaissance. A renaissance is a rebirth or flowering of art and learning.

Much of these artists' work promoted pride among African Americans. Many had long been shut out of the American dream, which promised everyone equal rights and opportunities. The poet Langston Hughes claimed the right to share in that dream when he wrote, "I, Too." Through her stories, Zora Neale Hurston showed African Americans as people with goals and problems just like those of all Americans. At the end of the era, Jacob Lawrence told stories of the African American experience through his paintings, like the one on the next page.

This flowering of culture gave a boost to a movement pushing for civil rights. One of the leaders of that movement, W.E.B. DuBois, worked for fair and equal treatment of African Americans.

3. ☑ **Reading Check Explain** who "they" refers to in the poem "I, Too" and how the poem reflects the time period. Would you consider this poem a primary or secondary source? Why?

_____

_____

_____

_____

_____

_____

Quest Connection

Read Langston Hughes' poem, "I, Too," and circle powerful words that illustrate a message. Write the message or theme of the poem.

I, Too
by Langston Hughes

I, too, sing America.

I am the darker brother.
They send me to eat in the kitchen
When company comes,
But I laugh,
And eat well,
And grow strong.

Tomorrow,
I'll be at the table
When company comes.
Nobody'll dare
Say to me,
"Eat in the kitchen,"
Then.

Besides,
They'll see how beautiful I am
And be ashamed—

I, too, am America.

Langston Hughes

Movement and Change

African Americans continued to stream from the South after World War I in search of jobs. The flow north grew so large that it was called the **Great Migration**. By the end of the 1920s, more than 1 million had moved north, mainly to cities.

In many ways, life was better in the North for African Americans. They did not have to sit in a special section on buses or in movie theaters. They were not **prevented** from voting. Wages were higher in the North, too. But African Americans, as a rule, did not move out of lower-paying jobs as fast as white people did.

4. ☑ **Reading Check** **Identify** and list three factors that caused African Americans to leave the South. **Identify** and list three factors that drew African Americans to the North.

_____

_____

_____

_____

Jacob Lawrence painted a well-known mural called *The Great Migration*. This panel shows the special guards called in by the over-packed railroad stations to keep order.

Academic Vocabulary

prevent • *v.*, to make someone not do something

 **INTERACTIVITY**

Explore how a poet's choice of words can impact the power of a poem.

A Tough Time for Immigrants

Many immigrants from Latin American countries also made little economic progress. In the West and Southwest, great numbers of Latin Americans came to the United States as **migrant workers** to harvest crops. They moved around with the seasons, never putting down roots. They also faced a wave of anti-immigrant feelings.

Migrant workers, like these people from Latin America, often faced discrimination in the 1920s.

Some Americans had long opposed immigration. They thought all immigrants took Americans' jobs. They also thought that immigrants threatened American culture and values. In the 1920s, the Ku Klux Klan were spreading ideas of hatred against African Americans. They also opposed people who had different values and religious beliefs. Anti-immigrant groups gained support, as well.

In 1924, Congress passed the Immigration Act of 1924. It limited the number of people from Asia and southern and eastern Europe who could move into the United States each year.

Reforms to the Constitution

During the early 1900s, several changes had been made to the United States Constitution. In 1913, two amendments were added. The Sixteenth Amendment gave Congress the power to collect a tax on people's incomes. The Seventeenth Amendment allowed the direct election of United States senators by the people. Before this, most senators were elected by state legislatures. In 1920, Congress passed the Nineteenth Amendment giving women the right to vote.

At the same time, Progressive reformers worked for prohibition, or the complete ban, of alcohol. In 1920, the Eighteenth Amendment outlawed the making, selling, or shipping of alcohol anywhere in the United States.

The law stayed in effect throughout the 1920s. Some people still wanted alcohol, though, even if it meant breaking the law to get it. Otherwise law-abiding people found ways to get alcohol illegally. Soon criminals were smuggling and selling it. Their competition led to violence. Police spent much time and effort to find and destroy illegal alcohol while the law was in effect.

By 1933, however, the country had changed its mind. The Twenty-first Amendment was passed in that year, ending Prohibition.

5. ☑ **Reading Check** **Explain** the change that occurred because of the Seventeenth Amendment.

_____

_____

👆 **INTERACTIVITY**

Check your understanding of the key ideas of this lesson.

☑ **Lesson 2 Check**

6. **Cause and Effect Explain** why Prohibition led to crime and violence.

_____

_____

7. **Summarize Describe** how mass production led to economic growth in the nation.

_____

_____

_____

_____

8. **Understand the _Quest_ Connections** How did music reflect the mood of the 1920s?

_____

_____

The Great Depression

👆 **INTERACTIVITY**

Participate in a class discussion to preview the content of this lesson.

Unlock The BIG Question

I will know the different ways in which Americans responded to the hardships of the Great Depression.

Vocabulary

Great Depression
unemployment
stock market
credit
tariff
Dust Bowl

Academic Vocabulary

test
expand

JumpStart Activity

You open a lemonade stand and sell each glass for 50 cents. Subtracting what it costs to make the lemonade, you earn 25 cents per glass. Another lemonade stand opens on the next block. They offer their lemonade for 40 cents per glass. What will you do in response? How would your business be affected if a third stand opens and sells its lemonade for 25 cents per glass?

During the 1920s, under Presidents Warren G. Harding and Calvin Coolidge, the United States economy seemed strong. But in 1929, the year when Herbert Hoover became president, the country went from good times to bad in a hurry. In that year, a long and severe decline in the economy began. This decline became known as the **Great Depression**.

Many Americans made a living as farmers in the 1920s. But by the 1930s, they barely made enough to survive.

Trouble for Farmers

The United States economy seemed to be booming in the 1920s. As the decade passed, though, several signs suggested that the economy was not as strong as it seemed. Trouble was growing in the lives of farmers and factory workers.

Most farmers never fully enjoyed the good times of the 1920s. New technology should have made their work more profitable. Gas-powered tractors and other machinery allowed farmers to grow more crops. But growing more crops turned out to be a problem. The supply of food became greater than people's demand for it.

INTERACTIVITY

Explore the key ideas of this lesson.

More Supply, Less Demand

Lower demand caused food prices to fall. Many farmers had taken out loans to pay for their expensive new machines. Now they couldn't make enough money to pay back the loans.

Farmers who didn't buy modern equipment also suffered. Their costs for producing food were too high. They couldn't compete with the larger farms. Farm workers couldn't compete with tractors. It seemed that their labor was no longer needed. In the 1920s, many migrated to the cities to find other work.

These migrants often found that the supply of jobs was limited even in the cities. Companies had built new factories and hired more workers to meet growing consumer demand. But Americans could not consume all the goods being produced. Companies now had to cut production and jobs.

1. ☑ **Reading Check** **Summarize** the trouble for farmers.

_____

_____

_____

The Stock Market Crash

By the late 1920s, the signs of trouble were clear. Factories were letting workers go or not hiring new workers. **Unemployment**—the condition of being out of work—was rising. Without jobs, Americans could not afford to buy new products. People began to buy less. In his inaugural address, President Hoover told the American people:

Primary Source

"I have no fears for the future of our country. It is bright with hope."

—President Herbert Hoover, Inaugural Address, 1929

2. ☑ **Reading Check**
Turn and talk with a partner about how you think unemployment may have led to the stock market crash.

Seven months later, the stock market crashed. The **stock market** is where people buy and sell stocks. A crash is a sudden, steep drop in stock prices. Stocks are shares in the ownership of a company. If a company wants to raise money, it sells stocks. The value or price of a stock generally rises when a company does well, but it falls if a company does poorly.

Buying on Credit

During the 1920s, some people got rich and many others hoped to. People bought stocks hoping to resell them for a big profit. But many did not buy stocks with their own money. Instead, they used **credit**, or borrowed money.

These people expected stock prices to keep rising. Then they could pay back their loans and still make a profit. If stock prices fell, they might owe more money than their stocks were worth. They could lose everything.

In the 1920s, stock prices rose unusually fast and people invested. Then in late 1929, stock prices began to fall. Many people worried about losing money, so they sold their stocks. Others panicked. They sold their stocks for whatever price they could get. As a result, stock prices fell by one third. People rushed to sell more stocks, and prices kept falling. Many people had paid much more for their stocks than they were now worth. These people were ruined financially.

The Great Depression Begins

The crash was just one of several causes of what is known as the Great Depression. The Great Depression was the longest and most severe economic decline in United States history.

The economy goes through ups and downs all the time. A depression begins as a normal downturn in the economy. In the late 1920s, the overproduction of goods caused a downturn. The stock market crash and the buying of stocks with borrowed money helped the downturn grow into a depression.

A year after the crash came the first bank panics. Consumers had bought cars and other goods on credit. Now they could not pay their loans. Many banks ran out of funds and had to close. People who had savings in those banks lost them. Customers of other banks raced to withdraw their savings. Many of those banks ran out of cash and had to close, too.

During the Great Depression, crowds gathered to remove their money from the banks. This became known as a "run on the bank" and caused the collapse of many banks.

3. **☑ Reading Check** Early in the Great Depression, people rushed to banks, like the one in the photograph, to find out if they had lost money. **Explain** at least one way you think a bank run like this one could affect a family.

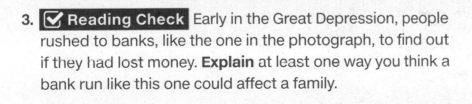

_____

_____

_____

_____

The Depression Deepens

The stock market crash caused Americans to believe that the future might not be very bright. Fearing a loss of income, consumers cut back on their purchases. Businesses began to limit spending, too. Production declined, so people lost their jobs. Jobless people, and those who feared losing their jobs, bought even fewer goods than before. This slowdown in consumption lowered production further. Even greater unemployment resulted. As this downward spiral continued, the economy grew weaker and weaker.

High tariffs added to the economic problems. A **tariff** is a tax on imports, or goods from other countries. To protect American farmers against competition from cheaper imported crops, Congress passed a tariff in 1930. This caused other countries to pass their own tariffs. These "tariff walls" kept many American companies from selling goods overseas.

Early in the Great Depression, President Hoover took steps to try to pull the country out of its economic slump. He thought government had an important role to play in the economy. Hoover urged companies not to cut jobs or wages. He urged Congress to put money into building roads, bridges, and other public works. These projects, he said, would create jobs. He supported loans to help banks and industries. Yet the Great Depression only got worse.

Causes of the Great Depression

Consumers cut spending.

↓

Companies _____

↓

Companies cut jobs.

↓

Consumers spend even less.

↓

_____ _____

↓

_____ _____

4. ☑ **Reading Check** **Cause and Effect** Identify and fill in the missing information to complete the cause-and-effect diagram on the left side of the page.

Surviving the Depression

For many Americans the Great Depression became a **test** of their survival skills. People cut their spending down to the most basic needs. But everyone needed food, clothing, and shelter.

President Hoover urged local, private agencies to help. They did. In cities around the country, charity and other organizations offered free aid to people in need. Jobless people stood in long lines to receive free bread or a bowl of soup. In 1933, the unemployment rate rose higher than 25 percent. One of every four American adults was out of work. Unemployment stayed above 14 percent for the rest of the 1930s. Most of the jobless were former factory workers and other laborers.

Many people lost their homes when they could not pay their housing loans. Some moved in with relatives. Others moved to public areas, where they built shacks of cardboard or other materials they could find. These people blamed President Hoover for their troubles and called their shack towns "Hoovervilles."

Academic Vocabulary

test • *n.*, a trial that shows how strong someone is in a difficult situation

5. ☑ **Reading Check** This photo shows a typical Hooverville. Write a sentence **explaining** why a family might have lived there.

_____

_____

Problems on the Great Plains

Before the Great Depression, farmers had already faced hardship. By the early 1930s, many had lost their farms. On the Great Plains, farmers who had managed to keep their land now had to deal with a new challenge. Their region was hit by a drought.

Before World War I, the Great Plains region had been mainly grassland used to support cattle. During the war, farmers began to plant wheat instead. In the 1920s, new technology allowed farming to **expand**. Now the soil was in poor shape.

When the drought came, the sun baked the weakened topsoil, turning it to dust. Then the strong winds of the Plains blew the soil into the air. Great clouds of dust blocked the sun. Farmers fought a losing battle to keep the dust out of their homes. American novelist John Steinbeck describes their efforts:

Primary Source

"Houses were shut tight, and cloth wedged around doors and windows, but the dust came in so thinly that it could not be seen in the air, and it settled like pollen on the chairs and tables. . . ."

–John Steinbeck, *The Grapes of Wrath*

Academic Vocabulary

expand • *v.*, to extend in one or more directions

In the Dust Bowl, massive dust storms rolled across the plains.

The Dust Bowl

Even worse than the dust was the damage that wind caused. After the topsoil blew away, nothing would grow. Much of the Plains became known as the **Dust Bowl**.

Farmers in the damaged areas still owned their land, but it would no longer grow enough crops to support their families. More than 2 million people from the region packed up their belongings, left their farms behind, and headed west. Many of them ended up in California working as migrant workers or day laborers.

6. ☑ **Reading Check**
Talk and Turn and discuss with a partner what may have resulted from the migration of farmers and their families out of the Dust Bowl region.

👆 **INTERACTIVITY**

Check your understanding of the key ideas of this lesson.

☑ Lesson 3 Check

7. **Draw Conclusions** What effect do you think bank panics had on the ability of consumers or businesses to take out new loans? **Explain** your conclusion.

_____

_____

_____

8. **Draw Conclusions** If you were living during the Dust Bowl, how would you describe life on your farm?

_____

_____

_____

9. **Summarize** Explain how lower demand hurt farmers during the late 1920s.

_____

_____

_____

_____

_____

The Photography of Dorothea Lange

Dorothea Lange was a documentary photographer who is well known for her Depression-era photography. During the Great Depression, she brought her camera to the streets. In the process, she captured the life of many Americans and the living conditions of farmworkers and their families in the western states during this difficult time in American history.

This family lived in a tent on a Farm Security Administration migratory labor campsite in the Imperial Valley in California.

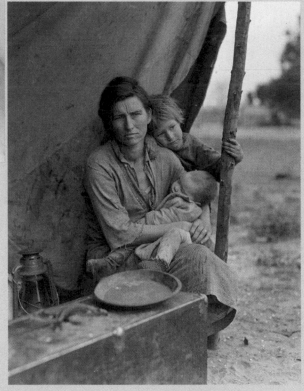

This thirty-year-old mother of seven is shown in a migrant camp in California. She and her family were destitute pea pickers.

Close Reading

1. Compare List two to three similarities in Lange's photos.

_____

_____

_____

2. Explain how Lange's images captured the life of many Americans during the 1930s, and **describe** the message she was trying to communicate through her photographs.

_____

_____

_____

_____

_____

_____

_____

Wrap It Up

Describe what life must have been like for the majority of Americans during the Great Depression. Support your answers with information from these images and the chapter.

_____

_____

_____

_____

_____

The New Deal

 INTERACTIVITY

Participate in a class discussion to preview the content of this lesson.

Vocabulary

New Deal
First Hundred Days
Social Security

Academic Vocabulary

measure
stability

President Roosevelt used the power of radio to speak directly to the American people.

Unlock The BIG Question

I will know that the purpose of the New Deal was to improve people's lives during the Great Depression.

JumPstart Activity

Think of a time you were upset, sad, or frustrated. Make a list of things or activities that you use to help change your attitude when you have these feelings. Share your list with a partner. Draw a picture of something that makes you happy.

For the first two years of the Great Depression, many Americans suffered. They lost jobs, homes, and hope. The United States government did little to help. President Hoover had faith that the economy would bounce back. But the crisis only grew worse. Many people blamed Hoover. In 1932, they would choose a new leader: Franklin D. Roosevelt, also known as FDR.

Roosevelt and the New Deal

Roosevelt realized that Americans were afraid of the future. He also had once feared for his own future. Early in his career he had been a state senator and then Assistant Secretary of the Navy. By 1921, he was a rising star in the Democratic Party. But in that year, he caught a terrible disease, polio.

Franklin Roosevelt survived polio, but his legs were damaged—he would never walk again without help. But he did not give up. He stayed active in politics. In 1928, he was elected governor of New York.

During the 1932 presidential election, Roosevelt told the American people that, if he won, he would use the power of the government to try to solve their problems. He made them a promise: "I pledge you, I pledge myself, to a new deal for the American people." Once elected, the programs President Roosevelt set up to end the Great Depression became known as the **New Deal**.

Immediately, Roosevelt tried to give the American people hope. In his first presidential speech he told them, "The only thing we have to fear is fear itself." He would work right away to restore confidence in the economy. His New Deal programs would take aim at the major problems facing the nation.

New Laws

On his second day as president, March 5, 1933, Roosevelt took a bold step. To deal with bank panics, he declared a "bank holiday." For four days, all banks would be closed. Each bank would only be able to reopen when it was judged to be stable.

Soon, Roosevelt also gave the first of his "fireside chats." He spoke on the radio directly to the American people. Through these informal talks, the President kept the public informed about the progress of the New Deal. He hoped these talks would help lift their spirits.

INTERACTIVITY

Explore the key ideas of this lesson.

Much happened in the first three months of Roosevelt's presidency. This period, from March to June, became known as the **First Hundred Days**. During this time, the President worked with Congress to pass many new laws. The new laws focused on three goals: relief, recovery, and reform.

Relief **measures** aimed to help the unemployed. One of them, the Civilian Conservation Corps (CCC), put 250,000 young men to work right away. They built roads, planted trees, and did other work on public lands. By 1941, the CCC had employed more than 2 million people.

Academic Vocabulary

measure • *n.*, an action taken to cause a desired result

The TVA project needed a lot of laborers, especially to build the dams. This dam measures 161 feet high and 1,682 feet long.

The goal of the recovery programs was to boost the economy. A major recovery project was the Tennessee Valley Authority (TVA). One task of the TVA was to control flooding in the region of the Tennessee River Valley. Another job was to provide electricity to the people of the region. Workers did both by building dams and power plants.

1. ☑ **Reading Check** Look at the photo. **Explain** why the TVA provided jobs to many workers.

_____

_____

_____

_____

_____

_____

More New Deal Reforms

Some New Deal reforms were meant to prevent future problems, like those that had caused the Great Depression. The Banking Act of 1933 improved banking practices. One of its most important features was the Federal Deposit Insurance Corporation (FDIC). This agency insures bank deposits up to a certain amount. It ended bank panics, since people trusted that their savings were safe. In 1934, the Securities and Exchange Commission (SEC) was formed to protect people in the stock market. That is still the SEC's main job.

The FDIC, TVA, and CCC, as well as a dozen or more other programs, were all put in place during the First Hundred Days. Some, including the FDIC and the TVA, still exist. The CCC ended in 1942.

After the First Hundred Days, the New Deal produced many other programs. Later in 1933, Congress passed the Social Security Act. **Social Security** is an insurance system to help support the disabled and provide funds to retired people. Today, this program still provides benefits to millions of retired, disabled, and other Americans.

Other programs included the Works Progress Administration (WPA), created in 1935. This agency, like the CCC, put jobless people to work—more than 8 million in all. They built roads, bridges, parks, airports, and public buildings. The WPA also employed many writers, actors, and artists. It ended in 1943.

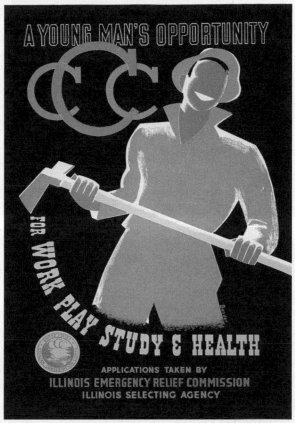

Posters, such as this one for the CCC, help spread the word that jobs were available for those who needed work.

2. ☑ **Reading Check** **Cause and Effect** What effect did the New Deal programs have on the majority of Americans?

_____

_____

_____

Word Wise

Compound Words are made up of two smaller words and act as a single word. Each word in the compound word gives clues about its meaning. Circle the compound words that you find on this page. What do you think each compound word means?

Quest Connection

Study the mural on this page. Make a list of encouraging images shown in the mural. What message do you think the artist is trying to communicate?

The Government Expands

Many people complained about the New Deal and its programs. They said the national government was playing too large a role in the economy.

Before the New Deal, most politicians took a hands-off approach to business. Under the New Deal, the national government gained much more power over the economy. It not only oversaw private business; it also competed against it. For example, the TVA, a public agency, provided electricity that could have come from a private company.

During the 1930s, government expanded greatly to deal with the crisis of the Great Depression. That expansion lessened the hardships of millions of Americans. But it cost a great deal of money. Much of that money came from higher taxes.

When the Depression ended, so did many New Deal programs. But many Americans now believed government should take a larger and more active role in safeguarding the economy and improving society. The role of government had changed forever.

During the Great Depression, the federal government hired artists to create public art, such as this mural in Trenton, New Jersey.

A Global Depression

The Great Depression did not strike only the United States. It was a global economic disaster. Canada, France, and other industrial countries faced the same problems as the United States did. Around the world, consumers stopped buying goods, businesses failed, and unemployment soared.

In Germany and other nations, the Great Depression led to the loss of democracy. People in some countries were willing to give up freedoms for **stability** and security. For example, the new German government became a dictatorship. It improved its economy earlier than other countries, partly by spending large sums on weapons. This militarism in Germany would lead to another world war in the coming years.

 **INTERACTIVITY**

Explore the ideas and messages expressed in the art of the 1930s.

Academic Vocabulary

stability • *n.*, the state of being stable, not likely to change

INTERACTIVITY

Check your understanding of the key ideas of this lesson.

☑ Lesson 4 Check

3. **Cause and Effect Explain** how the New Deal changed the role of the United States government.

_____

_____

_____

4. **Identify** some of Franklin D. Roosevelt's accomplishments.

_____

_____

_____

5. **Understand the** **Connections** Why would the government spend money to create murals or other pieces of art?

_____

_____

_____

Generate New Ideas

When you need to solve a problem, it is helpful to have tools you can use to generate, or come up with, new ideas. The first step in generating new ideas is to gather information about the problem. For example, what caused it? Why did it happen? What resources can you use to solve it? Once you have listed the main information about the problem, you can then use these steps to generate solutions.

- **State the problem.** Write, in clear language, exactly what the problem is.

- **Analyze the causes.** Think about how things were before the problem started. What caused the problem or made it worse?

- **Think about the goal of the solution.** Decide what the goal of a solution must be. Ask, "What do we want to accomplish?" or "What would improve this situation?"

- **Brainstorm ideas.** Alone or in a group, list whatever ideas come to mind, even if they seem unrealistic at first. Consider each idea; then keep the best one or two, and delete the others.

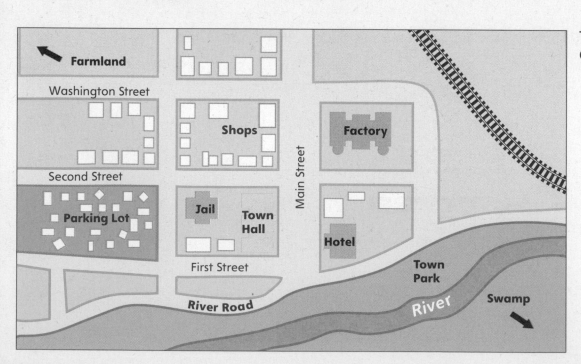

The Town of Caznor, 1931

Your Turn!

The map on the opposite page shows an imaginary town, Caznor, in 1931. The factory in Caznor closed a year ago, and all 30 workers lost their jobs. Now most are homeless, living in shacks in the Second Street parking lot. The state has given the town emergency funds, which could help, but the mayor asks you to come up with a way to help the workers. You know some facts. You have a map of the town. Follow the steps for generating new ideas to develop a solution.

▶ VIDEO

Watch a video on how to generate new ideas.

1. Write a statement of the problem.

   _____

2. List the cause or causes.

   _____

   _____

3. Write the main goal of your solution.

   _____

   _____

4. **Brainstorm** solutions. On another sheet of paper, record all your ideas. Then cut down the list to include only the best one.

5. **Describe** your best solution here:

   _____

   _____

   _____

6. **Apply** Think of a problem in your school or community. Then follow the steps to generate two new ideas that might solve it.

   _____

   _____

   _____

Quality:
Patriotism

Private Marcelino Serna (1896–1992)
An American Hero

Marcelino Serna was born in Chihuahua, a Mexican state, in 1896. When he was a teenager, he came to the United States. He worked hard as a farm hand and ended up in Denver, Colorado, where he soon enlisted in the U.S. Army.

In April of 1917, the United States declared war on Germany, and it wasn't long after when Serna and his unit were sent overseas. After the Army realized that he wasn't an American citizen, they offered to discharge him. However, Serna decided to stay and fight with his new friends.

During a battle in France, Serna's unit came under attack. He saw an opportunity and got close enough to the German attackers to launch several hand grenades at them. The eight survivors surrendered to Serna and his unit. Two weeks later, another act of bravery on the front led Serna to take 24 German prisoners.

Serna risked his life to protect our nation's freedom and the safety of his fellow soldiers. For his service and patriotism, he was awarded the Distinguished Service Cross. This is the second highest military decoration of the United States Army. He was the first Mexican-American to receive this medal. In 1924, he became an American citizen.

Find Out More

1. Identify one act of patriotism that Private Serna exhibited. Explain why his actions were patriotic.

_____

_____

_____

2. Think of people who have fought for what they believe in for our country. **Compare** their story with Serna's. How did this person show patriotism? Report your findings to your class.

Use these graphics to review some of the key terms, people, and ideas from this chapter.

Positive Events	Hardships
Mass production of products helps make life easier.	World War I erupts, resulting in death and destruction.
Women gain the right to vote.	Great Depression develops, leading to unemployment and poverty.
Popular culture develops across the nation.	Dust Bowl arises, forcing farmers to abandon their farms.
Harlem Renaissance takes place, promoting African American pride and creativity.	Global depression sets in, leading to economic and political instability around the world.

Key Events and People

In June of 1914, a Serbian nationalist assassinates Archduke Ferdinand and his wife. In July, the Austro-Hungarian Empire declares war on Serbia, starting World War I.

In April of 1917, the United States joins the Allied Powers in the Great War.

On November 11, 1918, the Central Powers surrender and World War I ends.

In October of 1929, the stock market crashes and helps trigger the Great Depression.

During the mid-1930s, the Plains states suffer from a series of dust storms.

In 1932, Franklin D. Roosevelt is elected president of the United States and leads the country through the Great Depression with a series of reforms known as the New Deal.

⊙⊙ **GAMES**

Play the vocabulary game.

Vocabulary and Key Ideas

1. **Define** What is **nationalism**?

_____

_____

2. Complete the sentences below. Choose from these words: *isolationism, scarcity, migrant worker, unemployment, credit, New Deal.*

   (A) In order to stay neutral at the beginning of World War I, the United States followed a policy of _____.

   (B) Many Latin American immigrants moved to the United States and harvested crops as _____.

   (C) By the end of the 1920s, there were many signs of looming economic troubles, especially with rising _____.

3. **Explain** Roosevelt's New Deal.

_____

_____

_____

4. **Generate New Ideas** Look at the map of Caznor. The river flooded up to Second Street and completely destroyed the area. The state has provided emergency funds, but they don't cover all of the expenses. Generate two ideas that will help Caznor rebuild.

_____

_____

_____

_____

_____

Map of Caznor showing Farmland, Washington Street, Shops, Factory, Second Street, Main Street, Parking Lot, Jail, Town Hall, Hotel, First Street, River Road, Town Park, River, Swamp.

Critical Thinking and Writing

5. **Explain** why Roosevelt expanded government power during his time in office.

_____

_____

_____

_____

6. **Identify** The New Deal agency that helped bring an end to bank panics was called the

(A) FDIC.

(B) SEC.

(C) TVA.

(D) CCC.

7. **Analyze** how the consumption of goods changed between the 1920s and the 1930s.

_____

_____

_____

_____

8. **Revisit the Big Question** How do people respond to good times and bad times?

_____

_____

_____

9. **Writing Workshop: Write an Opinion** It is 1915 and the United States is maintaining a policy of isolationism. However, you read in today's newspaper that the *Lusitania* has been sunk by a German U-boat. On a separate piece of paper, write a letter to President Wilson explaining your opinion on whether the United States should enter the war now or maintain its isolationist policy.

Analyze Primary Sources

10. This picture was taken during the Great Depression era. Dorothea Lange, a well-known photographer of the Great Depression and Dust Bowl, captured the daily lives of many who pushed through and survived the difficulties they faced. How does this photo help you to understand the hardships of many Americans during this time?

_____

_____

_____

_____

_____

Documents and Biographies

11. Suppose you are writing a report on the Great Depression. What types of primary sources would you use? List five types of documents you might use. What types of secondary sources would you use? List five different types of secondary sources. Write a brief explanation about why you would choose these sources for your report.

_____

_____

_____

_____

_____

_____

Quest Findings

INTERACTIVITY
Use this activity to help you create your poem or artwork.

Expressing Change!

You have read the lessons in this chapter and now you are ready to plan and create your masterpiece. Remember that the goal of the poem or artwork you create is to express the mood of a particular era in time.

1 Prepare to Create

Think about the era you want to represent. Work with your group to write a list of powerful words that come to mind when you think about the good times and hardships of the era.

2 Create

Use your notes and thoughts from your Quest Connections to write a poem or create a piece of art that illustrates your era. Make sure you include a title for your work.

3 Describe

Write a paragraph that describes how your poem or artwork reflects the mood of the era.

4 Present

Present your finished poem, painting, collage, or mural to the class. Discuss the similarities and differences of the messages being communicated by members of the class.

GO ONLINE FOR
DIGITAL RESOURCES

▶ VIDEO

👆 INTERACTIVITY

🔊 AUDIO

🎮 GAMES

☑ ASSESSMENT

📖 eTEXT

The **BIG** Question

What is worth fighting for?

▶ VIDEO

JumpStart Activity

The day after the attack on Pearl Harbor, President Franklin Roosevelt addressed the nation with the following statement: "Yesterday—December 7, 1941—a date which will live in infamy—the United States was suddenly and deliberately attacked by naval and air forces of the Empire of Japan." In small groups, have a discussion about whether or not a surprise attack by an enemy is a good reason to enter a war.

_____

_____

_____

_____

♪ Rap About It! ♪

 AUDIO

The Price Is So Very Great

Preview the chapter vocabulary as you sing the rap.

Dictator, warmonger, and Poland's lands are taken,
Put Europe back into war and left the peace forsaken.
Spreading across the land like a wave of destruction,
The **Axis Powers** had the will, and feared no
repercussion.

In the east and not for peace, Japan was starting war,
Taking parts of China, the Philippines, and more.
So the U.S. stopped its aid to them including all its oil,
Which made them attack Pearl Harbor, the first on
American soil.

This finally brought the U.S. into the second
global fight,
Where it would show the Japanese the power
of its might.
Island hopping, land and sea, on their homelands we
would strike.
We went to Europe to fight that war to help the **Allies**
defeat the Third Reich.

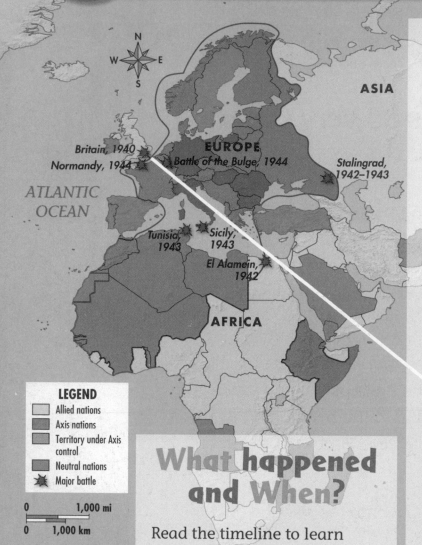

ASIA

ATLANTIC
OCEAN

EUROPE

Britain, 1940
Normandy, 1944
Battle of the Bulge, 1944

Stalingrad,
1942–1943

Tunisia,
1943

Sicily,
1943

El Alamein,
1942

AFRICA

LEGEND
☐ Allied nations
☐ Axis nations
☐ Territory under Axis control
☐ Neutral nations
✦ Major battle

0	1,000 mi
0	1,000 km

Where did the Blitz take place?

During the Blitz, the city of London was subjected to months of heavy air raid attacks by German forces, destroying much of the city. The British spirit was not broken, however.

A London street after an air raid during the Blitz

What happened and When?

Read the timeline to learn about some of the major events of World War II.

TODAY
London is a thriving, cosmopolitan capital city.

1920

1930

1929
Joseph Stalin rises to power in the USSR.

1933
Hitler rises to power in Germany.

Who will you meet?

Franklin D. Roosevelt
Served as the American president during most of World War II

Adolf Hitler
Became dictator of Germany in 1933, and his aggressive actions in Europe led to World War II

Tuskegee Airmen
Served their country during World War II in many successful missions

Anne Frank
Was forced into hiding during the war because of her Jewish heritage

 INTERACTIVITY

Complete the interactive digital activity.

1940

1941
Japanese attack on Pearl Harbor.

1944
Allies storm the beaches at Normandy.

1945
Victory in Europe Day; Japan surrenders to the Allies.

TODAY
Americans remember the bravery of the soldiers who fought during World War II.

A Story of World War II

Every person who lived through World War II witnessed events that changed the world forever. Each one of them has their own unique story. Some of them fought for their country, and some had to hide just to survive each day.

Quest Kick Off

Your mission is to write a biography of a person who lived through World War II and dealt with its challenges. You will choose a specific soldier, female pilot or nurse, or a Holocaust survivor to write about.

1 Ask Questions

Where did your subject live? What role did he or she play in the war? How did the war affect this person? Write two questions of your own.

....

....

....

....

2 Research

Write an outline: Follow your teacher's instructions to research each group and decide who you will write about. Write some of the important points about the person's life below and begin to plan your outline.

INTERACTIVITY

Use this activity to help you prepare your assignment.

....

....

....

....

....

....

3 Look for Quest Connections

Begin looking for Quest Connections that will help you write your biography.

4 Quest Findings
Write Your Biography

Use the Quest Findings page at the end of the chapter to help you write your biography.

The Holocaust

Key Figures in WWII

The Rise of Dictators in Europe

World War II Begins

Unlock
The **BIG**
Question

I will know the events that led to World War II.

Vocabulary

dictator
fascism
Axis
Allies
Lend-Lease Act

Academic Vocabulary

declare
draw

JumpStart Activity

Imagine that you are playing at recess and two classmates start having a disagreement. Soon, other students start taking sides in the argument. Have a discussion about if and why you would get involved in the argument. What would make it worth it to get involved? What would the argument have to be about? What would your involvement be?

After World War I, the United States returned to its prewar policy of isolationism. It chose not to get involved in foreign affairs. It even reduced the size of its armed forces. Americans wished never to go to war again. But events in Europe soon drew the United States into yet another global conflict.

Dictators Rise in Europe

The Great Depression of the 1930s had caused hard times everywhere. People in some countries blamed their governments. They began looking for strong leaders to take control and fix the problems. Some even turned to dictators. A **dictator** is a ruler who has total power over a country.

One such dictator was Benito Mussolini [beh NEE toh moo soh LEE nee] of Italy. Italy had been one of the victors of World War I. But the country had lost many lives in that war. It had also lost a lot of money and had gained little from the Treaty of Versailles that had ended the war. This angered many Italians.

Mussolini came to power in 1922. His party was called the Fascists, which gave us the word *fascism*. **Fascism** is a movement that gives all power to the government and does away with individual freedoms. It uses the military to enforce laws. Mussolini took control. He banned elections and ended free speech.

An even more dangerous dictator was Adolf Hitler. He and his political party, the Nazis, gained control of Germany in 1933. The Nazis turned the country into a fascist state. Hitler was its supreme leader.

Germans, too, were unhappy with the Versailles treaty. It stated that they were guilty of starting World War I. It had forced Germany to make payments to the victors of the war. It had also taken away some of Germany's land. Hitler vowed to get back that land, and more. To do so, he began rearming Germany and increasing its troop levels.

INTERACTIVITY

Explore the key ideas of this lesson.

Italian dictator Benito Mussolini inspired great crowds.

The Axis and the Allies

Mussolini set out to expand Italy's territory. In 1935, he took over the African country of Ethiopia, then made an agreement with Hitler. The two fascist countries planned to conquer other countries. They called their new alliance the **Axis**. Japan would later join the Axis. By 1937, Japan had invaded China and controlled much territory in the Pacific.

Starting in 1936, German armies began taking lands that the nation had lost in World War I. The leaders of Britain and France urged Hitler to stop his aggression, but they did not try to block him. The British and French people did not want to go to war again. Britain and France were known as the **Allies**.

1. ☑ **Reading Check** **Analyze** the map. On which continents did the Axis have control?

_____

_____

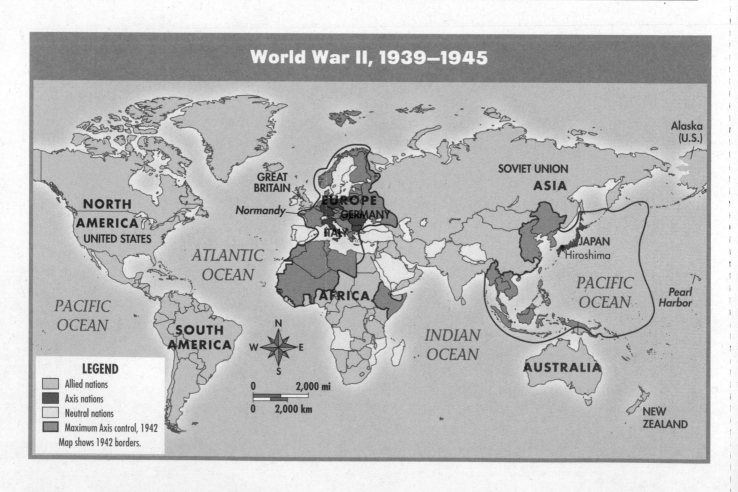

World War II, 1939–1945

Alaska (U.S.)

GREAT BRITAIN

NORTH AMERICA
UNITED STATES

Normandy

EUROPE
GERMANY
ITALY

SOVIET UNION
ASIA

JAPAN
Hiroshima

ATLANTIC OCEAN

PACIFIC OCEAN

PACIFIC OCEAN

SOUTH AMERICA

AFRICA

INDIAN OCEAN

Pearl Harbor

AUSTRALIA

NEW ZEALAND

N W E S

0   2,000 mi
0   2,000 km

LEGEND
- Allied nations
- Axis nations
- Neutral nations
- Maximum Axis control, 1942

Map shows 1942 borders.

In 1938, Germany took control of its neighbor, Austria. In 1939, Hitler prepared to invade Poland. Britain and France said they would fight if Hitler went ahead with his plans. In September, Nazi forces moved into Poland. The Allies then **declared** war on Germany. World War II had begun.

Academic Vocabulary

declare • *v.*, make known to the public

The Germans easily defeated the Polish army. A few months later, Hitler decided the time was right to invade France. First, his armies defeated the smaller and weaker countries west and north of Germany. British troops sent to block the Germans were forced to retreat. In May, the German army swept across northern France, all the way to the English Channel.

Then, in June 1940, German forces struck the heart of France. The French capital, Paris, fell. In less than three weeks of fighting, Germany had conquered France. Italy now declared war on the Allies, too.

2. ☑ **Reading Check Sequence Identify** and underline the dates and other time clues in the text under "The Axis and Allies" section that show the sequence of events that led to the start of World War II. Look at each date you identified. What do they have in common?

_____

_____

_____

The United States Debates Going to War

Great Britain now stood alone against Hitler. The British defense of their island nation is called the Battle of Britain. It took place mostly in the air. For months, night after night, German planes dropped bombs on London and other British cities. British fighter planes shot down many bombers, but the pounding continued.

Britain's prime minister, Winston Churchill, asked U.S. President Franklin Roosevelt for help. Many Americans still wanted to stay out of the conflict. With the Atlantic Ocean between them and Europe, they felt secure. Others, though, feared what might happen if Hitler were able to defeat the British. What would keep him from attacking the United States?

Roosevelt decided to take action but still remain neutral. In September 1940, he sent Britain 50 old destroyers, a type of warship, to help defend its coastline. Then in March 1941, Roosevelt signed the **Lend-Lease Act**. This bill allowed the United States to sell, lend, or give ships, planes, tanks, and other equipment to the Allies. Many Americans worried that this action would **draw** the country into war.

Meanwhile, Congress passed the Selective Service Act. This law required more than 1 million young men to serve in the military by the fall of 1941. The United States built up its army, air force, and navy.

The Attack on Pearl Harbor

By the spring of 1941, the British had won the Battle of Britain. The Germans had been stopped at the English Channel. But in the Pacific, Japan was steadily grabbing more land. It now controlled much of China and Southeast Asia.

Japan depended on the United States for many of its resources, including oil. But in July 1941, Congress banned all trade with Japan. As a result, tensions rose between the two countries. In Japan, the military ran the government. Leading general Hideki Tojo (hee DAY kee TOH joh) believed that the United States Navy stood in the way of Japan's complete control over East Asia. Japan decided to attack the United States Pacific fleet.

Academic Vocabulary

draw • v., to cause someone to become involved in something

During the Battle of Britain, people in London looked for shelter from air raids, or bombings, in the city's subway system, called the Underground.

On December 7, 1941, Japan launched a surprise attack on the United States Navy base at Pearl Harbor, Hawaii. The first Japanese bombers arrived early in the morning. They had taken off from the decks of aircraft carriers far out at sea. The Japanese sank or damaged 18 American warships and destroyed nearly 200 planes. More than 2,300 soldiers and sailors from the base died.

On December 8, President Roosevelt told Congress:

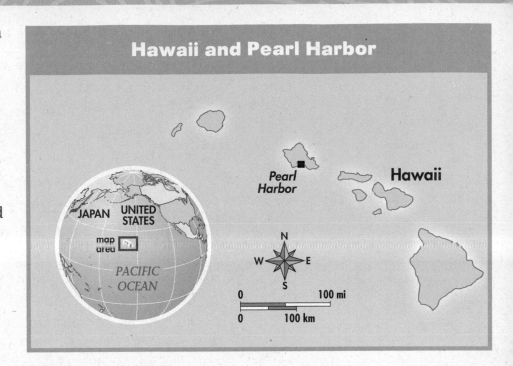

Hawaii and Pearl Harbor

Primary Source

Yesterday, December 7, 1941—a date which will live in infamy [shame]—the United States of America was suddenly and deliberately attacked by naval and air forces of the Empire of Japan.

—President Franklin D. Roosevelt, address to Congress, 1941

That same day, Congress declared war on Japan. The attitude of Americans quickly shifted. Now most of them supported joining the war.

3. ☑ **Reading Check** Find Hawaii on the globe. Use the globe and the information provided in the text to write two or three sentences explaining why the Japanese might have chosen to attack the United States at Pearl Harbor.

_____

_____

_____

_____

_____

_____

Germany Attacks the Soviet Union

Hitler's armies had easily moved west across Europe. But all that time, Hitler had his eye on a large area of rich farmland far to the east. The land was in Russia, then called the Soviet Union. In 1941, Hitler would try to claim it for Germany.

The Soviet Union was ruled by Joseph Stalin. Stalin, himself a brutal dictator, did not trust Hitler. In 1939, he and Hitler had made an agreement not to attack each other. That agreement had allowed Hitler to send his full forces west to conquer France. He did not have to worry about fighting the Soviet Union on a second front in the east. The pact had also left Stalin free to invade Finland, which he did in 1940.

In June 1941, Hitler broke the agreement with Stalin. He began an invasion of the Soviet Union. Hitler sent 3 million German troops, backed by 3,000 tanks and 2,500 planes, against the Soviets. The Germans destroyed much of the Soviet army and forced the remaining Soviet troops to retreat.

As the Soviets retreated, they burned crops and destroyed railways and factories. The goal of this "scorched-earth" policy was to leave nothing behind for the Germans to claim.

4. ☑ **Reading Check**
Identify and label each leader as *Axis* or *Allies* to show which side the leader's country fought on in the war.

Benito Mussolini
_____

Winston Churchill
_____

Joseph Stalin
_____

Adolf Hitler
_____

The Germans still pressed forward. By November, they had nearly reached Moscow, the Soviet capital.

Stalin needed help. He had never been friendly with Britain or the United States. But now he was forced to turn to them for equipment and supplies. The United States, through the Lend-Lease Act, gave the Soviet Union a loan of $1 billion to buy what it needed. Soon, the Soviet Union would become an important member of the Allies.

The Soviet scorched-earth policy slowed the advance of the German army. Then the Soviet winter, with its heavy snows and bitterly cold temperatures, stopped the Germans completely. Soviet forces were able to drive them back. In a few months, the Soviets had pushed the German troops well away from Moscow.

INTERACTIVITY

Check your understanding of the key ideas in this lesson.

☑ Lesson 1 Check

5. **Sequence** Number the events below from 1 to 4 to **show the correct sequence** in which they happened.

_____ Japan bombs Pearl Harbor.   _____ France falls to German forces.

_____ The Battle of Britain starts.   _____ Germany invades Poland.

6. In the attic of an old house, you and your friends find some newspapers from the late 1930s. One headline reads, "Hitler's Troops Continue to Advance." Write what you would say to your friends to **explain** the headline.

_____

_____

_____

7. **Analyze** how the treaty that ended World War I helped to cause World War II.

_____

_____

_____

Analyze Historical Visuals

When you analyze visuals from history, like this photo, you can uncover important details. Historical visuals can help you learn more about the period you are studying. Photos and other images are considered to be primary sources because they were taken at the time an event took place. These sources are often located at United States government Web sites such as the Library of Congress.

A rally at the Brooklyn Navy Yard, December 1941

To analyze a historical visual, follow these steps:

1. Identify what you see. What, exactly, is in this picture? Note people, objects, and major details.

2. Describe the action. What is going on in the picture?

3. Link the picture with any nearby text. If there is a caption or text in the image, how does it help you understand the picture?

4. Use your experience and what you have learned to draw a conclusion about the meaning or importance of the picture.

1. Complete the graphic organizer as you analyze the image. Then **describe** why you came to your conclusion.

▶ **VIDEO**

Watch a video about analyzing images.

What Do You See?	What Is Going On?	Conclusion

2. What other kinds of photographs do you think you would find that depict events in the United States after the Pearl Harbor attack? **Describe** three possible photographs.

_____

_____

_____

_____

_____

_____

INTERACTIVITY

Participate in a class discussion to preview the content of this lesson.

Vocabulary

rationing
war bond
internment camp

Academic Vocabulary

order
defend

Unlock **The BIG Question**

I will know that Americans at home during World War II played an important role in the war effort.

JumpStart Activity

With a small group, walk around your classroom and identify all the items that could be recycled and used for another purpose. As you identify objects, discuss how you would organize a recycling effort in your community.

Starting in 1941, many autoworkers learned a new trade. Their factories were converted to wartime use. The workers stopped making cars and started making planes or tanks or bombs. The assembly line of one auto plant near Detroit, Michigan, turned out a new plane every two hours. By the end of the war, about 200,000 companies had switched from producing consumer goods to military ones. This was just one of many changes that the war caused on the American home front.

Helping Win the War

Food and fuel became scarce during the war. Soldiers needed food. Their planes, tanks, and ships needed fuel. Other goods became scarce, too, as more goods were needed to help the war effort. Americans at home had to learn to get by without some things and with less of others.

The United States government tried to make sure that everyone had equal shares of scarce goods. In 1942, it set up a rationing system. **Rationing** is a system that limits the amount of scarce goods people can buy. President Roosevelt told Congress, ". . . where any important article becomes scarce, rationing is the democratic, equitable [fair] solution."

Rationed foods included sugar, butter, meat, eggs, and canned goods. Tires and gasoline were also rationed. Highway speed limits were lowered to save fuel.

Americans also helped the war effort by recycling. War industries needed metal, paper, and rubber. To do their part, children held "scrap drives." They went from door to door, collecting scrap materials. People contributed metal cans, tin foil, old cooking pots, piles of newspapers, and old tires.

Much of the food grown on American farms was shipped overseas to feed the Allied troops. As they had done in World War I, Americans made up for food shortages by planting victory gardens. These vegetable plots popped up in backyards and public spaces all over the country. In 1943, Americans planted about 20 million victory gardens.

Americans also supported their country by lending it money. The cost of fighting the war was about $350 billion. Taxes paid some of the cost, but the government borrowed the rest. It did so by selling **war bonds**. By purchasing bonds, Americans lent money to the government. People later earned money called interest on these bonds. More importantly, buying bonds helped to fund the war.

INTERACTIVITY

Explore the key ideas of this lesson.

Word Wise

Antonyms are words that have opposite meaning. The word *scarce* in the first paragraph on this page means "not having enough." What is an antonym for the word *scarce*?

Victory gardens helped free up food for the troops and provided Americans at home with fresh food.

African Americans Find New Opportunities

The Great Migration of African Americans continued, as more and more African Americans moved from the South to cities in the Northeast, Midwest, and West. They still came in search of work and better living conditions. But they faced unfair labor practices in many of the new war industries. The jobs they got were often low-paying and unskilled.

In 1941, President Roosevelt issued an **order** that banned discrimination in war industries. As the demand for war goods grew, so did the demand for labor. More African Americans got better-paying, skilled factory jobs. By the end of the war in 1945, African Americans held 8 percent of the jobs in war industries.

African Americans in the armed forces faced racial discrimination, too. Segregation in the military meant they could only serve in all-black units. They were not allowed to earn promotions to leadership roles and were kept out of many skilled jobs. Until 1941, African American pilots could not serve in the armed forces. Pressure from civil rights groups led to the formation of the Tuskegee Airmen. This squadron of African American pilots and support crew was named for its training location in Tuskegee, Alabama. By the end of the war, 355 Tuskegee pilots served overseas, flying hundreds of successful missions. For their bravery and service, many of the airmen received military awards, including Purple Hearts and Distinguished Flying Crosses.

Academic Vocabulary

order • *n.*, a command or instruction to do something

The Tuskegee Airmen trained to be fighter pilots at an army base in Tuskegee, Alabama. Serving in the Army Air Force, their unit won more than 850 medals.

Women Find New Opportunities

Around 10 million American men were drafted to serve in the armed forces. Some of their jobs went to unemployed men who stayed home. But millions of jobs remained open. Women filled many of those jobs.

During the war, about 6 million women joined the workforce. About a third of them ended up in war industries. They worked in aircraft factories and shipyards. Some did jobs they already knew, such as filing or typing. However, many trained for jobs that traditionally only men did, including building equipment and weapons.

Before World War II, women could serve as nurses, radio operators, or clerks in the armed forces, but most other military jobs were closed to them. A bill to allow women to enlist in the military was passed by Congress in 1942. The government urged women to join up. About 300,000 did.

Women served in a wide range of military jobs. Some were mapping specialists or language translators. A select few became pilots. They flew fighters and bombers from one base to another. Women did not take part in combat, although nurses tended the wounded in war zones. Some nurses were captured by enemy forces. More than 200 were killed.

Quest Connection

Some women went to Europe and Asia during the war. Write down three qualities that you think female pilots and nurses shared.

Women working in a factory during World War II

INTERACTIVITY

Find out more about what women did during World War II.

1. ☑ **Reading Check**

Analyze Images This photo shows women working in a steel mill in Indiana during World War II. **Identify** two things you can learn about women's work during this time period from this primary source.

_____

_____

_____

_____

The Japanese Experience

After Pearl Harbor, Americans began to fear what might happen next. Japanese forces, they thought, could cross the Pacific Ocean and invade the United States. Most Japanese Americans lived near the West Coast. Would they help **defend** the country against a Japanese attack? Many Americans believed they would, but others were not sure.

In February 1942, two months after Pearl Harbor, President Roosevelt issued an order. Americans, he said, could be forced to move out of certain areas if they might be a threat to the country's security. The order was aimed mainly at Japanese Americans.

About 110,000 people of Japanese ancestry were affected. Two thirds were American citizens. By the end of March, they had been forced to leave their homes in California, Oregon, Washington, and Arizona. They had to give up their ways of life and most of their possessions. They were moved to guarded camps away from the coast.

These places were called **internment camps**. They seemed like prisons to the families forced to live in them. Yuri Tateishi (YOO ree tah TAY shee) recalled what it was like: "You're kept inside a barbed-wire fence, and you know you can't go out."

Academic Vocabulary

defend • *v.*, to protect from harm or danger

Japanese Americans in an internment camp

Some young men from the camps did get out. Starting in 1943, they were allowed to volunteer for the armed forces. Many joined the 442nd Regimental Combat Team. This all-Japanese unit fought in Europe and was the most decorated unit in the United States Army. The actions of the 442nd were highly praised:

Primary Source

They were superb! That word correctly describes it: superb! They took terrific casualties. They showed rare courage and tremendous fighting spirit.

—U.S. Army General George C. Marshall

2. ☑ **Reading Check**
Sequence Identify which came first, the Pearl Harbor attack or the Japanese American internment. Underline the sentence in the text that supports your answer.

 **INTERACTIVITY**

Check your understanding of the key ideas in this lesson.

☑ Lesson 2 Check

3. **Cause and Effect Summarize** why so many women joined the workforce during the war.

_____

_____

_____

4. **Identify** the accomplishments of the 442nd Regimental Combat Team.

_____

_____

_____

_____

5. **Understand the Quest Connections** Around 300,000 women joined the military during World War II. What if very few women had signed up for duty? How do you think the war would have been different?

_____

_____

_____

A Letter Home

Corado "Babe" Ciarlo was one of five children. His older and younger brothers were exempt from the draft, meaning that they could not be drafted. Babe fought with the Fifth Allied Army in Italy. He sent letters home as often as he could to let his family know that he was safe.

Vocabulary Support

A small seaport city, located on the west coast of Italy

U.S. troops were tasked with taking Cisterna but were outnumbered and suffered a stinging defeat.

A body of water off Italy's western coast, where soldiers could relax between battles

deferment, n., the act of putting something off until another time, such as military service

Jerries, n., a nickname given to the German soldiers by Allied soldiers

April 30, 1944

Dearest Mom and Family:

Last night I received about ten letters. . . . It was certainly good to hear from all of you and also the good news about Dom getting 6 months (deferment). . . . Boy I almost broke down myself hearing all the good news.

I'm glad you enjoyed yourselves Easter. As for myself, I had a good time. . . . Don't worry about my money situation, because there isn't a thing to spend it on here in Anzio. . . .

I'm not in Cisterna because the Jerries still got it, but we were pretty darn close. This afternoon I might go swimming in the Tyrennian Sea—the salt water will do me good.

Tell Aunt Lucy that there is nothing to worry about, because it is safe here and the ocean is very, very safe. . . . Well, I've said enough for one day so take care of yourselves. . . .

Love, Babe

—Corado Ciarlo, letter to his family

A navy medic writes home during World War II

Close Reading

1. **Identify** and circle what Babe does not want his family to worry about.
2. **Explain** why you think he comments about their worrying.

_____

_____

_____

_____

_____

_____

_____

Wrap It Up

Describe the overall tone of the letter. What are some of the words and terms Corado uses to describe his situation? Are these words and terms you would expect from someone living on the frontlines of a war?

_____

_____

_____

_____

_____

_____

_____

Lesson 3

World War II in Europe

INTERACTIVITY

Participate in a class discussion to preview the content of this lesson.

Vocabulary

radar
code talker
D-Day
V-E Day

Academic Vocabulary

revealing
target

Unlock The BIG Question

I will know what sacrifices the American military made in the fight to free Europe.

Jumpstart Activity

Imagine that you were going to be away from home for a long period of time. What would you bring with you to remind you of home?

The war between the Allies and the Axis powers affected nearly every country on Earth. It was truly a "world war." Battles took place on land and at sea.

New War Technology

The Allied and Axis leaders knew that better technology would be required to win the war. Both sides worked to build more powerful ships, planes, tanks, and guns. They also came up with new ideas.

British fighter planes

The biggest advance in ships was the aircraft carrier. The warring countries soon realized that aircraft carriers could dominate sea battles. Also called "flattops," these huge vessels were floating runways. Bombers and fighter planes could take off from and land on aircraft carriers. This made it possible to attack an enemy far from any land-based runway. This was how Japanese aircraft were able to attack Pearl Harbor.

During the war, airplanes called bombers destroyed factories and parts of cities. The planes came in various sizes. The biggest carried a large number of bombs and could fly more than 2,000 miles without running out of fuel. Fighter planes were faster than bombers and carried machine guns. They often escorted bombers on missions.

In Poland and France, the Germans used tanks to smash through lines of defense. These heavy armored vehicles, introduced in World War I, improved throughout this war. They became faster, more powerful, and harder to destroy.

After World War I, all the major nations developed radar. **Radar** is an electronic system that uses sound to identify objects from a distance. A radar machine sends out little beeps of sound. The sound waves hit the object and show up on a screen, **revealing** the object's location. A major use of radar was, and still is, to spot enemy aircraft.

Radio played a big, new role in this war, too. Through radio, officers could talk with pilots or troops in the field. Radio helped armies to coordinate their tactics.

The enemy could listen in on radio conversations, so armies used codes to try to keep their messages secret. One kind of United States code proved very hard to break, or figure out. These codes were used by Navajo, Comanche, and other American Indians who served as **code talkers**. About 400 Navajo code talkers sent military messages by radio using the complex Navajo language. That language became an Allied secret weapon.

👆 **INTERACTIVITY**

Explore the key ideas of this lesson.

Navajo code talkers in the Pacific

Academic Vocabulary

reveal • *v.*, to make something hidden or secret known to others

The Battle for Europe and North Africa

The German invasion of the Soviet Union had stalled outside Moscow in December 1941. But the Germans did not give up. Soon they had the Soviets on the defensive again. Now the German goal was to conquer the Soviet city of Stalingrad. The Battle of Stalingrad was one of the turning points of World War II.

German troops had to deal with Russia's severe winter as they retreated after the Battle of Stalingrad.

The battle started in September 1942. The German army entered the city but met fierce resistance. Soviet troops defended every house on every block. Then, in November, a large Soviet force managed to break out of the city. Soon they had the German army surrounded. With winter coming on, the German troops were trapped. The battle ended in February 1943, when the invading Germans surrendered. Finally, the Soviets started pushing the rest of the German forces out of their country. Germany would never conquer the Soviet Union now.

In 1942, Axis forces held all of North Africa except Egypt. That June, Axis troops invaded Egypt. They aimed to take over the Suez Canal, a key Middle East shipping route. In October 1942, a British army unit forced the Axis troops to retreat. Again, it was a major victory for the Allies.

The next month, Allied troops landed in North Africa and started moving east. The British in Egypt moved west. The Axis troops were caught in Tunisia, between the two Allied forces. A series of hard battles followed. In May 1943, the Allies forced about 250,000 Germans and Italians to surrender.

Now the Allies were free to cross the Mediterranean Sea to invade Italy. The Allied campaign to take Italy began on the island of Sicily. By August 1943, the Allies controlled the island. Next, they began heavily bombing Italian cities on the mainland. The Allied invasion and constant bombing by air brought big changes. Mussolini resigned. In September, the Italians surrendered. A month later, the new Italian government declared war on Germany, its former ally.

1. ☑ **Reading Check**
Turn and Talk Study the photo above. **Discuss** with a partner how the Russian climate affected the German forces during and after the Battle of Stalingrad.

At the same time, American and British bombers were hitting **targets** inside Germany. One raid on the city of Dresden killed about 45,000 German people.

Academic Vocabulary

target • *n.*, a place selected as an object of attack

2. ☑ **Reading Check** **Sequence Identify** and draw a line from the timeline entries for 1942 and 1943 to the locations on the map where each event happened.

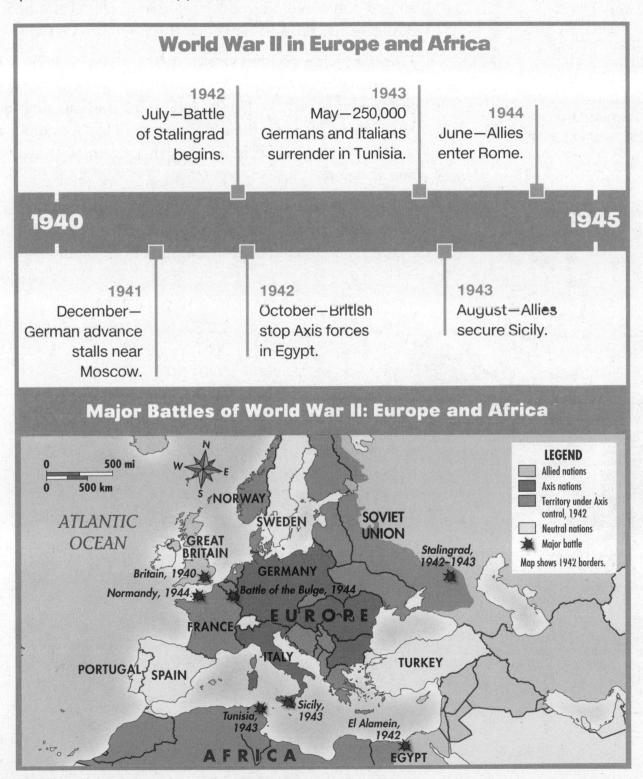

World War II in Europe and Africa

1942
July—Battle of Stalingrad begins.

1943
May—250,000 Germans and Italians surrender in Tunisia.

1944
June—Allies enter Rome.

1940

1945

1941
December—German advance stalls near Moscow.

1942
October—British stop Axis forces in Egypt.

1943
August—Allies secure Sicily.

Major Battles of World War II: Europe and Africa

0   500 mi
0   500 km

N
W   E
S

ATLANTIC OCEAN

NORWAY

SWEDEN

SOVIET UNION

GREAT BRITAIN

GERMANY

Stalingrad, 1942–1943

Britain, 1940

Normandy, 1944

Battle of the Bulge, 1944

EUROPE

FRANCE

ITALY

TURKEY

PORTUGAL

SPAIN

Tunisia, 1943

Sicily, 1943

El Alamein, 1942

AFRICA

EGYPT

LEGEND
Allied nations
Axis nations
Territory under Axis control, 1942
Neutral nations
✴ Major battle
Map shows 1942 borders.

The Normandy Invasion

Quest Connection

Make a list of words that describe what the Allied soldiers might have been feeling as they prepared to face Hitler's "Atlantic Wall" on the beaches at Normandy.

The Allies were making progress. But Germany still controlled most of western Europe. It was time for the Allies to push into the center of Europe and free it from German forces. Doing that would not be easy. By now, Germany had big guns in place all along the Atlantic coast of France. It also had half a million troops prepared to block an Allied assault on the coast. Hitler called this his "Atlantic Wall."

Once the Allies decided to invade, the planning began. American general Dwight D. Eisenhower was made Supreme Commander of all Allied forces in Europe, and directed the operation. Secrecy was the key to success. The Germans knew an invasion was coming; they did not know exactly when or where.

Eisenhower chose a 60-mile section of Normandy in northern France for the Allied invasion. This part of France lies directly across the English Channel from Great Britain.

Allied troops come ashore during the D-Day invasion.

3. ✓ **Reading Check** **Identify** and circle the route of the Allied invasion. Write why the Allies chose Great Britain as the place from which to launch their attack.

_____

_____

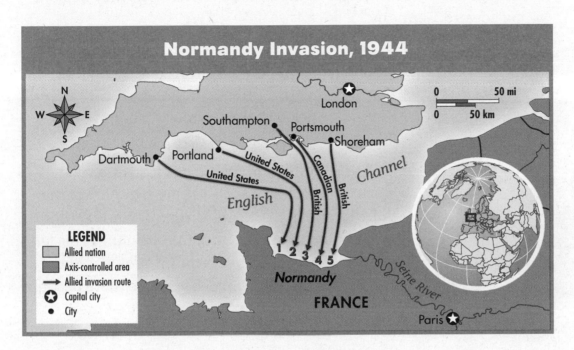

Normandy Invasion, 1944

LEGEND
- ▢ Allied nation
- ▢ Axis-controlled area
- → Allied invasion route
- ✪ Capital city
- • City

Eisenhower gathered more than 150,000 troops in Britain. He had about 4,000 ships and boats prepared, too. By the spring of 1944, the invasion forces from the United States, Canada, and Britain were finally ready to cross the English Channel.

The Allies hit the beaches at Normandy on June 6, 1944, known as **D-Day**. They faced a line of German guns and 70,000 soldiers. This part of Hitler's "Atlantic Wall" did not stop the Allies, but it cost them dearly. Many soldiers were killed or injured.

INTERACTIVITY

Take a closer look to learn more about the D-Day invasion.

The battle for one area was the most deadly. The spot was code-named Omaha Beach. Americans coming ashore there had to make their way from their ships to the shore. Carrying gear and weapons, they had to run across minefields on the beach, where explosives were hidden in the sand. They had to get through tangles of barbed wire. Then they had to climb over a concrete wall. All the time, they faced a storm of German gunfire.

The Americans showed great courage and willpower. They fought through the German defenses and pushed inland. By July, the Allies had brought ashore more than 1 million troops.

Victory in Europe

German defenses in France remained strong. After the D-Day invasion, every mile forward was a struggle for the Allied forces. But their victories kept coming. By mid-August, they had the shattered German army on the run. The Allies quickly won control of Paris and freed the rest of France. Then they headed toward Germany.

American troops march through the snow during the Battle of the Bulge.

The first American troops crossed through the nation of Belgium into Germany on September 12, 1944. In the next three months, they took several German cities. But the Germans fought hard to defend their homeland.

On December 16, the German army struck back. It launched a surprise strike at part of the Allied front line. The Americans defending that section had to retreat back into Belgium. This left a bulge surrounded by Germans that was about 45 miles deep in the line. The battle there became known as the Battle of the Bulge. The American forces bravely fought back in bitter cold. By December 26, they had taken back much of the lost ground.

By April 1, 1945, American and British armies were moving west toward the German capital, Berlin. At the same time, the Soviet Union's army was closing in on that city from the east.

Soviet troops reached Berlin first and started to attack the city on April 21. On April 30, Hitler killed himself. German forces fought on for another week, but they finally surrendered on May 7. The Allies named May 8 **V-E Day** for "Victory in Europe." Huge crowds celebrated throughout the Allied countries. But the war wasn't over yet.

4. ☑ **Reading Check** Working with a partner, write the first sentence of a news article describing the Battle of the Bulge.

_____

_____

_____

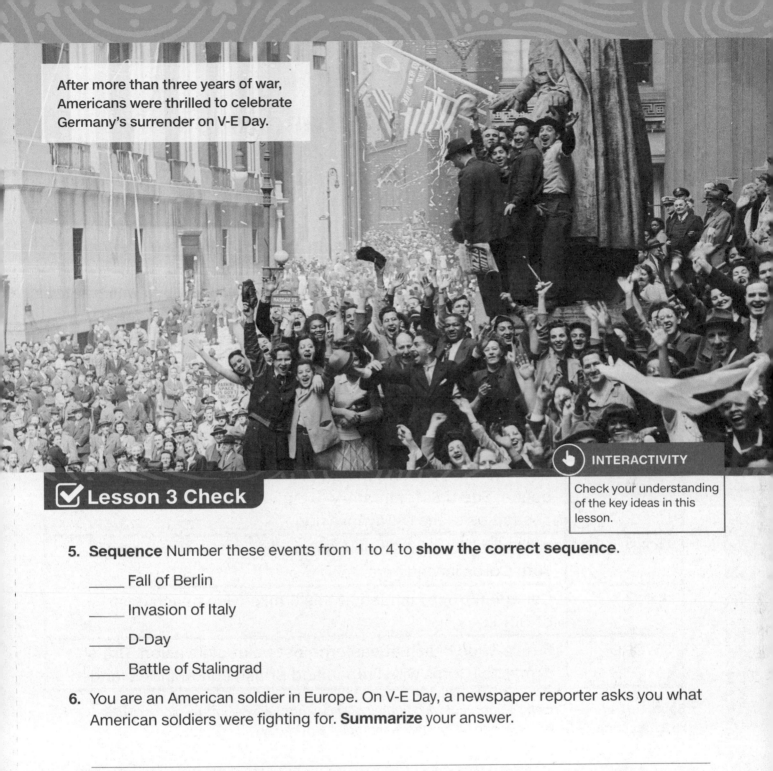

After more than three years of war, Americans were thrilled to celebrate Germany's surrender on V-E Day.

INTERACTIVITY

Check your understanding of the key ideas in this lesson.

☑ Lesson 3 Check

5. **Sequence** Number these events from 1 to 4 to **show the correct sequence**.

_____ Fall of Berlin

_____ Invasion of Italy

_____ D-Day

_____ Battle of Stalingrad

6. You are an American soldier in Europe. On V-E Day, a newspaper reporter asks you what American soldiers were fighting for. **Summarize** your answer.

_____

_____

7. **Understand the** Quest **Connections** What was the impact of the Allied forces invading Normandy?

_____

_____

_____

Analyze Tables and Maps

Social studies information can be presented in many different ways. Often it is presented in **tables**. To analyze and draw conclusions about certain topics, you have to organize and interpret that information. Let's say you wanted to learn more about the Allied casualties that occurred during the D-Day invasion. You also want to learn which beaches in Normandy were assigned to which Allied countries. Read the information in the table below.

Beach	Description
UTAH	The most western beach, 3 miles long, assigned to the U.S. 1st Army, 7th Corps. Casualties were the lightest of all the landings.
OMAHA	Second most western beach at 6 miles long, the largest beach. The U.S. 1st Infantry experienced the highest casualties of the D-Day invasion.
GOLD	First beach east of Omaha, 5 miles long. British 2nd Army, 30th Corps landed here.
JUNO	Canadian troops landed at this 6-mile-wide beach east of Gold.
SWORD	5-mile-wide beach at easternmost point of invasion. British Army, 1st Corps with French and British commandos landed.

Source: *The Royal British Legion: Facts and figures of D-Day http://www.britishlegion.org.uk/ remembrance/d-day-65/history-of-d-day/facts-and-figures-of-d-day*

Given this information, at which beach can you conclude that the Germans had the most guns and soldiers in place? Why did you come to this conclusion?

_____

_____

_____

_____

Your Turn!

The numbers in the map below identify the beaches of Normandy. Study the map and answer the questions using the information from the map as well as the table.

▶ VIDEO

Watch a video about drawing conclusions.

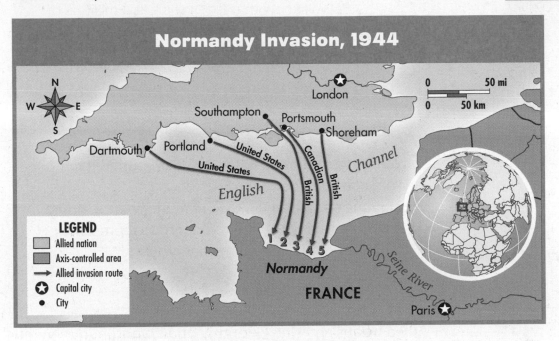

Normandy Invasion, 1944

1. Look at the map. Circle the name of beach 2 on the table. What sets it apart from other beaches?

_____

2. Organize information from the table about beach 4. Interpret the information and describe the conclusions you can draw from it.

_____

_____

3. Summarize the D-Day invasion based on your analysis and conclusions drawn from the information in the table and map.

_____

_____

_____

_____

Lesson 4 — The Holocaust

 INTERACTIVITY

Participate in a class discussion to preview the content of this lesson.

Vocabulary

concentration camp
genocide
Holocaust
anti-Semitism
ghetto

Academic Vocabulary

evidence
purpose

Jewish people arrive in Auschwitz in June of 1944.

Unlock The BIG Question

I will know that the Nazis killed millions of Jews and other people in the Holocaust.

JumpStart Activity

With a group of classmates, discuss your heritage. What countries do your ancestors come from? After everyone has explained their heritage, look at a map to see how many countries your group represents. Compare your results with other groups.

Allied troops entering Germany and Poland had seen much death and destruction. But they had never imagined the new horrors they would find. They discovered Nazi prisons packed with extremely weak, starving people. These people were mostly Jews. The Nazis had rounded them up and sent them to these prisons, or **concentration camps**.

Genocide

What the Allied soldiers first found shocked them. But they had not yet seen the worst. In several of the camps, they would find buildings designed just for killing people. They would uncover mass graves.

These soldiers had come across **evidence** of genocide. **Genocide** is the murder of an entire group of people, based on their race, culture, or beliefs. The Nazis wanted to get rid of all the Jewish people in Europe. In pursuing this goal during World War II, they murdered about 6 million Jews.

This period of Germany's genocide against the Jews is now known as the **Holocaust**. Jews were not the only victims of the Nazis, though. The Nazis also murdered millions of other innocent people. These included the disabled and other groups.

German Anti-Semitism

Hitler and the Nazis began to promote **anti-Semitism**, or hatred of Jews. They blamed Jews for all of Germany's problems. They said Jews were inferior. They claimed that Germans were superior. They forced Jews to wear yellow stars on their clothes, so they could be easily identified.

Abuse of Jews grew. The Nazis forced Jews out of government jobs, and even out of their homes. They declared them to be noncitizens and without rights. Germans were ordered not to buy from Jewish businesses.

The night of November 9, 1938, showed how terrible living in Germany had become for Jews. Around the country, their religious buildings were damaged or destroyed. Jewish businesses were robbed. So many windows were shattered that the event was called *Kristallnacht* (KRIS tahl nahkt), or "the Night of Broken Glass." The Nazis also captured thousands of Jewish men that night. They took away their property and sent them to concentration camps. Seeing these events, some Jews left Germany. More tried to leave, but most other countries would not accept them.

INTERACTIVITY

Explore the key ideas of this lesson.

Academic Vocabulary

evidence • *n.*, facts and information that prove whether or not something is true

Jewish-owned businesses and properties were the target of Nazi mobs during a night of vandalism known as "Kristallnacht."

Germany's government forced Jews and other groups into concentration camps.

Concentration Camps

The Nazis began rounding up Jews and placing them in ghettos. A **ghetto** is an area in a city where members of certain minority groups are forced to live. Jewish ghettos had existed in European cities and towns for centuries. But under the Nazis they now had a special **purpose**. Jews were held in ghettos until they could be sent to concentration camps.

The concentration camps had begun as prisons to hold political enemies of the Nazis. When Hitler started conquering new lands in 1938, he moved the Jews from those lands to the camps. Jews from Poland, France, and many other countries ended up in these places. Besides Jews, other groups considered inferior by the Nazis were put in the camps. After he invaded the Soviet Union, Hitler also filled camps with Soviet prisoners of war.

The Nazis began to locate concentration camps near factories. Prisoners were forced to work as slave laborers. Many were worked to death. Others died from beatings, disease, or lack of food.

In January 1942, the Nazis made a secret decision. They called it the "Final Solution" to the "Jewish problem." They would kill all the Jews in Europe. Several concentration camps in Poland were set aside as places for killing Jews. They became death camps. Many prisoners were killed as soon as they arrived.

Academic Vocabulary

purpose • *n.*, the reason for which something is done

Quest Connection

Underline the words that describe the treatment the Jewish people received in ghettos and concentration camps. What do you think America represented for the people who survived the Holocaust?

1. ☑ **Reading Check**

Discuss With a partner, discuss why concentration camps were so large and why they were located near factories.

The killing in the death camps was carefully planned and well organized. Jews were transported by train to a camp. They were herded into rooms that would then be filled with poison gas. At the largest death camp, Auschwitz (OWSH vihtz) in Poland, up to 8,000 Jews were killed each day.

Resisting the Nazis

Life in the ghettos was very harsh. Disease and starvation were common. The Warsaw ghetto in Poland was the largest. About 450,000 people lived there. The Nazis built a 10-foot wall around it to keep people from escaping.

Beginning in July 1942, the Nazis began regularly taking Jews from this ghetto to the death camps. By September 1942, nearly 300,000 Warsaw Jews had been killed. The remaining Jews decided to fight back, even though they had few weapons and they did not know if the rumors of the death camps were true.

When the Germans came to kill them in April 1943, the Warsaw Jews fired on them. This rebellion, called the Warsaw Ghetto Uprising, lasted nearly a month. By the end, the ghetto was in ruins and the remaining Jews were killed or sent to concentration camps.

Jews in many other ghettos fought back as well. They also resisted the Nazis from hiding places in the forest and even in the death camps themselves.

The Experience of Anne Frank

Anne Frank, a Jewish girl in the Netherlands, also resisted. When the Germans invaded, Anne and her family went into hiding in an office building of her father's. For two years in hiding, Anne kept a diary. The diary shows that she remained hopeful. She wrote, "In spite of everything I still believe that people are really good at heart." In 1944, the Nazis found the Franks. Anne ended up in a concentration camp, where she died of an illness at age 15.

Non-Jewish friends had helped Anne and her family. They had brought them food and other necessities. Across Europe, others resisted the Nazis by aiding Jews. Some helped Jews escape. Others hid them in their own homes.

👆 **INTERACTIVITY**

Learn more about the hardships faced by Jews held in concentration camps.

Ann Frank lived in hiding for two years before she was found and sent to a concentration camp.

Survival and Freedom

Millions of Jews died in the concentration camps. But some survived. They hoped and prayed that one day they would be free again.

In 1944, the Soviet army began to push into Poland. The Nazis tried to cover up their genocide as they retreated back to Germany. They destroyed some of the camps. They forced prisoners to march away, or they simply murdered them. But much evidence of their "Final Solution" remained.

In July 1944, the Soviets found thousands of Jews and others at the Majdanek (mye DAH nek) death camp in Poland. It was the first of many camps they would liberate, or make free. In April 1945, Americans and other Allies began to liberate camps in Germany.

For months after liberation, surviving Jews remained in the camps. Most could not return home. By now, their houses had been taken over by others. Many were not welcome back in their own towns.

Primary Source

I even find myself trying to deny what I am looking at with my own eyes. Certainly, what I have seen in the past few days will affect my personality for the rest of my life.

—U.S. soldier Harold Porter

2. ☑ **Reading Check**
Identify and list the emotions you see in this photograph.

_____

_____

_____

_____

Prisoners being set free from a concentration camp located in Germany.

Many Allied countries limited the number of Jewish immigrants they would accept. In time, however, the United States and other nations changed policies. Public pressure also built to let surviving Jews move to their historic homeland in the Middle East. In 1947, the United Nations voted to establish the Jewish state of Israel there.

Many Holocaust survivors settled in Israel, the United States, and elsewhere. Wherever they went, they made sure that people understood the Holocaust's lesson that good people must act against hatred. Today, memorials to Holocaust victims exist worldwide. They all make the same point: Nothing like the Holocaust should happen again.

3. ☑ **Reading Check**
Turn and Talk and discuss with a partner why memorials to the Holocaust are important.

INTERACTIVITY

Check your understanding of the key ideas in this lesson.

☑ Lesson 4 Check

4. **Generalize Explain** why the Nazis in Germany established a policy of anti-Semitism.

_____

_____

_____

5. **Make an inference** as to why you think other countries would not accept Jews who were trying to flee Nazi Germany.

_____

_____

6. **Understand the**  **Quest Connections** What do you think are the long-term consequences of the Holocaust? Consider family life, politics, and society in general.

_____

_____

_____

_____

5 World War II in the Pacific

INTERACTIVITY

Participate in a class discussion to preview the content of this lesson.

Vocabulary

island hopping
atomic bomb

Academic Vocabulary

result
determine

American warships USS *Maryland*, USS *West Virginia*, and USS *Pennsylvania* took part in battles in the Pacific during World War II.

Unlock The BIG Question

I will know how the Allies won the war in the Pacific.

JumPstart Activity

With your class, look at the map in this lesson showing the Major Battles of World War II: The Pacific. Volunteers should stand at the front of the room to represent the islands where the major battles took place. Look at their positions and discuss how warfare in the Pacific must have been different from it was in Europe. Do you think it was easier or harder? Why?

In the early 1940s, Germany enlarged the area it controlled in Europe. At the same time, Japan was gaining new territory in the Pacific. After Pearl Harbor, Japan invaded the Philippine Islands. Then it took the island of Guam and Wake Island. All three were parts of the United States. America would lead the effort to stop Japanese expansion.

War in the Pacific

Warfare in the Pacific was different from warfare in Europe. Unlike in Europe, the war in the Pacific was fought mostly by naval forces. Japan was a nation of several islands. It controlled land from China south through Southeast Asia. Much of Japan's growth was the **result** of its taking over other islands in the Pacific Ocean. The aircraft carrier would be at the center of many of the battles. The long-range bomber, too, would play a key role in the Pacific theater of the war.

In April 1942, United States Navy fliers launched the first air attack on Japan. They dropped bombs on Tokyo, Japan's capital. The attack did not do widespread damage, but it showed the Japanese people that their homeland was not secure.

In May 1942, Japan took control of the Philippines. The American commander there, General Douglas MacArthur, had left that island nation in March. Most of his troops were captured by the Japanese. He made a famous promise to those he left behind: "I shall return!"

Many people wondered if the Americans would really ever return. The Japanese forces seemed unstoppable. But few in Japan thought that beating the United States would be easy. One Japanese admiral wrote in early 1942:

Primary Source

This war will give us much trouble in the future. The fact that we have had a small success at Pearl Harbor is nothing.

—Admiral Isoroku Yamamoto

The Battle of Midway in June 1942 proved him right. It was a fierce battle over a tiny island, but it changed the course of the war.

Japan wanted to push the Americans out of Hawaii. But between the Japanese fleet and Hawaii lay Midway Island. There, the American forces took a stand against the Japanese. In a four-day clash of aircraft carriers and fighter planes, the United States earned its first victory. Japan's expansion in the Pacific had been stopped.

 **INTERACTIVITY**

Explore the key ideas of this lesson.

Academic Vocabulary

result • *n.*, an effect of something

To win in the Pacific, the United States had to invade a series of islands.

From Island to Island

In late 1942, Japanese leaders still dreamed of enlarging their empire. They wanted to claim the big prize of the South Pacific: Australia. But the island of Guadalcanal helped to end that dream. The fight with the Allies for that island lasted more than five months. After losing much of their navy there, the Japanese retreated in February 1943.

The United States military then went on the attack. American forces drove the Japanese off island after island. The fighting was fierce nearly everywhere. The Allies often had superior air and sea power. However, those alone could not capture an island. To do that they also needed ground forces. Ground forces meant the United States Marines.

The Marines were troops who were trained to fight both on land and at sea. Yet, on the jungle islands of the Pacific, the Marines lost many men. On some islands, the Japanese troops hid in tunnels and caves. These hideouts could not be overcome without great loss of life. But these battles had to be won. Otherwise, the Allies could not defeat Japan.

1. ☑ **Reading Check** **Identify** and underline sentences in the text on these two pages that describe why it was hard for American troops to capture a Pacific island.

The Allies needed a new strategy, or plan. They came up with the idea of **island hopping**. When they came to a heavily guarded island, United States bombers would pound it day after day. Ground troops would pass it by, moving on to an island that was less well defended.

By island hopping, the Allies caused Japanese food and supplies to begin running out. This gradually forced the Japanese forces to retreat to their home islands.

However, some islands could not be "hopped." For example, pounding the Philippines with bombs would have been too destructive to this crowded island nation. Therefore, winning those islands back from Japan became a long, hard struggle. In 1944, General MacArthur did return to the Philippines. But it took his forces nine months to overcome the Japanese. They finally succeeded in July 1945.

Two other islands also proved very hard to win. The nearer the Allies got to Japan's home islands, the more fiercely the Japanese fought. The battle of Iwo Jima took more than 6,000 American lives. More than 12,000 American soldiers died taking Okinawa. But those victories in 1945 brought the Allies major steps closer to ending the war with Japan.

Word Wise

A compound word is made up of two smaller words. When the two smaller words are joined together, a new word with a new meaning is formed. *Notebook* is an example of a compound word. What do you think the word *overcome* means?

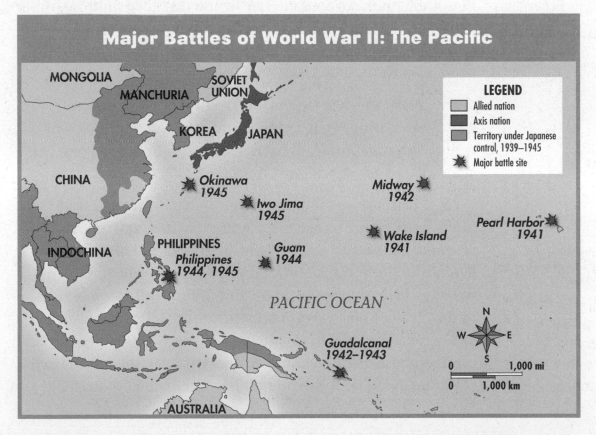

Major Battles of World War II: The Pacific

MONGOLIA

MANCHURIA

SOVIET UNION

KOREA JAPAN

CHINA

Okinawa 1945

Iwo Jima 1945

Midway 1942

INDOCHINA

PHILIPPINES

Philippines 1944, 1945

Guam 1944

Wake Island 1941

Pearl Harbor 1941

PACIFIC OCEAN

Guadalcanal 1942–1943

AUSTRALIA

LEGEND
Allied nation
Axis nation
Territory under Japanese control, 1939–1945
Major battle site

N W E S

0   1,000 mi
0   1,000 km

A Dangerous New Weapon

While American troops fought in Europe and the Pacific, a different kind of challenge was taking shape at home. Scientists were trying to create the first **atomic bomb**. Their secret work was given the code name the Manhattan Project.

The idea of engineering an atomic bomb went back to 1939. In that year, scientist Albert Einstein sent President Roosevelt a letter. He explained that a new source of energy might be used to create "extremely powerful bombs." He hinted that the Germans might be making such a weapon.

Two years later, the United States government approved the project. Scientists around the country worked on it. The first test of the atomic bomb took place in July 1945 in the desert of southern New Mexico. The explosion was a shocking success.

Hiroshima and Nagasaki

President Roosevelt died in April 1945. Now it was up to the new president, Harry S. Truman, to make a hard choice. He had to decide whether to drop an atomic bomb on Japan.

Truman knew that most Japanese believed death was more honorable than surrender. They would just keep fighting, never giving up. Truman hoped the powerful new weapon could end the war quickly. It would force the Japanese to surrender immediately. But it would also kill many Japanese civilians.

The alternative was to invade Japan. That would cost hundreds of thousands of American lives. A continued war would also cost hundreds of thousands of Japanese lives. Truman decided to use the bomb.

First, Truman warned Japan that it faced "prompt and utter destruction" unless it surrendered. The Japanese did not respond. On August 6, 1945, an American B-29 bomber flew over Japan's largest island. It dropped an atomic bomb on the city of Hiroshima. In an instant, a four-square-mile area of the city was destroyed. Temperatures reached thousands of degrees. The explosion killed more than 70,000 people. It injured about as many more. Radiation from the bomb would continue to kill people who had been near the bomb site.

2. ☑ **Reading Check**
Talk and turn and discuss with a partner why deciding to use the atomic bomb was such a difficult decision to make.

On August 9, United States forces dropped another atomic bomb, this time on the city of Nagasaki. The results were just as devastating. On August 14, Emperor Hirohito (hihr oh HEE toh) agreed to the Allies' terms for surrender.

That date became V-J Day, for "Victory Over Japan." The formal surrender, and the end of World War II, came on September 2, 1945.

3. ☑ **Reading Check** Complete the Venn diagram to **compare and contrast** the fighting tactics, or methods, during World War II in Europe and the Pacific.

World War II Tactics in Europe and the Pacific

A. War in Europe

C. War in both areas

B. War in the Pacific

The Effects of the War

The human cost of World War II was terribly high. As many as 60 million people may have died as a result of the fighting. Although the exact number is hard to estimate, half probably died serving in the armed forces. The other half were civilians, or people not in the military.

The United States lost about 298,000 people. Great Britain lost about 388,000, and France lost 810,000. China lost more than 11 million, mostly civilians. Japan lost almost 2 million, and Germany about 4 million. Nearly 7 million Polish people died. More than half of them were Jews killed in the Holocaust. The estimated number of Soviet war deaths was 18 million.

Academic Vocabulary

determine • *v.*, to find out through information gathering or research

The economic cost of the war is harder to **determine**. Governments probably spent more than $1 trillion to fight the war. But that figure does not cover the property destruction linked to the war.

To help restore order, British, Soviet, and United States forces remained in Germany. However, while Britain and the United States worked to make the parts of Germany they controlled independent, the Soviet Union kept control of its zone. The Soviets wanted to expand their territory. Not wanting another war, the Americans and British gave in to this.

Europe After World War II

LEGEND
Soviet Union before World War II
Land gained by the Soviet Union
Occupation zones in Germany
Map shows 1945 borders.

0   400 mi
0   400 km

ATLANTIC OCEAN

NORWAY
SWEDEN
FINLAND
GREAT BRITAIN
DENMARK
IRELAND
SOVIET UNION
GERMANY   Berlin
NETHERLANDS   British Zone   Soviet Zone   POLAND
BELGIUM
LUXEMBOURG   U.S. Zone   CZECHOSLOVAKIA
French Zone
FRANCE   SWITZ.   AUSTRIA   HUNGARY
ROMANIA
YUGOSLAVIA
BULGARIA
ITALY
SPAIN
ALBANIA   TURKEY
GREECE

4. **☑ Reading Check Analyze** this map. Which country benefited the most from changes to national boundaries as a result of World War II?

_____

_____

A New Role

By the end of the war, the United States had proven itself to be an important world leader. It could no longer return to its prewar isolationism.

The United States was willing to help Germany and Japan recover from the war. However, the Soviet Union, a former ally, would soon become a powerful enemy in a future and very different kind of war.

Winston Churchill, Harry Truman, and Joseph Stalin were allies during World War II. Afterward, their alliance broke down.

INTERACTIVITY

Check your understanding of the key ideas in this lesson.

5. **Cause and Effect Explain** why the Allies developed the Pacific strategy of island hopping.

_____

_____

_____

6. **Summarize** why the atomic bomb was used.

_____

_____

_____

7. **Describe** how World War II helped to make the United States into a new world power.

_____

_____

_____

Quality:
Determination

Dwight Eisenhower (1890–1969)
Handling Challenges

Throughout his early army career, Dwight Eisenhower excelled at his assignments. After Pearl Harbor, he was appointed to the army's war plans division in Washington, D.C. There he prepared a strategy for an invasion of Europe during World War II. Eisenhower led American troops to a hard-earned but decisive victory on D-day in 1944.

When the war was over, Eisenhower left the armed forces for a time to become president of Columbia University. In 1951, he was convinced by colleagues to run for president of the United States. His slogan during the campaign was "I like Ike," and Eisenhower won in a landslide victory.

As president, Eisenhower was determined to maintain world peace. He eased tensions during the Cold War between the United States and Russia in the 1950s. He also brought the Korean War to an end. At home, America enjoyed a period of prosperity during his presidency, and Eisenhower remained popular during his two terms.

Find Out More

1. **Identify** three situations when Dwight Eisenhower showed determination. **Explain** why his actions were those of a determined person.

_____

_____

_____

_____

2. Who are the strong leaders of today? How do they show determination? Take a survey at your school to find out who students think is a determined leader and why. Present your findings to the class.

Visual Review

Use these maps to review some of the key terms, people, and ideas from this chapter.

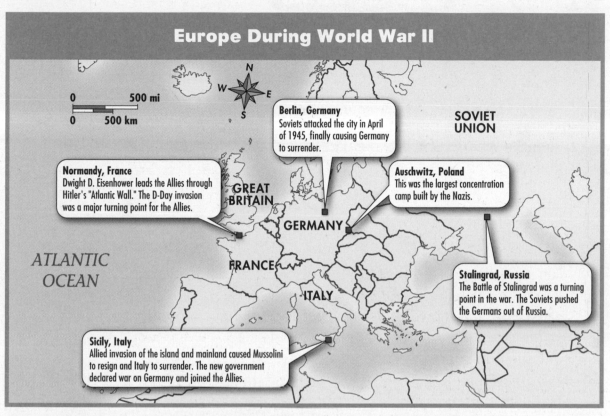

Europe During World War II

Berlin, Germany
Soviets attacked the city in April of 1945, finally causing Germany to surrender.

SOVIET UNION

Normandy, France
Dwight D. Eisenhower leads the Allies through Hitler's "Atlantic Wall." The D-Day invasion was a major turning point for the Allies.

Auschwitz, Poland
This was the largest concentration camp built by the Nazis.

GREAT BRITAIN

GERMANY

ATLANTIC OCEAN

FRANCE

Stalingrad, Russia
The Battle of Stalingrad was a turning point in the war. The Soviets pushed the Germans out of Russia.

ITALY

Sicily, Italy
Allied invasion of the island and mainland caused Mussolini to resign and Italy to surrender. The new government declared war on Germany and joined the Allies.

0   500 mi
0   500 km

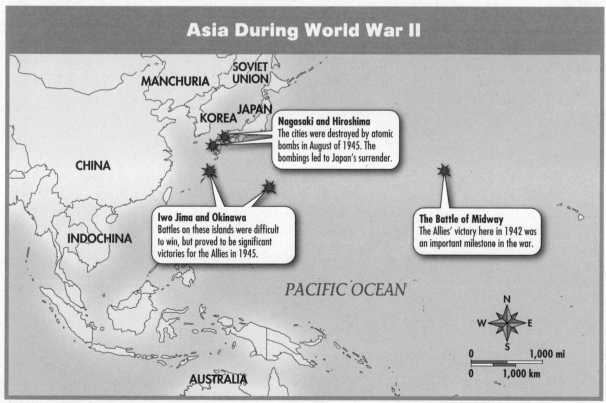

Asia During World War II

MANCHURIA

SOVIET UNION

KOREA   JAPAN

Nagasaki and Hiroshima
The cities were destroyed by atomic bombs in August of 1945. The bombings led to Japan's surrender.

CHINA

Iwo Jima and Okinawa
Battles on these islands were difficult to win, but proved to be significant victories for the Allies in 1945.

The Battle of Midway
The Allies' victory here in 1942 was an important milestone in the war.

INDOCHINA

PACIFIC OCEAN

AUSTRALIA

0   1,000 mi
0   1,000 km

GAMES

Play the vocabulary game.

Vocabulary and Key Ideas

1. Define What is **fascism**?

_____

_____

2. Identify What countries were part of the Axis? What countries made up the Allies?

_____

_____

_____

3. Describe How did World War II affect each of these groups?

African Americans _____

_____

Women _____

_____

Japanese Americans _____

_____

4. Define What was the "scorched-earth" policy?

_____

_____

_____

_____

_____

Critical Thinking and Writing

5. **Explain** Why were the D-Day invasions significant?

_____

_____

_____

_____

6. **Make Inferences** Why did General Eisenhower choose Normandy for the Allied invasion?

_____

_____

_____

7. **Analyze** What were the Nazi policies that led to *Kristallnacht*?

_____

_____

_____

_____

_____

8. **Revisit the Big Question** Why were so many Americans willing to fight in World War II? Why were Americans at home willing to deal with rationing? Was it worth fighting for? Use evidence from the text to support your answer.

_____

_____

_____

_____

_____

9. **Writing Workshop: Write an Opinion** On a separate sheet of paper, write an opinion about the strategy of island hopping. Given the outcome, do you think it was a wise strategy? Why or why not?

Analyze Primary Sources

"We must seek to bind up the wounds of a suffering world—to build an abiding peace, a peace rooted in justice and in law. We can build such a peace only by hard, toilsome, painstaking work—by understanding and working with our allies in peace as we have in war."

President Harry S. Truman, radio broadcast, May 8, 1945

10. Why does President Truman say that peace will be hard work?

_____

_____

_____

_____

Analyze Historical Visuals

11. This image shows people in the London Underground during World War II. Why are they there? Describe the conditions of the people in this image. Make Inferences about the condition of the city when this image was taken.

_____

_____

_____

_____

Quest Findings

A Story of World War II

You have read about what it was like to live during World War II, and now you are ready to write your biography about a specific person. Remember to include interesting details about the person's life as well as how he or she became involved in the war and how it affected him or her.

1 Prepare to Write

Review what you learned about your subject. Use the evidence that you gathered from your Quest Connections and your research about the challenges they lived through and how they responded.

2 Write a Draft

Use your notes to write your biography. Answer the following questions: What challenges did this person face during World War II? How did this person overcome them?

3 Share With a Partner

Exchange your draft story with a partner. Tell your partner what you like about the story and what could use improvement. Listen to their input and incorporate their suggestions.

4 Present Your Biography

Present your biography to your class. Encourage classmates to ask you questions about your person's life that might not have been fully covered in your presentation.

Chapter 15

The Cold War

GO ONLINE FOR DIGITAL RESOURCES

- VIDEO
- INTERACTIVITY
- AUDIO
- GAMES
- ASSESSMENT
- eTEXT

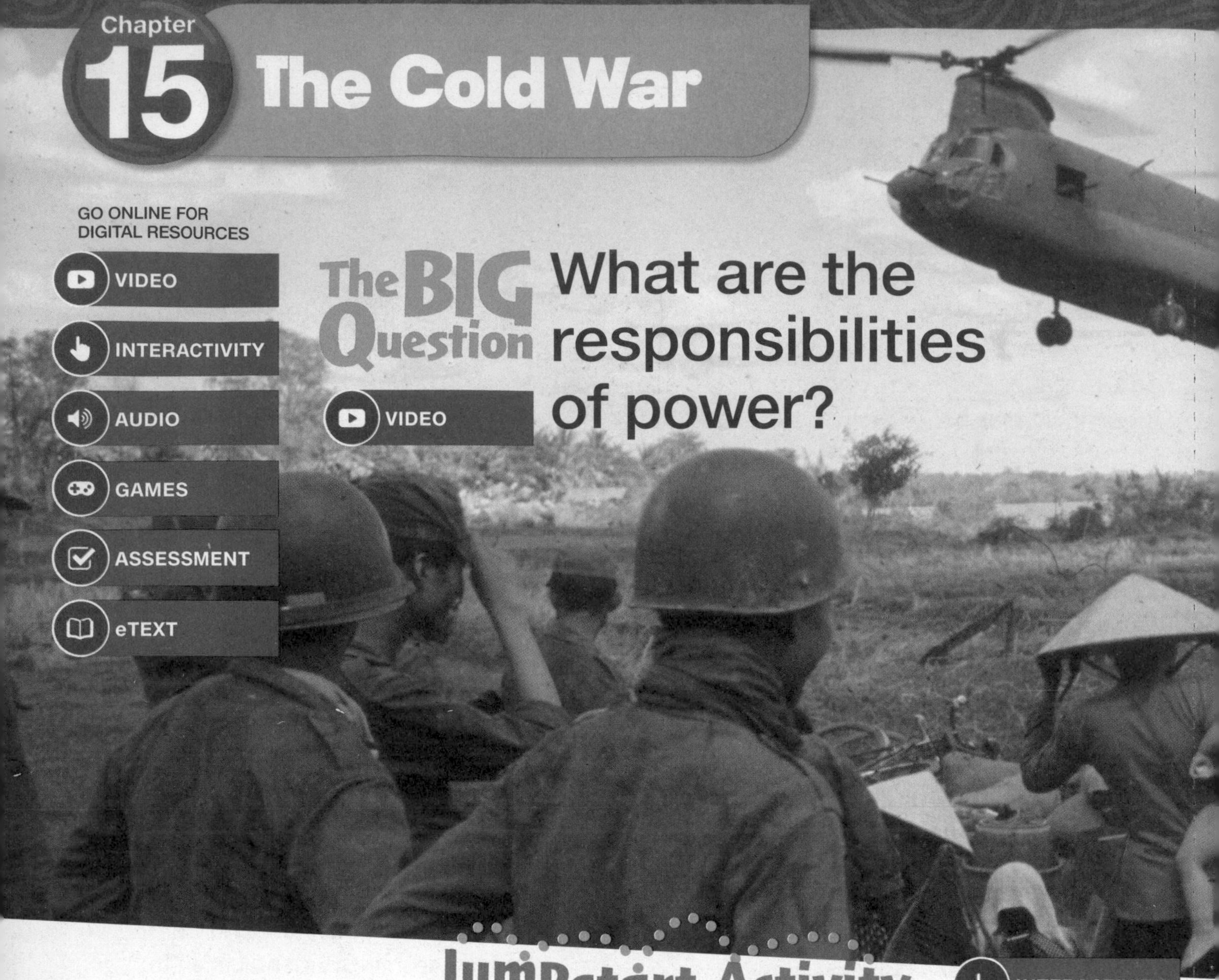

The BIG Question

VIDEO

What are the responsibilities of power?

Jumpstart Activity

INTERACTIVITY

Divide into two teams, Team A and Team B. Each team will work together to write three new class rules. Once both teams have written their rules, have a teammate write your team's rules on the board. What rules do the two teams have in common? What rules are different? Try to convince the other team to change the rules that are different. Keep a log of your results.

Lesson 1
A Divided World

Lesson 2
The Superpowers Compete

Lesson 3
Cold War Conflicts

Lesson 4
The End of the Cold War

AUDIO

Superpowers

Preview the chapter **vocabulary** as you sing the rap.

After World War II, the entire planet knew,
That the world was divided into views.
The U.S. and the West, the Soviets and the East,
A wall dividing Berlin did not help to keep the peace.

Around communist Europe arose an **Iron Curtain**,
And getting Europe back together was anything
    but certain.
To fight a war like never before was shocking to behold,
But nuclear missiles, the Red Scare, would fan
    fears untold.

To continue the ideas over East versus West,
The communists got involved because they thought
    they knew best.
The **Korean War** and the **Vietnam War** too,
Continued to split these countries in two.

The good news is that the **Cold War** finally ended,
But that didn't mean the conflict was suspended.
It took efforts and compromise from leaders from
    both sides,
To stop the wars, and end the race that created
    the divide.

What did Europe look like at the end of World War II?

After World War II, a human-made line divided Eastern and Western Europe. Winston Churchill called this border the "Iron Curtain" because the Soviet Union would not allow Eastern Europeans to leave the region.

Divided Berlin after World War II

TODAY
Berlin is one reunified city.

What happened and When?

Read the timeline to find out about events related to the Cold War.

1940	1950	1960	1970

1948
The Berlin Airlift begins.

1950
Korean War begins.

1957
Soviet Union launches *Sputnik* into space.

1969
U.S. astronauts land on the moon.

TODAY
Fifty-two nations operate satellites in Earth's orbit.

Who will you meet?

Joseph McCarthy
U.S. senator who spread panic about the spread of communism in the United States

Nikita Khrushchev
First leader of the Soviet Union to visit the United States

Ronald Reagan
U.S. president who worked to reduce nuclear arms during the Cold War

Mikhail Gorbachev
Soviet leader who worked to bring reforms to the Soviet Union

👆 **INTERACTIVITY**

Complete the interactive digital activity.

1980

1990

2000

1989
The Berlin Wall comes down.

1991
The Soviet Union ends.

Speak Out!

World leaders often need to express their thoughts and opinions to other leaders. One way they make their opinions known is by giving persuasive speeches. A persuasive speech clearly describes opinions on issues. However, it uses facts to support these opinions or points of view.

Quest Kick Off

I work as a speech writer for world leaders. I need your help to write a persuasive speech to present at a United Nations meeting. The topic is the Cold War. You may choose to write about leaders, conflicts, or negotiations during the Cold War. What is important for this mission is that you take a point of view.

1 Ask Questions

What is the Cold War? Who are the key people and events of the Cold War? Write two questions of your own.

....

....

....

....

INTERACTIVITY

Go online to get tips to help you write and give a speech.

2 Use Primary Sources

Reading speeches from the time will show you how Cold War leaders spoke. Some, like Nikita Khrushchev and Ronald Reagan, were very outspoken and passionate. Others were more careful and moderate. As you read the chapter, look for excerpts from speeches.

3 Look for *Quest* Connections

Begin looking for Quest Connections that will help you write your speech.

4 *Quest* Findings Write a Speech

Use the Quest Findings page at the end of the chapter to help you write your speech.

INTERACTIVITY

Participate in a class discussion to preview the content of this lesson.

Vocabulary

refugee
communism
capitalism
Iron Curtain
Cold War
propaganda

Academic Vocabulary

ongoing
promote

Unlock
The **BIG** Question

I will know that a powerful United States took responsibility for helping other countries after World War II.

JumpStart Activity

With a partner, make a list of two or three of your favorite fruits and vegetables. Discuss what it would feel like if these items were suddenly unavailable. What if the grocery stores and supermarkets in your neighborhood were empty of most food items? Discuss how you might be able to get food.

The United States came out of World War II as a leading world power, or superpower. Its economy was strong. Its government was strong and so were its people. In much of the rest of the world, the story was different.

The Postwar World

World War II left many European cities in ruins. Factories, stores, and homes had been destroyed. In the German capital, Berlin, people lived in cellars or shacks or on the street. They had little or no food to eat. The same was true for residents of many other cities and towns. Some 20 million **refugees**, or people who leave their countries to escape war or famine, roamed Europe, homeless.

The war had brought destruction to East Asia, too. Firestorms started by United States bombs had burned down more than 60 of Japan's cities. Much of Tokyo, the Japanese capital city, was in ruins. China had suffered greatly under Japanese rule. Farms were flooded and factories were destroyed. Things only got worse. Starvation and disease swept through the population.

Great Britain, France, Germany, and Japan had been major powers before the war. In the postwar 1940s, they no longer were. The United States and the Soviet Union had emerged as the two great powers. Their rivalry would shape the postwar world.

The Marshall Plan

In June 1947, Secretary of State George Marshall proposed a plan for rebuilding Europe and strengthening its economy. He described this plan by saying that

Primary Source

". . .the United States should do what ever it is able to do to assist in the return of normal economic health in the world, . . . Its purpose should be the revival of a working economy in the world. . . ."

—George Marshall, from a speech at Harvard University, June 5, 1947

Marshall explained that the countries that chose to take part would draw up the program. The United States would pay the costs. The recovery program became known as the Marshall Plan.

INTERACTIVITY

Explore the key ideas of this lesson.

1. ☑ **Reading Check**
Analyze the picture. **Turn and talk** to a partner about what it must have felt like to live in postwar Europe.

Sitting among bombed-out buildings in West Berlin, Germany, this family had escaped from communist-controlled East Germany after World War II.

Seventeen countries met in July 1947 to figure out what they needed. The Soviet Union and the Eastern European countries it controlled refused to participate. The Soviet Union accused the United States of using the Marshall Plan to try to take over Europe.

Academic Vocabulary

ongoing • *adj.*, continuing

In 1948, Congress approved the Marshall Plan. Over the next four years, the United States provided about $13 billion in aid to Europe. This money was used to rebuild houses and factories and to provide machinery, food, and supplies. As a result, industries grew and trade increased.

The Marshall Plan strengthened the bond between the United States and Western Europe. This bond would be of **ongoing** importance in the years to come. The United States would need support as it clashed with the Soviet Union.

Greek children line up to receive bread as part of the Marshall Plan.

2. ☑ **Reading Check**
Describe three effects of the Marshall Plan in the empty boxes below.

Effects of the Marshall Plan

Cause

The Marshall Plan

Effect	Effect	Effect

The United Nations

After World War I, the Allied countries had created the League of Nations. The United States did not join. Ultimately, the League proved too weak to stop World War II.

Now many countries, including the United States, said they were eager to form a new world organization to **promote** peace. On October 24, 1945, they founded the United Nations, or UN. The UN Charter states its goals:

Academic Vocabulary

promote • *v.*, to support, or actively encourage

Primary Source

"to save succeeding generations from the scourge [destruction] of war, . . . to reaffirm faith in fundamental human rights, . . . to promote social progress and better standards of life. . . ."

—UN Charter, 1945

The UN would soon be tested. Relations were growing worse between the Soviet Union and the West. *The West* refers to the countries that opposed Soviet expansion after World War II. It includes the United States and the countries in Western Europe.

In 1947, President Truman announced the Truman Doctrine. It stated that the United States would protect any nation from invasion or control by an outside power. This was a warning to the Soviet Union.

Adlai Stevenson, U.S. ambassador to the UN, addresses the General Assembly during the Cold War.

Communism and Capitalism

Communism is an economic and political system developed on a national level in the Soviet Union. In a communist country, the government owns all the land and most industries, in the name of the people. However, communism tends to limit personal freedoms. **Capitalism** is an economic system that encourages citizens to own businesses and property. A capitalist and democratic nation, like the United States, also protects personal freedoms. Most countries in the West were capitalist democracies.

A stronger Soviet Union opposed most Western nations. Differences in ideology, or belief, led to conflict. One goal of communism, to overthrow capitalist countries, turned the Soviet Union and the West into bitter enemies.

A Divided Europe

As World War II was ending, the Soviet army fought its way across Eastern Europe into Germany. After the war, the Soviets set up communist systems in the countries of Eastern Europe. As a result, Europe was divided between capitalism in the West and communism in the East.

Former British leader Winston Churchill described this divided world. In a famous speech in March 1946, he said,

3. **☑ Reading Check**
Distinguish Fact From Opinion Turn and talk to a partner. **Describe** how Churchill's quote expresses a fact. Support your answer.

Primary Source

"An Iron Curtain has descended across the Continent."
—Winston Churchill, 1946

The **Iron Curtain** meant the closing off of Eastern Europe from Western Europe. The "curtain" referred to the policy of isolation imposed by the Soviet Union.

Western countries feared the Soviet armies on the other side of the Iron Curtain. In 1949, the West formed a military alliance. It is called the North Atlantic Treaty Organization, or NATO. If one NATO country was attacked, the others pledged to come to its aid. In 1955, the countries east of the Iron Curtain signed their own treaty. It was called the Warsaw Pact. Warsaw Pact countries, too, promised to help defend one another.

The official North Atlantic Treaty signing ceremony was held in Washington, D.C.

The Berlin Airlift

Germany had been split into zones after the war. The Soviets controlled East Germany. The French, British, and Americans controlled West Germany. The capital, Berlin, was split in a similar way. But the city itself lay 110 miles inside East Germany. The roads into Berlin passed through Soviet-held land.

In June 1948, the Soviets tried to cut off the West's access to Berlin. They set up a blockade. No vehicles could pass through to West Berlin. Britain and the United States were worried that the Soviet Union would take over West Berlin. One U.S. general in Germany reported back,

Primary Source

"We are convinced that our remaining in Berlin is essential to our prestige [reputation] in Germany and in Europe. Whether for good or bad, it has become a symbol of the American intent."

—U.S. General Lucius D. Clay, a cable to Washington, D.C., June 13, 1948

The millionth bag of coal is loaded for the Berlin Airlift.

The U.S. and its allies started flying food, fuel, machinery, and other goods into West Berlin. This effort was called the Berlin Airlift. The Berlin Airlift kept the people of West Berlin supplied for nearly a year. During that time, both sides built up their troop strength in Germany. Tensions rose and stayed high. In May 1949, the Soviets finally lifted the blockade.

Although the blockade had been lifted, the Soviet Union still controlled the government of East Germany. It also controlled the people. Like everyone behind the Iron Curtain, the East Germans were not free to leave. Some East Germans left anyway, escaping to West Berlin.

Between 1949 and 1961, more than 2 million East Germans fled to the West. In 1961, the East German government built the Berlin Wall to stop them. This concrete wall divided the two parts of Berlin. Barbed wire sat on top of the wall. Armed guards watched it day and night.

By the 1980s, the government had added electrified fences. Still, over the years, about 5,000 East Germans risked their lives to cross the wall into the West.

The Soviet Union worked to keep control of Eastern Europe. It also tried to expand communism into other parts of the world. For example, it backed communist governments in China and North Korea. The United States opposed Soviet efforts wherever it could.

4. ☑ **Reading Check**
Turn and talk to a partner. **Describe** how the Berlin Airlift sought to stop the spread of communism.

East German troops add barbed wire to the wall as a West German family watches.

A New Kind of War

The two sides did not fight a traditional war. Usually, their struggle did not involve weapons. They fought this **Cold War** for about 40 years.

The clash over Berlin was typical. A crisis would put the two sides on edge, but they did not attack each other directly. Sometimes they might fight a "hot war" indirectly by supporting two opposing groups in other countries. For the most part, however, the Americans and Soviets fought the Cold War with propaganda.

Propaganda is the spreading of ideas or beliefs to gain support for a cause. The United States used a radio network in Europe to spread anticommunist propaganda to countries behind the Iron Curtain. The Soviet Union used propaganda to influence its own people and those in other countries.

This Soviet propaganda poster says, "We Also Want to be Pilots!"

INTERACTIVITY

Check your understanding of the key ideas of this lesson.

☑ Lesson 1 Check

5. **Sequence Identify** and circle the event that happened last.

building of the Berlin Wall   founding of NATO   signing of Warsaw Pact treaty   Berlin Airlift

6. It is 1961, and you have a job as a reporter for a magazine with a feature titled "Cold War Diary." You are sent around the world to witness important events. Your first assignment is to **describe** the Iron Curtain.

_____

_____

_____

7. **Analyze** the difference between a "cold war" and a "hot war." **Describe** the way military actions influenced the Cold War.

_____

_____

_____

Writing Persuasive Speeches

Have you ever written a persuasive speech? A **speech** is a spoken address to an audience. Persuasive speeches can be useful because they show an opinion about a topic. They are often controversial. Speeches often include written scripts you can read. The script plans the argument and wording of the speech. The speaker reads from the script. A script is a **primary source** because it shows the words of a person who experienced an event.

When you write a persuasive speech, be sure to include important information. Ask and answer the following questions: *Who will give the speech? Who will listen to the speech? What point does the speaker wish to make?*

The passage below is a good example of a persuasive speech. It was given by Eleanor Roosevelt in 1948. Roosevelt's speech talks about the upcoming presentation to the UN of an International Declaration of Universal Rights, which she had helped to write.

Primary Source

"It is interference [involvement] in other countries that especially stirs up antagonism [strong feelings of dislike] against the Soviet Government. If it wishes to feel secure in developing its economic and political theories [ideas] within its territory, then it should grant others that same security. [. . .]

The basic problem confronting the world today . . . is the preservation of human freedom for the individual and consequently [as a result] for the society of which he is a part. We are fighting this battle again today as it was fought at the time of the French Revolution and at the time of the American Revolution."

—Eleanor Roosevelt,
"The Struggle for Human Rights," 1948

Your Turn!

Reread the section titled **The Berlin Airlift** in Lesson 1. Then complete
the activity about speechwriting.

1. Imagine you are an American politician who wants to help the
   people of West Berlin. Answer the questions to help you figure out
   details you might need in order to **create** a speech.

   What would you like to convince people to do?

   _____

   What might happen if people do not take the action you suggest?

   _____

   _____

   Why would the event described above be important to your audience?

   _____

   _____

   What words or phrases can you use to capture your audience's
   attention?

   _____

   _____

2. Use your answers from the questions to **write** the opening lines to a
   speech. Be sure to include your issue and plan.

   _____

   _____

   _____

   _____

   _____

   _____

The Superpowers Compete

INTERACTIVITY

Participate in a class discussion to preview the content of this lesson.

Vocabulary

McCarthyism
arms race
Cuban Missile Crisis

Academic Vocabulary

nuclear
tense

Unlock
The **BIG**
Question

I will know that one goal of the superpowers during the Cold War was to avoid a "hot" war.

JumpStart Activity

With a small group, quickly sketch the design of a poster that warns Americans about the spread of communism during the Cold War. Think of designs, words, and ideas that would inspire fear of communism.

At the end of World War II, the United States was a military superpower. One reason for this was because the United States had the atomic bomb. By 1950, the Soviet Union had tested its own atomic bomb. Americans were horrified at the thought that the Soviet Union had such a weapon.

In the 1950s, billboards like this one added to the panic during the Red Scare.

wake up !!!
the SHADOW is SPREADING
FOOD INDUSTRY FOR AMERICA

The Red Scare and McCarthyism

Communists had taken control of Russia in 1918. They then conquered many of the surrounding countries. The communists said they would conquer the United States, too. The Soviet flag was red, and the Soviets were known as "Reds." So the fear of a communist takeover of the United States became known as the Red Scare.

The panic grew in the early 1950s. Communists had taken control of China. They had invaded Korea. In the years after World War II, the Soviets had set up communist governments in most of Eastern Europe.

U.S. Senator Joseph McCarthy of Wisconsin helped spread feelings of fear. McCarthy encouraged people to feel panic. In 1950, he gave a speech which said,

Primary Source

> "In my opinion the State Department, which is one of the most important government departments, is thoroughly infested with communists."
> –Joseph McCarthy, Speech to the State Department, 1950

He claimed he had a list of about 200 communists working in the U.S. government. He said they were loyal to the Soviets and might be spies.

Investigations found spies in government, so McCarthy's claim caught the attention of the news media and the American people. A 1947 law required federal employees to sign a loyalty oath. McCarthy used this law, and many Americans lost their jobs when they refused to sign the oath, even though there was no proof that they were spies.

McCarthy began to get too aggressive, accusing too many people. Eventually, the Senate said he had gone too far. McCarthy's career was over. This political bullying of innocent people came to be known as **McCarthyism**.

1. ☑ **Reading Check**
   Turn and talk to a partner. Explain how Joseph McCarthy helped to spread fear and panic.

INTERACTIVITY

Explore the key ideas of this lesson.

Quest Connection

McCarthy used the word *infested* to make Americans think communists were everywhere. Think about words you might use to help complete your Quest.

INTERACTIVITY

Learn more about how language was used to cause panic and fear during the Cold War.

Senator Joseph McCarthy used the new medium of television to spread his message.

The Arms Race

nuclear • *adj.*, atomic

During the Cold War, the United States and the Soviet Union competed in an arms race. An **arms race** is a contest to build more and better weapons than those of your enemy. Both sides continued to make **nuclear** weapons.

In the 1950s, Americans feared a nuclear war between the Cold War superpowers. They realized that Soviet planes or rockets could drop nuclear bombs on the United States.

Americans began to prepare for a nuclear attack. Some built underground bomb shelters in their backyards. They stocked the shelters with food and other supplies. In schools, students learned how to "duck and cover" in case of attack. This was a drill in which students practiced ducking under their desks for protection from falling debris.

Students practiced the safety drill "duck and cover" to prepare for a nuclear attack.

2. ☑ **Reading Check** **Summarize** How did Americans prepare for a possible nuclear attack?

_____

_____

The Cuban Missile Crisis

Americans' fears almost came true. The nation of Cuba lies about 90 miles off southern Florida. In 1959, Fidel Castro led a revolution in Cuba. Then he formed a communist government. The Soviets supported him. In 1962 the Soviet Union secretly began to install nuclear weapons in Cuba. These weapons had the power to reach many cities in the United States.

On October 14, 1962, American spy planes took photos of the weapon sites being built. President John F. Kennedy sent the United States Navy to blockade Cuba. Navy ships prevented any more weapons from reaching the island. In addition, Kennedy demanded that the Soviets remove the sites that were already there.

This incident was called the **Cuban Missile Crisis**. It lasted for nearly two weeks. Kennedy and Nikita Khrushchev, the Soviet leader, exchanged messages. Meanwhile, the American people wondered what would happen if the Soviets did not back down. Would there be a nuclear war? It was a **tense** time for people around the world.

Finally, on October 28, the Soviets agreed to Kennedy's demands. In return, the United States pledged never to invade Cuba. The crisis was over. But both sides realized how close they had come to war.

The Cuban Missile Crisis did not end the tension over nuclear weapons. Instead, it led to an idea that would shape the relationship of the two superpowers. The idea was called "Mutual Assured Destruction," or MAD. It was based on the likelihood that each superpower could destroy the other in a nuclear war. According to the theory of MAD, neither side would dare use their nuclear weapons.

Academic Vocabulary

tense • *adj.*, anxious

3. ☑ **Reading Check**
Analyze the map. About how far would a missile from Cuba have had to travel to hit Washington, D.C.?

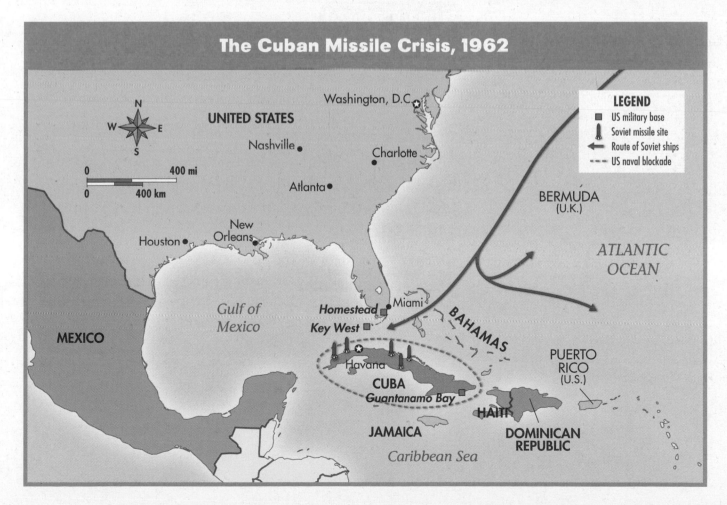

The Cuban Missile Crisis, 1962

LEGEND
■ US military base
⚊ Soviet missile site
← Route of Soviet ships
--- US naval blockade

UNITED STATES
Washington, D.C.
Nashville
Charlotte
Atlanta
Houston
New Orleans
Miami
Homestead
Key West
Gulf of Mexico
MEXICO
BAHAMAS
BERMUDA (U.K.)
ATLANTIC OCEAN
Havana
CUBA
Guantanamo Bay
PUERTO RICO (U.S.)
HAITI
DOMINICAN REPUBLIC
JAMAICA
Caribbean Sea

0   400 mi
0   400 km

N
W   E
S

The Space Race

While the arms race continued, another "race" began. The space race would eventually send American astronauts all the way to the moon and back.

The space race started with a satellite called *Sputnik*, which the Soviet Union launched in October 1957. The *Sputnik* launch took the United States by surprise. American scientists scrambled to catch up. In 1958, the U.S. government created the National Aeronautics and Space Administration, or NASA, to plan U.S. missions to space.

However, the Soviets had a big head start. One month after *Sputnik 1*, they sent the first living creature, a dog named Laika (LAY kah), into orbit. Then, in April 1961, the Soviets sent the first human into space. Cosmonaut Yuri Gagarin (gah GAH rhin) successfully orbited Earth.

Two months later, President Kennedy announced to Congress:

Primary Source

"I believe that this nation should commit itself to achieving the goal, before this decade is out, of landing a man on the moon and returning him safely to the earth."

—John F. Kennedy, Address to Congress, 1961

American competitive spirit and know-how helped fulfill this goal. In February 1962, U.S. astronaut John Glenn safely piloted the *Friendship 7* craft through three orbits around Earth.

4. ☑ **Reading Check** **Underline** the U.S. achievements in the space race. **Explain** how the launch of *Sputnik* and the space race were part of the Cold War.

_____

_____

_____

_____

Americans Reach the Moon

Many other United States space flights followed. NASA used them to figure out how to land an American on the moon. On July 16, 1969, NASA was ready. People worldwide watched on television as a rocket blasted off. The *Apollo 11* spacecraft carried three astronauts named Neil Armstrong, Edwin "Buzz" Aldrin, and Michael Collins.

Four days later, on July 20, Armstrong and Aldrin boarded a landing craft named *Eagle*. They flew it to the moon's surface. Armstrong then became the first person to walk on the moon. Aldrin soon joined him. The three astronauts returned safely to Earth on July 24. On the moon, they left an American flag and a plaque to mark their accomplishment. It said, "We Came In Peace For All Mankind."

This postage stamp shows the moon landing in 1969.

 **Lesson 2 Check**

INTERACTIVITY

Check your understanding of the key ideas of this lesson.

5. **Draw Conclusions** If the Soviet Union had not launched *Sputnik,* would there have ever been a space race? **Explain**.

_____

_____

6. You are asked to report on the Cuban Missile Crisis. **Explain** how the president has handled the crisis. Also **describe** what ordinary families fear about these events.

_____

_____

_____

7. **Understand the** *Quest* **Connections** Why do you think Joseph McCarthy chose dramatic words for his speeches?

_____

_____

_____

Primary Source

Life Magazine Cover

On August 3, 1959, President Eisenhower announced to Americans that Nikita Khrushchev would soon visit the United States. This announcement shocked many people. They thought that Khrushchev was our enemy. Many Americans did not want a communist leader visiting their country.

These objections did not change President Eisenhower's mind. In September, Khrushchev became the first Soviet leader to visit the United States. Khrushchev was very interested in American farms. He saw farming as the way for communism to succeed. During his visit, he gave a speech that said that the earth should be "furrowed by plows, not rockets and tanks."

Khrushchev traveled to visit an American farm in Coon Rapids, Iowa. He was excited and impressed by the prize pigs and fields of corn he saw there. This *Life Magazine* cover was published a few days after Khrushchev left the United States to return to the Soviet Union. It shows the farmers with Khrushchev.

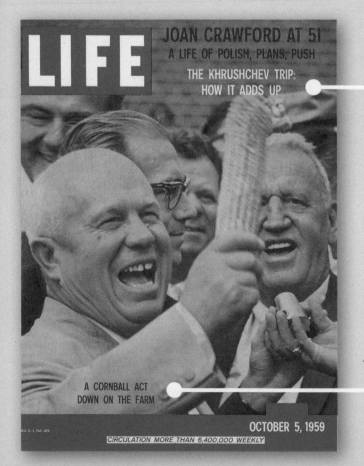

LIFE

JOAN CRAWFORD AT 51
A LIFE OF POLISH, PLANS, PUSH

THE KHRUSHCHEV TRIP:
HOW IT ADDS UP

A CORNBALL ACT
DOWN ON THE FARM

OCTOBER 5, 1959

CIRCULATION MORE THAN 6,400,000 WEEKLY

**THE KHRUSHCHEV TRIP:
HOW IT ADDS UP**

**A CORNBALL ACT
DOWN ON THE FARM**

Close Reading

1. **Circle** the headline at the bottom of the magazine cover that describes Khrushchev's visit. Then **underline** the headline about Khrushchev at the top. How does it compare with the title at the bottom?

_____

_____

_____

_____

2. **Explain** what is happening in the photograph. Why do you think the magazine editors chose this picture for the cover?

_____

_____

_____

_____

Wrap It Up

The title of one of the magazine's cover stories is "A Cornball Act Down On The Farm." To act like a cornball means to be silly or strange. How does this title help you understand how the author might have felt about Khrushchev's visit?

_____

_____

_____

_____

_____

_____

INTERACTIVITY

Participate in a class discussion to preview the content of this lesson.

Vocabulary

proxy war
Korean War
guerrilla
Vietnam War
Tet Offensive

Academic Vocabulary

crucial
widespread

U.S. troops evacuate civilians during the Korean War.

Unlock
The **BIG**
Question

I will know that the United States felt a responsibility to fight against the spread of communism.

JumpStart Activity

Divide into three groups to plan a class field trip. Draw slips of paper to determine two class leaders. Each of the two leaders must visit all three groups and add to or change the group's plans. Each leader should also oppose any plan that the other has suggested. Discuss the challenges your group faced in planning the field trip.

During the Cold War, the conflict between the United States and the Soviet Union sometimes led to proxy wars. A *proxy* is a stand-in or substitute. In these **proxy wars**, capitalist and communist forces battled each other.

The Korean War

After World War II, the Soviets continued to support the communist government in North Korea. The United States backed the government of South Korea.

On June 25, 1950, the North Korean army invaded the capitalist area of South Korea. The United Nations ordered it to withdraw. However, it did not. The **Korean War** had begun.

If North Korea won, all of Korea would be united under a communist government. Right away, President Harry Truman sent United States troops to assist the South Korean army. In a speech to Americans, Truman said,

Primary Source

An act of aggression such as this creates a very real danger to the security of all free nations.

–Harry S. Truman, speech, 1950

They would later be joined by troops from 15 other countries. These soldiers would fight as a United Nations force. The UN forces pushed the North Koreans north almost to their border with China. Then communist China entered the war, and Chinese troops drove the UN forces out of North Korea.

In July, 1951, both sides began peace talks. The negotiations dragged on for two years. Finally, on July 27, 1953, the fighting ended. Korea was divided into two nations, as it remains today. The United States had stopped the spread of communism into South Korea. The United States paid a high price for the victory, however. More than 36,000 Americans died in the war.

1. ☑ **Reading Check** **Use Evidence From Text** How was the Korean War a proxy war in the conflict between capitalism and communism?

_____

_____

_____

INTERACTIVITY

Explore the key ideas of this lesson.

Quest **Connection**

In the text, underline the events that led to President Truman's speech. Think about the events or issues that you might use in your Quest.

INTERACTIVITY

Learn how to use language to write an effective speech.

The Vietnam War

The country of Vietnam was also split after World War II. The communists of North Vietnam started fighting to unify the country under a communist government. The Soviet Union and China supported this goal. They helped communists in the north arm guerrillas in South Vietnam.

Guerrillas are fighters who do not fight directly but make surprise raids or quick attacks from under cover. They usually fight in small bands. The guerrillas battling the government of South Vietnam were known as the Viet Cong.

American troops march through the countryside of Vietnam.

Most people in South Vietnam did not want communism. The United States feared what might happen if South Vietnam fell to the communists. Maybe Vietnam's neighbors, such as Cambodia and Laos, might also fall, like dominoes in a line. Americans called this effect of one nation after another falling to communism the "domino theory."

In 1964, President Lyndon Johnson ordered bombers to attack North Vietnam. The next year, U.S. combat troops joined the conflict. By 1968, half a million U.S. soldiers were fighting in the **Vietnam War**.

Part of South Vietnam is hilly land covered with thick jungle. Viet Cong guerrillas could hide in the jungle, fire on U.S. troops, and then escape. The Americans often did not see their enemy or know where the shots were coming from. To destroy the Viet Cong's cover, the Americans sprayed the chemical Agent Orange. It killed the vegetation.

American bombers destroyed roads and bridges in North Vietnam. They also bombed Viet Cong bases in South Vietnam. Bombs often fell on villages, killing civilians.

In 1968, the North Vietnamese launched a widespread attack on South Vietnam. It happened during the Vietnamese holiday of Tet, and it took the Americans by surprise. This attack is known as the **Tet Offensive**. The Tet Offensive was a **crucial** turning point in the war, in favor of North Vietnam. The Tet Offensive proved that the war was far from over.

Academic Vocabulary

crucial • *adj.*, very important

Protests at Home

Even before the Tet Offensive, many Americans at home had begun to question the United States' role in Vietnam. On television, they could see how brutal the war was. They were shocked to see how many American soldiers were injured or killed. Antiwar protests became common.

College students held rallies against the conflict. In 1970, President Richard Nixon announced that the United States had bombed Viet Cong bases in Cambodia. At this, protests increased. Then a protest at Kent State University in Ohio turned deadly. Troops were called in to keep order. But during the event, soldiers shot and killed four unarmed protesters. Americans were horrified.

2. **☑ Reading Check** **Distinguish Fact From Opinion Describe** the antiwar rally shown in the picture by writing two statements. Make one statement a fact and the other an opinion.

_____

_____

This antiwar rally was held in Washington, D.C., in 1969.

The End of the Vietnam War

In May 1968, peace talks began. They continued for years with little progress. In 1969, President Nixon started relying more on the South Vietnamese to fight the war. He withdrew 25,000 U.S. soldiers.

In January 1973, the peace talks finally ended in a cease-fire. That allowed the United States to pull all its combat troops out of Vietnam. But the withdrawal did not stop the fighting between North and South Vietnamese soldiers.

By 1975, the North Vietnamese had taken control of some regions of the South. In April 1975, with the capital city, Saigon, about to fall to the North Vietnamese, South Vietnam surrendered. The nation was then unified as the communist country of Vietnam.

The Vietnam War was hard on both soldiers and civilians.

3. ☑ **Reading Check** **Analyze** this photograph of American soldiers. Write how it captures the hardships of war.

_____

_____

_____

_____

The Vietnam War caused **widespread** death and destruction. Bombs smashed whole villages and towns. Chemicals like Agent Orange destroyed the countryside. Millions of Vietnamese soldiers and civilians were killed. Thousands of South Vietnamese fled their country in small, flimsy boats. Many immigrated to the United States.

The Vietnam War cost the United States a great deal as well. More than 58,000 Americans died, and many more were wounded in this war. The war had also failed to contain communism. The unified nation of Vietnam was now communist. Many Americans feared that communism would continue to spread in Asia.

Academic Vocabulary

widespread • *adj.*, across a large area

INTERACTIVITY

Check your understanding of the key ideas of this lesson.

☑ Lesson 3 Check

4. **Distinguish Fact From Opinion Describe** the Korean War in two sentences. Make the first one a fact and the second one an opinion.

_____

_____

_____

5. In 1968, you take a dangerous trip to Vietnam to report on the war there. **Describe** what officials and soldiers tell you.

_____

_____

_____

6. **Understand the** **Connections** What kind of political system did Harry Truman refer to when he described the Korean conflict as a danger to "free nations"? **Explain** how this idea connects to the Cold War.

_____

_____

_____

Recognize Bias

Suppose you are writing about a sporting event for your school newspaper. Would your story treat your team the same as its big rival? Probably not. In fact, you would likely show a bias in favor of your team. Bias is a point of view that is affected by strongly held beliefs. Bias can appear in history sources, too. Look at the cartoon below. The caption talks about a dove with an olive branch, which is an ancient symbol of peace. Is the cartoon biased?

SHAKING THE OLIVE BRANCH

Use the following steps to identify bias.

1. Look for exaggeration or one-sided language. They suggest opinions, not facts.

2. Look for words or images that ask you to feel a certain way.

3. Identify the source. Sources often express bias for a reason.

4. Summarize the information. Using your own words to describe the information can make any bias more obvious.

Your Turn!

Answer the questions below about the cartoon you just studied.
Decide whether the cartoonist was biased or not.

 VIDEO

Watch a video about
recognizing bias.

1. **Identify** who the person in the cartoon stands for. **Explain** how
   you know.

   _____

   _____

2. **Identify** what the person in the cartoon is doing. **Explain** what
   his actions mean.

   _____

   _____

   _____

3. **Identify** the cartoonist's possible nationality. Then **identify** the
   details that support your answer.

   _____

   _____

   _____

4. **Identify** the cartoon's message. **Describe** its message in your
   own words.

   _____

   _____

5. Reread the section titled **Protests at Home** in Lesson 3. Think
   about the Vietnamese point of view. Use a separate sheet of
   paper to **create** a protest sign with a Vietnamese bias.

The End of the Cold War

INTERACTIVITY

Participate in a class discussion to preview the content of this lesson.

Unlock The BIG Question

I will know that American leaders worked to try to end the Cold War.

Vocabulary

arms control
embargo
diplomacy

Academic Vocabulary

collapse
cease

JumpStart Activity

A diplomat is a representative of a country. Work with a partner to act out a quick dialogue between U.S. and Soviet diplomats. After your dialogue, think about what each side wants and what compromises each side might need to make for peace.

During the 1950s, the Cold War was a struggle between two superpowers. In the 1960s, some things changed. The United States and the Soviet Union began to talk about limiting the production of weapons.

A 1971 parade in Moscow shows Soviet military strength.

Arms Control

The United States and the Soviet Union both knew the arms race was dangerous, but they were not sure how to stop it. After the Cuban Missile Crisis in 1962, the two nations took small steps. In 1963, they agreed to new guidelines to limit nuclear testing. Only underground tests would be allowed. In 1968, they agreed, by treaty, not to spread nuclear weapons to other countries. But neither agreement slowed the arms race.

INTERACTIVITY

Explore the key ideas of this lesson.

In 1967, President Lyndon Johnson met with the Soviet leader, Leonid Brezhnev. They talked about **arms control**, or limiting the production of weapons. Their discussion began what were called the Strategic Arms Limitation Talks, or SALT.

When Richard Nixon became president, the talks became more serious. In May 1972, President Nixon traveled to the Soviet Union. He was the first U.S. president to visit the capital, Moscow. There, he and Leonid Brezhnev signed SALT I.

Carter (left) and Brezhnev (right) at the SALT II talks

The SALT I agreement froze the number of certain kinds of nuclear weapons. Neither nation would produce more than it already had. It put a cap on the number of missiles that could be launched from submarines. SALT I also stated that each side would destroy a given number of older nuclear weapons.

In 1979, the SALT II agreement put even more limits on the number of missiles each side could produce. But it still did not stop the arms race.

1. ☑ **Reading Check** Draw Inferences Explain why there was a danger of spreading nuclear weapons to other countries.

_____

_____

_____

Tensions Rise and Fall

The quest for arms control helped ease tensions during the Cold War. Improving United States–Soviet relations was a key part of American foreign policy. But it was not the only part.

U.S. and Chinese players compete

In 1972, before he went to the Soviet Union, President Nixon became the first United States president to go to China. China had been a fierce rival and enemy of the United States. Nixon's goal was to establish friendly ties with this growing communist power. He met with Mao Zedong, China's leader.

Nixon's trip was possible because of actions the United States had already taken. In 1969, the United States loosened restrictions on travel by Americans to China. In 1971, it ended an **embargo**, or ban, on trade with that nation, too. The Chinese responded with a surprising invitation.

2. ☑ **Reading Check**
Analyze the steps the United States took to improve relations with China.

In 1971, they asked the United States ping-pong team to come to China. The next year the Chinese team visited the United States. Journalists called it "ping-pong diplomacy." **Diplomacy** is the art of handling relations between nations.

During the same year, the United States proposed that China take a seat in the UN Security Council. At the time, the seat was held by an American ally, Taiwan.

Anticommunist Chinese had fled to Taiwan and separated from mainland China. American recognition of Taiwan as the rightful government of China was a very sore point. During his visit, Nixon accepted that Taiwan was a part of China.

Nixon's trips were great diplomatic successes. He helped bring about friendlier relations between the United States and the world's two most powerful communist countries. However, a new conflict soon emerged in central Asia.

In 1956, Soviet leader Nikita Khrushchev had begun providing military and economic support to Afghanistan. Then, in 1978, the Afghan Communist Party overthrew the ruling government. At first, it seemed like communism had successfully spread to Afghanistan. However, a movement of rebel guerrillas, the *mujahedin* (moo jayh heh DEEN), developed later that year. They began fighting the communist government.

Then, in December 1979, the Soviet Union invaded Afghanistan. The Soviets' goal was to keep Afghanistan's communist government in power. But that government had little support from its people. Soviet troops took control of most cities, but the *mujahedin* controlled the countryside.

The United States supported the *mujahedin*. President Jimmy Carter cut grain sales to the Soviets. He stopped sales of technology to them, as well. In 1980 the Olympic Games were held in Moscow, but the United States refused to send its athletes. The Cold War had regained some of its old chill.

Words From Other Languages The term *mujahedin* comes from the Arabic word *mujahid*. It means those who are engaged in a rightful struggle. The rebel guerillas in Afghanistan took the name because they saw themselves as leaders of a struggle against the communist government.

3. ☑ **Reading Check** **Complete** the timeline on the conflict in Afghanistan.

Conflict in Afghanistan, 1950s–1980s

1978
The *mujahedin* begin to battle the Soviet-backed government.

| 1950 | 1960 | 1970 | 1980 | 1990 |

1956
_____
_____

1979
_____
_____

1989
The Soviet Union agrees to withdraw 100,000 troops from Afghanistan.

Reagan and Gorbachev

U.S. President Ronald Reagan took a strong stand against communism. He called the Soviet Union "an evil empire." He also spent billions of dollars on new weapons and on building up the United States military. Reagan thought the Soviets had a weak economy. His actions pressured them to spend more money on arms than they could afford.

In 1983, Reagan announced a new program called the Strategic Defense Initiative, or SDI. Its goal was to build a defensive shield over the United States to protect the country against a nuclear attack. It would use high-tech weapons to shoot down incoming nuclear missiles. Critics said that SDI was too expensive and would not work. The program was never fully developed.

During the Reagan years, however, the United States did make progress in arms control. Reagan did not want just to limit arms. He wanted to reduce them. In 1982, Strategic Arms Reduction Talks (START) began. They led to a new agreement with the Soviets. START called for both superpowers to begin destroying nuclear weapons. In 1991, President George H. W. Bush signed START for the United States. Mikhail Gorbachev signed it for the Soviet Union.

Gorbachev (right) and Reagan (left) chat during an official meeting in the Soviet Union in 1988.

Mikhail Gorbachev played a key role in ending the Cold War. In the mid-1980s, he led the Soviet Union into a new era. Gorbachev was a reformer. He introduced some basic capitalist elements to the Soviet economy. He allowed some democratic freedoms. He tried to open the Soviet Union to the outside world.

The spirit of reform spread from the Soviet Union to other communist countries under Soviet control. In 1989, communist governments began to fall in Eastern Europe and within Soviet states. Democratic governments took their place. In Poland, Hungary, and elsewhere, the people started freely electing their own leaders. Gorbachev did not try to stop them.

4. **☑ Reading Check**
Distinguish Fact From Opinion Identify and circle one opinion expressed by President Reagan on this page.

Germans break down the Berlin Wall, which divided their nation for almost 30 years.

The Berlin Wall Comes Down

East Germany was another place where people demanded reform. In 1987, President Reagan visited West Berlin. In a speech at the Brandenberg Gate, near the Berlin Wall, he said:

Primary Source

"General Secretary Gorbachev, if you seek peace [. . .] come here to this gate. Mr. Gorbachev, open this gate! Mr. Gorbachev, tear down this wall!"

—Ronald Reagan, speech in West Berlin, 1987

On November 9, 1989, East German leaders were forced to open the checkpoints. They allowed free passage into West Berlin. By the end of 1990, East Germans and others had torn down much of the wall.

5. **☑ Reading Check** **Describe** how President Reagan contributed to the removal of the Berlin Wall.

_____

_____

_____

Breakup of the Soviet Union, 1991

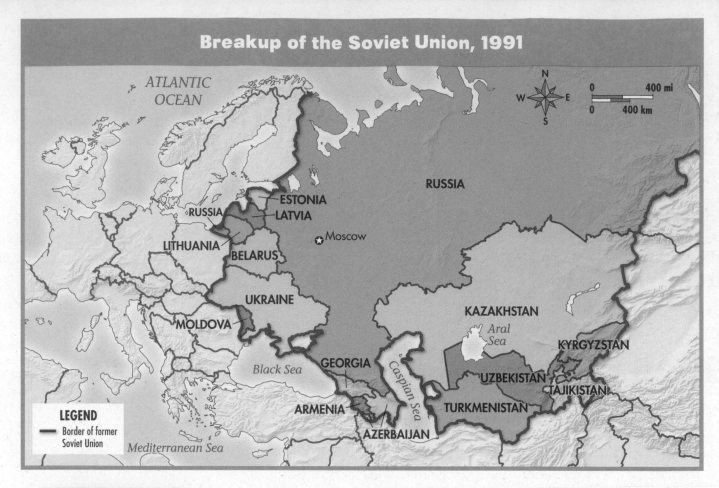

6. ☑ **Reading Check**
Analyze the map.
Circle the names of the countries in Europe that came from the old Soviet Union.

The End of Communism and the Cold War

In 1990, the Cold War was clearly ending. The reforms Reagan and Gorbachev began had led to reduced Soviet power in Europe. Gorbachev withdrew troops from the nations the Soviets had controlled in Eastern Europe. East and West Germany were reunified into a single Germany.

Communism had been strong and long-lived in the Soviet Union. The Communist Party there was still powerful. Some Soviet officials saw Gorbachev's reforms as a threat to their influence and way of life. In 1991, they tried to overthrow him. Their plot failed.

Academic Vocabulary

collapse • *v.*, to fall apart
cease • *v.*, to stop; to end

The Soviet Union had begun to **collapse**. Several republics within the Soviet Union decided to secede, or leave. The Soviet Union had been made up of 15 republics, or separate states. These republics wanted to form democratic governments and become independent. By the end of 1991, they achieved this goal. The Soviet Union had **ceased** to exist.

7. ☑ **Reading Check** **Identify** two important events and dates about the end of communism in Europe and add them to the timeline.

The End of Communism

1989

_____

_____

_____

1991

_____

_____

_____

| **1981** | **1986** | **1991** |

INTERACTIVITY

Check your understanding of the key ideas of this lesson.

☑ Lesson 4 Check

8. Compare and Contrast Describe the main difference between the SALT and START agreements.

_____

_____

9. You interview the leaders who signed the SALT treaty and decide you can tell the story best with a political cartoon. Write some of your ideas below. Then on a separate sheet of paper, **draw** a cartoon.

_____

_____

_____

10. Why did Ronald Reagan's speech use the words "if you seek peace"? Explain the context of his speech.

_____

_____

_____

Quality
Leadership

Ellen Ochoa (1958–)
American Astronaut

Born in Los Angeles, California, Ellen Ochoa grew up during the Cold War. Ochoa followed the news of the *Apollo* missions. When she was 11 years old, she watched Neil Armstrong walk on the moon. At that time, there were no women flying on space missions. Ochoa did not consider becoming an astronaut.

Ochoa studied physics and electrical engineering. In 1988, she joined NASA as a researcher. It was not long before Ochoa was selected to be a NASA astronaut! She became a mission specialist and flight engineer for the space shuttle. Ochoa was the first Hispanic woman to go into space.

Ellen Ochoa served on four space shuttle missions. Altogether, she spent nearly 1,000 hours in space. Today, Ochoa serves as the director of NASA's Lyndon B. Johnson Space Center, in Houston, Texas. She is its first Hispanic director. She welcomes each new class of astronauts. Of the 2017 astronaut recruits, Ochoa said, "Children all across the United States right now dream of being in their shoes someday."

Find Out More

1. How do you think the space race influenced Ellen Ochoa? Explain your answer.

_____

_____

_____

2. Ellen Ochoa is a physicist and engineer. What qualities do you think astronauts need? Discuss with a partner.

_____

_____

_____

Visual Review

Use these graphics to review some of the key terms, people, and ideas from this chapter.

A Look at the Cold War

Money spent on the Space Race
1957-1964 (USD)

USA 15.9 billion

Soviet Union about 10.2 billion

Nuclear Weapons
1982

USA 22,886

Soviet Union 33,486

USA

Soviet Union

East Germans fleeing to West Germany

1949-1961: about 2,500,000 🏃🏃🏃🏃🏃🏃🏃🏃🏃🏃🏃🏃🏃🏃🏃🏃🏃🏃🏃🏃

1962-1989: 5,000 🏃

Actions Contributing to Cold War Tensions

United States	Soviet Union
Developed atomic weapons during World War II	Took over Eastern European states
Became more active in Europe due to the Marshall Plan	Built the Berlin Wall
Used the American military to back NATO	Secretly built military installations in Cuba
Led the Red Scare and anti-communist ideas	Gained atomic power in 1949

Vocabulary and Key Ideas

1. **Describe** What was the Cold War?

_____

_____

2. **Explain** What was the Cuban Missile Crisis?

_____

_____

3. **Analyze** the line graph. It shows the number of nuclear weapons the United States had during the Cold War arms race. During which decade was the number the highest?

_____

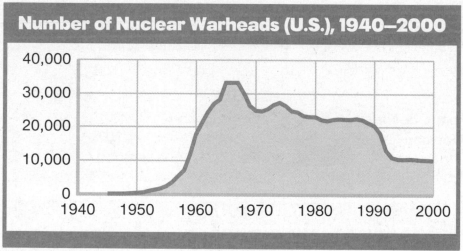

Number of Nuclear Warheads (U.S.), 1940–2000

Source: Nuclear Threat Initiative Project

4. Why do you think the number of nuclear weapons fell during the 1970s and 1980s?

_____

_____

_____

Critical Thinking and Writing

5. **Analyze** Why did Winston Churchill call the divide in Europe an Iron Curtain?

_____

_____

_____

6. **Identifying Points of View** How did Senator Joseph McCarthy feel about communism?

_____

_____

_____

7. **Summarize** How did the Cold War change throughout the presidencies of Lyndon Johnson, Richard Nixon, and Ronald Reagan?

_____

_____

_____

_____

_____

8. **Revisit the Big Question** Why did the leaders of the United States and the Soviet Union choose to avoid open warfare during the Cold War?

_____

_____

_____

9. **Writing Workshop: Narrative** Taking the role of a citizen of East Berlin, describe your plan for escape over the Berlin Wall. Use a separate sheet of paper to write your plan.

Analyze Primary Sources

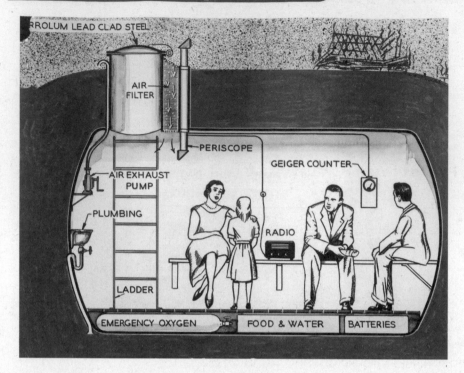

Illustration of a family bomb shelter

10. What is happening in this Cold War drawing? Use details from the text to support your answer.

_____

_____

11. What three types of supplies are shown at the base of the shelter? Why are these included?

_____

_____

_____

Writing Persuasive Speeches

12. Work with a partner to write a short speech about the Berlin Airlift. What is the who, what, where, and when of your speech? Use a separate sheet of paper for your speech.

Quest Findings

Write Your Speech

Now you are ready to write your speech. Decide what topic you will use in your speech. How will you persuade people? What facts and opinions will you use? What persuasive language will you use?

INTERACTIVITY

Use this interactivity to help you write your speech.

1 **Make Your Choices**

Choose the Cold War topic for which you want to write a speech. Decide which issue you will write about.

2 **Gather Evidence**

Use resources from your classroom, Library Media Center, or the Internet. Decide on the primary sources you will use and the tone you will use in your speech.

3 **Write Your Speech**

Write and revise your speech. Be sure to describe the issue and propose an action or idea. Write in a persuasive style. Use language and tone to create a strong speech.

4 **Talk About It**

Work with a partner. Explain how and why you took a specific persuasive approach in your speech.

16 America Changes

GO ONLINE FOR
DIGITAL RESOURCES

▶ VIDEO

👆 INTERACTIVITY

🔊 AUDIO

🎮 GAMES

☑ ASSESSMENT

📖 eTEXT

The **BIG** Question

When does change become necessary?

▶ VIDEO

Lesson 1
Postwar America

Lesson 2
Civil Rights

Lesson 3
From the Great Society to Reagan

Jumpstart Activity

👆 INTERACTIVITY

Work with a partner. Describe something in your school or community that you think should be changed. Make a list of ideas that you could do to help bring about the change.

Rap About It!

🔊 AUDIO

Changing Times

Preview the chapter **vocabulary** as you sing the rap.

All of the **veterans** who fought in the war,
Wanted to come home and finally buy more.
New cars, new houses, and the **baby boom**,
"We have more stuff, we need more room!"

New TVs washers and **credit cards**,
They allowed us to live in suburban yards.

African Americans had the right to be,
Came at a cost that only they could see.
Even though they had to suffer, they still
   could make a choice,
Through Martin Luther King they could find a voice.

From the 60s and on, **the Great Society**
Demanded change from all the sides to ease anxiety.

The 1970s were full of actions that would scare,
President Nixon resigned in an act of despair.

The 1980s brought with it a surprise,
Cut taxes, cut spending, get out of peoples lives.

16 America Changes

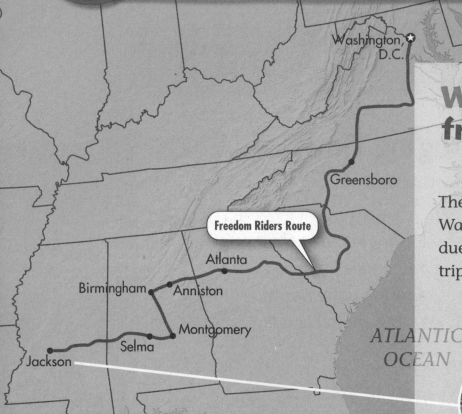

Washington, D.C.

Greensboro

Freedom Riders Route

Atlanta

Birmingham — Anniston

Montgomery

Selma

Jackson

ATLANTIC OCEAN

Where did the first freedom ride begin and end?

The first Freedom Riders left Washington, D.C., in May 1961, and due to attacks, they shortened their trip to end in Jackson, Mississippi.

Freedom Riders

TODAY
The Freedom Riders National Monument is located in Anniston, Alabama. It was established by President Barack Obama in January 2017.

What happened and When?

Read the timeline to discover all the changes that occurred from the 1950s to the 1980s.

1950   1955   1960   1965

1951
Scientists introduce the Universal Automatic Computer.

1963
Martin Luther King, Jr. leads the March on Washington.

1964
Civil Rights Act becomes law.

TODAY
85 percent of American homes have some type of a computer.

Who will you meet?

Thurgood Marshall
First African American Supreme Court justice

Rachel Carson
A scientist who wrote about her concerns about the effects of pollution and pesticides on the environment

Jackie Robinson
The first African American major league baseball player

César Chávez
A Latino American labor leader and civil rights activist

INTERACTIVITY

Complete the interactive digital activity.

1970   **1975**   **1980**   **1985**

1983
Astronaut Sally Ride is the first American woman in space.

TODAY
As of July 2017, 50 women have flown with NASA.

Equality Once and for All

In this chapter, you will learn about a number of groups and their leaders who fought for civil rights, the rights that all people should have. You will learn about Martin Luther King, Jr., and César Chávez. These are two leaders who believed in using nonviolent protests to gain rights. They also used moving speeches to inspire their groups. For example, King's "I Have a Dream" speech is a famous example of an inspiring speech.

Quest Kick Off

Your task is to write and deliver a speech to give at a peaceful protest march to convince participants of your point of view. Choose from one of the important postwar era movements you will learn about in this chapter.

1 Ask Questions

What movement will you choose? What was the purpose of the movement? Write two questions you have about your chosen movement.

....

....

....

2 Research

Follow your teacher's instructions to find examples of speeches given at protests or marches for different movements and to analyze speeches. How do the speakers try to persuade and motivate their audiences? Write some of your ideas on the lines.

INTERACTIVITY

Complete the interactivity to learn more about important speeches.

3 Look for Quest Connections

Begin looking for Quest Connections that will help you write your speech.

4 Quest Findings
Write Your Speech

Use the Quest Findings page at the end of the chapter to help you write your speech.

INTERACTIVITY

Participate in a class discussion to preview the content of this lesson.

Vocabulary

veteran
baby boom
credit card
G.I. Bill of Rights
suburb

Academic Vocabulary

benefit
decade

Unlock
The **BIG**
Question

I will know how America changed after World War II.

JumpStart Activity

After World War II, many new and improved household items and new technologies made life easier for Americans. Today, technology continues to affect the way we learn and live. Work with a partner to list three ways technology has affected your lives.

When World War II was over, Americans were ready for change. Soldiers came home, and families were reunited. Marion Gurfein had not seen her soldier husband for three years. Almost 60 years later she remembered the day he returned from the war: "[T]he door opened and there was Joe and I guess that was one of the greatest moments of my life." Then she turned to introduce him to his daughter, who had been born while he was away fighting.

A World War II soldier is reunited with his family.

Boom Years

During the war, millions of soldiers had put their lives on hold as they fought for freedom. Now the returning soldiers and Americans who had been on the home front were ready to enjoy life.

Many **veterans**, people who have fought in a war, wanted to start families. So many babies were born in the years from 1945 to 1964 that historians call this wave of births after World War II the **baby boom**. About 76 million babies were part of the baby boom. All these new families needed new houses, more goods, and more services. These were "boom times" for the economy as well as for the population.

The Changing Workplace

During World War II, many women took factory jobs that were usually held by men. By the end of the war, women made up one third of the workforce. When veterans came home, however, they took their jobs back. Soon, most women were once again at home, working as housewives and mothers.

There was no shortage of jobs. Manufacturing grew because employed Americans could afford to buy more. In this booming economy, many American consumers had a high standard of living. During the war, scarce items like meat, rubber, and gasoline had been rationed, or given out sparingly. Now people wanted the plentiful goods that went with their new modern lives, including cars, washing machines, televisions, and refrigerators.

Credit cards helped them pay for these goods. A **credit card** lets a user charge goods and services and pay for them later. Users pay a fee if they do not repay the charge within a certain time period.

By the end of the 1950s, the American economy was changing. It had been based on manufacturing since the Industrial Revolution. By 1960, more and more people were starting careers in service industries such as sales, teaching, or medicine.

INTERACTIVITY

Explore the key ideas of this lesson.

The Growth of Suburbs

As millions of G.I.s, or United States soldiers, returned from the war, they wanted better lives. For many, this meant raising their new families in homes of their own. Thanks to the law known as the G.I. Bill of Rights, many of them could afford homes. The **G.I. Bill of Rights** gave veterans funds for education, home loans, and other **benefits**.

It wasn't easy to find housing, however. The nation had a shortage of about 5 million houses. However, there was no shortage of space outside cities. Builders like William Levitt had an answer. They built massive developments of inexpensive houses in the suburbs. A **suburb** is a community outside a city. The first of these "instant suburbs" was Levitt's own Levittown in New York. The almost 18,000 two-bedroom houses sold for less than $10,000. "We had achieved the American dream," said one Levittown homeowner.

1. ☑ **Reading Check** **Analyze** and **describe** the trend the graph shows you about home ownership at this time.

_____

_____

A suburban family enjoys a backyard barbeque.

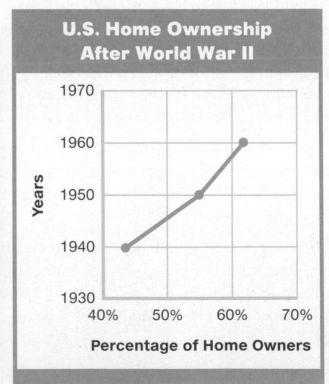

U.S. Home Ownership After World War II

Years

Percentage of Home Owners

Source: U.S. Census Bureau

As the nation's population exploded, more and more people moved out of cities and into suburbs. By 1950, more Americans lived in suburbs than in any other kind of community. By the end of the **decade**, more than 60 percent of Americans owned their own homes.

Life in the suburbs depended on transportation. Trains and buses carried workers in and out of nearby cities. However, in sprawling suburban neighborhoods, people needed cars. They drove to buy groceries, take children to school, or go to the train station. Having a car was not a luxury. It was a necessity.

Growing car ownership affected other parts of American life. Better roads were needed, for example. In 1954, President Dwight Eisenhower announced funding for a new interstate highway system. The roads modified the environment by cutting through landscapes. Today the system is called the Dwight D. Eisenhower System of Interstate and Defense Highways. New roads connected suburbs with cities and cities with one another. More efficient distribution of goods by trucks contributed further to the booming economy.

2. ☑ Reading Check **Main Idea and Details** Based on what you have read in this lesson, **describe** details in the diagram to support the main idea.

The Booming Fifties

Main Idea
The 1950s were a time of economic growth.

Detail
Veterans returned home and started families.

Detail
_____
_____
_____

Detail
_____
_____
_____

New Technology

After the war, American scientists and engineers could concentrate on peacetime technology. The result was an explosion of inventions. Many changed people's lives forever.

In the field of medicine, a vaccine was introduced in 1955 to prevent a widespread, serious disease called polio. The vaccine nearly eliminated the disease in the United States within just a few years.

Transistor radios made music portable. Direct-dial telephone service connected the nation. Jet planes let travelers cross the country in just hours. Americans came to expect a more comfortable and convenient life.

A new field—computer science—was just developing. In 1951, scientists introduced the UNIVAC (Universal Automatic Computer). The UNIVAC was 7 feet tall and 14 feet wide. It was first used to sort data from the 1950 United States Census.

Television might have changed life more than any other invention. Television was not new. But in 1946 only 8,000 American homes had a TV. By 1950 the number had skyrocketed to more than 5 million. By 1959 almost 44 million American homes had television sets.

Watching TV became a popular family pastime in the 1950s.

3. ☑ **Reading Check** How do you think television changed family life? **Identify** some things this family might have done together before television.

_____

_____

_____

_____

Television in 1950s America

Television broadcasts expanded during the 1950s. Three radio networks, NBC, CBS, and ABC, became television networks. They produced news shows, sports, comedies, and dramas.

Television not only entertained but also affected politics. The first coast-to-coast television broadcast was a speech by President Harry Truman in 1951. In 1960, 70 million viewers watched the first-ever televised debates between presidential candidates Richard Nixon and John Kennedy. Many people thought Kennedy won the debates because he looked so much better on television than Nixon did.

Television had a huge impact on people's lives. By the end of the 1950s, Americans watched an average of six hours of television a day. Families watched TV together. One food company even packaged "TV dinners" so that families could eat while watching a TV show.

The televised Nixon-Kennedy debates helped John F. Kennedy (right) win the 1960 presidential election.

American Popular Culture

In the 1950s, new technology let people across the country share culture. Television and portable radios helped. Musicians, sports figures, and actors became major national stars. Some even became popular in other countries.

Elvis Presley (left) appeared on *The Ed Sullivan Show* in 1956.

A new kind of music, called rock-and-roll, swept the nation. Rock-and-roll used old-style country and western sounds. It added in the rhythm and blues of African American music. In the mid-1950s, its most famous performer was Elvis Presley. Presley appeared on *The Ed Sullivan Show* in 1956. About 60 million people watched. It was the largest TV audience up to that time.

Throughout the 1950s, many African American rock-and-rollers became world-famous. Musicians such as Chuck Berry and Little Richard helped make rock-and-roll popular. In 1959, Detroit's Motown Records became a center of African American popular music. Motown helped bring African American music to a worldwide audience.

4. ☑ **Reading Check** **Draw a conclusion** about why you think appearing on television was important for Elvis Presley's career.

_____

_____

_____

_____

In the 1960s, folk singers began to sing about the need for political and social change. One of the most famous folk singers was Bob Dylan. Dylan protested old ways and urged listeners to think seriously about the nation's problems.

The 1960s also saw popular singers like the Beatles, Johnny Cash, Hank Williams, and Aretha Franklin rise to stardom. These artists and their music still influence popular music and culture today.

The Four Tops, a band from Detroit, Michigan, perform.

 INTERACTIVITY

Check your understanding of the key ideas of this lesson.

☑ Lesson 1 Check

5. **Main Idea and Details** Cars were important in the growth of suburbs and benefited people's lives. **Identify** at least two details to support that idea.

_____

_____

_____

6. **Draw Conclusions** If you were a reporter working in postwar America, what important changes caused by new technology would you describe?

_____

_____

7. **Summarize** Reread American Popular Culture and create an outline of the main idea and supporting details. Then use your outline to write a summary.

_____

_____

_____

_____

_____

_____

Make a Difference

How can you make a difference? Your first step should be to identify the problem you want to help solve. What problems do you hear about in the news? What problems do you see around you every day?

Your next step is to develop a solution. What will you need to do to solve the problem? Who can help you? What are some advantages and disadvantages of the solution?

Finally, it's time to put your plan into action. Share your plan with people to get them involved. A huge movement can start with just a few people.

Now read about an elementary school student who used these simple steps to make a big difference.

When Brandon Keefe was in elementary school, he decided to make a difference. One day he visited the Hollygrove Children's Home, a place for children in trouble. Brandon found out that Hollygrove wanted to start a library, but they did not have money to buy books. Brandon thought about all the books he had at home. He could give away those he had already read. So could his friends.

The next day at school, Brandon talked to his classmates. He suggested that they hold a book drive. Brandon decided collecting books for Hollygrove would help the children. However, he could not collect all of the books himself. Brandon asked his classmates and teachers to help. They made fliers. They gave speeches at school. Soon they had collected almost 900 books for Hollygrove.

Brandon's idea led to an organization called BookEnds. Robin Keefe, Brandon's mother, founded BookEnds more than 10 years ago.

BookEnds helps students organize book drives. They give books to places that need them. So far they have donated about 2 million books to almost 500,000 children.

Young Brandon Keefe

How did Brandon Keefe make a difference?

1. What problem did Brandon identify?

_____

_____

2. What solution did he develop?

_____

_____

3. How did Brandon put his plan into action?

_____

_____

_____

4. **Apply** How can you make a difference? Work in a small group
to identify a problem in your school or in your community.
Think of at least one solution that you can all agree on. Identify
the advantages and disadvantages of the solution. Then describe
how this solution would make a difference to your fellow students
or the people in your community.

_____

_____

_____

_____

_____

_____

VIDEO

Watch a video about working in cooperative teams to learn about making a difference with others.

2 Civil Rights

👆 INTERACTIVITY

Participate in a class discussion to preview the content of this lesson.

Unlock The BIG Question

I will know how African Americans struggled for civil rights.

Vocabulary

civil rights
discrimination
integration
sit-in
freedom ride

Academic Vocabulary

challenge
alternative

Jumpstart Activity

Civil rights are basic freedoms and protections. Work with a partner to make a list of all the freedoms you have as Americans. Then share your list with another group.

Thelma Williams grew up in the South before World War II. It was a time and place where African Americans and white Americans were kept separate in many ways. "There were these hard separation lines that you simply did not cross," Ms. Williams remembered. In the postwar years, those lines of separation were strong. But they were about to weaken.

COLORED WAITING ROOM

PRIVATE PROPERTY NO PARKING
Driving through or Turning Around

Laws that separated black and white Americans were called Jim Crow laws. Segregated facilities, like waiting areas, were common before civil rights reform.

COACH COMPANY

45

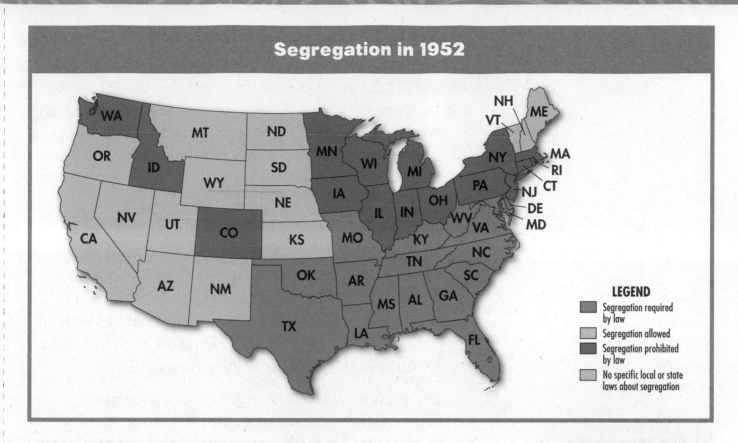

Segregation in 1952

LEGEND
- Segregation required by law
- Segregation allowed
- Segregation prohibited by law
- No specific local or state laws about segregation

A Long History of Segregation

The United States Constitution guarantees civil rights to free Americans of all races. **Civil rights** are basic freedoms and protections, such as the right to a fair trial. In the late 1800s, African Americans were being denied their civil rights. This was especially true in the South.

In 1896, the Supreme Court judged a now-famous legal case, *Plessy* v. *Ferguson*. It said that separation of races in public places was legal if the facilities, though separate, were equal. This ruling made racial segregation, or separation, legal.

Look at the map. It shows where segregation was required or allowed by 1952. Even in places where segregation was not the law, African Americans often faced **discrimination**, or the unfair treatment of people based on race or gender.

African Americans built strong communities across the nation. They ran successful businesses. There were African American colleges, clubs, and theaters. African American scientists, entertainers, and authors were famous for their achievements. Nonetheless, segregation isolated African Americans. In reality, "separate but equal" did not work.

INTERACTIVITY

Explore the key ideas of this lesson.

Breaking the Color Barrier

On April 15, 1947, Jack Roosevelt Robinson stepped onto the field at Dodger Stadium in Brooklyn, New York. It was a historic moment. African Americans had played in their own Negro League since the late 1800s. No African Americans had been allowed to play in Major League Baseball. Dodgers manager Branch Rickey hired Jackie Robinson from the Negro League. Robinson was a brave and outstanding player, and he now broke the "color barrier." However, he still faced terrible racism from white players and fans.

A year later, President Harry Truman issued an executive order. He stated that "there shall be equality of treatment and opportunity for all persons in the armed services without regard to race, color, religion, or national origin." The United States armed services were officially no longer segregated.

Like Robinson, other African Americans were also breaking down the color barrier. In 1950, Ralph Bunche became the first African American to win the Nobel Peace Prize. In that same year, Gwendolyn Brooks became the first African American poet to win the Pulitzer Prize. Meanwhile, something larger was going on. The National Association for the Advancement of Colored People (NAACP) was planning to overturn *Plessy* v. *Ferguson*.

1. ☑ **Reading Check**
Main Idea and Details
Examine the chart. Fill in supporting details using examples from the text.

Fighting Discrimination

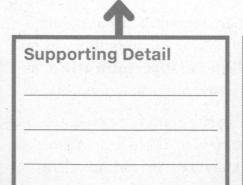

Main Idea
People worked to break the color barrier.

Supporting Detail
President Truman ordered equal treatment of African Americans in the military.

Supporting Detail

_____
_____
_____

Supporting Detail

_____
_____
_____

Ending School Segregation

In the early 1950s, the NAACP asked for legal trials in Kansas, South Carolina, Virginia, and Delaware. All the trials claimed that separate education was not equal education. Eventually, these court cases went to the Supreme Court. Together they were called *Brown* v. *Board of Education of Topeka*. Topeka is a community in Kansas.

The lawyer for the NAACP was the gifted Thurgood Marshall. Marshall spent his career fighting segregation, arguing 32 cases before the Supreme Court and winning 29 of them.

At the center of the *Brown* case was a young girl named Linda Brown. She lived in Topeka and went to an all-African American school far from her house. Why couldn't Linda go to the all-white school close to home?

In 1954, the Supreme Court agreed that she could. It said that "separate educational facilities are inherently [basically] unequal." This decision changed American life.

It would be years before **integration**, or the mixing of different groups, came to all American schools. But the *Brown* decision had improved civil rights for millions of African Americans.

Mother and daughter sit on the Supreme Court steps after the *Brown* v. *Board of Education* ruling, which ended segregation in public schools.

The News
HIGH COURT BANS SEGREGATION IN PUBLIC SCHOOLS

The Montgomery Bus Boycott

In the 1950s, Montgomery, Alabama, was one of the most segregated cities in the nation. However, the movement for change would come to Montgomery, too.

Academic Vocabulary

challenge • *v.*, to say or show that an idea may not be legal or true

alternative • *n.*, other choice

A woman named Rosa Parks was in the local NAACP. Parks **challenged** one of Montgomery's Jim Crow laws. The law said that African Americans had to sit in the back of public buses. On December 1, 1955, Parks refused to move to the back of a bus. She was jailed for it.

In response, African Americans in Montgomery organized a boycott of city buses. A majority of Montgomery's bus riders were African American. In the end, the bus company was forced to give in and let everyone sit where they wished on the city's buses, or go out of business.

The boycott's leader was a 26-year-old minister named Martin Luther King, Jr. "We have no **alternative** but to protest," King said. He understood that the African American community could no longer be patient "with anything less than freedom and justice."

Peaceful but powerful protests like the Montgomery bus boycott were at the heart of King's belief in nonviolence. He urged peaceful resistance to injustice, not violence. "Nonviolence is a powerful and just weapon," he said. "It is a sword that heals." Martin Luther King, Jr., shaped the nation's civil rights movement with this belief in nonviolence.

Protests Spread

Over the next ten years, the strength of the civil rights movement grew. School integration began slowly, however. Arkansas was one of the few states to start integrating schools. In September 1957, nine African American students were ready to integrate Central High School in the city of Little Rock. But the governor of Arkansas refused to let them begin classes. Violence erupted. Finally, President Eisenhower sent 1,000 United States Army soldiers to Little Rock. They were ordered to protect "the Little Rock Nine" at school.

Meanwhile, African Americans and white supporters tried to integrate other public places. In 1960, four African American college students in North Carolina staged the first **sit-in**. They sat quietly at a whites-only lunch counter. The manager asked them to leave, but they refused. Soon, sit-ins were happening in cities across the South.

Nonviolence was sometimes met with violence. In the summer of 1961, 13 civil rights protestors went on the first freedom ride. On **freedom rides**, African American and white protesters rode buses together to integrate bus lines. The Freedom Riders were often in danger from those who did not want segregation to end. Rider John Lewis was 21 years old that summer. He remembered the violence. "I thought I was going to die," he said after his bus was burned and he was beaten.

Still, the protests continued. In Birmingham, Alabama, in 1963, children and adults, including Martin Luther King, Jr., marched and went to jail to protest segregation. Reverend Fred Shuttlesworth was a leader of the African American community in Birmingham. To bring about change, he said, you might have "to suffer for what you believe in. . . . That's what the movement is all about."

2. ☑ **Reading Check**
Summarize Turn and talk to your partner about how peaceful protests contributed to the civil rights movement.

Sit-ins were a form of peaceful protest.

New Civil Rights Laws

On August 28, 1963, Martin Luther King, Jr., stood on the steps of the Lincoln Memorial in Washington, D.C. He called the crowd of more than 200,000 people in front of him "the greatest demonstration for freedom in the history of our nation." In the most famous part of his "I Have a Dream" speech, King said that day,

Primary Source

I have a dream that my four little children will one day live in a nation where they will not be judged by the color of their skin but by the content of their character.

—Martin Luther King, Jr., speech in Washington, D.C., August 28, 1963

Martin Luther King, Jr.

Quest Connection

What point of view was Martin Luther King, Jr. trying to share with the crowd on August 28, 1963?

INTERACTIVITY

Learn more about how to use words to create powerful speeches that inspire people for your Quest by going online.

In March 1965, King led protests in Selma, Alabama, to demand voting rights. Protesters marched from Selma to the state capitol in Montgomery. The protesters were met with tear gas and beatings. The event, known as Bloody Sunday, was televised. People from around the United States and the world were angered by this treatment of peaceful marchers.

Just a few months later, Congress passed the Voting Rights Act of 1965. When he signed it, President Lyndon Johnson called it "one of the most monumental laws in the entire history of American freedom."

The victories of the 1960s were powerful. But tragedy struck when Martin Luther King, Jr., was assassinated in 1968. Today, his birthday, January 15, is a national holiday.

3. ☑ **Reading Check** **Explain** how television affected the civil rights movement. Do you think hearing protests on the radio would have had the same effect as television?

_____

_____

_____

_____

The Movement Continues

Strengthened by the civil rights movement, African Americans achieved new successes. Thurgood Marshall became the first African American justice on the United States Supreme Court in 1967. In 1968, Shirley Chisholm was the first African American woman elected to Congress. Mae Jemison became the first African American female astronaut to reach space in 1992. The list of achievements goes on and on.

In 2008, Americans elected the first African American president, Barack Obama. Obama spoke in Selma before his election. Honoring the civil rights movement, he told the crowd, "I am here because somebody marched."

Mae Jemison

INTERACTIVITY

Check your understanding of the key ideas of this lesson.

✓ Lesson 2 Check

4. **Compare and Contrast** What were similarities and differences in the Supreme Court rulings in *Plessy* v. *Ferguson* (1896) and *Brown* v. *Board of Education of Topeka* (1954)?

_____

_____

_____

_____

5. **Identify** the main goal of the civil rights movement. **Describe** two ways the movement reached its goals.

_____

_____

6. **Understand the**  **Connections** **Explain** how Martin Luther King, Jr.'s nonviolent approaches to battling segregation, such as giving speeches, was successful.

_____

Outlines and Graphic Organizers

How do writers stay organized when they are writing an expository text? Outlines and graphic organizers help to make the writing process smoother and easy to follow. An outline helps organize your research. Outlines include numbers for each main idea you plan to write about. A letter can be used to indicate supporting ideas.

Graphic organizers are helpful for seeing your notes in a visual way. There are graphic organizers to help with each kind of writing. Read the outline and graphic organizer below. Then read the paragraph that resulted from those organizing tools.

Civil Rights Leaders

1. **Linda Brown**
   A. Could not go to an all-white school
   B. Supreme Court decided she could go

2. **Rosa Parks**
   A. Refused to follow law; sat at front of city bus
   B. Actions started boycott that changed laws

3. **Dr. Martin Luther King, Jr.**
   A. Leader in the civil rights struggle
   B. Promoted nonviolence

Many people helped in the civil rights movement. A young girl named Linda Brown brought attention to the problem of segregation. The Supreme Court decided that she could attend an all-white school. Rosa Parks also challenged laws. When she refused to follow the laws of the Montgomery bus system, people boycotted and the rules were changed. Dr. Martin Luther King, Jr., led many people through the civil rights struggle by promoting nonviolence.

Civil Rights Leaders

Linda Brown | Rosa Parks | Dr. Martin Luther King, Jr.

Reread the section titled **Protests Spread**. Make an outline to help organize and summarize and interpret the section. Then complete the graphic organizer and activity at the bottom of the page.

Protests Spread

1. _____

   A. _____

   B. _____

New Civil Rights Laws

2. _____

   A. _____

   B. _____

3. _____

   A. _____

   B. _____

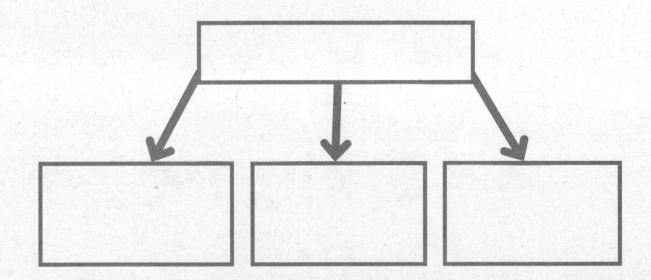

From the Great Society to Reagan

Vocabulary

the Great Society
minority group
affirmative action
impeach

Academic Vocabulary

decline
expansion

Unlock
The **BIG** Question

I will know that Americans made important social and political changes.

JumpStart Activity

Work with a partner make a list of changes you would like to see your school or community make. Then sketch a quick poster or slogan to promote one of the changes on your list.

On November 22, 1963, President John F. Kennedy was assassinated. The nation was in shock. Kennedy had been a popular president, and now a new president had to carry on his work.

President Johnson is sworn in as president.

The Great Society

Lyndon Johnson, Kennedy's vice president, became president on the same day Kennedy was assassinated. Along with leading a grieving nation, Johnson needed Congress to pass key laws. President Kennedy's civil rights bill. President Johnson got it passed. The 1964 Civil Rights Act said that there could be no discrimination in jobs and no segregation in public housing.

President Johnson did not stop there. He wanted to use his power as president to help more people. In a speech in 1964 he gave his plan a name: **the Great Society**. "The Great Society rests on abundance and liberty for all," he said. "It demands an end to poverty and racial injustice. . . . But that is just the beginning."

Americans showed Lyndon Johnson that they approved of his plans. They elected him president in 1964, with the biggest majority in United States history. President Johnson created an Office of Economic Opportunity. It managed programs like the Job Corps, which trained young people in job skills.

President Johnson's war on poverty included the Food Stamp Act to help poor people afford food. Members of the Volunteers in Service to America (VISTA) program worked on many projects, such as building homes and fighting illiteracy, to help less-fortunate Americans.

Congress passed bills to reform health and education. Medicare and Medicaid were designed to provide assistance to older or disadvantaged citizens. Other programs, like Head Start, provided money for early education.

The war in Vietnam eroded President Johnson's popularity, however. Antiwar protests focused on problems with his leadership. In 1968, Lyndon Johnson said he would not run for president again.

Head Start preschoolers listen as First Lady Johnson reads to them.

1. ☑ **Reading Check**
Describe Why do you think First Lady Johnson posed with children from the Head Start program?

_____

_____

_____

_____

_____

_____

The Women's Movement

In the 1960s, many women wanted more opportunities for education and work. In a new reform movement, women began to push for more changes.

Overall, women were paid less than men. Congress passed the Equal Pay Act in 1963. In 1964 the Equal Employment Opportunity Commission was set up.

Betty Friedan (center) was an important leader of the women's rights movement.

In 1963, Betty Friedan's book *The Feminine Mystique* was published. It was about the problems women faced. A few years later, Betty Friedan became a founder of the National Organization for Women (NOW). NOW's goal is still to fight for and to protect women's rights.

In 1972, the Senate approved a new constitutional amendment. The Equal Rights Amendment (ERA) would have guaranteed equality for women. NOW and other groups gave the ERA their strong support, but it did not pass.

Even though many people opposed these activities, the push for equality had powerful results. A federal law called Title IX, or Title Nine, opened school athletics to girls and women. At the same time, more and more women got better jobs, in new fields, with more pay. In 1981, Sandra Day O'Connor became the first female justice on the Supreme Court. In 1983, astronaut Sally Ride became the first American woman in space. Women's roles and opportunities were expanding.

Improved Rights for Others

The civil rights movement opened doors for African Americans and women. It also inspired other groups to work to improve their lives. In California, César Chávez (SAY zahr CHAH vez) followed the nonviolent teachings of Martin Luther King, Jr. Chávez was a Hispanic farm worker. In the 1960s, Chávez organized a group that became the United Farm Workers (UFW).

In 1965, the UFW went on strike against grape growers in California. The workers protested their low wages and terrible working conditions. Many Americans joined in by refusing to buy grapes. The UFW improved conditions for its members.

American Indians also demanded better treatment. American Indians were the nation's poorest minority group. A **minority group** is a group that is distinct from the majority, or largest group in a society. Many American Indians lived on reservations, where conditions were terrible. In the 1950s and 1960s, American Indians began to work together. Groups such as the American Indian Movement (AIM) marched in Washington for fair and better treatment.

In 1990, Congress passed the Americans with Disabilities Act. This law protects the civil rights of people with disabilities of all kinds. For example, the law says that public buildings and public transportation must be accessible to disabled people.

Affirmative action is one path to change. The goal of affirmative action is to make up for past discrimination. For example, businesses might try to hire more women or minorities than in the past.

Some people have challenged this policy. They feel it is a form of discrimination that gives some people special treatment based on their race or gender. Others think it is the only way to make up for past wrongs.

The United States has always been a diverse nation. Together, Americans have shown that they can work to protect the civil rights of all of the country's citizens.

Quest Connection

What were members of the UFW trying to change for the people of their movement? Locate a speech given by César Chávez and determine his message as a leader of the UFW.

👆 INTERACTIVITY

Go online to find out more about how speeches are written and analyze a speech.

A student using the wheelchair ramp on a public school bus.

2. ✅ **Reading Check** Public transportation must be available to everyone. **Identify** other protections for disabled people.

_____

_____

_____

The Environmental Movement

During the 1960s, people began to worry that the environment was in serious trouble. One was scientist Rachel Carson. She wrote about her concern in a best-selling book, *Silent Spring*. Carson warned about chemicals, such as pesticides, that were poisoning the environment. *Silent Spring* sparked a national debate about pollution.

There was a lot to worry about. Two events in 1969 made the environmental crisis very real. In January, an oil rig blew up off the coast of Santa Barbara, California. About 200,000 gallons of oil spread across the ocean surface. Thousands of birds and animals were killed. A few months later, in Cleveland, Ohio, the Cuyahoga River actually caught fire because there was so much oil and garbage in it. Americans were horrified. What was happening to the environment?

People formed groups to clean up the land, air, and water. In April 1970, the nation celebrated the first Earth Day. Also in 1970, President Richard Nixon set up the Environmental Protection Agency (EPA). The EPA's job is to make and enforce guidelines to protect the environment.

Rachel Carson

Primary Source

"These [chemicals] are now applied almost universally ... —chemicals that have the power to kill every insect, the 'good' and the 'bad,' to 'still' the song of birds, and the leaping of fish in the streams, ... and to linger on in soil. ..."

—Excerpt from Rachel Carson's book *Silent Spring*

3. ☑ **Reading Check** **Analyze** the quotation. Then circle words that show the effects of using poisonous chemicals.

A Loss of Confidence in Government

Republican candidate Richard Nixon was elected United States president in 1968. As the 1960s came to an end, the war in Vietnam deeply divided the nation. The nation would also become deeply divided over President Nixon.

After Nixon won a landslide victory in the 1972 election, the *Washington Post* newspaper reported a troubling story. Five men had been arrested during the presidential campaign. They had broken into Democratic Party offices at the Watergate Hotel in Washington, D.C. Over the next two years a national scandal developed, known simply as Watergate. It became clear that Nixon was involved in trying to hide the role of the White House in the break-in.

Nixon feared that he would be **impeached**, or charged with a crime, and maybe removed from office by Congress. On August 9, 1974, Richard Nixon resigned, or voluntarily quit, as president.

4. ☑ **Reading Check** **Identify** why Americans might have lost confidence in government after Nixon's resignation.

_____

_____

_____

_____

Former President Nixon says goodbye after his resignation.

After Nixon

Vice President Gerald Ford became president upon Nixon's resignation. Ford believed that a legal trial of the former president would harm the nation, so he pardoned Nixon. This meant Nixon would not be tried in court for any crimes. This made many Americans angry because they thought that Nixon should have been tried and punished.

Ford lost the 1976 election to Democrat Jimmy Carter. President Carter negotiated a peace treaty between Israel and Egypt. But the United States faced several crises during his presidency. One was the energy crisis. Due to an increased use of oil and gas, the Organization of Petroleum Exporting Countries (OPEC) was raising the price of oil. Americans had become dependent on their cars and needed a steady supply of oil and gas. They faced long lines and shortages when they tried to buy gasoline. Another crisis developed in 1979 when 66 Americans were taken hostage by Iranian militants.

President Carter tried to restore Americans' confidence in government. "We simply must have faith in each other," he said, "faith in our ability to govern ourselves and faith in the future of this nation."

The Reagan Years

Republican Ronald Reagan defeated Carter in the 1980 election. Reagan's ideas were different from Carter's. He once said, "Government is not the solution to our problem; government is the problem."

Reagan set out to restore the economy by reducing the role of government in people's lives. He cut taxes with the idea that people would have more money to spend. He also cut government spending in areas such as education, Medicare, and food stamps. He also increased spending in others, especially on the military.

Two years into Reagan's presidency, the nation fell deeper into a recession, or economic **decline**. Reagan responded by raising taxes. The economy began to recover.

Reagan remained a popular president and was reelected in 1984. The economy continued to improve during his second term. Reagan supporters said this was "the longest peacetime **expansion** in American history." However, the United States government had to borrow money from other countries to pay its bills. By the end of Reagan's second term, the national debt had tripled.

Academic Vocabulary

decline • *n.*, the process of a condition becoming worse

expansion • *n.*, the act of becoming larger or bigger

Ronald Reagan delivering a speech in the oval office.

Lesson 3 Check

5. **Compare and Contrast** how Lyndon Johnson and Ronald Reagan viewed the role of government.

_____

_____

_____

6. **Identify** how groups such as the National Organization for Women, the American Indian Movement, and the United Farm Workers made political contributions to America.

_____

_____

7. **Understand the** *Quest* **Connections Draw Conclusions** What methods did various groups use to improve the rights of others?

_____

_____

_____

Ronald Reagan's Inaugural Speech, 1981

Ronald Reagan delivered his inaugural speech on January 20, 1981. The mood of much of the country was low. The nation had endured the oil crisis. Then Americans had been taken hostage during a revolution in Iran. During Reagan's address, Iran released the 52 American hostages it had held for 444 days.

Ronald Reagan spoke about his confidence in the nation and its citizens. He described the type of government he believed in. Reagan reminded Americans that he had been elected because he planned to limit the power of the federal government.

Vocabulary Support

It is not surprising that the nation's problems are related to the growth of government control.

expression meaning the end of the United States

Fun Fact

Ronald Reagan's inauguration was the first to be held on the West Front of the U.S. Capitol.

"It is no coincidence that our present troubles parallel and are proportionate to the intervention and intrusion in our lives that result from unnecessary and excessive growth of government. It is time for us to realize that we're too great a nation to limit ourselves to small dreams. We're not, as some would have us believe, doomed to an inevitable decline. I do not believe in a fate that will fall on us no matter what we do. I do believe in a fate that will fall on us if we do nothing. So, with all the creative energy at our command, let us begin an era of national renewal. Let us renew our determination, our courage, and our strength. And let us renew our faith and our hope."

—Ronald Reagan, Inauguration Speech, 1981

Close Reading

1. **Summarize** What did President Ronald Reagan express as the nation's greatest trouble?

_____

_____

2. **Draw Conclusions** How does Reagan suggest to move ahead as a nation?

_____

_____

_____

_____

_____

_____

Wrap It Up

What was Reagan's main message in his speech? Write a paragraph explaining this excerpt from Reagan's inaugural speech. Support your response with information from the chapter and a quote from the speech.

_____

_____

_____

_____

_____

_____

_____

_____

Quality:
Individual Responsibility

Bella Abzug (1920–1998)
A Passionate Perfectionist

Bella Savitzky was born to Russian Jewish immigrants. She grew up in New York City where she earned a degree from Hunter College. Then she won a scholarship to Columbia Law School where she earned her law degree in 1947. During law school she married Martin Abzug.

Abzug began working in labor law and then worked on civil rights cases. She also defended people accused of communist activities by Senator Joseph McCarthy. Abzug was passionate about speaking up for civil rights of women, the poor, and minorities.

Her passion led Abzug to successfully run for Congress in 1970. She was quoted as saying "This woman's place is in the House—the House of Representatives." Abzug boldly introduced a bill to remove all U.S. troops from Vietnam on her very first day in Congress! The bill did not pass, but it demonstrated her dedication to causes she believed in.

In Congress, Abzug was a leader in women's issues. She also wrote laws that made government information and activities more open to citizens. Abzug was among the first to call for President Richard Nixon's impeachment.

After serving in Congress, she worked with other leading activists. President Jimmy Carter asked her to work on his committee on women. She continued to work on women's rights issues until her death in 1998.

Find Out More

1. Identify how Bella Abzug represents individual responsibility.

_____

_____

_____

2. On a separate sheet of paper, design a memorial that pays respect to the work of Bella Abzug.

Use these graphics to review some of the key terms, people, and ideas from this chapter.

1945
Harry S. Truman sworn into office.

1960
President John F. Kennedy becomes president.

1974
Gerald Ford becomes president after Nixon resigned.

1980
Ronald Reagan is elected president.

1945	1950	1955	1960	1965	1970	1975	1980	1985	1990

1952
Dwight D. Eisenhower is elected president.

1963
Lyndon B. Johnson becomes president.

1968
Richard Nixon is elected president.

1976
James Carter sworn into office.

Important Dates in the Civil Rights Movement

1947 – Jackie Robinson breaks the color barrier in major league baseball.

1954 – Supreme Court rules that separate educational facilities are unequal.

1955 – Rosa Park is jailed for where she sat on a public bus.

1961 – Freedom Rides takes place to protest segregation in the South.

1963 – Dr. Martin Luther King Jr delivers his "I Have a Dream" Speech.

1967 – Thurgood Marshall becomes first African American Supreme Court justice.

GAMES

Play the vocabulary game.

Vocabulary and Key Ideas

1. **Identify** What is **the Great Society**?

_____

_____

_____

2. Complete the sentences below. Choose from these words: civil rights, discrimination, integration, sit-in, freedom ride.

   Many people had to fight for their basic freedoms and protections known as _____.

   Protestors demanded fair treatment and an end to segregation in restaurants, so they refused to move until they were served. This is known as a _____.

   _____ is unfair treatment based on race and color.

3. **Main Idea and Details** Read the two details from the chart. Then write the main idea the details support.

   Main Idea

   _____

   _____

   Details
   Martin Luther King, Jr., led a march from Selma to Montgomery.

   Details
   Congress passed the 1965 Voting Rights Act.

Critical Thinking and Writing

4. **Explain** what contributed to the growth of the suburbs after the war.

_____

_____

_____

_____

5. **Analyze** the issues Americans had with getting oil and gas in the 1970s.

_____

_____

_____

6. **Analyze** Why did Richard Nixon resign from the presidency?

_____

_____

7. **Revisit the Big Question** When does change become necessary?

_____

_____

_____

8. **Analyze** What aspects of life did the Great Society try to change?

_____

_____

9. **Writing Workshop: Expressing an Opinion** Choose one of the U.S. presidents that you learned about in this chapter. Write three paragraphs expressing your opinion about the president's accomplishments and possible shortcomings or failures during his time in office. In the first paragraph, write about the president's accomplishments. In the second paragraph, write about his shortcomings. In the third paragraph, sum up your opinions about the president.

Analyze Primary Sources

"Peace is no mere matter of men fighting or not fighting. Peace, to have meaning for many who have known only suffering in both peace and war, must be translated into bread or rice, shelter, health, and education, as well as freedom and human dignity—a steadily better life. If peace is to be secure, long-suffering and long-starved, forgotten peoples of the world, the underprivileged and the undernourished, must begin to realize without delay the promise of a new day and a new life."

—Ralph Bunche

10. These words were spoken by Ralph Bunche at a nobel lecture. He won the Nobel Peace Prize in 1950 for his work in mediating peace in Israel in the late 1940s. How do these words help you to understand what peace looks like to war-torn countries?

_____

_____

_____

_____

_____

Outlines and Graphic Organizers

11. Reread the section "Breaking the Color Barrier" and review the graphic organizer in the Worktext. Then complete the outline about the section.

Breaking the Color Barrier

1. _____

    A. _____

    B. _____

2. _____

    A. _____

    _____

3. _____

    A. _____

    B. _____

Quest Findings

INTERACTIVITY

Learn more about speech writing with an online activity.

Write Your Speech

You have read the lessons in this chapter, and now you are ready to plan and write your speech. Remember that the goal of the speech is to persuade people to have a similar point of view about one of the movements from the chapter.

1 Prepare to Write

Determine your message for the speech. Write a sentence that delivers your point of view. Then write three facts or statements that support your argument. Use these notes to help you write your speech.

2 Write a Draft

Use your notes and the evidence from your Quest Connections to write the strongest speech you can. Make sure your speech answers the following questions:

- What does the movement stand for?
- Why is change needed?
- How do you suggest to make this change?

3 Share With A Partner

Exchange your draft speech with a partner. Tell your partner what you like about the speech and what could be improved. Make sure to provide positive criticism. Make changes to your speech.

4 Deliver the Speech

Read your speech to your classmates. Discuss the importance of each movement and how freedom and equality are common ideas among the movements.

GO ONLINE FOR DIGITAL RESOURCES

- ▶ VIDEO
- 👆 INTERACTIVITY
- 🔊 AUDIO
- 🎮 GAMES
- ☑ ASSESSMENT
- 📖 eTEXT

The BIG Question What goals should we set for our nation?

▶ VIDEO

JumpStart Activity

👆 INTERACTIVITY

Divide into three groups. Each group will choose a student who will be the group leader. As a group, discuss a few ways to volunteer in the community and suggest activities and projects that your group could complete. The final decision about which activity or project your group will perform will be up to the leader. Share your group's choice with the class. What kind of impression does each group's choice suggest about their leader's goals? Do you agree with the choice of your group's leader?

_____

_____

_____

What Do We Want to Be?

Preview the chapter vocabulary as you sing the rap.

The Cold War was ended, so now what do we do?
Use the power to conquer or to help other nations to.
We could broker peace in the Middle East,
Till the fear of different views could finally be deceased.

But this wouldn't be as easy as we thought,
There were still wars to be won and fights to be fought.
Iraq, Kuwait, and Afghanistan,
Told us that we might have to change our plan.

To our horror and to our surprise,
September 11th took many **civilian** lives.
This put **terrorism** and Bin Laden firmly in our sites,
And we forced the Taliban to grant **human rights**.

From war to peace, or to make the wrongs right,
To recast our past decisions, or to move to the light.
And other challenges await us to behold,
For the history yet to come and yet to be told.

TURKEY

CYPRUS

LEBANON

SYRIA

ISRAEL

West Bank

JORDAN

EGYPT

IRAQ

IRAN

Kabul ★

AFGHANISTAN

PAKISTAN

KUWAIT

BAHRAIN

QATAR

SAUDI
ARABIA

UNITED
ARAB
EMIRATES

OMAN

Arabian
Sea

N
W   E
S

0   400 mi
0   400 km

YEMEN

Where did the United States go to war in the Middle East?

Following the terrorist attacks of September 11, 2001, the United States invaded Afghanistan. Two years later, the U.S. invaded Iraq. The Middle East remains a major focus of American foreign policy.

What happened and When?

Read the timeline to learn about several major national and world events since the 1970s.

1975	1985	1995

1978
Camp David Accords are signed.

1990
Operation Desert Storm is carried out.

1997
Madeleine Albright becomes the first female secretary of state.

Who will you meet?

Madeleine Albright
Under President Bill Clinton, served as the first female secretary of state

Saddam Hussein
Iraqi president who invaded Kuwait, which led to the United States taking military action against Iraq

George W. Bush
Served as president during the September 11 terrorist attacks and declared a War on Terror

Barack Obama
Served as the first African American president, helping the nation through economic and political hardships

 INTERACTIVITY

Complete the Interactive digital activity.

2005 **2015**

2001
Terrorists attack New York City and the Pentagon.

2008
Barack Obama is elected the first African American president.

TODAY
The United States continues to meet challenges of the modern age.

Quest

Project-Based Learning

Mapping the Middle East

The Middle East is a region made up of many countries. It has a long and rich history. Mesopotamia, which is widely believed to be the home of the earliest civilizations, was located in modern-day Iraq. Countries of the Middle East have experienced many conflicts since the mid-twentieth century. To protect its interests, the United States has sometimes chosen to become involved in these conflicts.

Quest Kick Off

Your mission is to create an annotated class map of the Middle East. Partners will choose a country and provide key details about that country to include on the map.

1 Ask Questions

What are some of the conflicts that have taken place between the United States and Middle Eastern countries? What issues did these conflicts involve? Write two questions of your own.

....

....

....

....

2 Research

Follow your teacher's instructions to research your country's history, culture, and its interactions with the United States. Did these factors influence the conflicts in which your country was involved?

INTERACTIVITY

Complete the digital activities to get started on your map.

....

....

....

....

....

....

ASIA

EUROPE

MIDDLE EAST

AFRICA

3 Look for *Quest* Connections

Begin looking for Quest Connections that will help you illustrate your map.

4 *Quest* Findings
Write Your Annotations

Use the Quest Findings page at the end of the chapter to help you create your notecards and images.

Trials at Home and Abroad

👆 **INTERACTIVITY**

Participate in a class discussion to preview the content of this lesson.

Unlock The **BIG** Question

I will know that the United States played a new, important role in world events after the Cold War.

Vocabulary

human rights
coalition
Electoral College
levee

Academic Vocabulary

criticize
crisis

Jumpstart Activity

In small groups, have a discussion about how you meet challenges. Talk about what happens when you have a disagreement at home with a sibling or parent and what happens when you have a disagreement with a friend. How are these situations similar, and how are they different? Do the members of your group deal with these situations in the same manner as you do?

After the Cold War ended, the United States played a new role in international events. It was now the world's only superpower. Americans had to decide how the nation would use its power. Many believed that the United States should work to help settle conflicts around the world.

From left to right, Sadat, Carter, and Begin celebrate the Camp David Accords at the White House in 1978.

The United States Works for Peace

Even before the Cold War ended, the United States had worked for peace between Egypt and Israel. Those two Middle Eastern nations had been enemies for many years. The Middle East is a region also known as Southwest Asia, which includes Israel, Egypt, Iraq, Iran, and other nations. In 1948, Israel was founded as a Jewish state in the ancient Jewish homeland where Jews had always lived. The majority of people living in the new state were Jewish.

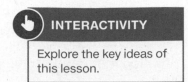
The Muslim nations that surround Israel did not want a Jewish state there. These countries fought several wars trying to destroy Israel. In 1977, Egypt decided to make peace with Israel.

In 1978, United States President Jimmy Carter invited the leaders of the two countries, Israeli Prime Minister Menachem Begin (muh NAHK um BAY gihn) and Egyptian President Anwar El Sadat (AHN wahr el suh DAHT) to a meeting at Camp David in Maryland. There they signed peace agreements known as the Camp David Accords.

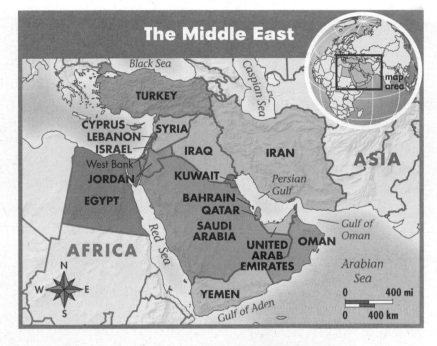

The Middle East

Carter also tried to make human rights a more important part of his foreign policy. **Human rights** are the rights and freedoms that everyone should have as human beings. To encourage the protection of human rights around the world, Carter sometimes **criticized** other nations, even American allies, for human rights violations.

After Carter left office, American presidents continued to work for peace in the Middle East. In 1994, President Bill Clinton met with Jordan's King Hussein and Israeli Prime Minister Yitzhak Rabin as they signed a peace treaty. Conflicts in the Middle East continue, and the United States still works for peace in the region.

Academic Vocabulary

criticize • *v.*, to find fault with

Trouble in the Persian Gulf

Academic Vocabulary

crisis • *n.*, a dangerous situation that needs serious attention

Quest Connection

In the text, underline the Middle Eastern countries that were involved in the 1990 conflict. With a partner, make inferences about why there might be continued unrest in this region.

INTERACTIVITY

Take a closer look at the conflicts in the Middle East.

Another **crisis** occurred in the Middle East in 1990. The nation of Iraq invaded the neighboring country of Kuwait (koo WAYT). Saddam Hussein (hoo SAYN) was the leader of Iraq. Hussein wanted to take over the rich oil fields of Kuwait. People feared he might also invade Saudi Arabia, which bordered Kuwait. Saudi Arabia had many oil fields, too.

American President George H. W. Bush worked with other nations to try to stop Iraq. The United Nations demanded that Iraq leave Kuwait. When this peaceful tactic failed, troops from the United States and other nations formed a coalition. A **coalition** is a group of allies who work together.

The coalition's attack on Iraqi forces was called Operation Desert Storm. American General Colin Powell helped to plan the invasion. Forces led by the United States won the war in only six weeks. The Iraqis were pushed out of Kuwait, but Hussein remained in power.

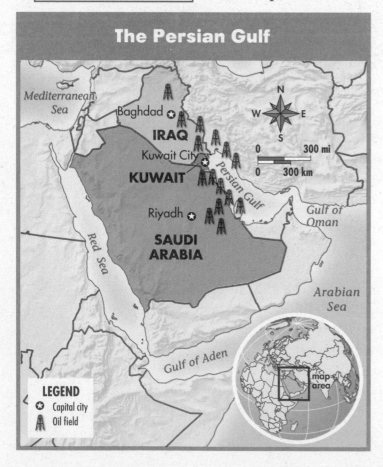

The Persian Gulf

Mediterranean Sea

Baghdad ✪

IRAQ

Kuwait City ✪

KUWAIT

Persian Gulf

Riyadh ✪

SAUDI ARABIA

Red Sea

Gulf of Oman

Arabian Sea

Gulf of Aden

map area

LEGEND
✪ Capital city
⛏ Oil field

1. ☑ **Reading Check** **Analyze** How does the international response to the invasion of Kuwait illustrate the global aim to maintain peace in the Middle East?

_____

_____

_____

_____

_____

_____

_____

_____

_____

_____

The Clinton Years

Democrat Bill Clinton was elected president in 1992. Before his second term, he chose Madeleine Albright as Secretary of State. She was the first woman to hold this position. Together, they worked to resolve conflicts around the world. In 1990, the country of Yugoslavia, in Eastern Europe, split apart. Different regions declared themselves to be independent republics. Several ethnic groups fought for control in the new republics. The United States and other nations sent troops to restore peace. Fighting there ended in 1995.

In Northern Ireland, which was ruled by Great Britain, Catholics and Protestants had been fighting for hundreds of years. President Clinton worked with both groups to sign a peace treaty in 1998. Clinton also worked to keep peace between Saddam Hussein in Iraq and his neighbors.

During his second term, President Clinton faced a serious scandal. During an official investigation, Clinton lied in court. As outlined in the Constitution, the House of Representatives voted to impeach him. *Impeach* means to charge someone with a crime. The Senate held a trial. They found Clinton not guilty. He was not removed from office.

Madeleine Albright was Secretary of State for President Clinton.

Saddam Hussein was the Iraqi leader who invaded Kuwait.

President Clinton responding to his impeachment acquittal.

Challenges at Home

In the 2000 United States presidential election, former Texas governor George W. Bush, son of President George H. W. Bush, ran against Clinton's Vice President Al Gore. The election was one of the closest in American history. Democrat Gore received 50.9 million votes. Republican Bush received almost 50.5 million votes.

However, American presidents are not elected directly by the people. The people vote for electors, who cast their votes as part of a group called the **Electoral College**. The electors determine who wins a presidential election. The candidate who wins the most votes in a state wins all of that state's electoral votes.

2. ☑ **Reading Check**
Analyze the map. How many electoral votes did Florida have?

_____

How many more electoral votes did Bush get than Gore?

_____

Identify the winner and his political party.

_____

_____

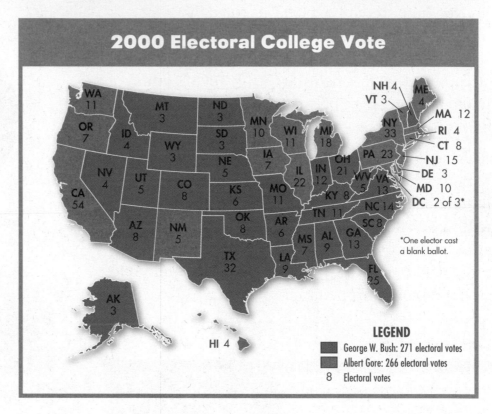

2000 Electoral College Vote

LEGEND
George W. Bush: 271 electoral votes
Albert Gore: 266 electoral votes
8 Electoral votes

*One elector cast a blank ballot.

The 2000 election was so close that whoever got the most votes in Florida would win the election. The Florida vote was so close that it had to be counted several times. Eventually, the Supreme Court decided which count was official. Based on their decision, George W. Bush won the election.

Early in his presidency, President Bush supported a law known as "No Child Left Behind." This law was designed to improve public schools by testing students regularly to see whether they were making good progress.

Bush faced many challenges during his presidency. One of the worst was Hurricane Katrina. This storm hit the states along the coast of the Gulf of Mexico in August 2005.

During the storm, New Orleans, Louisiana, flooded completely when levees protecting the city broke. A **levee** is an earthen barrier built to prevent flooding. The city was evacuated. Thousands of people were rescued from their homes, many in boats or helicopters. Hurricane Katrina was, to that point, the most deadly and costly disaster in American history.

3. ☑ **Reading Check** **Make Inferences** What can you infer were challenges Americans faced following Hurricane Katrina?

_____

_____

_____

The aftermath of Hurricane Katrina

✋ **INTERACTIVITY**

Check your understanding of the key ideas in this lesson.

☑ Lesson 1 Check

4. **Main Idea and Details Identify** the American foreign policy goal reflected in the Camp David Accords and Operation Desert Storm.

_____

5. **Analyze** the events that made the election of 2000 unusual.

_____

_____

_____

6. **Understand the** *Quest* **Connections** What do you think neighboring countries thought about America's actions in the Persian Gulf in 1990?

_____

_____

_____

Critical Thinking Skills

Evaluate Media Content

Suppose you want to learn more about the events leading up to the Syrian refugee crisis and what is being done to address it. How would you find this information? One way is to read the news in a print newspaper or online at a news site such as nytimes.com, cnn.com, or BBC.com.

Be sure you understand the types of articles you may find. News articles, such as the one below, are secondary sources based on facts. Editorials are people's opinions about events in the news. Feature articles contain information that is interesting to readers, but they may not contain only factual information.

 http://www.globalnews.com

Page last updated 8:25 GMT Friday, 31 March 2017

The Syrian Refugee Crisis

During the Arab Spring, many countries, including Syria, took part in countrywide protests. Syrians took to the streets to demand better treatment from their oppressive government. Soon, the country was engulfed in an all-out civil war.

As a result of the destructive conflict between the government and ordinary citizens, over 4 million Syrians have had to flee their country. Mostly women and children have gone to neighboring Lebanon, Turkey, and Jordan. About 10 percent of the refugees have gone to Europe. Another 6 million people have had to leave their homes but are still in Syria.

According to the United Nations, $3.2 billion are needed to help the refugees who require some form of humanitarian assistance. Most of the people still living in Syria do not have access to clean drinking water and do not have enough food. Many children are unable to attend school. The warring groups have made the problem worse by not allowing humanitarian groups to gain access to the people who need help. The civil war in Syria has created the worst humanitarian crisis of the twenty-first century.

Your Turn!

Read the article on the previous page from a news Web site.

▶ **VIDEO**

Watch a video about evaluating media content.

1. Is this an objective, formal news article, a feature article, or an editorial? How do you know?

   _____

   _____

   _____

2. When was the article written?

   _____

3. **Write** two facts or supporting ideas you learned from this article.

   _____

   _____

   _____

   _____

4. **Apply Locate** a print or online news article about a recent international event. Write the title of the article and list the main and supporting ideas. Then **summarize** the content below.

   _____

   _____

   _____

   _____

INTERACTIVITY

Participate in a class discussion to preview the content of this lesson.

Unlock The BIG Question

I will know that, in the early 2000s, the United States faced terrorist attacks and fought in several wars.

Vocabulary

terrorism
weapons of mass destruction
civilian

Academic Vocabulary

controversial
base

JumpStart Activity

A large area within your community has been destroyed by a serious fire. With a small group, create a list of things the people affected would need. Then discuss and create a list of ways that you and your community could help them out. Compare your lists with those of the other groups.

Today, much of the world is worried about terrorism. **Terrorism** is the use of violence and fear to achieve political goals. Terrorists, the people who use terrorism, come from all over the world.

September 11, 2001

On September 11, 2001, terrorists hijacked, or took over, four airplanes. They crashed two of the airplanes into the Twin Towers of the World Trade Center in New York City. These buildings were completely destroyed. The terrorists crashed a third airplane into the Pentagon in Arlington, Virginia. The Pentagon is the headquarters of the United States military.

The fourth airplane crashed in a Pennsylvania field. This plane's passengers learned what the terrorists were planning and tried to take control of the plane. Their actions prevented the plane from crashing into another important building.

The Twin Towers housed more than 430 companies from 28 countries. Many were engaged in banking and finance.

Rescue workers at the site of the September 11 attacks.

More than 3,000 people were killed in the September 11 attacks. The attackers were part of al Qaeda (al KYE dah), a Muslim terrorist group. The group's leader, Osama bin Laden, was from Saudi Arabia. He and the members of al Qaeda strongly opposed American influence in Islamic lands.

Americans Respond

Immediately after the attacks, people from all over the country lined up to donate blood for injured victims and rescue workers. They also donated food, clothing, and money to help the victims' families.

The attacks led the United States to place a greater emphasis on the security of the nation. The Department of Homeland Security was created. This department's job is to protect the country from terrorism and to prepare for natural disasters.

War in Iraq

Soon after the September 11 attacks, President George W. Bush announced a "War on Terror." This meant that the nation would use its military to find and capture terrorists around the world.

Al Qaeda had been based in Afghanistan. A group called the Taliban controlled Afghanistan's government. They refused to help find Osama bin Laden. In October 2001, American troops invaded Afghanistan. Within months, the Taliban government surrendered. Some terrorists were captured, but bin Laden escaped.

INTERACTIVITY

Explore the key ideas of this lesson.

Quest Connection

Underline the text that explains why the United States invaded Afghanistan. With a partner, discuss the costs and benefits of this invasion.

INTERACTIVITY

Learn more about the invasion of Afghanistan.

President Bush then turned his focus toward Iraq. The treaty that had ended the war in Iraq in 1991 called for that country to destroy all its **weapons of mass destruction**, or WMDs. These weapons can kill large numbers of people. They include nuclear weapons and weapons that spread poison or disease over large areas.

But in early 2003, President Bush and British Prime Minister Tony Blair declared that Hussein was hindering U.N. inspections. This action along with the reports that there might be ties between Iraq's government and al Qaeda caused the U.S. government to support an invasion of Iraq to remove Hussein from power.

In March 2003, American troops, as well as troops from 30 other nations, went to war in Iraq. A few months later, the Iraqis were defeated and Hussein was arrested. The rebels continued to fight, and American troops stayed in the region. By 2009, the rebels were weakening and President Barack Obama began to withdraw troops from Iraq.

After the war began, people learned that Iraq did not have WMDs. Also, it turned out that Hussein was not connected to al Qaeda. The war in Iraq remains **controversial** today.

Afghanistan and Other Challenges

After defeating the Taliban in 2001, American troops stayed in Afghanistan to help establish a new government. While the Taliban were in power, they had denied many human rights to Afghani citizens, especially women. The new government promised the citizens of Afghanistan more rights. Today, however, Afghani women still do not have the same rights as Afghani men.

Many of the Taliban fled from Afghanistan to the neighboring country of Pakistan. There, the Taliban began to regain strength. Its members attacked American soldiers and Afghan civilians.

Academic Vocabulary

controversial • *adj.*, to cause much discussion or argument

1. **☑ Reading Check Generalize** Many statues of Saddam Hussein were destroyed after the war. With a partner discuss what this action might have represented.

Areas of Conflict After September 11, 2001

Civilians are people who are not in the military. In response, President Obama sent more soldiers to Afghanistan, beginning in 2009. The United States also attacked areas of Pakistan where they believed Taliban members were **based**.

As American forces fought the Taliban, the search continued for the al Qaeda leader Osama bin Laden, who had planned the September 11 attacks on the United States. After years of investigation, the United States government discovered bin Laden's hiding place. In May 2011, American forces raided a house in Pakistan and bin Laden was killed. According to reports, the raid also uncovered evidence that bin Laden was planning more attacks on the United States.

The Arab Spring

Political unrest in the Middle East was not restricted to Iraq and Afghanistan. The desire to become free of oppressive governments led protesters in several Arab countries to take to the streets. They wished to end decades of brutal dictatorship and demanded a more democratic form of government.

What became known as the "Arab Spring" began in Tunisia in December 2010. It spread to Egypt, Bahrain, Yemen, and Syria. The Middle East and North Africa were swept up in an unprecedented series of protests organized by everyday people.

Academic Vocabulary

base • *v.*, to have a specific location that is the center of operations

Word Wise

Root words are the most basic part of a word when the prefixes and suffixes are taken away. *Precedent* means an earlier action that is considered an example or guide in later circumstances. What do you think *unprecedented* means?

A few oppressive leaders were removed from power. In many cases, however, the protests resulted in a strong response from harsh leaders. War and violence broke out in some of the countries involved in the protests.

Civil War in Syria

Syria's protests began in March of 2011. When government forces began to arrest protesters, it triggered nationwide unrest. Citizens demanded the resignation of their president, Bashar al-Assad. When the government responded with force, it incited the protesters. Armed protesters began to force troops out of their towns and cities. This was the beginning of a civil war in Syria.

As the war raged on, many were killed and injured and cities were destroyed. Millions of Syrians fled their homeland resulting in the largest refugee crisis of the 21st century. Refugees are people who have been forced out of their own country. Neighboring nations struggled to deal with the many people looking for shelter.

The Rise of ISIS

A terrorist group known as the Islamic State in Iraq and Syria (ISIS) took part in the Syrian civil war. It first developed during the war in Iraq. Rejected by other terrorist groups for being too brutal, ISIS destroyed territories in battle and then put its own government in place.

ISIS became known around the world in 2014 when it drove Iraqi forces out of large cities in Iraq and Syria. The group planned, executed, and took credit for many terrorist attacks over the next few years. These actions caused President Obama to order U.S. air strikes against key positions of ISIS. The group remains a threat to the United States and other nations today.

Rebel soldiers on their way to battle in Syria

2. 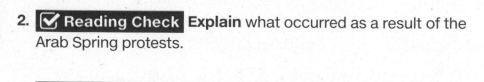 **Reading Check** **Explain** what occurred as a result of the Arab Spring protests.

_____

_____

_____

Businessman Elected President

In 2016, Donald Trump, a wealthy real estate developer with no prior experience in government, was elected president of the United States. Trump's direct way of speaking resonated with many people across the country. During his presidency, Trump pledged to defeat ISIS and continued to work with allies in the Middle East toward this goal.

He faced many critics, however, for some of his policies. Although he ordered air strikes against Syria in response to its use of chemical weapons against civilians, Trump refused to lift his ban on Arab immigrants in order to help Syrian refugees.

 INTERACTIVITY

Check your understanding of the key ideas in this lesson.

✓ Lesson 2 Check

3. **Generalize** Why were the invasions of Afghanistan and Iraq part of the War on Terror?

_____

_____

_____

4. **Summarize** the different outcomes of the Arab Spring protests.

_____

_____

_____

5. **Understand the** *Quest* **Connections** How do you think learning that there were no weapons of mass destruction affected Americans' feelings about the war in Iraq?

_____

_____

_____

Write Reports and Bibliographies

Writing a report is easier if you break it down into small steps and organize information. Here are some steps to include:

- Decide on a topic, the purpose of your report, and your target audience.

- Begin locating information. Search a library or online encyclopedia for your topic.

- Gather and organize information. Write each new piece of information on an index card. Include the title, author, and source of the information. You will need this for your *bibliography*—a list of your sources.

- Quotations add interest to your report. Copy the exact words of quotations onto your index cards and place them in quotes. Add information about the source.

- Choose the key ideas and supporting details you will include. Arrange the cards in order. Write an outline.

- As you write your draft, put information in your own words.

- Use footnotes to cite references or make a comment about a part of the text. Footnotes are placed at the bottom of a page.

- Edit and proofread your draft. Correct and improve grammar, spelling, punctuation, and sentence structure.

- Write a bibliography for your report. List your sources in alphabetical order. Ask your teacher what format you should use.

Here is part of a bibliography you might include for a report on the War on Terror.

Barber, Benjamin. *Jihad vs. McWorld: Terrorism's Challenge to Democracy*, New York, Ballantine Books, 1995. Print.

"Bush's War on Terror." Editorial. *Centerville Chronicle*, Oct. 3, 2001. Print.

Savage, Charlie. "Debating the Legal Basis for the War on Terror." *New York Times*, May 16, 2013. Web.

1. Fill in the chart with ideas for a report about a person or event that you have learned about so far in this chapter.

Topic	Key Ideas	Search Terms

2. How will you organize and record the information you find on this topic? What is the advantage of recording information this way?

_____

_____

_____

_____

3. Write a fictional bibliography entry for a source that you will use for your report on this topic. Remember to include the author and title of the source, where the information appeared, the date it was written, and whether it is a print book or from the Internet.

_____

_____

_____

Meeting Today's Challenges

INTERACTIVITY

Participate in a class discussion to preview the content of this lesson.

Unlock The BIG Question

I will know that the United States and the world are meeting many challenges.

Vocabulary

recession
national debt
globalization
nonrenewable resource
climate change

JumPstart Activity

With a group, discuss what the impact would be if banks were unable to loan money. Think about the kinds of loans that banks provide, such as loans for buying homes and to start small businesses. Share your ideas with the class.

Academic Vocabulary

enforce
controversy

The 2008 presidential election was a historic event. Candidates used the Internet to reach supporters. Women candidates ran for the top offices. Many Americans who had never voted did so now. On November 4, the nation elected Barack Obama as President of the United States. He was the first African American to achieve that office.

On November 4, 2008, Barack Obama was elected the 44th United States president.

Challenges at Home

Many people were excited about Obama's election because he was the first African American president and because he represented change. But he faced many challenges. Republicans opposed many of the laws that Democrat Obama proposed, and the nation's economy was in serious decline.

The economic decline began in the mid-2000s. Industries started to let go, or lay off, workers. These workers could not pay their mortgages, so the banks lost money. As a result, banks could not lend money to businesses, and more layoffs occurred. Everyone was buying less, which put more stress on businesses. In addition, banks had made bad decisions about some loans. These were not repaid, and many banks closed.

By 2009, the United States, and the world as a whole, was in a serious recession. A **recession** is a long economic slowdown. In response, Congress passed a stimulus bill that put almost $500 billion into public works projects, such as road repairs, to create jobs. The government also provided billions of dollars to banks so that they could keep operating and lending money. Unfortunately, this dramatically increased the **national debt**, or money that the country has borrowed to pay its bills.

👆 **INTERACTIVITY**

Explore the key ideas of this lesson.

Government programs created jobs to stimulate the economy.

Conflict Over Jobs

Throughout the economic slowdown, immigrants continued to come to the United States. Most came legally, but many came illegally. Some Americans worried that illegal immigrants would get jobs that should go to citizens. They wanted tougher laws against illegal immigrants.

When Donald Trump took office in 2017, he tried to put a hold on immigration, especially from Muslim countries. This caused conflict among Americans because many felt this was too harsh. America has always welcomed immigrants. Trump argued that he was only **enforcing** existing immigration laws. Some courts overturned what became known as the "immigration ban." However, the Supreme Court supported parts of the executive order and it went into effect in mid-2017.

Academic Vocabulary

enforce • v., to effectively carry out

The Global Economy

Globalization is another factor that has affected the United States economy. **Globalization** is the development of a world economy, in which people, goods, and ideas move freely from one country to another.

Globalization has created interdependence among nations. This has both benefits and drawbacks. Many Americans worry that American jobs are going overseas, where the companies pay lower wages. Globalization also helps explain why the recession that began in 2008 did not just affect the United States. When American banks started lending less money around the world, businesses in other nations were hurt. Also, with Americans buying fewer foreign-made goods, the countries that exported those goods to the United States lost money.

Examples of globalization are trade agreements, such as the North American Free Trade Agreement (NAFTA) and the Trans-Pacific Partnership (TPP). The United States signed NAFTA with Canada and Mexico in 1992. Twelve nations, including the United States, signed the TPP in 2016.

1. ☑ **Reading Check**
Identify and circle the top three U.S. trading partners on the map. **Turn and Talk** and discuss why you think Mexico and Canada are among the top ten U.S. trading partners.

United States Trade Partners

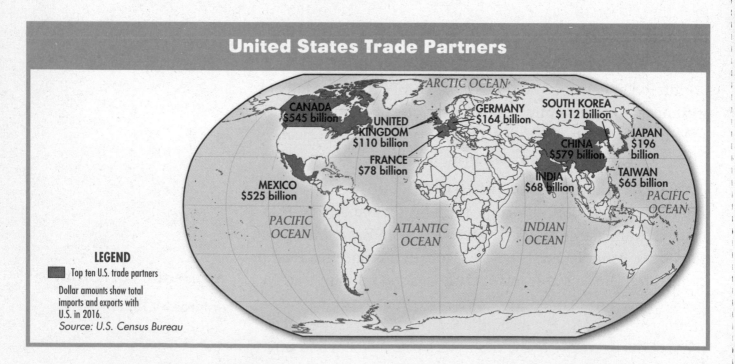

ARCTIC OCEAN

CANADA $545 billion
UNITED KINGDOM $110 billion
GERMANY $164 billion
SOUTH KOREA $112 billion
JAPAN $196 billion
CHINA $579 billion
FRANCE $78 billion
MEXICO $525 billion
INDIA $68 billion
TAIWAN $65 billion
PACIFIC OCEAN
PACIFIC OCEAN
ATLANTIC OCEAN
INDIAN OCEAN

LEGEND
Top ten U.S. trade partners
Dollar amounts show total imports and exports with U.S. in 2016.
Source: U.S. Census Bureau

Trade agreements allow member countries to import and export goods to each other without paying import fees, or tariffs. When imported goods don't have tariffs added, they cost less. This helps American consumers because imports are less expensive to buy.

During his presidential campaign, Donald Trump promised he would renegotiate existing trade agreements to protect American workers. This was a popular idea with many voters, but it made some companies uneasy.

Within days of taking office, Trump pulled the United States out of the TPP. Although it had not yet gone into effect, many businesses were unhappy with the change because it took away their ability to sell products to a large part of the global population. The idea of renegotiating NAFTA also created unease for businesses that had been built with the trade deal in mind. American companies worried that they were becoming isolated in an increasingly global economy.

Future Jobs for Americans

Globalization has changed manufacturing in the United States. Many goods once solely produced in the United States are now produced in other countries where labor costs are lower. The goods imported by the United States from those countries are often less costly than the same goods made in America.

Globalization has also had an effect on American workers. As manufacturing in China has dramatically increased, jobs in the United States have been focusing on other industries. A goal of President Trump was to bring manufacturing jobs back to the United States. Many were skeptical about this goal, since not being involved in major trade deals hurt America's chances of bringing these jobs back.

Technology has also changed the kinds of jobs people have. Many people have jobs in the computer industry. Millions work faster and more productively because of technology. Who knows how future technologies will change the way we all work, play, and live?

Students using technology in the classroom

2. ☑ **Reading Check**
Explain Technology, like this tablet, allows people around the world to meet without leaving home. With a partner, discuss how new technology has affected how and where people work.

Environmental Issues

A trip across the United States on the transcontinental railroad in the 1800s took about a week. Today, thanks to the nation's interstate highway system, you can drive it in three or four days. But this convenience comes at a cost.

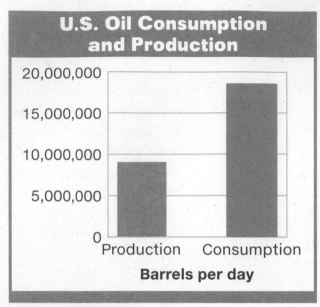

U.S. Oil Consumption and Production

20,000,000
15,000,000
10,000,000
5,000,000
0

Production   Consumption

Barrels per day

Source: World Factbook

Most cars run on fuels made from oil. Americans use more oil than any other country in the world. The graph on the left shows how much oil the United States produces compared to how much it uses. This means we need to buy our oil from other countries.

Oil is a **nonrenewable resource**, which means that once it is used, it cannot be replaced. Someday, the world's supply of oil will run out.

Because it uses such large quantities of oil, the United States wants to be on good terms with the countries that export the oil. This affects our relations with those countries. For example, tensions in the Middle East have arisen, in part, over protecting oil resources.

Burning fuels like gasoline releases carbon dioxide into the atmosphere. Carbon dioxide, which occurs both naturally and through human activities, is called a greenhouse gas, because it traps heat. As the amounts of carbon dioxide and other greenhouse gases increase, the Earth warms. Scientists warn that **climate change**, caused by this warming, will pose challenges to society. These include rising sea levels and changes in rainfall patterns.

Some people, however, do not believe that climate change exists and that laws created to address it have a negative impact on the economy. Early in his term, President Trump made deep cuts to the Environmental Protection Agency (EPA). This caused great **controversy** among Americans since the EPA is responsible for addressing problems related to the environment, including climate change.

Academic Vocabulary

controversy • *n.*, public dispute or debate

Going Green

In the twenty-first century, Americans are more aware of their role in conserving oil and protecting the environment. Some businesses and factories now use renewable sources of energy, such as the sun and wind. These resources do not run out. The federal government rewards companies that develop solar and wind-powered energy.

Some people are buying hybrid cars that use less gas and produce less pollution. However, everything from toothpaste and contact lenses to cell phones and bicycle helmets contain oil-based materials.

Using up oil is only part of the problem. In 2014, Americans produced about 258 million tons of trash. Over time, trash in landfills decays. This produces carbon dioxide and other hazardous gases. Reducing trash by recycling is almost like taking millions of cars off the road!

People are "going green" in many ways. For example, we can reuse cloth shopping bags instead of plastic. We can recycle metal, paper, plastic, and glass.

3. ☑ **Reading Check** **Summarize** Briefly summarize what Americans can achieve by "going green."

_____

_____

_____

Recycling reduces the oil used to make many products and reduces the trash in landfills.

America's Place in the World Today

In 2013, more than 765 million people, about 1 out of every 10 people on Earth, lived on less than $1.90 per day. Extreme poverty such as this is only one of many challenges facing people around the world today.

Hunger, disease, and lack of education are often caused by poverty. About 1 billion people cannot read a book or write their names. Millions of people don't have access to healthcare. People around the world also suffer from wars or terrorism or are denied their basic human rights.

Governments and international organizations are working to solve these problems. The United Nations, for example, has set "17 Goals to Transform Our World." These goals include reducing poverty, improving education and healthcare, and ending diseases, such as Acquired Immunodeficiency Syndrome, or AIDS.

Because the United States is such a wealthy country, its government works to address many international challenges. Individual Americans also contribute to solving the world's problems. They donate money or time, and even go overseas to help teach, work as doctors, or protect the oppressed.

There are many stories of Americans helping to solve international problems and improve people's lives. September 11 widow Susan Retik's group, Beyond the 11th, helps widows and other women in Afghanistan improve their lives. Doctor Paul Farmer established medical clinics for poor people in Haiti and other countries. Of helping others, Farmer said,

Primary Source

"You're in front of someone who is suffering and you have the tools [to end] that suffering . . . you act."

—Paul Farmer

4. ☑ **Reading Check** **Identify** a challenge facing the world today and describe something an individual could do to help solve it.

_____

_____

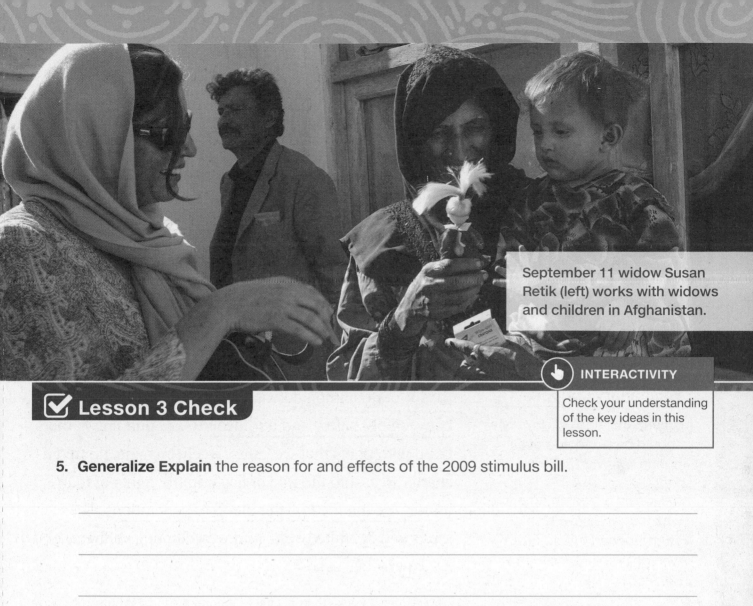

September 11 widow Susan Retik (left) works with widows and children in Afghanistan.

INTERACTIVITY

Check your understanding of the key ideas in this lesson.

☑ Lesson 3 Check

5. **Generalize Explain** the reason for and effects of the 2009 stimulus bill.

_____

_____

_____

6. **Analyze** the effect globalization has had on the economy of the United States.

_____

_____

_____

7. **Analyze** and **explain** a positive and negative consequence of changing the environment in the United States.

_____

_____

_____

President Barack Obama's First Inaugural Address

In 2008, Barack Obama was elected president of the United States. He was the first African American to hold the nation's highest office. At the time, the country was in the middle of a severe economic downturn and involved in wars with two countries in the Middle East. Still, there was a feeling of hope among many Americans that we would overcome these obstacles.

Vocabulary Support

Americans' right to privacy should be protected even during the War on Terror

the ideals on which America was founded have been strengthened by those who gave their lives in their defense

peril, *n.*, a danger

charter, *n.*, a document describing how a government will be organized

expedience, *n.*, the quality of being easy in order to reach a desired result

"As for our common defense, we reject as false the choice between our safety and our ideals. Our Founding Fathers, faced with perils that we can scarcely imagine, drafted a charter to assure the rule of law and the rights of man— a charter expanded by the blood of generations. Those ideals still light the world, and we will not give them up for expedience sake."

–President Barack Obama, First Inaugural Address, January 21, 2009

Fun Fact

On Inauguration Day in 2009, Chief Justice John Roberts misstated a few words as President Obama took the oath of office. As a result, Obama was sworn in again the next day. In 2013, after being reelected, he took the oath privately on January 20 because it fell on a Sunday, and then publicly on January 21. Franklin Roosevelt, who was elected four times, was the only other president to be sworn in four times.

President Barack Obama

Close Reading

1. **Identify** and write down the name of the "charter" that President Obama was referring to when he said "a charter to assure the rule of law and the rights of man."

_____

2. Explain why he mentions this document in his speech.

_____

_____

_____

_____

_____

_____

_____

Wrap It Up

Summarize the threats to our common defense to which President Obama was referring.

_____

_____

_____

_____

_____

_____

_____

Lesson 4

Science and Technology

 INTERACTIVITY

Participate in a class discussion to preview the content of this lesson.

Vocabulary

science
technology

Academic Vocabulary

observation
operation

Scientific discoveries about light led to three-dimensional holograms. The hologram can then help scientists understand more about the human body.

Unlock The BIG Question

I will know how scientific and technological discoveries have affected life in America.

JumpStart Activity

With a group, talk about the most recent scientific or medical advance each of you have heard about. Discuss why the advance is important and how it will affect people's lives. Then talk about advances that you would like to see achieved in your lifetime.

The Impact of Science

At the beginning of the twentieth century, Americans marveled at the Wright Brothers' flight and the Model T Ford. In the 1950s, the first commercial computer was built. It took up an entire room! In 1969, Americans landed on the moon. By the 1970s, desktop computers were available for the home. By the year 2000, the Internet and e-mail were household words. Where do we go from there?

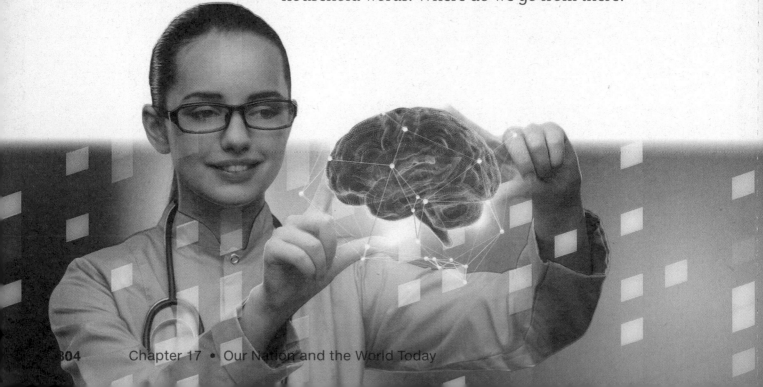

Science and Technology

Science is the study of the natural world through **observation** and experiment. For example, chemists found that some elements, such as silicon, had unusual electrical properties. That was interesting, but it wasn't particularly useful to ordinary people.

Technology is the application of scientific knowledge for practical purposes. Engineers used what the chemists had learned to reduce the size and increase the power of that first huge computer. Over time, science and technology worked together to give you the smartphone.

Academic Vocabulary

observation • *n.*, the act of viewing or noting facts for a scientific purpose

INTERACTIVITY

Explore the key ideas of this lesson.

The Space Program

On October 4, 1957, the United States got a wake-up call. The Soviet Union had sent the first satellite into orbit around Earth. The satellite, named *Sputnik*, was about the size of a beach ball. This marked the dawn of the Space Age. It also led directly to the formation of the National Aeronautics and Space Administration (NASA).

In January 1958, the United States successfully launched its first satellite, *Explorer I*. Since then, NASA has achieved goals that seemed like science fiction 100 years ago. In 1969, American Neil Armstrong became the first human to set foot on the moon. In August 2012, NASA safely landed the rover *Curiosity* on Mars. In 2014, *Curiosity* was still sending information back to Earth.

In 1969, American astronaut Neil Armstrong became the first man on the moon.

Spinoffs From Space

Some people think that money should be spent solving problems on Earth instead of exploring space. However, many everyday consumer products had their start in the space program. These are called "spinoffs" from space.

For example, to keep food fresh, NASA perfected freeze-dried foods. Cordless power tools were also first developed for space missions. The space program is responsible for many of the scientific discoveries used in today's technology. These new technologies are a key part of America's economic growth.

Science and Technology in Medicine

In the early 1900s, a simple cut finger could be fatal. Then the first antibiotic, penicillin, was discovered in the 1920s. Since then, scientists have developed many new drugs to treat a variety of illnesses.

The goal of other scientists was to understand the human genetic code. The genetic code is the set of instructions that cells use to determine how a person grows, functions, and looks. Understanding how the human body works and why it fails is the first step in developing new medical treatments.

In 2016, engineers built the first dust-sized, wireless sensors. This "neural dust" can be implanted in the body to monitor nerves or organs. These sensors could be a step toward treating problems such as epilepsy or to decrease inflammation in the body.

Other advances have led to safer and more effective surgery. New tests can detect problems earlier, while they can still be fixed. As a result, people are living longer and healthier lives.

Advances in Transportation

The most important advance in transportation in the late twentieth century wasn't electric cars or jet planes. It was computers. Most new vehicles today have built-in computers. These devices constantly monitor all of the car's systems. Global Positioning System (GPS) units know exactly where the car is. In many cases, the driver simply asks the computer how to get to the next destination.

GPS units use satellites to help drivers navigate more easily.

Today's transportation requires complex control systems. Computers control traffic lights that keep traffic moving safely. They allow air traffic controllers to safely guide over 30,000 flights a day. Computers automatically control trains and mass transit systems in cities.

Mass transit systems could look very different in the coming years. After being proposed by entrepreneur Elon Musk, three startup companies began testing a high-speed railway in 2016. Called the Hyperloop, the system would have passengers traveling in pods through low-pressure tubes, surrounded by a cushion of air. The air reduces friction and allows the pods to travel, using magnetic levitation, at speeds as high as 670 miles per hour.

Radar and GPS satellites make ship travel safer. Computers linked to satellites keep track of every ship, train, and truck in a delivery system. In the future, computers might only be tracking delivery drones. In late 2016, the first package was delivered in the United Kingdom using a drone.

A high-speed railway called the Hyperloop is being tested in the Nevada desert.

Advances in Communication

In the early 1900s, getting news from a distant town might take days or even weeks. Today, a post to a social network is seen around the world in seconds. People carry on text conversations as if they were in the same room. With satellites, they watch live events around the world.

In 1946, the world's first computer, which weighed over 25 tons, could perform 385 multiplications per second. Today's smartphone can perform over 2 billion **operations** per second. Some people believe that instant communication is like an addiction. There is also the challenge of keeping the Internet safe for all users. Cyberbullying and sharing too much personal information are problems that have come along with the conveniences of new technologies. Only time will tell if the benefits are greater than the risks.

Academic Vocabulary

operation • *n.*, a single step in a computer program

1. **☑ Reading Check** **Identify** and **explain** scientific discoveries and technological innovations in transportation that have benefited individuals and society.

_____

_____

_____

Technology and the Economy

In 1938, Stanford graduates William Hewlett and David Packard began working on a few product ideas in a garage in Palo Alto, California. They soon founded Hewlett-Packard (HP). Within 20 years, the area around San Francisco Bay became a breeding ground for high-tech companies known as Silicon Valley.

The popularity of computers created a huge demand that contributed to economic growth. Computers allowed employees to get more work done in less time, and companies could now sell their product worldwide.

The effect on jobs was mixed. Jobs once done by human hands were now done by robots, causing some workers to lose their jobs. On the other hand, computers created new jobs. People had to build them, program them, operate them, or fix them.

What the Future Holds

In 1971, scientist and writer Arthur C. Clarke predicted that the first Mars landing would be in 1994. *Viking 1* landed on July 20, 1976. In 1951, he predicted a mission to the moon in 1978. *Apollo 11* landed in 1969. Today, scientists at NASA are planning the first manned trip to Mars for the 2030s. Maybe we will exceed that goal, too.

The only thing we can be sure of in the future is that things will change. How will changes in science and technology affect society? How will they affect individuals?

2. **✓ Reading Check**
With a partner, **identify** and **discuss** two ways in which scientific discoveries and technological changes have affected the economy of the United States.

These robots have replaced human workers in an automobile assembly line.

In medicine, work is underway to allow people to control artificial limbs with their mind and 3-D printers will create custom prosthetics. In transportation, trains that travel over 300 mph are already operating. In communication, clothing with built-in computers will become common.

With all the possibilities, where should our efforts lie? What goals will we set for the future? Will they focus on building our society, personal convenience, the needs of the less fortunate, or something else?

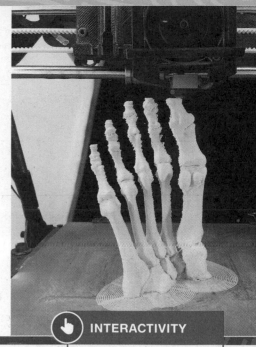

A 3D-printing model of a human foot

INTERACTIVITY

Check your understanding of the key ideas in this lesson.

☑ Lesson 4 Check

3. **Draw Conclusions Explain** how scientific or technological developments in medicine have benefited individuals and society in the United States.

_____

_____

4. **Predict** and **explain** the goals the U.S. should set for science or technology that will bring the greatest benefit to American society.

_____

_____

_____

5. **Analyze** how computers and satellites have affected communications and transportation.

_____

_____

_____

_____

Quality:
Leadership

Sonia Sotomayor (1954–)
Leading By Example

Sonia Sotomayor graduated with high honors from Princeton University in 1976. She went on to Yale Law School where she advocated for an increase in minority students. After graduation, she became assistant district attorney in Manhattan in 1980. In 1984, while working as a partner at a private law firm, she served on the board of the Puerto Rican Legal Defense and Education Fund as a top policy member. Her work at these agencies got the attention of a number of U.S. senators.

In 1992, President George H. W. Bush nominated her for a position as U.S. District Court Judge for the Southern District of New York State. She was the youngest judge in this court. Six years later, she was confirmed as a judge for the U.S. Second Circuit Court of Appeals. Even while holding high positions, Sotomayor continued doing what she loved—educating others. She taught law at New York University in 1998 and at Columbia Law School in 1999.

In 2009, President Barack Obama nominated Sotomayor for a Supreme Court justice. She was confirmed and became the first Latina Supreme Court justice in American history.

Find Out More

1. **Explain** why Sonia Sotomayor is a strong leader especially for the Hispanic community.

_____

_____

_____

_____

_____

2. Make a quick timeline of Sonia Sotomayor's career. Show your timeline to students at your school who are not familiar with her career. Are they inspired by her work?

Use this information to review some of the key terms, people, and ideas from this chapter.

President Jimmy Carter helped broker the Camp David Peace Accords.

After peaceful tactics failed, President George H. W. Bush led a coalition against an Iraqi invasion.

Iraqi leader Saddam Hussein's refusal to allow the UN to confirm the destruction of Iraq's WMD led to his downfall.

As Secretary of State, Madeleine Albright worked to resolve conflicts in areas of unrest around the world.

President Barack Obama led the country through the worst economic downturn since the Great Depression and two wars in the Middle East.

Elected in 2016, Donald Trump, dealt with issues involving trade, immigration, the environment, and political unrest.

1977
NASA launches *Voyager 1* to explore our solar system.

1969
Neil Armstrong is the first human to walk on the moon.

1992
The first smartphone is used.

2016
Elon Musk begins testing for a high speed railway.

1945 **1965** **1985** **2005** **2025**

1946
The first computer is developed.

1993
The first bionic limb is developed.

2012
The rover *Curiosity* lands on Mars.

☑ **Assessment**

🎮 **GAMES**

Play the vocabulary game.

Vocabulary and Key Ideas

1. **Define** What is the **Electoral College?**

_____

_____

2. **Identify** the main cause of the invasion of Iraq in 2001.

_____

_____

_____

_____

3. **Define** Draw a line to match the definitions to the correct terms.

1. people who are not in the military   a. **coalition**

2. a large economic slowdown   b. **civilians**

3. the application of science for   c. **recession**
   practical purposes

4. a group of allies who work together   d. **technology**

4. **Analyze** the effects of American dependence on oil as a source of energy. Use evidence from the graph to support your answer.

_____

_____

_____

_____

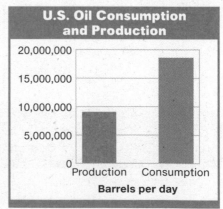

Source: World Factbook

Critical Thinking and Writing

5. **Analyze** and **explain** how globalization has affected the United States.

_____

_____

_____

_____

_____

6. **Analyze** and **explain** how technology developed by NASA affected the economic development of the United States.

_____

_____

_____

_____

7. **Revisit the Big Question** What goals do you think the United States should set for itself regarding energy and developing new technology?

_____

_____

_____

_____

_____

8. **Writer's Workshop: Write an Explanatory Essay** On a separate sheet of paper, write an explanatory essay about how the lives of Americans would be better if we actually meet the goals that you outlined in question 7. How would these goals change lives? How far do you think we are from achieving them?

Analyze Primary Sources

"Good evening. Today our fellow citizens, our way of life, our very freedom came under attack in a series of deliberate and deadly terrorist acts.

The victims were in airplanes or in their offices—secretaries, businessmen and women, military and federal workers. Moms and dads. Friends and neighbors."

—President George W. Bush, speech, September 11, 2001

9. To what was President Bush referring in this speech? What was the response of Americans to this event?

_____

_____

_____

_____

_____

Write Reports and Bibliographies

Gillis, Justin. "An Effect of Climate Change You Could Really Lose Sleep Over."
New York Times, May 26, 2017. Web.

10. Look at the bibliography entry above. Write a title and a topic sentence for a report that you would write, using this article as a source.

_____

_____

_____

_____

_____

Quest Findings

INTERACTIVITY

Use this activity to help you prepare your map.

Mapping the Middle East

You have read about what occurred between the United States and several Middle Eastern countries during the late twentieth century and beginning of the twenty-first century. Now you are ready to illustrate and annotate your country's portion of the class map of the Middle East. Remember to include historical and cultural information.

1 Collaborate With Your Partner

Review what you learned about the Middle East. Use the evidence that you gathered from your Quest Connections and your research and decide what kinds of details you will include about your country.

2 Gather Evidence

Create notecards with information about leaders, conflicts, the role of the United States, and any other relevant information.

3 Create Visuals

Look at the information that you have gathered. Decide what visuals would be most helpful for your audience.

4 Present Your Map

Create the class map by joining together your map with those of the rest of the class. Pairs should then take turns presenting the information that they gathered for their country.

The Declaration of Independence

In Congress, July 4, 1776
The Unanimous Declaration of the Thirteen
United States of America

The first part of the Declaration of Independence is called the Preamble. A preamble is an introduction, or the part that comes before the main message. The Preamble states why the Declaration was written.

The second paragraph lists the basic rights that all people should have. The founders called these **unalienable** rights, meaning that these rights cannot be taken or given away. If a government cannot protect these rights, the people must change the government or create a new one.

1. According to the Declaration, what are three "unalienable rights"? Circle these words in the text.

The third paragraph introduces the List of Grievances. Each part of this list begins with the words, "He has…." These words refer to King George III's actions in the colonies. To prove that the king had abused his power over the colonies, this list of 27 complaints described how the British government and the king had treated the colonists.

When in the Course of human events it becomes necessary for one people to dissolve the political bands which have connected them with another, and to assume among the powers of the earth, the separate and equal station to which the Laws of nature and of nature's God entitle them, a decent respect to the opinions of mankind requires that they should declare the causes which impel them to the separation.

We hold these truths to be self-evident, that all men are created equal, that they are endowed by their Creator with certain unalienable Rights, that among these are Life, Liberty and the Pursuit of Happiness. That to secure these rights, Governments are instituted among Men, deriving their just powers from the consent of the governed; That whenever any Form of Government becomes destructive of these ends it is the Right of the People to alter or to abolish it, and to institute new Government, laying its foundation on such principles and organizing its powers in such form, as to them shall seem most likely to effect their Safety and Happiness. Prudence, indeed, will dictate that Governments long established should not be changed for light and transient causes; and accordingly all experience hath shown, that mankind are more disposed to suffer, while evils are sufferable, than to right themselves by abolishing the forms to which they are accustomed. But when a long train of abuses and usurpations, pursuing invariably the same Object evinces a design to reduce them under absolute Despotism, it is their right, it is their duty, to throw off such Government, and to provide new Guards for their future security.

Such has been the patient sufferance of these Colonies; and such is now the necessity which constrains them to alter their former Systems of Government. The history of the present King of Great Britain is a history of repeated injuries and usurpations, all having in direct object the establishment of an absolute Tyranny over these States. To prove this, let Facts be submitted to a candid world.

He has refused his Assent to Laws, the most wholesome and necessary for the public good.

He has forbidden his Governors to pass Laws of immediate and pressing importance, unless suspended in their operation till his

Assent should be obtained; and when so suspended, he has utterly neglected to attend to them.

He has refused to pass other Laws for the accommodation of large districts of people, unless those people would relinquish the right of Representation in the Legislature, a right inestimable to them and formidable to tyrants only.

He has called together legislative bodies at places unusual, uncomfortable, and distant from the depository of their Public Records, for the sole purpose of fatiguing them into compliance with his measures.

He has dissolved Representative Houses repeatedly, for opposing with manly firmness his invasions on the rights of the people.

He has refused for a long time, after such dissolutions, to cause others to be elected; whereby the Legislative powers, incapable of Annihilation, have returned to the People at large for their exercise; the State remaining in the mean time exposed to all the dangers of invasions from without, and convulsions within.

He has endeavored to prevent the population of these States; for that purpose obstructing the Laws for Naturalization of Foreigners; refusing to pass others to encourage their migration hither, and raising the conditions of new Appropriations of Lands.

He has obstructed the Administration of Justice, by refusing his Assent to Laws for establishing Judiciary powers.

He has made Judges dependent on his Will alone for the tenure of their offices, and the amount and payment of their salaries.

He has erected a multitude of New Offices, and sent hither swarms of Officers to harass our people and eat out their substance.

He has kept among us in time of peace, Standing Armies, without the Consent of our legislatures.

He has affected to render the Military independent of, and superior to, the Civil Power.

He has combined with others to subject us to a jurisdiction foreign to our constitutions, and unacknowledged by our laws; giving his Assent to their Acts of pretended Legislation:

For quartering large bodies of armed troops among us;

For protecting them, by a mock Trial, from punishment for any Murders which they should commit on the Inhabitants of these States;

In the List of Grievances, the colonists complain that they have no say in choosing the laws that govern them. They say that King George III is not concerned about their safety and happiness. They list the times when the king denied them the right to representation. The colonists also state that the king has interfered with judges, with the court system, and with foreigners who want to become citizens.

2. There are many words in the Declaration that may be unfamiliar to you. Circle three words you do not know. Look the words up in the dictionary. Write one word and its meaning on the lines below.

_____

_____

_____

_____

_____

_____

_____

This page continues the colonists' long List of Grievances.

3. In your own words, briefly sum up three grievances.

_____

_____

_____

_____

4. Match each word from the Declaration with its meaning. Use a dictionary if you need help with a word.

abolishing	tried to achieve
plundered	changing
suspending	doing away with
altering	stopping for a time
endeavored	robbed

Statement of Independence
After listing their many grievances, the signers begin their statement of independence. Because the king has refused to correct the problems, he is an unfair ruler. Therefore, he is not fit to rule the free people of America.

For cutting off our Trade with all parts of the world;

For imposing Taxes on us without our Consent;

For depriving us, in many cases, of the benefits of Trial by Jury;

For transporting us beyond Seas to be tried for pretended offenses;

For abolishing the free System of English Laws in a neighboring Province, establishing therein an Arbitrary government, and enlarging its Boundaries so as to render it at once an example and fit instrument for introducing the same absolute rule into these Colonies;

For taking away our Charters, abolishing our most valuable Laws, and altering fundamentally the Forms of our Governments;

For suspending our own Legislatures, and declaring themselves invested with Power to legislate for us in all cases whatsoever.

He has abdicated Government here, by declaring us out of his Protection, and waging War against us.

He has plundered our seas, ravaged our Coasts, burned our towns, and destroyed the lives of our people.

He is at this time transporting large Armies of foreign mercenaries to complete the works of death, desolation and tyranny, already begun with circumstances of Cruelty and perfidy scarcely paralleled in the most barbarous ages, and totally unworthy the Head of a civilized nation.

He has constrained our fellow Citizens taken Captive on the high Seas to bear Arms against their Country, to become the executioners of their friends and Brethren, or to fall themselves by their Hands.

He has excited domestic insurrections amongst us, and has endeavored to bring on the inhabitants of our frontiers the merciless Indian Savages whose known rule of warfare, is an undistinguished destruction of all ages, sexes, and conditions.

In every stage of these Oppressions We have Petitioned for Redress in the most humble terms. Our repeated Petitions have been answered only by repeated injury. A Prince, whose character is thus marked by every act which may define a Tyrant, is unfit to be the ruler of a free People.

Nor have We been wanting in attentions to our British brethren. We have warned them from time to time of attempts by their legislature to extend an unwarrantable jurisdiction over us. We have reminded them of the circumstances of our emigration and settlement here. We have appealed to their native justice and magnanimity, and we have conjured them by the ties of our common kindred to disavow these usurpations, which, would inevitably interrupt our connections and correspondence. They too have been deaf to the voice of justice and of consanguinity. We must, therefore, acquiesce in the necessity, which denounces our Separation, and hold them, as we hold the rest of mankind, Enemies in War, in Peace Friends.

We, therefore, the Representatives of the United States of America, in General Congress, Assembled, appealing to the Supreme Judge of the world for the rectitude of our intentions, do, in the Name, and by the Authority of the good People of these Colonies, solemnly publish and declare, That these United Colonies are, and of right ought to be Free and Independent States; that they are Absolved from all Allegiance to the British Crown, and that all political connection between them and the State of Great Britain, is and ought to be totally dissolved, and that as Free and Independent States, they have full Power to levy War, conclude Peace, contract Alliances, establish Commerce, and to do all other Acts and Things which Independent States may of right do. And for the support of this Declaration, with a firm reliance on the protection of Divine Providence, we mutually pledge to each other our Lives, our Fortunes, and our sacred Honor.

New Hampshire:
Josiah Bartlett
William Whipple
Matthew Thornton

Massachusetts Bay:
John Hancock
Samuel Adams
John Adams
Robert Treat Paine
Elbridge Gerry

Rhode Island:
Stephan Hopkins
William Ellery

Connecticut:
Roger Sherman
Samuel Huntington
William Williams
Oliver Wolcott

New York:
William Floyd
Philip Livingston
Francis Lewis
Lewis Morris

New Jersey:
Richard Stockton
John Witherspoon
Francis Hopkinson
John Hart
Abraham Clark

Delaware:
Caesar Rodney
George Read
Thomas M'Kean

Maryland:
Samuel Chase
William Paca
Thomas Stone
Charles Carroll of
   Carrollton

Virginia:
George Wythe
Richard Henry Lee
Thomas Jefferson
Benjamin Harrison
Thomas Nelson, Jr.
Francis Lightfoot Lee
Carter Braxton

Pennsylvania:
Robert Morris
Benjamin Rush
Benjamin Franklin
John Morton
George Clymer
James Smith
George Taylor
James Wilson
George Ross

North Carolina:
William Hooper
Joseph Hewes
John Penn

South Carolina:
Edward Rutledge
Thomas Heyward, Jr.
Thomas Lynch, Jr.
Arthur Middleton

Georgia:
Button Gwinnett
Lyman Hall
George Walton

In this paragraph, the signers point out that they have asked the British people for help many times. The colonists hoped the British would listen to them because they have so much in common. The British people, however, paid no attention to their demand for justice. This is another reason for why the colonies must break away from Great Britain.

In the last paragraph, the members of the Continental Congress declare that the thirteen colonies are no longer colonies. They are now a free nation with no ties to Great Britain. The United States now has all the powers of other independent countries.

5. List three powers that the signers claim the new nation now has.

_____

_____

_____

_____

_____

6. The signers promised to support the Declaration of Independence and each other with their lives, their fortunes, and their honor. On a separate sheet of paper, tell what you think this means. Then explain why it was a brave thing to do.

United States Constitution

PREAMBLE

This **Preamble** gives the reasons for writing and having a Constitution. The Constitution will form a stronger and more united nation. It will lead to peace, justice, and liberty and will defend American citizens. Finally, it will improve the lives of people.

We the People of the United States, in Order to form a more perfect Union, establish Justice, insure domestic Tranquility, provide for the common defense, promote the general Welfare, and secure the Blessings of Liberty to ourselves and our Posterity, do ordain and establish this Constitution for the United States of America.

ARTICLE I

Section 1. Congress
The legislative branch of government makes the country's laws. Called the Congress, it has two parts, or houses: the House of Representatives and the Senate.

Section 1.
All legislative Powers herein granted shall be vested in a Congress of the United States, which shall consist of a Senate and House of Representatives.

Section 2. The House of Representatives
Members of the House of Representatives are elected every two years. Representatives must be 25 years old and United States citizens. They must also live in the states that elect them.

The number of Representatives for each state is based on the population, or number of people who live there.

Section 2.
1. The House of Representatives shall be composed of Members chosen every second Year by the People of the several States, and the Electors in each State shall have the Qualifications requisite for Electors of the most numerous Branch of the State Legislature.
2. No Person shall be a Representative who shall not have attained to the age of twenty-five Years, and been seven Years a Citizen of the United States, and who shall not, when elected, be an Inhabitant of that State in which he shall be chosen.
3. Representatives and direct Taxes shall be apportioned among the several States which may be included within this Union, according to their respective Numbers, which shall be determined by adding to the whole Number of free Persons, including those bound to Service for a Term of Years and excluding Indians not taxed, three fifths of all other Persons. The actual Enumeration shall be made within three Years after the first Meeting of the Congress of the United States, and within every subsequent Term of ten Years, in such Manner as they shall by Law direct. The Number of Representatives shall not exceed one for every thirty Thousand, but each State shall have at Least one Representative; and, until such enumeration shall be made, the State of New Hampshire shall be entitled to choose three, Massachusetts eight, Rhode Island and Providence Plantations one, Connecticut five, New York six, New Jersey four, Pennsylvania eight, Delaware one, Maryland six, Virginia ten, North Carolina five, South Carolina five, and Georgia three.

1. Why do some states have more Representatives in Congress than other states?

_____

_____

_____

_____

Over the years, the Constitution has been altered, or changed. These altered parts are shown here in gray type.

4. When vacancies happen in the Representation from any State, the Executive Authority thereof shall issue Writs of Election to fill such Vacancies.
5. The House of Representatives shall choose their Speaker and other Officers; and shall have the sole Power of Impeachment.

Section 3.

1. The Senate of the United States shall be composed of two Senators from each State chosen by the Legislature thereof for six Years; and each Senator shall have one Vote.
2. Immediately after they shall be assembled in Consequences of the first Election, they shall be divided, as equally as may be, into three Classes. The Seats of the Senators of the first Class shall be vacated at the Expiration of the second Year; of the second Class, at the Expiration of the fourth Year; and of the third Class, at the Expiration of the sixth Year; so that one-third may be chosen every second Year; and if Vacancies happen by Resignation, or otherwise, during the Recess of the Legislature of any State, the Executive thereof may make temporary Appointments until the next Meeting of the Legislature, which shall then fill such Vacancies.
3. No Person shall be a Senator who shall not have attained to the Age of thirty Years, and been nine Years a Citizen of the United States, and who shall not, when elected, be an Inhabitant of that State for which he shall be chosen.
4. The Vice President of the United States shall be President of the Senate but shall have no Vote, unless they be equally divided.
5. The Senate shall choose their other Officers, and also a President pro tempore, in the Absence of the Vice President, or when he shall exercise the Office of President of the United States.
6. The Senate shall have the sole Power to try all Impeachments. When sitting for that Purpose, they shall be on Oath or Affirmation. When the President of the United States is tried, the Chief Justice shall preside: And no Person shall be convicted without the Concurrence of two thirds of the Members present.
7. Judgment in Cases of Impeachment shall not extend further than to removal from Office, and disqualification to hold and enjoy any Office of honor, Trust, or Profit under the United States: but the Party convicted shall nevertheless be liable and subject to Indictment, Trial, Judgment and Punishment, according to Law.

A state governor calls a special election to fill an empty seat in the House of Representatives.

Members of the House of Representatives choose their own leaders. They also have the power to impeach, or accuse, government officials of crimes.

Section 3. Senate
Each state has two Senators. A Senator serves a six-year term.

At first, each state legislature elected its two Senators. The Seventeenth Amendment changed that. Today, the voters of each state elect their Senators.

Senators must be 30 years old and United States citizens. They must also live in the states they represent.

2. How is the length of a Senator's term different from a Representative's term?

_____

_____

The Vice President is the officer in charge of the Senate but only votes to break a tie. When the Vice President is absent, a temporary leader (President Pro Tempore) leads the Senate.

The Senate holds impeachment trials. When the President is impeached, the Chief Justice of the Supreme Court is the judge. A two-thirds vote is needed to convict. Once convicted, an official can be removed from office. Other courts of law can impose other punishments.

Section 4. Elections and Meetings of Congress

The state legislatures determine the times, places, and method of holding elections for senators and representatives.

Section 5. Rules for Congress

The Senate and House of Representatives judge the fairness of the elections and the qualifications of its own members. At least half of the members must be present to do business. Each house may determine the rules of its proceedings and punish its member for disorderly behavior. Each house of Congress shall keep a record of its proceedings and from time to time publish the record.

3. Why is it important for Congress to publish a record of what they do?

_____

_____

_____

_____

Section 6. Rights and Restrictions of Members of Congress

The Senators and Representatives shall receive payment for their services to be paid out of the Treasury of the United States. Members of Congress cannot be arrested during their attendance at the session of Congress, except for a very serious crime, and they cannot be arrested for anything they say in Congress. No person can have a government job while serving as a member of Congress.

Section 4.

1. The Times, Places and Manner of holding Elections for Senators and Representatives, shall be prescribed in each State by the Legislature thereof; but the Congress may at any time by law make or alter such Regulations, except as to the Places of choosing Senators.

2. The Congress shall assemble at least once in every Year, and such Meeting shall be on the first Monday in December, unless they shall by Law appoint a different Day.

Section 5.

1. Each House shall be the Judge of the Elections, Returns and Qualifications of its own Members, and a Majority of each shall constitute a Quorum to do Business; but a smaller Number may adjourn from day to day, and may be authorized to compel the Attendance of absent Members, in such Manner, and under such Penalties, as each House may provide.

2. Each House may determine the Rules of its Proceedings, punish its Members for disorderly Behavior, and, with the Concurrence of two thirds, expel a Member.

3. Each House shall keep a Journal of its Proceedings, and from time to time publish the same, excepting such Parts as may in their Judgment require Secrecy; and the Yeas and Nays of the Members of either House on any question shall, at the Desire of one fifth of those Present, be entered on the Journal.

4. Neither House, during the Session of Congress, shall, without the Consent of the other, adjourn for more than three days, nor to any other Place than that in which the two Houses shall be sitting.

Section 6.

1. The Senators and Representatives shall receive a Compensation for their Services, to be ascertained by Law, and paid out of the Treasury of the United States. They shall in all Cases, except Treason, Felony, and Breach of the Peace, be privileged from Arrest during their Attendance at the Session of their respective Houses, and in going to and returning from the same; and for any Speech or Debate in either House, they shall not be questioned in any other Place.

2. No Senator or Representative shall, during the Time for which he was elected, be appointed to any civil Office under the Authority of the United States, which shall have been created, or the Emoluments whereof shall have been increased during such time; and no Person holding any Office under the United States, shall be a Member of either House during his Continuance in Office.

Section 7.

1. All Bills for raising Revenue shall originate in the House of Representatives; but the Senate may propose or concur with amendments as on other Bills.

2. Every Bill which shall have passed the House of Representatives and the Senate, shall, before it become a law, be presented to the President of the United States: If he approve, he shall sign it, but if not he shall return it, with his Objections to that House in which it shall have originated, who shall enter the Objections at large on their Journal, and proceed to reconsider it. If after such Reconsideration two thirds of the House shall agree to pass the Bill, it shall be sent, together with the Objections, to the other House, by which it shall likewise be reconsidered, and if approved by two thirds of that House, it shall become a Law. But in all such Cases the Votes of both Houses shall be determined by Yeas and Nays, and the Names of the Persons voting for and against the Bill shall be entered on the Journal of each House respectively. If any Bill shall not be returned by the President within ten Days (Sunday excepted) after it shall have been presented to him, the Same shall be a law, in like Manner as if he had signed it, unless the Congress by their Adjournment, prevent its Return, in which Case it shall not be a Law.

3. Every Order, Resolution, or Vote to which the Concurrence of the Senate and House of Representatives may be necessary (except on a question of adjournment) shall be presented to the President of the United States; and before the Same shall take Effect, shall be approved by him, or, being disapproved by him, shall be repassed by two thirds of the Senate and House of Representatives, according to the Rules and Limitations prescribed in the Case of a Bill.

Section 8.

The Congress shall have Power

1. To lay and collect Taxes, Duties, Imposts and Excises to pay the Debts and provide for the common Defense and general Welfare of the United States; but all Duties, Imposts and Excises, shall be uniform throughout the United States;

2. To borrow Money on the credit of the United States;

3. To regulate Commerce with foreign Nations, and among the several States, and with the Indian Tribes;

4. To establish an uniform Rule of Naturalization, and uniform Laws on the subject of Bankruptcies throughout the United States;

Section 7. How Laws are Made

All bills for raising money shall begin in the House of Representatives. The Senate may suggest or agree with amendments to these tax bills, as with other bills.

Every bill which has passed the House of Representatives and the Senate must be presented to the President of the United States before it becomes a law. If the President approves of the bill, the President shall sign it. If the President does not approve, then the bill may be vetoed. The President then sends it back to the house in which it began, with an explanation of the objections. That house writes the objections on their record and begins to reconsider it. If two thirds of each house agrees to pass the bill, it shall become a law. If any bill is neither signed nor vetoed by the President within ten days, (except for Sundays) after it has been sent to the President, the bill shall be a law. If Congress adjourns before ten days have passed, the bill does not become a law.

Section 8. Powers of Congress

Among the powers of Congress listed in Section 8 are:

- establish and collect taxes on imported and exported goods and on goods sold within the country. Congress also shall pay the debts and provide for the defense and general welfare of the United States. All federal taxes shall be the same throughout the United States.
- borrow money on the credit of the United States;
- make laws about trade with other countries, among the states, and with the American Indian tribes;
- establish one procedure by which a person from another country can become a legal citizen of the United States;
- protect the works of scientists, artists, authors, and inventors;
- create federal courts lower than the Supreme Court;

- declare war;
- establish and support an army and navy;
- organize and train a National Guard and call them up in times of emergency;
- govern the capital and military sites of the United States; and
- make all laws necessary to carry out the powers of Congress.

4. The last clause of Section 8 is called "the elastic clause" because it stretches the power of Congress. Why do you think it was added to the Constitution?

_____

_____

_____

_____

_____

_____

_____

5. To coin Money, regulate the Value thereof, and of foreign Coin, and fix the Standard of Weights and Measures;
6. To provide for the Punishment of counterfeiting the Securities and current Coin of the United States;
7. To establish Post Offices and post Roads;
8. To promote the Progress of Science and useful Arts, by securing, for limited Times to Authors and Inventors the exclusive Right to their respective Writings and Discoveries;
9. To constitute Tribunals inferior to the supreme Court;
10. To define and punish Piracies and Felonies committed on the high Seas, and Offences against the Law of nations;
11. To declare War, grant Letters of Marque and Reprisal, and make Rules concerning Captures on Land and Water;
12. To raise and support Armies; but no Appropriation of Money to that Use shall be for a longer Term than two Years;
13. To provide and maintain a Navy;
14. To make Rules for the Government and Regulation of the land and naval Forces;
15. To provide for calling forth the Militia to execute the Laws of the Union, suppress Insurrections and repel Invasions;
16. To provide for organizing, arming, and disciplining the Militia, and for governing such Part of them as may be employed in the Service of the United States, reserving to the States respectively the Appointment of the Officers, and the Authority of training the Militia according to the discipline prescribed by Congress;
17. To exercise exclusive Legislation in all Cases whatsoever, over such District (not exceeding ten Miles square) as may, by Cession of Particular States, and the Acceptance of Congress, become the Seat of the Government of the United States, and to exercise like Authority over all Places purchased by the Consent of the Legislature of the State in which the Same shall be, for the Erection of Forts, Magazines, Arsenals, Dockyards and other needful Buildings;—And
18. To make all Laws which shall be necessary and proper for carrying into Execution the foregoing Powers and all other Powers vested by this Constitution in the Government of the United States, or in any Department or Officer thereof.

Section 9.

1. The Migration or Importation of such Persons as any of the States now existing shall think proper to admit, shall not be prohibited by the Congress prior to the Year one thousand eight hundred and eight, but a Tax or duty may be imposed on such Importation, not exceeding ten dollars for each Person.

2. The Privilege of the Writ of Habeas Corpus shall not be suspended, unless when in Cases of Rebellion or Invasion the public safety may require it.

3. No Bill of Attainder or ex post facto Law shall be passed.

4. No Capitation, or other direct, Tax shall be laid, unless in Proportion to the Census of Enumeration herein before directed to be taken.

5. No Tax or Duty shall be laid on Articles exported from any State.

6. No Preference shall be given by any Regulation of Commerce or Revenue to the Ports of one State over those of another: nor shall Vessels bound to, or from, one State, be obliged to enter, clear or pay Duties in another.

7. No Money shall be drawn from the Treasury, but in Consequence of Appropriations made by Law; and a regular Statement and Account of the Receipts and Expenditures of all public Money shall be published from time to time.

8. No Title of Nobility shall be granted by the United States: And no Person holding any Office of Profit or Trust under them, shall, without the Consent of the Congress, accept of any present, Emolument, Office, or Title, of any kind whatever, from any King, Prince, or foreign State.

Section 10.

1. No State shall enter into any Treaty, Alliance, or Confederation; grant Letters of Marque and Reprisal; coin Money; emit Bills of Credit; make any Thing but gold and silver Coin a Tender in Payment of Debts; pass any Bill of Attainder, ex post facto Law, or Law impairing the Obligation of Contracts, or grant any Title of Nobility.

2. No State shall, without the Consent of the Congress, lay any Imposts or Duties on Imports or Exports, except what may be absolutely necessary for executing its inspection Laws; and the net Produce of all Duties and Imposts, laid by any State on Imports or Exports, shall be for the Use of the Treasury of the United States; and all such Laws shall be subject to the Revision and Control of the Congress.

Section 9: Powers Denied to Congress

Congress cannot

- stop slaves from being brought into the United States until 1808;
- arrest and jail people without charging them with a crime, except during an emergency;
- punish a person without a trial; punish a person for something that was not a crime when he or she did it;
- pass a direct tax, such as an income tax, unless it is in proportion to the population;
- tax goods sent out of a state;
- give the seaports of one state an advantage over another state's ports; let one state tax the ships of another state;
- spend money without passing a law to make it legal; spend money without keeping good records;
- give titles, such as king and queen, to anyone; allow federal workers to accept gifts or titles from foreign governments.

5. Why do you think the writers included the last clause of Section 9?

_____

_____

_____

_____

_____

Section 10: Powers Denied to the States

After listing what Congress is not allowed to do, the Constitution tells what powers are denied to the states.

State governments do not have the power to

- make treaties with foreign countries; print money; do anything that Section 9 of the Constitution says the federal government cannot;
- tax goods sent into or out of a state unless Congress agrees;
- keep armed forces or go to war; make agreements with other states or foreign governments unless Congress agrees.

6. What problems might arise if one state went to war with a foreign country?

_____

_____

_____

_____

_____

Article 2 describes the executive branch.

Section 1. Office of President and Vice President

The President has power to execute, or carry out, the laws of the United States.

Electors from each state choose the President. Today, these electors are called the Electoral College and are chosen by the voters.

Before 1804, the person with the most electoral votes became President. The person with the next-highest number became Vice President. The Twelfth Amendment changed this way of electing Presidents.

3. No State shall, without the Consent of Congress, lay any Duty of Tonnage, keep Troops, or Ships of War in time of Peace, enter into any Agreement or Compact with another State, or with a foreign Power, or engage in War, unless actually invaded, or in such imminent Danger as will not admit of delay.

ARTICLE II

Section 1.

1. The executive Power shall be vested in a President of the United States of America. He shall hold his Office during the Term of four Years, and, together with the Vice President, chosen for the same Term, be elected as follows:

2. Each State shall appoint, in such Manner as the Legislature thereof may direct, a Number of Electors, equal to the whole Number of Senators and Representatives to which the State may be entitled in the Congress: but no Senator or Representative, or Person holding an Office of Trust or Profit, under the United States, shall be appointed an Elector.

3. The Electors shall meet in their respective States, and vote by Ballot for two Persons, of whom one at least shall not be an Inhabitant of the same State with themselves. And they shall make a List of all the Persons voted for, and of the Number of Votes for each; which List they shall sign and certify, and transmit sealed to the Seat of the Government of the United States, directed to the President of the Senate. The President of the Senate shall, in the Presence of the Senate and House of Representatives, open all the Certificates, and the Votes shall then be counted. The Person having the greatest Number of Votes shall be the President, if such Number be a majority of the whole Number of Electors appointed; and if there be more than one who have such Majority, and have an equal Number of Votes, then, the House of Representatives shall immediately choose by Ballot one of them for President; and if no Person have a Majority, then from the five highest on the List the said House shall in like Manner choose the President. But in choosing the President, the Votes shall be taken by States, the Representatives from each State having one Vote; a quorum for this Purpose shall consist of a Member or Members from two thirds of the States, and a Majority of all the States shall be necessary to a Choice. In every Case, after the Choice of the President, the Person having the greatest Number of Votes of the Electors shall be the Vice President. But if there should remain two or more who have equal Votes, the Senate shall choose from them by Ballot the Vice President.

4. The Congress may determine the Time of choosing the Electors, and the Day on which they shall give their Votes; which Day shall be the same throughout the United States.

5. No Person except a natural born Citizen, or a Citizen of the United States, at the time of the Adoption of this Constitution, shall be eligible to the Office of President; neither shall any person be eligible to that Office who shall not have attained to the Age of thirty-five Years, and been fourteen Years a Resident within the United States.

6. In Case of the Removal of the President from Office, or of his Death, Resignation, or Inability to discharge the Powers and Duties of the said Office, the Same shall devolve on the Vice President, and the Congress may by Law provide for the Case of Removal, Death, Resignation or Inability, both of the President and Vice President, declaring what Officer shall then act as President, and such Officer shall act accordingly, until the Disability be removed, or a President shall be elected.

7. The President shall, at stated Times, receive for his Services, a Compensation, which shall neither be increased nor diminished during the Period for which he shall have been elected, and he shall not receive within that Period any other Emolument from the United States, or any of them.

8. Before he enter on the Execution of his Office, he shall take the following Oath or Affirmation: "I do solemnly swear (or affirm) that I will faithfully execute the Office of President of the United States, and will to the best of my Ability, preserve, protect and defend the Constitution of the United States."

Section 2.

1. The President shall be Commander in Chief of the Army and Navy of the United States, and of the Militia of the several States, when called into the actual Service of the United States; he may require the Opinion, in writing, of the principal Officer in each of the executive Departments, upon any Subject relating to the Duties of their respective Offices, and he shall have Power to Grant Reprieves and Pardons for Offences against the United States, except in Cases of Impeachment.

Congress decides when electors are chosen and when they vote for President. Americans now vote for the electors on Election Day, the Tuesday after the first Monday in November.

To become President, a person must be born in the United States and be a citizen. Presidents also have to be at least 35 years old and have lived in the United States for at least 14 years.

If a President dies or leaves office for any reason, the Vice President becomes President. If there is no Vice President, Congress decides on the next President. (In 1967, the Twenty-fifth Amendment changed how these offices are filled.)

7. Why is it important to agree on how to replace the President or Vice President if one should die or leave office?

_____

_____

_____

_____

The President's salary cannot be raised or lowered while he is in office. The President cannot accept other money or gifts while in office. Before taking office, the President must swear to preserve, protect, and defend the Constitution.

Section 2. Powers of the President

The President controls the armed forces and National Guard, and can ask for advice of those who run government departments. (These advisers to the President are members of the Cabinet.) The President can pardon, or free, people convicted of federal crimes.

The President can make treaties, but two thirds of the Senate must approve them. The President, with Senate approval, can name Supreme Court judges, ambassadors, and other important officials.

8. What is the Senate's ability to approve or reject treaties an example of?

_____

_____

Section 3. Duties of the President

From time to time, the President must talk to Congress about the condition of the nation. (Today, we call this speech the State of the Union address. It is given once a year in late January.) In an emergency, the President can call on Congress to meet. The President also meets with foreign leaders, makes sure the nation's laws are carried out, and signs the orders of military officers.

Section 4. Removal From Office

The President, Vice President, and other high officials can be impeached. If proved guilty, they are removed from office.

2. He shall have Power, by and with the Advice and Consent of the Senate, to make Treaties, provided two thirds of the Senators present concur; and he shall nominate, and by and with the Advice and Consent of the Senate, shall appoint Ambassadors, other public Ministers and Consuls, Judges of the supreme Court, and all other Officers of the United States, whose Appointments are not herein otherwise provided for, and which shall be established by Law: but the Congress may by Law vest the Appointment of such inferior Officers, as they think proper, in the President alone, in the Courts of Law, or in the Heads of Departments.

3. The President shall have Power to fill up all Vacancies that may happen during the Recess of the Senate, by granting Commissions which shall expire at the End of their next Session.

Section 3.

He shall from time to time give to the Congress Information of the State of the Union, and recommend to their Consideration such Measures as he shall judge necessary and expedient; he may, on extraordinary Occasions, convene both Houses, or either of them, and in Case of Disagreement between them, with Respect to the Time of Adjournment, he may adjourn them to such Time as he shall think proper; he shall receive Ambassadors and other public Ministers; he shall take Care that the Laws be faithfully executed, and shall Commission all the Officers of the United States.

Section 4.

The President, Vice President and all Civil Officers of the United States, shall be removed from Office on Impeachment for and Conviction of, Treason, Bribery, or other high Crimes and Misdemeanors.

ARTICLE III

Section 1.

The judicial Power of the United States, shall be vested in one supreme Court, and in such inferior Courts as the Congress may from time to time ordain and establish. The Judges, both of the supreme and inferior Courts, shall hold their Offices during good Behavior, and shall, at stated Times, receive for their Services, a Compensation, which shall not be diminished during their Continuance in Office.

Section 2.

1. The judicial Power shall extend to all Cases, in Law and Equity, arising under this Constitution, the Laws of the United States, and Treaties made, or which shall be made, under their Authority;— to all Cases affecting Ambassadors, other public ministers, and Consuls;— to all Cases of Admiralty and maritime Jurisdiction;— to Controversies to which the United States shall be a Party;— to Controversies between two or more States;— between a State and Citizens of another State;— between Citizens of different States;— between Citizens of the same State claiming Lands under Grants of different States, and between a State, or the Citizens thereof, and foreign States, Citizens, or Subjects.

2. In all Cases affecting Ambassadors, other public Ministers and Consuls, and those in which a State shall be a Party, the supreme Court shall have original Jurisdiction. In all the other Cases before mentioned, the supreme Court shall have appellate Jurisdiction, both as to Law and Fact, with such Exceptions, and under such Regulations as the Congress shall make.

3. The trial of all Crimes, except in Cases of Impeachment, shall be by Jury; and such Trial shall be held in the State where the said Crimes shall have been committed; but when not committed within any State, the Trial shall be at such Place or Places as the Congress may by Law have directed.

Article 3 deals with the judicial branch.

Section 1. Federal Courts
The judges of the Supreme Court and other federal courts have the power to make decisions in courts of law. If they act properly, federal judges hold their offices for life.

9. Do you think it's a good idea that federal judges hold their offices for life? Why?

_____

_____

_____

_____

_____

_____

Section 2. Powers of Federal Courts
Federal Courts have legal power over
- laws made under the Constitution
- treaties made with foreign nations
- cases occurring at sea
- cases involving the federal government
- cases involving states or citizens of different states
- cases involving foreign citizens or governments

Only the Supreme Court can judge cases involving ambassadors, government officials, or states. Other cases begin in lower courts, but they can be appealed, or reviewed, by the Supreme Court. In criminal cases other than impeachment, trials are held in the state in which the crime took place. A jury decides the case.

Section 3. Treason

Treason is waging war against the United States or helping its enemies. To be found guilty of treason, a person must confess to the crime; or, two people must have seen the crime committed.

10. Name the three branches of federal government described in Articles 1-3.

_____

_____

_____

Congress decides the punishment for a traitor. The traitor's family cannot be punished if innocent.

Article 4 deals with relationships between the states.

Section 1. Recognition by Each State

Each state must respect the laws and court decisions of the other states.

Section 2. Rights of Citizens in Other States

Citizens keep all their rights when visiting other states.

A person charged with a crime who flees to another state must be returned to the state in which the crime took place.

A slave who escapes to another state must be returned to his or her owner. (The Thirteenth Amendment outlawed slavery.)

Section 3. New States

Congress may let new states join the United States. New states cannot be formed from the land of existing states unless Congress approves.

Congress has the power to make laws to govern territories of the United States.

Section 3.

1. Treason against the United States shall consist only in levying War against them, or in adhering to their Enemies, giving them Aid and Comfort. No Person shall be convicted of Treason unless on the Testimony of two Witnesses to the same overt Act, or on Confession in open Court.
2. The Congress shall have Power to declare the Punishment of Treason, but no Attainder of Treason shall work Corruption of Blood, or Forfeiture except during the Life of the Person attainted.

ARTICLE IV

Section 1.

Full Faith and Credit shall be given in each State to the public Acts, Records, and judicial Proceedings of every other State. And the Congress may by general Laws prescribe the Manner in which such Acts, Records and Proceedings shall be proved, and the Effect thereof.

Section 2.

1. The Citizens of each State shall be entitled to all Privileges and Immunities of Citizens in the several States.
2. A Person charged in any State with Treason, Felony, or other Crime, who shall flee from justice, and be found in another State, shall on Demand of the executive Authority of the State from which he fled, be delivered up, to be removed to the State having Jurisdiction of the Crime.
3. No Person held to Service or Labor in one State, under the Laws thereof, escaping into another, shall, in Consequence of any Law or Regulation therein, be discharged from Service or Labor, but shall be delivered up on Claim of the Party to whom such Service or Labor may be due.

Section 3.

1. New States may be admitted by the Congress into this Union; but no new State shall be formed or erected within the Jurisdiction of any other State; nor any State be formed by the Junction of two or more States, or Parts of States, without the Consent of the Legislatures of the States concerned as well as of the Congress.

2. The Congress shall have Power to dispose of and make all needful Rules and Regulations respecting the Territory or other Property belonging to the United States; and nothing in this Constitution shall be so construed as to Prejudice any Claims of the United States, or of any particular State.

Section 4.

The United States shall guarantee to every State in this Union a Republican Form of Government, and shall protect each of them against Invasion; and on Application of the Legislature, or of the Executive (when the Legislature cannot be convened) against domestic Violence.

ARTICLE V

The Congress, whenever two thirds of both Houses shall deem it necessary, shall propose Amendments to this Constitution, or, on the Application of the Legislatures of two thirds of the several States, shall call a Convention for proposing Amendments, which, in either Case, shall be valid to all Intents and Purposes, as Part of this Constitution, when ratified by the Legislatures of three fourths of the several States, or by Conventions in three fourths thereof, as the one or the other Mode of Ratification may be proposed by the Congress; Provided that no Amendment which may be made prior to the Year One thousand eight hundred and eight shall in any Manner affect the first and fourth Clauses in the Ninth section of the first Article; and that no State, without its Consent, shall be deprived of its equal Suffrage in the Senate.

ARTICLE VI

Section 1.

All Debts contracted and Engagements entered into, before the Adoption of this Constitution, shall be as valid against the United States under this Constitution, as under the Confederation.

Section 2.

This Constitution, and the Laws of the United States which shall be made in Pursuance thereof; and all Treaties made, or which shall be made, under the Authority of the United States, shall be the supreme Law of the Land; and the Judges in every State shall be bound thereby, anything in the constitution or Laws of any State to the Contrary notwithstanding.

Section 4. Guarantees to the States
The federal government guarantees that each state has the right to elect its leaders. The federal government will also protect the states from invasion and violent disorders.

11. There were only thirteen states when the Constitution was written. Do you think the framers expected the United States to grow in size? Why?

_____

_____

_____

_____

Article 5 describes the two ways the Constitution can be amended. Two thirds of the Senate and House of Representatives can suggest an amendment, or two thirds of the state legislatures can have a special convention to suggest an amendment. Once an amendment has been suggested, three fourths of the state legislatures or three fourths of the special conventions must approve the amendment.

Article 6 deals with national law and the national debt. The federal government promises to pay all its debts and keep all agreements made under the Articles of Confederation.
The Constitution and federal laws are the highest laws in the land. If state laws disagree with them, the federal laws must be obeyed.

Section 3. Supporting the Constitution

Federal and state officials must promise to support the Constitution. A person's religion cannot disqualify him or her from holding office. Nine of the thirteen states must approve the Constitution for it to become the law of the land.

Article 7 deals with ratifying the Constitution. On September 17, 1787, twelve years after the Declaration of Independence, everyone at the Constitutional Convention agreed that the Constitution was complete.

The delegates to the Constitutional Convention signed their names below the Constitution to show they approved of it.

12. "The power under the Constitution will always be in the people," wrote George Washington in 1787. Explain what you think he meant.

_____

_____

_____

_____

_____

_____

Section 3.

The Senators and Representatives before mentioned, and the Members of the several State legislatures, and all executive and judicial Officers, both of the United States and of the several States, shall be bound by Oath or Affirmation, to support this Constitution; but no religious Test shall ever be required as a Qualification to any Office or public Trust under the United States.

ARTICLE VII

The ratification of the Conventions of nine States, shall be sufficient for the Establishment of this Constitution between the States so ratifying the same.

Done in Convention by the Unanimous Consent of the States present the Seventeenth Day of September in the Year of our Lord one thousand seven hundred and Eighty-seven and of the Independence of the United States of America the twelfth. In witness whereof We have hereunto subscribed our Names.

Attest:
William Jackson,
Secretary
George Washington,
President and Deputy from Virginia

New Hampshire
John Langdon
Nicholas Gilman

Massachusetts
Nathaniel Gorham
Rufus King

Connecticut
William Samuel
  Johnson
Roger Sherman

New York
Alexander Hamilton

New Jersey
William Livingston
David Brearley
William Paterson
Jonathan Dayton

Pennsylvania
Benjamin Franklin
Thomas Mifflin
Robert Morris
George Clymer
Thomas FitzSimons
Jared Ingersoll
James Wilson
Gouverneur Morris

Delaware
George Read
Gunning Bedford, Jr.
John Dickinson
Richard Bassett
Jacob Broom

Maryland
James McHenry
Dan of St. Thomas
  Jenifer
Daniel Carroll

Virginia
John Blair
James Madison, Jr.

North Carolina
William Blount
Richard Dobbs
  Spaight
Hugh Williamson

South Carolina
John Rutledge
Charles
  Cotesworth Pinckney
Charles Pinckney
Pierce Butler

Georgia
William Few
Abraham Baldwin

AMENDMENTS
Amendment 1

Congress shall make no law respecting an establishment of religion, or prohibiting the free exercise thereof, or abridging the freedom of speech, or of the press; or the right of the people peaceably to assemble, and to petition the Government for a redress of grievances.

Amendment 2

A well-regulated Militia being necessary to the security of a free State, the right of the people to keep and bear Arms, shall not be infringed.

Amendment 3

No Soldier shall, in time of peace be quartered in any house, without the consent of the Owner, nor, in time of war, but in a manner to be prescribed by law.

Amendment 4

The right of the people to be secure in their persons, houses, papers, and effects, against unreasonable searches and seizures, shall not be violated, and no Warrants shall issue, but upon probable cause, supported by Oath or affirmation, and particularly describing the place to be searched, and the persons or things to be seized.

Amendment 5

No person shall be held to answer for a capital, or otherwise infamous crime, unless on a presentment or indictment of a Grand Jury, except in cases arising in the land or naval forces, or in the Militia, when in actual service in time of War, or public danger; nor shall any person be subject for the same offence to be twice put in jeopardy of life or limb; nor shall be compelled in any criminal case to be a witness against himself, nor be deprived of life, liberty, or property, without due process of law; nor shall private property be taken for public use, without just compensation.

The first ten amendments to the Constitution are called the Bill of Rights.

First Amendment—1791
Freedom of Religion and Speech
Congress cannot set up an official religion or stop people from practicing a religion. Congress cannot stop people or newspapers from saying what they want. People can gather peacefully to complain to the government.

Second Amendment—1791
Right to Have Firearms
People have the right to own and carry guns.

Third Amendment—1791
Right Not to House Soldiers
During peacetime, citizens do not have to house soldiers.

Fourth Amendment—1791
Search and Arrest Warrant
People or homes cannot be searched without reason. A search warrant is needed to search a house.

Fifth Amendment—1791
Rights of People Accused of Crimes
Only a grand jury can accuse people of a serious crime. No one can be tried twice for the same crime if found not guilty. People cannot be forced to testify against themselves.

13. Write the amendment number that protects each right.

_____ to speak freely

_____ to be protected against unreasonable searches

_____ to not be put on trial twice for the same crime

Sixth Amendment—1791
Right to a Jury Trial
People have the right to a fast trial by a jury and to hear the charges and evidence against them. They also have the right to a lawyer and to call witnesses in their own defense.

Seventh Amendment—1791
Right to a Jury Trial in a Civil Case
In a civil, or noncriminal case, a person also has the right to a trial by jury.

Eighth Amendment—1791
Protection From Unfair Punishment
A person accused of a crime cannot be forced to pay a very high bail. A person convicted of a crime cannot be asked to pay an unfairly high fine or be punished in a cruel or unusual way.

Ninth Amendment—1791
Other Rights
People have other rights that are not specifically mentioned in the Constitution.

Tenth Amendment—1791
Powers of the States and the People
Some powers are not given to the federal government or denied to states. These rights belong to the states or to the people.

Eleventh Amendment—1795
Limits on Rights to Sue States
People from another state or foreign country cannot sue a state.

Amendment 6
In all criminal prosecutions, the accused shall enjoy the right to a speedy and public trial, by an impartial jury of the State and district wherein the crime shall have been committed, which district shall have been previously ascertained by law, and to be informed of the nature and cause of the accusation; to be confronted with the witnesses against him; to have compulsory process for obtaining witnesses in his favor, and to have the Assistance of Counsel for his defense.

Amendment 7
In Suits at common law, where the value in controversy shall exceed twenty dollars, the right of trial by jury shall be preserved, and no fact tried by a jury, shall be otherwise re-examined in any Court of the United States, than according to the rules of the common law.

Amendment 8
Excessive bail shall not be required, nor excessive fines imposed, nor cruel and unusual punishment inflicted.

Amendment 9
The enumeration in the Constitution, of certain rights, shall not be construed to deny or disparage others retained by the people.

Amendment 10
The powers not delegated to the United States by the Constitution, nor prohibited by it to the States, are reserved to the States respectively, or to the people.

Amendment 11
The Judicial power of the United States shall not be construed to extend to any suit in law or equity, commenced or prosecuted against one of the United States by Citizens of another State, or by Citizens or Subjects of any Foreign State.

Amendment 12

The Electors shall meet in their respective States and vote by ballot for President and Vice President, one of whom, at least, shall not be an inhabitant of the same State with themselves; they shall name in their ballots the person voted for as President, and in distinct ballots the person voted for as Vice President, and they shall make distinct lists of all persons voted for as President, and of all persons voted for as Vice President, and of the number of votes for each, which lists they shall sign and certify, and transmit sealed to the seat of the government of the United States, directed to the President of the Senate;— The President of the Senate shall, in the presence of the Senate and the House of Representatives, open all the certificates and the votes shall then be counted;— the person having the greatest Number of votes for President shall be the President, if such number be a majority of the whole number of Electors appointed; and if no person have such a majority, then, from the persons having the highest numbers not exceeding three on the list of those voted for as President, the House of Representatives shall choose immediately, by ballot, the President. But in choosing the President, the votes shall be taken by States, the representation from each State having one vote; a quorum for this purpose shall consist of a member or members from two thirds of the States, and a majority of all the States shall be necessary to a choice. And if the House of Representatives shall not choose a President whenever the right of choice shall devolve upon them, before the fourth day of March next following, then the Vice President shall act as President, as in case of death or other constitutional disability of the President. The person having the greatest number of votes as Vice President, shall be the Vice President, if such number be a majority of the whole number of Electors appointed, and if no person have a majority, then from the two highest numbers on the list, the Senate shall choose the Vice President; a quorum for the purpose shall consist of two thirds of the whole number of Senators, a majority of the whole number shall be necessary to a choice. But no person constitutionally ineligible to the office of President shall be eligible to that of Vice-President of the United States.

Twelfth Amendment—1804
Election of President and Vice President

This amendment changed the way the Electoral College chooses the President and Vice President. Before this amendment, candidates for President and Vice President ran separately, and each elector had two votes—one for President and one for Vice President. The candidate receiving the most votes became President, and the runner-up became Vice President.

Under this amendment, a candidate for President and a candidate for Vice President must run together. Each elector has only one vote, and the pair of candidates that receives more than half the electoral votes become the President and Vice President. If no one receives a majority of the electoral votes, the House of Representatives votes for the President from a list of the top three vote getters. In this situation, each state has one vote, and the candidate must receive more than half of the votes to become President.

If the Representatives fail to elect a President by March 4 (later changed to January 20), the Vice President serves as President. If no candidate receives at least half the electoral votes for Vice President, the names of the two top vote getters are sent to the Senate. The Senators then vote on the names, and the person receiving more than half the votes becomes Vice President.

Thirteenth Amendment—1865
Abolition of Slavery

The United States outlaws slavery. Congress can pass any laws that are needed to carry out this amendment.

Fourteenth Amendment—1868
Rights of Citizens

People born in the United States are citizens of both the United States and of the state in which they live. States must treat their citizens equally. States cannot deny their citizens the rights outlined in the Bill of Rights.

This section of the amendment made former slaves citizens of both the United States and their home state.

Based on its population, each state has a certain number of Representatives in Congress. The number of Representatives from a state might be lowered, however, if the state does not let certain citizens vote.

This section tried to force states in the South to let former slaves vote.

14. Why would a state not want to have its number of Representatives in Congress cut?

_____

_____

_____

_____

_____

Amendment 13

Section 1. Neither slavery nor involuntary servitude, except as a punishment for crime whereof the party shall have been duly convicted, shall exist within the United States, or any place subject to their jurisdiction.

Section 2. Congress shall have power to enforce this article by appropriate legislation.

Amendment 14

Section 1. All persons born or naturalized in the United States and subject to the jurisdiction thereof, are citizens of the United States and of the State wherein they reside. No State shall make or enforce any law which shall abridge the privileges or immunities of citizens of the United States; nor shall any State deprive any person of life, liberty, or property, without due process of law; nor deny to any person within its jurisdiction the equal protection of the laws.

Section 2. Representatives shall be apportioned among the several States according to their respective numbers, counting the whole number of persons in each State, excluding Indians not taxed. But when the right to vote at any election for the choice of electors for President and Vice President of the United States, Representatives in Congress, the Executive and Judicial officers of a State, or the members of the Legislature thereof, is denied to any of the male inhabitants of such State, being twenty-one years of age and citizens of the United States, or in any way abridged, except for participation in rebellion, or other crime, the basis of representation therein shall be reduced in the proportion which the number of such male citizens shall bear to the whole number of male citizens twenty-one years of age in such State.

Section 3. No person shall be a Senator or Representative in Congress, or elector of President and Vice President, or hold any office, civil or military, under the United States, or under any State, who, having previously taken an oath, as a member of Congress, or as an officer of the United States, or as a member of any State legislature, or as an executive or judicial officer of any State, to support the Constitution of the United States, shall have engaged in insurrection or rebellion against the same, or given aid or comfort to the enemies thereof. But Congress may, by a vote of two thirds of each House, remove such disability.

Section 4. The validity of the public debt of the United States, authorized by law, including debts incurred for payment of pensions and bounties for services in suppressing insurrection or rebellion, shall not be questioned. But neither the United States nor any State shall assume or pay any debt or obligation incurred in aid of insurrection or rebellion against the United States, or any claim for the loss or emancipation of any slave; but all such debts, obligations and claims shall be held illegal and void.

Section 5. The Congress shall have power to enforce, by appropriate legislation, the provisions of this article.

Amendment 15

Section 1. The right of citizens of the United States to vote shall not be denied or abridged by the United States or by any State on account of race, color, or previous condition of servitude.

Section 2. The Congress shall have power to enforce this article by appropriate legislation.

Officials who took part in the Civil War against the United States cannot hold federal or state office. Congress can remove this provision by a two-thirds vote.

The United States will pay back the money it borrowed to fight the Civil War. The money that the South borrowed to fight the Civil War will not be paid back to lenders. The former owners of slaves will not be paid for the slaves that were set free. Congress can pass any necessary laws to enforce this article.

15. List two ways in which the Fourteenth Amendment tended to punish those who rebelled against the United States.

_____

_____

_____

_____

_____

_____

_____

Fifteenth Amendment—1870 Voting Rights
The federal and state government cannot stop people from voting based on race or color. Former slaves must be allowed to vote.

Sixteenth Amendment—1913
Income Tax

Congress has the power to collect an income tax regardless of the population of a state. (Originally, Section 9 of Article 1 had denied this power to Congress.)

Seventeenth Amendment—1913
Direct Election of Senators

The voters of each state will elect their Senators directly. (Originally, Article 1, Section 3 said state legislatures would elect Senators.)

A state can hold a special election to fill an empty Senate seat. Until then, the governor can appoint a Senator to fill an empty seat.

Eighteenth Amendment—1919
Prohibition

Making, importing, or selling alcoholic drinks is illegal in the United States. This was called Prohibition because the amendment prohibited, or outlawed, alcohol.

Congress and the states can make any laws to prohibit alcohol.

This amendment becomes part of the Constitution if it is approved within seven years.

This amendment was repealed, or cancelled, in 1933 by the Twenty-first Amendment.

16. Write the amendment number that did each of the following:

_____ let the Federal Government collect income tax

_____ guaranteed voting rights for African Americans

_____ outlawed the sale of alcohol

_____ abolished slavery

_____ let voters elect their Senators

Amendment 16

The Congress shall have power to lay and collect taxes on incomes, from whatever source derived, without apportionment among the several States, and without regard to any census or enumeration.

Amendment 17

The Senate of the United States shall be composed of two Senators from each State, elected by the people thereof, for six years; and each Senator shall have one vote. The electors in each State shall have the qualifications requisite for electors of the most numerous branch of the State legislatures.

When vacancies happen in the representation of any State in the Senate, the executive authority of such State shall issue writs of election to fill such vacancies: Provided, That the legislature of any State may empower the executive thereof to make temporary appointments until the people fill the vacancies by election as the legislature may direct.

This amendment shall not be so construed as to affect the election or term of any Senator chosen before it becomes valid as part of the Constitution.

Amendment 18

Section 1. After one year from the ratification of this article the manufacture, sale, or transportation of intoxicating liquors within, the importation thereof into, or the exportation thereof from the United States and all territory subject to the jurisdiction thereof for beverage purposes is hereby prohibited.

Section 2. The Congress and the several States shall have concurrent power to enforce this article by appropriate legislation.

Section 3. This article shall be inoperative unless it shall have been ratified as an amendment to the Constitution by the legislatures of the several States, as provided in the Constitution, within seven years of the date of the submission hereof to the States by Congress.

Amendment 19

The right of citizens of the United States to vote shall not be denied or abridged by the United States or by any State on account of sex.

Congress shall have power to enforce this article by appropriate legislation.

Amendment 20

Section 1. The terms of the President and Vice President shall end at noon on the 20th day of January, and the terms of Senators and Representatives at noon on the 3d day of January, of the years in which such terms would have ended if this article had not been ratified; and the terms of their successors shall then begin.

Section 2. The Congress shall assemble at least once in every year, and such meeting shall begin at noon on the 3d day of January, unless they shall by law appoint a different day.

Section 3. If, at the time fixed for the beginning of the term of the President, the President elect shall have died, the Vice President elect shall become President. If a President shall not have been chosen before the time fixed for the beginning of his term, or if the President-elect shall have failed to qualify, then the Vice President elect shall act as President until a President shall have qualified; and the Congress may by law provide for the case wherein neither a President elect nor a Vice President elect shall have qualified, declaring who shall then act as President, or the manner in which one who is to act shall be selected, and such person shall act accordingly until a President or Vice President shall have qualified.

Section 4. The Congress may by law provide for the case of the death of any of the persons from whom the House of Representatives may choose a President whenever the right of choice shall have devolved upon them, and for the case of the death of any of the persons from whom the Senate may choose a Vice President whenever the right of choice shall have devolved upon them.

Section 5. Sections 1 and 2 shall take effect on the 15th day of October following the ratification of this article.

Section 6. This article shall be inoperative unless it shall have been ratified as an amendment to the Constitution by the legislatures of three fourths of the several States within seven years from the date of its submission.

**Twenty-first
Amendment—1933
Repeal of Prohibition**

The Eighteenth Amendment, which outlawed alcohol, is no longer in effect.

Any state may pass laws to prohibit alcohol.

17. How long was the Eighteenth Amendment in effect in the United States?

_____

**Twenty-second
Amendment—1951
Limit on Terms of the President**

A President can only be elected to the office for two terms (eight years). If a President serves more than two years of the last President's term, then the President may only be re-elected once.

18. Do you think a President should be limited to just two terms in office? Why or why not?

_____

_____

_____

_____

_____

_____

Amendment 21

Section 1. The eighteenth article of amendment to the Constitution of the United States is hereby repealed.

Section 2. The transportation or importation into any State, Territory, or possession of the United States for delivery or use therein of intoxicating liquors, in violation of the laws thereof, is hereby prohibited.

Section 3. This article shall be inoperative unless it shall have been ratified as an amendment to the Constitution by conventions in the several States, as provided in the Constitution, within seven years from the date of the submission hereof to the States by the Congress.

Amendment 22

Section 1. No person shall be elected to the office of the President more than twice, and no person who has held the office of President, or acted as President, for more than two years of a term to which some other person was elected President shall be elected to the office of the President more than once. But this Article shall not apply to any person holding the office of President, when this Article was proposed by the Congress, and shall not prevent any person who may be holding the office of President, or acting as President, during the term within which this Article becomes operative from holding the office of President or acting as President during the remainder of such term.

Section 2. This article shall be inoperative unless it shall have been ratified as an amendment to the Constitution by the legislatures of three fourths of the several states within seven years from the date of its submission to the States by the Congress.

Amendment 23

Section 1. The District constituting the seat of Government of the United States shall appoint in such manner as the Congress may direct:

A number of electors of President and Vice President equal to the whole number of Senators and Representatives in Congress to which the District would be entitled if it were a State, but in no event more than the least populous State; they shall be in addition to those appointed by the States, they shall be considered, for the purposes of the election of President and Vice President, to be electors appointed by a State; and they shall meet in the District and perform such duties as provided by the twelfth article of amendment.

Amendment 24

Section 1. The right of citizens of the United States to vote in any primary or other election for President or Vice President, for electors for President or Vice President, or for Senator or Representative in Congress, shall not be denied or abridged by the United States or any State by reason of failure to pay any poll tax or other tax.

Section 2. The Congress shall have power to enforce this article by appropriate legislation.

Amendment 25

Section 1. In case of the removal of the President from office or of his death or resignation, the Vice President shall become President.

Section 2. Whenever there is a vacancy in the office of the Vice President, the President shall nominate a Vice President who shall take office upon confirmation by a majority vote of both Houses of Congress.

Section 3. Whenever the President transmits to the President pro tempore of the Senate and the Speaker of the House of Representatives his written declaration that he is unable to discharge the powers and duties of his office, and until he transmits to them a written declaration to the contrary, such powers and duties shall be discharged by the Vice President as Acting President.

Twenty-third Amendment—1961 Presidential Elections for District of Columbia

People living in Washington, D.C., have the right to vote in presidential elections. Washington, D.C., can never have more electoral votes than the state with the smallest number of people.

Twenty-fourth Amendment—1964 Outlawing of Poll Tax

No one can be stopped from voting in a federal election because he or she has not paid a poll tax or any other kind of tax.

Congress can make laws to carry out this amendment.

Twenty-fifth Amendment—1967 Presidential Succession

If the President dies or resigns, the Vice President becomes President. If the office of Vice President is empty, the President appoints a new Vice President.

When the President is unable to carry out the duties of the office, Congress should be informed. The Vice President then serves as Acting President. The President may resume the duties of the office after informing Congress.

If the Vice President and half the President's top advisers, or Cabinet, inform Congress that the President cannot carry out his or her duties, the Vice President becomes Acting President. If the President informs Congress that he or she is able to carry out these duties, the President returns to office. However, after four days, if the Vice President and half the Cabinet again tell Congress that the President cannot carry out his or her duties, the President does not return to office. Instead, Congress must decide within 21 days whether the President is able to carry out his or her duties. If two thirds of Congress votes that the President cannot continue in office, the Vice President becomes Acting President. If two thirds do not vote in this way, the President remains in office.

19. Write the number of the amendment that:

_____ gave votes to women

_____ gave votes to citizens in Washington, D.C.

_____ gave votes to 18-year-old people

_____ outlawed taxes that blocked voting

Section 4. Whenever the Vice President and a majority of either the principal officers of the executive departments or of such other body as Congress may by law provide, transmit to the President pro tempore of the Senate and the Speaker of the House of Representatives their written declaration that the President is unable to discharge the powers and duties of his office, the Vice President shall immediately assume the powers and duties of the office as Acting President.

Thereafter, when the President transmits to the President pro tempore of the Senate and the Speaker of the House of Representatives his written declaration that no inability exists, he shall resume the powers and duties of his office unless the Vice President and a majority of either the principal officers of the executive department or of such other body as Congress may by law provide, transmit within four days to the President pro tempore of the Senate and the Speaker of the House of Representatives their written declaration that the President is unable to discharge the powers and duties of his office. Thereupon Congress shall decide the issue, assembling within forty-eight hours for that purpose if not in session. If the Congress, within twenty-one days after receipt of the latter written declaration, or, if Congress is not in session, within twenty-one days after Congress is required to assemble, determines by two-thirds vote of both Houses that the President is unable to discharge the powers and duties of his office, the Vice President shall continue to discharge the same as Acting President; otherwise, the President shall resume the powers and duties of his office.

Amendment 26

Section 1. The right of citizens of the United States, who are eighteen years of age or older, to vote shall not be denied or abridged by the United States or by any State on account of age.

Section 2. The Congress shall have the power to enforce this article by appropriate legislation.

Amendment 27

No law varying the compensation for the services of the Senators and Representatives, shall take effect, until an election of Representatives shall have intervened.

The United States of America, Political

Washington
★ Olympia

★ Salem

Oregon

Montana
★ Helena

North
Dakota
★ Bismarck

Minnes

St. Pau

★ Boise

Idaho

Wyoming

South Dakota
Pierre ★

Iow

Sacramento ★

Carson
★ City

Salt Lake ★
City

Cheyenne ★

Nebraska

Lincoln ★

Nevada

Utah

Denver ★

Colorado

Topeka ★

Kansas

California

Arizona

★ Phoenix

Santa Fe ★

New
Mexico

Oklahoma
★ Oklahoma
City

Texas

Austin ★

Alaska

Juneau ★

Honolulu
★

Hawaii

New Hampshire

Vermont

Maine

Augusta

Montpelier

Concord

Massachusetts

Boston

esota

Paul

Wisconsin

Michigan

Albany

New York

Providence

Madison

Lansing

Hartford

Rhode Island

Connecticut

Iowa

Pennsylvania

Trenton

New Jersey

Des Moines

Harrisburg

Illinois

Indiana

Ohio

Dover

Delaware

Springfield

Columbus

Annapolis

Maryland

Indianapolis

West
Virginia

Virginia

Washington, D.C.

Jefferson
City

Charleston

Frankfort

Richmond

Missouri

Kentucky

Raleigh

Nashville

North Carolina

Arkansas

Tennessee

Columbia

Little
Rock

Alabama

Atlanta

South
Carolina

Mississippi

Louisiana

Montgomery

Georgia

Jackson

Baton
Rouge

Tallahassee

Florida

LEGEND

⊗ National capital

★ State capital

N
W   E
S

LEGEND

Elevation

Feet	Meters
10,000	3,048
6,000	1,829
3,000	914
1,000	305
500	152
0	0

— National border

▲ Mountain

PACIFIC OCEAN

Columbia R.

Snake R.

Great Salt Lake

Colorado R.

ROCKY MOUNTAINS

SIERRA NEVADA

0   400 mi

0   400 km

ARCTIC CIRCLE

Brooks Range

Denali
20,310 ft (6,190 m) ▲

Alaska Range

Bering Sea

Aleutian Islands

0   300 mi

0   300 km

22°N

PACIFIC OCEAN

20°N

0   100 mi

0   100 km

160°W

Missouri R.

Platte R.

Red R.

Rio Grande

G R E A T   P L A I N S

Lake
Superior

Great Lakes

Lake
Huron

Lake
Ontario

Lake
Michigan

Lake Erie

**CENTRAL
PLAINS**

Ohio R.

Mississippi R.

A P P A L A C H I A N   M O U N T A I N S

C O A S T A L   P L A I N

**ATLANTIC
OCEAN**

80°W

70°W

Gulf of Mexico

90°W

PACIFIC
OCEAN

Hawaii

154°W

TROPIC OF CANCER

20°N

map
area

North America, Political

ARCTIC OCEAN

GREENLAND
(Denmark)

Bering Strait

Bering Sea

Viscount Melville Sound

Beaufort Sea

Baffin Bay

ALASKA
(U.S.)

Fairbanks

Anchorage

Gulf of Alaska

Juneau

Great Bear Lake

Great Slave Lake

CANADA

Lake Athabasca

Foxe Basin

Hudson Strait

Davis Strait

Labrador Sea

Hudson Bay

James Bay

Lake Winnipeg

Gulf of St. Lawrence

ATLANTIC OCEAN

Edmonton

Calgary

Vancouver

Puget Sound

Seattle

Regina

Winnipeg

Quebec

Ottawa ✪ Montreal

Boston

Toronto

New York City

Portland

Great Salt Lake

Salt Lake City

Great Lakes

Detroit

Philadelphia
Washington, D.C.

Chicago

San Francisco

Denver

St. Louis

30° N

30° N

Las Vegas

UNITED STATES

Los Angeles

Phoenix

Atlanta

San Diego

Dallas

New Orleans

Savannah

60° W

TROPIC OF CANCER

San Antonio

Houston

Miami

BAHAMAS

DOMINICAN
REPUBLIC

Gulf of Mexico

Nassau

PUERTO
RICO (U.S.)

PACIFIC OCEAN

MEXICO

Havana

CUBA

Santo Domingo

BELIZE

Port-au-Prince

Kingston

Mexico City

Belmopan

JAMAICA

HAITI

Caribbean Sea

GUATEMALA

HONDURAS

Guatemala City

Tegucigalpa

San Salvador

Managua

Panama City

LEGEND
—— National border
✪ National capital
• Other city

EL SALVADOR

NICARAGUA

San José

COSTA RICA

PANAMA

PACIFIC OCEAN

0°
EQUATOR

R32

120° W

90° W

60° N

0°

30° W

60° N

ARCTIC OCEAN

Point Barrow
Viscount Melville Sound
Ellesmere Island
Greenland
Queen Elizabeth Islands
Baffin Bay
Beaufort Sea
Banks Island
Melville I. Devon I.
Bering Strait
Bering Sea
Denali 20,310 ft (6,190 m)
Brooks Range
Victoria Island
Baffin Island
Davis Strait
Cape Farewell
Aleutian Islands
Alaska Range
Yukon River
Foxe Basin
Labrador Sea
ATLANTIC OCEAN
Alaska Peninsula
Mackenzie R.
Great Bear Lake
Hudson Strait
Kodiak Island
Yukon Plateau
Mt. Logan 19,524 ft (5,951 m)
Gulf of Alaska
Liard R.
Great Slave L.
Hudson Bay
Labrador
Newfoundland
Haida Qwaii (Queen Charlotte Islands)
Peace R.
Athabasca R.
Lake Athabasca
CANADIAN SHIELD
James Bay
St. Lawrence R.
Gulf of St. Lawrence
Vancouver Island
Saskatchewan R.
Lake Winnipeg
Nova Scotia
Puget Sound
GREAT PLAINS
Great Lakes
Bay of Fundy
Coast Ranges
Cascade Range
Snake
Mississippi R.
Missouri R.
APPALACHIAN MOUNTAINS
Cape Cod
Long Island
Great Salt Lake
Sierra Nevada
ROCKY MOUNTAINS
Black Hills
Platte R.
INTERIOR PLAINS
Ohio R.
Cape Hatteras
GREAT BASIN
Arkansas
Ozark Plateau
COASTAL PLAIN
Mt. Whitney 14,495 ft (4,418 m)
Colorado
Death Valley (lowest point in N.A.) −282 ft (−86 m)
Sonoran Desert
Rio Grande
Bahamas
Baja California
Sierra Madre Occidental
Sierra Madre Oriental
Gulf of Mexico
Cuba
Greater Antilles
Puerto Rico
Lesser Antilles
TROPIC OF CANCER
Citlaltépetl 18,701 ft (5,700 m)
Yucatán Peninsula
Jamaica
Hispaniola
Caribbean Sea
Isthmus of Panama
Lake Nicaragua
PACIFIC OCEAN
EQUATOR

ARCTIC CIRCLE

LEGEND
Elevation

Feet	Meters
10,000	3,048
6,000	1,829
3,000	914
1,000	305
500	152
0	0

▲ Peak
▼ Below sea level

R33

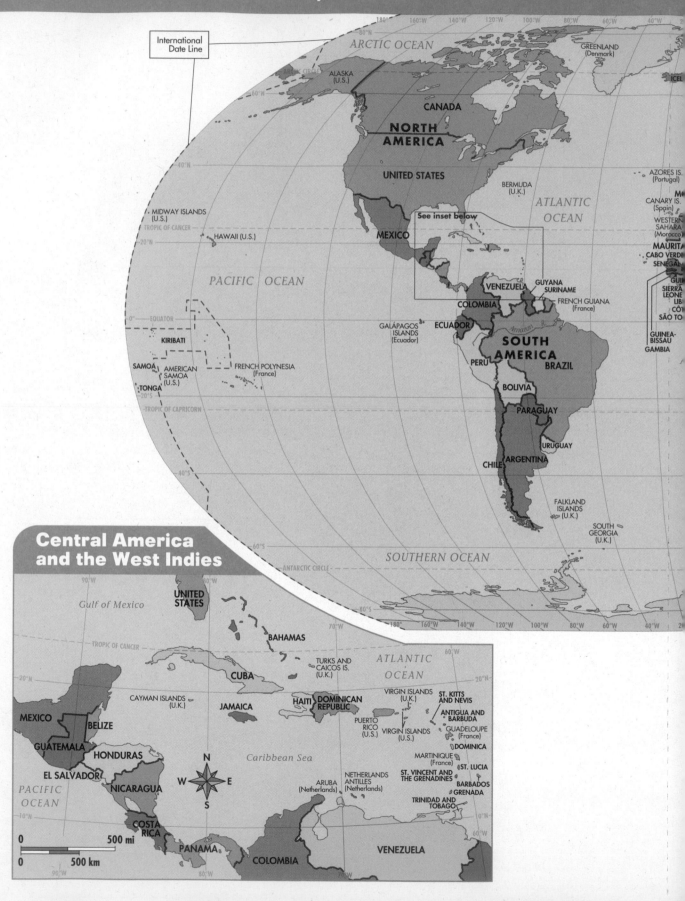

International
Date Line

ARCTIC OCEAN

GREENLAND
(Denmark)

ALASKA
(U.S.)

CANADA

NORTH
AMERICA

UNITED STATES

ICEL

AZORES IS.
(Portugal)

BERMUDA
(U.K.)

ATLANTIC
OCEAN

M

CANARY IS.
(Spain)

WESTERN
SAHARA
(Morocco)

MAURITA

CABO VERDE
SENEGAL

MIDWAY ISLANDS
(U.S.)

TROPIC OF CANCER

HAWAII (U.S.)

See inset below

MEXICO

PACIFIC OCEAN

VENEZUELA

GUYANA
SURINAME

FRENCH GUIANA
(France)

GUI
SIERRA
LEONE
LIB
CÔT
SÃO TO

COLOMBIA

EQUATOR

GALÁPAGOS
ISLANDS
(Ecuador)

ECUADOR

Amazon R.

SOUTH
AMERICA

BRAZIL

GUINEA-
BISSAU

GAMBIA

KIRIBATI

PERU

SAMOA

AMERICAN
SAMOA
(U.S.)

FRENCH POLYNESIA
(France)

TONGA

BOLIVIA

PARAGUAY

URUGUAY

TROPIC OF CAPRICORN

CHILE

ARGENTINA

FALKLAND
ISLANDS
(U.K.)

SOUTH
GEORGIA
(U.K.)

SOUTHERN OCEAN

ANTARCTIC CIRCLE

Central America and the West Indies

Gulf of Mexico

UNITED
STATES

BAHAMAS

TROPIC OF CANCER

TURKS AND
CAICOS IS.
(U.K.)

ATLANTIC
OCEAN

CUBA

CAYMAN ISLANDS
(U.K.)

JAMAICA

HAITI

DOMINICAN
REPUBLIC

VIRGIN ISLANDS
(U.K.)

ST. KITTS
AND NEVIS

MEXICO

BELIZE

PUERTO
RICO
(U.S.)

VIRGIN
ISLANDS
(U.S.)

ANTIGUA AND
BARBUDA

GUADELOUPE
(France)

GUATEMALA

HONDURAS

Caribbean Sea

DOMINICA

N

W   E

S

MARTINIQUE
(France)

ST. LUCIA

EL SALVADOR

NICARAGUA

PACIFIC
OCEAN

NETHERLANDS
ANTILLES
(Netherlands)

ARUBA
(Netherlands)

ST. VINCENT AND
THE GRENADINES

BARBADOS

GRENADA

TRINIDAD AND
TOBAGO

COSTA
RICA

0   500 mi

0   500 km

PANAMA

COLOMBIA

VENEZUELA

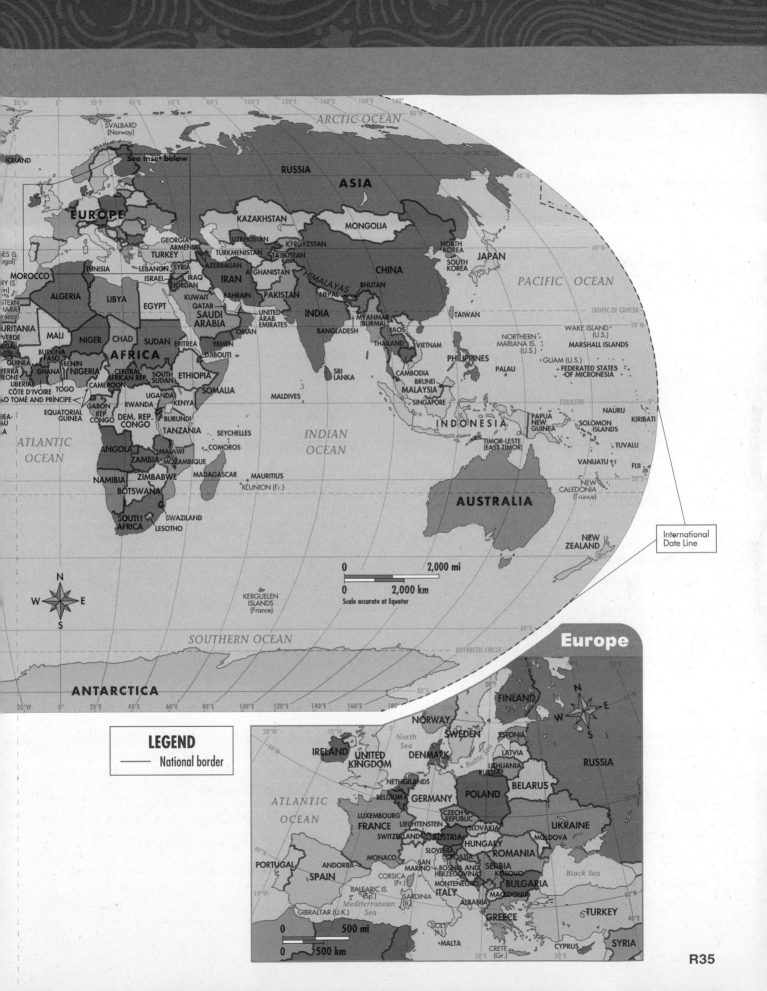

ARCTIC OCEAN

SVALBARD (Norway)

ICELAND

See inset below

EUROPE

RUSSIA

ASIA

ES IS.

KAZAKHSTAN

MONGOLIA

NORTH KOREA

JAPAN

GEORGIA
ARMENIA
TURKEY

UZBEKISTAN
KYRGYZSTAN
TURKMENISTAN
TAJIKISTAN
AZERBAIJAN

SOUTH KOREA

PACIFIC OCEAN

MOROCCO

TUNISIA

LEBANON SYRIA
ISRAEL JORDAN
IRAQ

AFGHANISTAN

HIMALAYAS

CHINA

IRAN

TAIWAN

TROPIC OF CANCER

RY IS.
in)
occo)

ALGERIA

LIBYA

EGYPT

KUWAIT
QATAR
SAUDI
ARABIA

BAHRAIN
UNITED
ARAB
EMIRATES

PAKISTAN

BHUTAN

NEPAL

MYANMAR
(BURMA)

LAOS

WAKE ISLAND
(U.S.)

NORTHERN
MARIANA IS.
(U.S.)

MARSHALL ISLANDS

URITANIA

VERDE
gal)

MALI

NIGER

CHAD

SUDAN

ERITREA

YEMEN

OMAN

INDIA

BANGLADESH

THAILAND

VIETNAM

GUAM (U.S.)

erra
EONE

BURKINA
FASO

GHANA

BENIN

AFRICA

DJIBOUTI

PHILIPPINES

PALAU

FEDERATED STATES
OF MICRONESIA

NIGERIA

CENTRAL
AFRICAN REP.

SOUTH
SUDAN

ETHIOPIA

SRI
LANKA

CAMBODIA

LIBERIA
CÔTE D'IVOIRE TOGO
O TOMÉ AND PRÍNCIPE

CAMEROON

SOMALIA

MALDIVES

BRUNEI
MALAYSIA

SINGAPORE

EAU

EQUATORIAL
GUINEA

GABON
REP.
CONGO

UGANDA

KENYA

EQUATOR

NAURU

DEM. REP.
CONGO

RWANDA
BURUNDI

INDONESIA

PAPUA
NEW
GUINEA

SOLOMON
ISLANDS

KIRIBATI

TANZANIA

SEYCHELLES

ATLANTIC
OCEAN

ANGOLA

ZAMBIA

MALAWI
MOZAMBIQUE

COMOROS

INDIAN
OCEAN

TIMOR-LESTE
(EAST TIMOR)

TUVALU

VANUATU

NAMIBIA

ZIMBABWE

MADAGASCAR

MAURITIUS

NEW
CALEDONIA
(France)

FIJI

BOTSWANA

RÉUNION (Fr.)

AUSTRALIA

SOUTH
AFRICA

SWAZILAND

LESOTHO

2,000 mi

NEW
ZEALAND

International
Date Line

0   2,000 km
Scale accurate at Equator

N
W   E
S

KERGUELEN
ISLANDS
(France)

SOUTHERN OCEAN

ANTARCTIC CIRCLE

ANTARCTICA

20°W   0   20°E   40°E   60°E   80°E   100°E   120°E   140°E   160°E   180°

Europe

LEGEND
— National border

NORWAY

FINLAND

SWEDEN

ESTONIA

North
Sea

IRELAND

UNITED
KINGDOM

DENMARK

LATVIA

RUSSIA

Baltic Sea

LITHUANIA
RUSSIA

BELARUS

ATLANTIC
OCEAN

NETHERLANDS

BELGIUM

GERMANY

POLAND

LUXEMBOURG
LIECHTENSTEIN
FRANCE
SWITZERLAND AUSTRIA

CZECH
REPUBLIC
SLOVAKIA

UKRAINE

HUNGARY

MOLDOVA

SLOVENIA
CROATIA

ROMANIA

PORTUGAL

ANDORRA

MONACO

SAN
MARINO

BOSNIA AND
HERZEGOVINA

SERBIA

Black Sea

SPAIN

CORSICA
(Fr.)

KOSOVO

MONTENEGRO

BULGARIA

BALEARIC IS.
(Sp.)

SARDINIA
(It.)

ITALY

MACEDONIA

GIBRALTAR (U.K.)

Mediterranean
Sea

ALBANIA

TURKEY

GREECE

SICILY
(It.)

500 mi

0   500 km

MALTA

CRETE
(Gr.)

CYPRUS

SYRIA

R35

Glossary

A

abolitionist (ab uh LIHSH un ihst) A person who supported the movement to end slavery.

abundant (uh BUN dunt) Having plenty of something.

according (uh KAWR ding) In agreement.

advocate (AD vuh kut) A person who supports a particular cause.

affirmative action (uh FUR muh tiv AK shun) A plan established by some businesses and educational organizations to make up for past discrimination against minorities or women by hiring or admitting more minorities or women than in the past.

alliance (uh LYE uns) A formal agreement of friendship between countries.

Allied Powers (AL eyd POU urz) During World War I, the nations who fought together against the Central Powers; mainly Great Britain, France, Russia, and later the United States.

Allies (AL eyz) During World War II, the nations who fought together against the Axis; mainly Great Britain, the United States, France, and the Soviet Union.

alternative (awl TUR nuh tiv) Other choice.

amendment (uh MEND muh nt) A change or addition, especially to the U.S. Constitution.

annex (uh NEKS) To take over a territory.

announce (uh NOUNS) To make known officially or publicly.

anti-Semitism (an tee SEH muh tiz um) A hatred of Jewish people.

appeal (uh PEEL) To be interesting or attractive to someone.

arms control (armz kun TROHL) Limiting the production of weapons.

arms race (armz rays) A contest to build more and better weapons than those of your enemy.

assassinate (uh SAS un neyt) To murder someone famous or powerful, usually for political reasons.

assembly line (uh SEM blee lyn) A factory system in which a product is put together as it moves past a line of workers, each of whom does one part of the whole job.

atomic bomb (uh TAH mik bahm) A type of bomb developed during World War II that uses atomic reactions to create a massive explosion; Atomic bombs were dropped by the United States on Japan to end that war.

Axis (AK sis) During World War II, the nations who fought together against the Allies; mainly Germany, Italy, and Japan.

B

baby boom (BAY bee boom) The years between 1945 and 1964 when 76 million babies were born in the United States.

base (bays) To have a specific location that is the center of operations.

benefit (BEN uh fit) A gift or advantage made by a government or a company.

black codes (blak kohdz) A group of laws passed in the late 1800s that denied African American men the right to vote, kept African Americans from owning guns or taking certain types of jobs.

blockade (blah KAYD) A barrier of troops or ships to keep people and supplies from moving in or out of an area.

boycott (BOI kaht) An agreement not to buy goods from a company.

C

capitalism (KA puh tuh liz um) An economic system that encourages citizens to own businesses and property.

carpetbaggers (KAHR pit bag erz) Northern people who moved South to start businesses after the Civil War.

cattle drive (KA tul dryv) The movement by cowboys of large herds of cattle from grazing areas to towns where they could be shipped to market.

cease (sees) Bring to an end.

Central Powers (SEN trul POU urz) During World War I, the nations who fought together against the Allied Powers; mainly Germany, Austria-Hungary, and the Ottoman Empire.

challenge (CHAH lunj) Something difficult.

challenge (CHAH lunj) To say or show that an idea may not be legal or true.

civil rights (SIV ul ryts) Basic legal freedoms and protections, such as the right to a fair trial.

civilian (suh VIL yun) A person who is not in the military.

climate change (KLY mut chanj) The slow heating of Earth's overall climate.

coalition (koh uh LISH un) A temporary arrangement among groups to work together for a certain purpose or to achieve certain goals.

code talker (kohd TAW kur) A member of the Navajo nation who used his tribe's language as a code to send military messages during war.

Cold War (kold wahr) A struggle that did not involve direct warfare.

collapse (kuh LAPS) Fall apart.

communism (KAHM yuh niz um) An economic and political system developed on a national level in the Soviet Union.

competitor (kum PEH tuh tur) A rival, someone selling or buying goods in the same market.

compromise (KAHM pruh myz) People on both sides of an issue giving up something to reach an agreement.

concentration camp (kahn sun TRAY shun kamp) One among many prisons set up by the German Nazis during World War II to contain mostly Jews but also other people considered enemies of the state.

Confederacy (kun FED ur uh see) Another name for the Confederate States of America, the southern states during the U.S. Civil War

conservation (kahn sur VAY shun) To preserve something.

consumer (kun SOO mur) Someone who buys or uses goods and services.

controversial (KAHN truh vur shul) To cause much discussion or argument.

controversy (KAHN truh vur see) Public dispute or debate.

corporation (kor puh RAY shun) A large business owned by investors.

create (kree YET) To design or invent something.

credit (KREH dit) Borrowed money.

credit card (KREH dit kard) A card that a person uses to borrow the money to buy goods and services; the cardholder then pays the total amount later by a set due date.

crisis (KRY sis) A dangerous situation that needs serious attention.

criticize (KRIH tuh syz) To express disapproval of.

crucial (KROO shul) Very important.

Cuban Missile Crisis (KYOO bun MIH sul KRY sis) A crisis in Cuba in which the United States and Soviet Union almost went to war.

D

D-Day (dee day) June 6, 1944, the day when Allied forces launched a major invasion of German-occupied lands in France.

decade (deh KAYD) A period of ten years.

declaration (deh kluh RAY shun) The act of making an official statement about something.

declare (dih KLAYR) Make known to the public.

decline (dih KLYN) The process of a condition becoming worse.

defend (dih FEND) To protect from harm or danger.

determine (dih TER min) To find out through information gathering or research.

dictator (DIK tay tur) A ruler who has total power over a country.

diplomacy (dih PLOH muh see) The art of handling relations between nations.

discrimination (dih skrim ih NAY shun) Unfair treatment of people based on their race, gender, age, or other characteristic.

distribute (dih STRIH byoot) To divide out.

diversity (duh VURS uh tee) Variety within a group.

draw (draw) To cause someone to become involved in something.

drought (drout) A long period of low or no rainfall.

dry farming (drye FAR ming) A method of crop production in which moisture is conserved in the soil during dry weather.

Dust Bowl (dust bohl) During the 1930s, the name for the area of the Great Plains where drought and damaging farming practices had turned topsoil into infertile dust.

E

Electoral College (ih LEK tur ul KAH lij) The group of people chosen by each state to vote for the United States president and vice president.

emancipation (ih man suh PEY shuh n) The setting free of enslaved African Americans.

embargo (em BAR goh) A ban.

enforce (in FORS) To effectively carry out. To make people obey a law or rule.

enlist (en LIHST) To join the military.

entrepreneur (ahn truh pruh NOOR) Someone who takes a risk to start a business.

evidence (EV uh duns) Facts and information that prove whether or not something is true.

exchange (iks CHAYNJ) The act of giving or taking something for something else of equal value.

exhibit (eg ZIB it) A collection of items put out so that people can see them.

expand (ik SPAND) To extend in one or more directions.

expansion (ik SPAN shun) The act of becoming larger or bigger.

F

fascism (FAH shih zum) A form of government that gives all power to the state, does away with individual freedoms, and uses the military to enforce the law.

fiercely (FEERS lee) In a violent manner.

First Hundred Days (furst HUN drud dayz) The first three months of Franklin Roosevelt's presidency, during which the president and Congress passed many new laws that focused on relief, recovery, and reform during the Great Depression.

free enterprise system (free EN tur pryz SIS tum) An economic system in which people are free to start their own businesses or to do whatever work they want; also called capitalism or free market system.

freedom ride (FREE dum ryd) A form of protest in which African Americans and whites rode buses together to integrate bus lines.

G

G.I. Bill of Rights (jee eye bil uv ryts) A federal program that gave veterans funds for education, home loans, and other benefits.

genocide (JEN uh syd) The murder of an entire group of people, based on their race, culture, or beliefs.

ghetto (GEH toh) An area in a city in which members of a certain minority group are forced to live.

globalization (gloh buh luh ZAY shun) The development of a world economy, in which people, goods, and ideas move freely from one country to another.

gold rush (gohld rush) The quick movement of people to a place where gold has been discovered.

Great Depression (grayt dih PREH shun) A long and severe decline in the economy that existed from 1929 until the early 1940s.

Great Migration (grayt mye GRAY shun) The movement of African Americans from farming areas in the South to big cities in the North.

Great Society (grayt suh SYE uh tee) A set of programs begun by President Lyndon Johnson and Congress in 1965 to improve the lives of Americans by working to end poverty and racial injustice.

guerrilla (guh RIL uh) A fighter who does not fight directly, but makes surprise raids or quick attacks from under cover.

H

Holocaust (HAHL uh kawst) The period, from about 1933 to 1945, of Germany's genocide against Jewish people.

Homestead Act (HOHM sted akt) A law passed in 1862, in which the United States federal government promised settlers 160 acres of land in the West for a fee of $18.00, as long as they built a home on the land within six months and lived there for at least five years.

homesteader (HOHM sted ur) A person who migrated to the West to take advantage of the Homestead Act; a settler or pioneer.

honor (AH nur) To show respect and admiration for someone in a public way.

horrific (haw RIF ik) Having the power to horrify; frightening or shocking.

human rights (HYOO mun ryts) The basic rights and freedoms that every human should have.

I

impeach (im PEECH) To bring charges of wrongdoing against a high government official by the House of Representatives.

impeachment (im PEECH muh nt) The process by which charges of wrongdoing is brought against an elected official.

imperialism (im PEER ee ul ih zum) A national policy of expanding power by taking control of other lands and peoples.

imply (im PLYE) To strongly suggest.

integration (in tuh GRAY shun) The mixing of different groups, usually of different races.

interfere (in tur FEER) To become involved in the affairs of others.

internment camp (in TURN munt kamp) During World War II, guarded camps away from the Pacific Coast, where Japanese immigrants and Japanese Americans were forced to move.

investor (in VES tur) Someone who puts money into a business hoping to make a profit.

Iron Curtain (EYE urn KUR tun) The closing off of Eastern Europe from Western Europe.

irrigation (ir uh GAY shun) The use of technology to bring water to crops.

island hopping (EYE lund HAHP ing) The United States military strategy during World War II in the Pacific, in which bombers would pound an island with bombs, but ground troops would pass that island by to attack one that was less well-defended; The goal was to force the enemy Japanese to retreat to their home islands.

isolationism (eye suh LAY shun iz um) The policy of avoiding political ties with other nations.

isthmus (IH smus) A narrow strip of land connecting two landmasses.

J

Jazz Age (jaz ayj) Another name for the decade of the 1920s when the jazz style of music became widely known and popular.

Juneteenth (JOON teenth) The name of a celebration for the day enslaved African Americans in Texas learned of the Emancipation Proclamation.

K

Korean War (kuh REE un wahr) A proxy war fought in Korea.

L

labor union (LAY bur YOON yun) A group of workers, usually in the same type of job, who have united to demand better wages and working conditions.

Lend-Lease Act (lend lees akt) A law passed by Congress that allowed the United States to sell, lend, or give ships, planes, tanks, and other equipment to the Allies before the United States joined World War II.

levee (LEV ee) A barrier of earth built to prevent flooding.

M

Manifest Destiny (MAN uh fest DES tuh nee) The idea, popular in the 1800s, that the United States had a right to add territory until it reached the Pacific Ocean.

mass consumption (mas kun SUMP shun) The large-scale demand for goods.

mass production (mas pruh DUK shun) To produce many things at once, usually with machinery.

McCarthyism (mih KAR thee is um) The political bullying of innocent people.

measure (MEH zhur) An action taken to cause a desired result.

melting pot (MEL ting paht) A place where different peoples, cultures, and ideas are mixed together.

migrant worker (MYE grunt WUR kur) Seasonal workers who move from place to place to harvest crops.

militarism (MIH luh tuh riz um) A policy in which a country keeps building up its troops and making plans for war.

minority group (muh NOHR uh tee groop) A group that is different from the majority in a society.

monopoly (muh NAHP uh lee) A company that has control of an entire industry.

Monroe Doctrine (mun ROH DAHK trun) U.S. foreign policy established by President James Monroe in 1823, warning European leaders not to establish colonies in the Western Hemisphere.

motivation (moh tih VAY shun) Reason to take an action.

muckraker (muk RAY kur) A writer who uncovered "muck," or shameful conditions in American business and society.

N

national debt (NASH uh nul det) The money a country has borrowed to pay its bills.

nationalism (NASH uh nul iz um) A strong feeling of pride in one's nation.

New Deal (noo deel) The programs President Franklin Roosevelt and his administration set up to end the Great Depression.

nonrenewable resource (non rih NOO uh bul REE sors) A material that, once it is used, cannot be replaced, such as oil.

nuclear (NOO klee ur) Atomic.

O

observation (ahb zur VAY shun) The act of viewing or noting facts for a scientific purpose.

obtain (uhb TEYN) To get or acquire.

official (uh FISH ul) Relating to a position of authority and its activities.

ongoing (AHN goh ing) Continual.

operation (ah puh RAY shun) A single step in a computer program.

oppression (uh PREH shun) Unjust treatment of a person or group by a government.

order (AWR dur) A command or instruction to do something.

overwhelm (oh ver HWELM) Beaten or vanquished.

overwhelming (oh ver HWELM ing) Causing strong emotions; overpowering.

P

pioneer (pye uh NEER) A person who built a home on the edge of the wilderness.

plantation (plan TAY shun) A large farm on which a single crop is usually grown.

prejudice (PREJ uh dis) Unfair, negative opinions about a group of people.

prevent (prih VENT) To make someone not do something.

process (PRAH ses) System by which something is done.

proclamation (prok luh MEY shuhn) An official announcement, usually by the government.

productive (proh DUK tiv) Able to produce a large amount of something.

profit (PRAHF it) The money a business earns after all its expenses are paid.

Progressive (proh GRES iv) People trying to find solutions to problems during the late 1800s.

promote (pruh MOHT) To support, or actively encourage.

propaganda (prah puh GAN duh) The spreading of ideas or beliefs to gain support for a cause.

propose (pruh POHZ) To suggest.

prove (proov) Find out something is difficult or a problem.

proxy war (PRAHK see wahr) A war with stand-ins or substitutes.

purpose (PUR puhs) The reason for which something is done.

R

radar (RAY dar) An electronic system that uses sound to find distant and approaching objects.

rationing (RAH shun ing) The system of limiting the amount people can buy of scarce goods.

raw material (raw muh TEER ee ul) A natural product used in manufacturing, such as wood.

recession (rih SEH shun) A long slowdown in the economy.

Reconstruction (ree kuh n STRUHK shun) The name of the plan by President Lincoln to help rebuild and heal the country after the Civil War.

refinery (rih FYN ur ee) A type of factory that turns oil into diffrent products, such as gasoline.

refugee (ref yoo JEE) A person who leaves his or her country to escape war or famine.

remain (rih MAYN) To continue in a specific condition.

renew (rih NOO) To begin again.

reservation (reh zuhr VAY shun) An area of land granted, often by force, to an American Indian tribe, usually in exchange for their own homeland.

result (rih ZULT) An effect of something.

revealing (rih VEEL ing) Making something hidden or secret known to others.

root (root) The origin of something.

S

scarcity (SKER suh tee) A shortage.

science (SY uns) The study of the natural world through observation and experiment.

secession (sih SESH uhn) To formally stop being part of something.

segregation (seg ri GEY shun) The separation of groups of people, usually by race.

sharecropping (SHAYR krop ing) A system in which someone who owns land rents the land to others in exchange for some of the crops raised on the land.

siege (seej) A military blockade designed to make a city surrender.

sit-in (SIT in) A nonviolent protest in which people sit quietly and refuse to leave.

Social Security (SOH shul seh KYUR uh tee) An insurance system funded by the United States federal government to help support disabled or retired Americans.

sodbuster (SAHD buh stur) The nickname given to a person who settled on the Great Plains and had to break up the thickly rooted grass, or sod, to build a home and plant crops.

stability (stuh BIL ih tee) The state of being stable, not likely to change.

stage (stayj) A period or step in an activity or process.

states' rights (steyts ryts) The right of each U.S. state to make its own local laws.

stock (stahk) A financial share of ownership of a company.

stock market (stahk MAR kut) Central location where people buy and sell stocks in companies.

strategy (stra TEH gee) A thought-out plan to accomplish a goal over a long time.

strike (STRYK) A refusal to work until a group's demands are met.

strikebreaker (STRYK bray kur) A worker who replaces striking workers.

style (stihl) A distinctive, particular, or characteristic of acting or way of moving.

suburb (SUH burb) A community outside of a city but not far into the countryside.

suffrage (SUF rij) The right to vote.

suffragist (SUF rih jist) People who worked for women's suffrage.

T

target (TAR git) A place selected as an object of attack.

tariff (TER if) A tax on imports.

technology (tek NAHL uh jee) The application of scientific knowledge for practical purposes.

telegraph (TEL uh graf) A communications system invented by Samuel Morse that uses coded bursts of electricity to send messages over long distances.

temperance (TEM puh runs) A call for people to reduce or stop drinking alcohol.

tenement (TEN uh munt) A building that has been divided into many small apartments.

tense (tens) Anxious.

tepee (TEE pee) A type of portable home used by many American Indians of the Great Plains made of wood poles covered with bark and animal skins.

terrorism (TER ur iz um) The use of violence and fear to achieve political goals.

test (test) A trial that shows how strong someone is in a difficult situation.

Tet Offensive (tet uh FEN siv) A North Vietnamese attack launched during the Tet holiday.

total war (TOHT l wawr) A method of warfare that seeks to destroy civilian as well as military targets to force a surrender.

transcontinental railroad (TRANS kahn tih nen tul RAYL rohd) A railroad that spans an entire continent.

trust (trust) Large and powerful groups of companies.

U

Underground Railroad (UHN der GROUND REYL rohd) A secret organization that helped escaped enslaved African Americans to get to the North or to Canada.

unemployment (un em PLOI munt) The condition of being out of work.

Union (YOON yuhn) Another name for the United States, especially the northern states during the Civil War.

urbanization (ur bun ih ZAY shun) The growth or spreading of cities.

V

V-E Day (VEE EE day) May 8, 1945, the day Germany surrendered, ending World War II in Europe.

veteran (VET ur un) A person who has fought in a war.

Vietnam War (VEE ut nahm wahr) A proxy war fought in Vietnam.

W

war bond (wahr bahnd) An investment paid by American citizens to the government to help pay for a war that, after the war, will be paid back with interest.

weapons of mass destruction (WMD) (WEH punz ov mas duh STRUK shun) Weapons designed to kill a large number of people.

widespread (WYD spred) Found across a large area.

Y

yellow journalism (YEL oh JUR nal iz um) False or exaggerated reporting by the news media, especially newspapers of the late 1800s.

Glosario

A

abolitionist/abolicionista Persona que apoyaba el movimiento para poner fin a la esclavitud.

abundant/abundante Con mucha cantidad de algo.

according/según Conforme a.

advocate/defensor Persona que apoya una causa.

affirmative action/acción afirmativa Plan que establecen algunas empresas y organizaciones educativas para reparar la discriminación del pasado contra las minorías o las mujeres, y que consiste en contratar o aceptar más mujeres o integrantes de minorías que en el pasado.

alliance/alianza Acuerdo formal de amistad entre naciones.

Allied Powers/Potencias Aliadas Durante la Primera Guerra Mundial, las naciones que lucharon juntas contra las Potencias Centrales; principalmente Gran Bretaña, Francia, Rusia y, más tarde, los Estados Unidos.

Allies/Aliados Durante la Segunda Guerra Mundial, las naciones que lucharon juntas contra el Eje; principalmente Gran Bretaña, los Estados Unidos, Francia y la Unión Soviética.

alternative/alternativa Otra opción.

amendment/enmienda Cambio o incorporación, especialmente a la Constitución de los Estados Unidos.

annex/anexar Ocupar un territorio.

announce/anunciar Dar a conocer de forma oficial o pública.

anti-Semitism/antisemitismo Odio a los judíos.

appeal/gustar Resultarle interesante o atractivo a alguien.

arms control/control de armas Limitación de la producción de armas.

arms race/carrera armamentista Competencia que consiste en construir más y mejores armas que las del enemigo.

assassinate/asesinar Matar a alguien famoso o poderoso, generalmente por razones políticas.

assembly line/línea de montaje Sistema de fabricación en el que el producto se va armando a medida que pasa por una hilera de obreros; cada obrero hace una parte de todo el trabajo.

atomic bomb/bomba atómica Tipo de bomba que se desarrolló durante la Segunda Guerra Mundial y que utiliza reacciones nucleares para generar una explosión masiva. Los Estados Unidos arrojaron bombas atómicas sobre el Japón para poner fin a esa guerra.

Axis/Eje Durante la Segunda Guerra Mundial, las naciones que lucharon juntas contra los Aliados; principalmente Alemania, Italia y el Japón.

B

baby boom/*baby boom* Período entre los años 1945 y 1964, en el que nacieron 76 millones de bebés en los Estados Unidos.

base/tener base Tener una ubicación específica que es el centro de las operaciones.

benefit/beneficio Ganancia o ventaja obtenida por el gobierno o una compañía.

black codes/códigos negros Conjunto de leyes aprobadas a finales del siglo xix que les negaban el derecho a votar a los hombres afroamericanos y les impedían poseer armas y tomar ciertos tipos de empleo.

blockade/bloqueo Barrera de tropas o barcos colocada con el fin de evitar que las personas y los suministros entren o salgan de una zona

boycott/boicot Acuerdo para negarse a comprar bienes de una empresa.

C

capitalism/capitalismo Sistema económico que alienta a los ciudadanos a ser dueños de negocios y propiedades.

carpetbaggers/*carpetbaggers* Norteños que iban al Sur después de la Guerra Civil para empezar negocios.

cattle drive/arreo de ganado Traslado de grandes manadas de ganado que hacían los vaqueros desde las zonas de pastoreo hasta los pueblos, donde se enviaba el ganado a los mercados.

cease/interrumpir Poner fin a algo.

Central Powers/Potencias Centrales Durante la Primera Guerra Mundial, las naciones que lucharon juntas contra las Potencias Aliadas; principalmente Alemania, Austria-Hungría y el Imperio Otomano.

challenge/desafío Situación difícil.

challenge/desafiar Decir o mostrar que una idea tal vez no sea legal o verdad.

civil rights/derechos civiles Libertad y protecciones legales fundamentales, como el derecho a un juicio justo.

civilian/civil Toda persona que no forma parte de las fuerzas armadas.

climate change/cambio climático Lento calentamiento del clima global de la Tierra.

coalition/coalición Acuerdo temporal entre distintos grupos para trabajar en conjunto con un propósito determinado o para lograr ciertos objetivos.

code talker/locutor de claves Miembro de la Nación Navajo que usaba el idioma de su tribu como código para enviar mensajes militares durante la guerra.

Cold War/Guerra Fría Lucha que no consistió en un conflicto armado directo.

collapse/colapsar Derrumbarse.

communism/comunismo Sistema económico y político desarrollado a nivel nacional en la Unión Soviética.

competitor/competidor Rival, alguien que vende o compra bienes en el mismo mercado.

compromise/acuerdo Situación donde las personas de los dos lados de una disputa renuncian a algo para llegar a un acuerdo.

concentration camp/campo de concentración Tipo de prisión que establecieron los nazis alemanes durante la Segunda Guerra Mundial para encerrar mayormente a los judíos, pero también a otras personas consideradas enemigas del Estado.

Confederacy/Confederación Otro nombre para los Estados Confederados de América, los estados sureños durante la Guerra Civil.

conservation/conservación Preservar algo.

consumer/consumidor Toda persona que compra o usa bienes y servicios.

controversial/controvertido Que causa mucho debate o mucha discusión.

controversy/controversia Disputa o debate público.

corporation/corporación Negocio grande cuyos dueños son los inversionistas.

create/crear Diseñar o inventar algo.

credit/crédito Dinero prestado.

credit card/tarjeta de crédito Tarjeta que una persona usa para pedir prestado dinero y comprar bienes y servicios; el titular de la tarjeta paga la cantidad total más tarde, en una fecha acordada.

crisis/crisis Situación peligrosa que requiere mucha atención.

criticize/criticar Expresar desaprobación.

crucial/crucial Muy importante.

Cuban Missile Crisis/crisis de los misiles de Cuba Crisis en Cuba en la que los Estados Unidos y la Unión Soviética casi fueron a la guerra.

D

D-Day/Día D 6 de junio de 1944, el día que las fuerzas Aliadas lanzaron una gran invasión sobre territorios ocupados por los alemanes en Francia.

decade/década Período de diez años.

declaration/declaración Acción de dar un comunicado oficial sobre algo.

declare/declarar Dar a conocer al público.

decline/declive Proceso de una condición que empeora.

defend/defender Proteger de daño o peligro.

determine/determinar Descubrir a través de la recopilación de información o de la investigación.

dictator/dictador Gobernante que tiene el control total sobre un país.

diplomacy/diplomacia Arte de manejar las relaciones entre naciones.

discrimination/discriminación Trato injusto de personas por motivos de raza, sexo, edad u otra característica.

distribute/distribuir Dividir algo entre varias personas.

diversity/diversidad Variedad dentro de un grupo.

draw/atraer Hacer que alguien participe en algo.

drought/sequía Largo período con poca lluvia o sin lluvias.

dry farming/cultivos en zonas áridas Método de cultivo en el que se conserva la humedad del suelo durante el tiempo seco.

Dust Bowl/*Dust Bowl* Durante la década de 1930, el nombre del área de las Grandes Llanuras donde la sequía y las prácticas de cultivo dañinas habían convertido la capa superior del suelo en polvo estéril.

E

Electoral College/Colegio Electoral Grupo de personas que elige cada estado para votar por el presidente y el vicepresidente de los Estados Unidos.

emancipation/emancipación La liberación de los afroamericanos esclavizados.

embargo/embargo Prohibición.

enforce/hacer cumplir Ejecutar de manera efectiva. Hacer que las personas obedezcan una ley o regla.

enlist/alistarse Unirse al ejército.

entrepreneur/empresario Persona que se arriesga para empezar un negocio.

evidence/evidencia Hechos e información que demuestran si algo es verdad o no.

exchange/intercambio Acción de dar o tomar algo a cambio de otra cosa de igual valor.

exhibit/exhibición Colección de objetos que se muestra para que las personas la vean.

expand/expandir Extender en una o más direcciones.

expansion/expansión Acción de volverse más extenso o grande.

F

fascism/fascismo Forma de gobierno que le da todo el poder al Estado, elimina las libertades individuales y usa al ejército para hacer cumplir la ley.

fiercely/ferozmente De manera violenta.

First Hundred Days/Los primeros 100 días Tres primeros meses de la presidencia de Franklin Roosevelt, durante los cuales el presidente y el Congreso aprobaron muchas leyes nuevas que se enfocaban en el alivio, la recuperación y la reforma durante la Gran Depresión.

free enterprise system/sistema de libre empresa Sistema económico en el que las personas son libres de iniciar sus propias empresas o de trabajar en lo que deseen; también llamado capitalismo o sistema de libre mercado.

freedom ride/viaje por la libertad Forma de protesta en la que activistas blancos y afroamericanos viajaban juntos para integrar las líneas de autobús.

G

G.I. Bill of Rights/Declaración de Derechos del Soldado Conocida en inglés como G.I. Bill of Rights, es un programa federal que daba a los veteranos fondos para educación, préstamos para vivienda y otros beneficios.

genocide/genocidio Asesinato de un grupo entero de personas, a causa de su raza, su cultura o sus creencias.

ghetto/gueto Zona de una ciudad en la que se obliga a vivir a los miembros de ciertas minorías.

globalization/globalización Desarrollo de una economía mundial en que las personas, los bienes y las ideas se desplazan libremente de un país a otro.

gold rush/fiebre del oro El movimiento rápido de personas hacia un lugar donde se descubrió oro.

Great Depression/Gran Depresión Largo y severo deterioro de la economía que se dio desde 1929 hasta comienzos de la década de 1940.

Great Migration/Gran Migración El traslado de afroamericanos desde zonas agrícolas del Sur a grandes ciudades del Norte.

Great Society/Gran Sociedad Conjunto de programas que iniciaron el presidente Lyndon Johnson y el Congreso en 1965 para mejorar la vida de los estadounidenses; buscaba poner fin a la pobreza y a la injusticia racial.

guerrilla/guerrillero Combatiente que no pelea directamente, sino que ataca por sorpresa o realiza ataques rápidos en secreto.

H

Holocaust/Holocausto Período de genocidio alemán contra los judíos, desde alrededor de 1933 hasta 1945.

Homestead Act/Ley de Fincas Ley aprobada en 1862, por la que el gobierno federal de los Estados Unidos prometía a los pobladores 160 acres de tierra en el Oeste por una tarifa de $18.00, siempre que construyeran una casa en esa tierra dentro de los primeros seis meses y vivieran allí al menos cinco años.

homesteader/nuevo colono Persona que migró al Oeste para aprovechar la Ley de Fincas; pionero.

honor/honrar Mostrar respeto y admiración por alguien de forma pública.

horrific/horrible Tener el poder de causar horror; espantoso o estremecedor.

human rights/derechos humanos Derechos y libertades fundamentales que debe tener todo ser humano.

impeach/enjuiciar políticamente Presentar cargos de mal desempeño contra un alto funcionario del gobierno por parte de la Cámara de Representantes.

impeachment/juicio político Proceso por el cual cargos son presentados contra un funcionario.

imperialism/imperialismo Política de una nación con la cual intenta expandir su poder controlando otros territorios y pueblos.

imply/insinuar Dar a entender.

integration/integración Mezcla de diferentes grupos de personas, por lo general de distintas razas.

interfere/interferir Involucrarse en los asuntos de los demás.

internment camp/campo de internamiento Durante la Segunda Guerra Mundial, campos vigilados lejos de la costa del Pacífico, donde se obligó a vivir a los inmigrantes japoneses y a los japonesesestadounidenses.

investor/inversionista Alguien que pone dinero en un negocio con la esperanza de recibir una ganancia.

Iron Curtain/Cortina de Hierro El bloqueo de Europa oriental a Europa occidental.

irrigation/irrigación El uso de tecnología para llevar agua a los cultivos.

island hopping/salto de isla en isla Estrategia militar de los EE. UU. durante la Segunda Guerra Mundial en el Pacífico, mediante la cual los bombarderos atacaban una isla, pero las tropas terrestres la salteaban y atacaban una isla menos defendida. El objetivo era obligar al enemigo japonés a retirarse a sus islas de origen.

isolationism/aislacionismo Política de evitar lazos políticos con otras naciones.

isthmus/istmo Franja estrecha de tierra que conecta dos masas continentales.

J

Jazz Age/era del jazz Otro nombre para la década de 1920, en la cual el estilo musical del jazz se hizo muy conocido y popular.

Juneteenth/fiesta del 19 de junio Nombre de la celebración del día en que afroamericanos esclavizados en Texas supieron sobre la Proclamación de Emancipación.

K

Korean War/Guerra de Corea Guerra por delegación librada en Corea.

L

labor union/sindicato Grupo de trabajadores, generalmente del mismo tipo de trabajo, que se ha unido para exigir mejores sueldos y condiciones de trabajo.

Lend-Lease Act/Ley de Préstamo y Arriendo Ley aprobada por el Congreso que permitía a los Estados Unidos vender, arrendar o dar barcos, aviones, tanques y otro equipamiento a los Aliados antes de que los Estados Unidos participaran de la Segunda Guerra Mundial.

levee/dique Barrera de tierra que se construye para evitar una inundación.

M

Manifest Destiny/destino manifiesto La idea, popular en el siglo XIX, de que los Estados Unidos tenían derecho a incorporar territorio hasta alcanzar el océano Pacífico.

mass consumption/consumo masivo Demanda a gran escala de bienes.

mass production/producción en serie Producir muchas cosas al mismo tiempo, generalmente con la ayuda de máquinas.

McCarthyism/macartismo Acoso político a personas inocentes.

measure/medida Acción tomada para lograr un resultado deseado.

melting pot/crisol de culturas Lugar donde se mezclan distintos pueblos, culturas e ideas.

migrant worker/trabajador migratorio Trabajadores que se mudan de lugar en lugar según las estaciones para cosechar.

militarism/militarismo Política por la cual un país continuamente prepara a sus tropas y hace planes de guerra.

minority group/grupo minoritario Grupo distinto de la mayoría dentro de una sociedad.

monopoly/monopolio Cuando una compañía tiene el control de toda una industria.

Monroe Doctrine/Doctrina Monroe Política exterior de los Estados Unidos creada por el presidente James Monroe en 1823, que advertía a los líderes europeos que no establecieran colonias en el hemisferio occidental.

motivation/motivación Razón para actuar.

muckraker/periodista de denuncia Periodista que denunciaba el estado vergonzoso de las empresas y la sociedad estadounidenses.

N

national debt/deuda pública Dinero que un país ha tomado prestado para pagar sus cuentas.

nationalism/nacionalismo Fuerte sentimiento de orgullo por la nación a la que se pertenece.

New Deal/Nuevo Trato Programas que el presidente Franklin Roosevelt y su gobierno pusieron en marcha para poner fin a la Gran Depresión.

nonrenewable resource/recurso no renovable Material que una vez que se usa, no se puede reemplazar, como el petróleo.

nuclear/nuclear Atómico.

O

observation/observación Acción de ver o notar hechos con un fin científico.

obtain/obtener Conseguir o adquirir.

official/oficial Relativo a una posición de autoridad y a sus actividades.

ongoing/constante Continuo.

operation/operación Un solo paso en un programa informático.

oppression/opresión Trato injusto de una persona o grupo por parte de un gobierno.

order/orden Comando o instrucción para hacer algo.

overwhelm/asolado Dominado o vencido.

overwhelming/abrumador Que causa emociones fuertes; agobiante.

P

pioneer/pionero Persona que construye una casa en el límite con las tierras vírgenes.

plantation/plantación Granja de gran tamaño en la que se suele cultivar solo un tipo de planta.

prejudice/prejuicio Opiniones negativas e injustas sobre un grupo de personas.

prevent/impedir Hacer que alguien no haga algo.

process/proceso Sistema con el que se hace algo.

proclamation/proclamación Anuncio oficial, generalmente del gobierno.

productive/productivo Que puede producir una gran cantidad de algo.

profit/ganancia Dinero que le queda a una empresa una vez que se han pagado todos los gastos.

Progressive/progresista Personas que intentaban hallar soluciones a los problemas durante fines del siglo XIX.

promote/promover Apoyar o alentar activamente.

propaganda/propaganda Difusión de ideas o creencias para conseguir apoyo para una causa.

propose/proponer Sugerir.

prove/validar Encontrar que algo tiene particular valor o mérito.

proxy war/guerra por delegación Guerra con suplentes o sustitutos.

purpose/propósito Razón por la que se hace algo.

R

radar/radar Sistema electrónico que usa el sonido para identificar objetos lejanos o que se acercan.

rationing/racionamiento Sistema que limita la cantidad de bienes escasos que pueden comprar las personas.

raw material/materia prima Producto natural, como por ejemplo la madera, que se usa en la manufacturación.

recession/recesión Situación en que la economía se hace más lenta durante un tiempo largo.

Reconstruction/Reconstrucción Nombre del plan del presidente Lincoln para ayudar a reconstruir y sanar el país después de la Guerra Civil.

refinery/refinería Tipo de fábrica que transforma el petróleo en productos útiles, como la gasolina.

refugee/refugiado Persona que abandona su país para escapar de la guerra o la hambruna.

remain/permanecer Continuar en una condición específica.

renew/recomenzar Volver a empezar.

reservation/reserva Territorio asignado, en general por la fuerza, a una tribu indígena americana, a menudo a cambio de su propia tierra.

result/resultado Efecto de algo.

revealing/revelador Que hace que los demás sepan algo oculto o secreto.

root/raíz Origen de algo.

S

scarcity/escasez Poca cantidad de algo.

science/ciencia Estudio del mundo natural a través de la observación y la experimentación.

secession/secesión Acción de separarse formalmente de algo.

segregation/segregación Separación de un grupo de personas, generalmente por su raza.

sharecropping/aparcería Sistema en el que alguien que posee tierras se las alquila a otros a cambio de parte de sus cultivos.

siege/sitio Bloqueo militar diseñado para hacer que una ciudad se rinda.

sit-in/sentada Protesta no violenta en la que las personas se sientan en silencio en un lugar y se niegan a irse.

Social Security/seguridad social Sistema de seguros fundado por el gobierno federal de los EE. UU. para brindar apoyo a los estadounidenses discapacitados o jubilados.

sodbuster/*sodbuster* Sobrenombre dado a una persona que se asentaba en las Grandes Llanuras y tenía que cortar un pasto con raíces muy gruesas, el tepe (sod en inglés), para construir su casa o plantar cultivos.

stability/estabilidad Estado de ser estable, que es improbable que cambie.

stage/etapa Período o paso en una actividad o proceso.

states' rights/derechos de los estados Derecho de cada estado de los Estados Unidos a crear sus propias leyes locales.

stock/acciones Propiedad de parte de las finanzas de una compañía.

stock market/bolsa de valores Lugar donde la gente compra y vende acciones de empresas.

strategy/estrategia Plan bien pensado para alcanzar una meta durante un largo período de tiempo.

strike/huelga Acción de negarse a trabajar hasta que se cumplan las exigencias de un grupo.

strikebreaker/rompehuelgas Persona que reemplaza a un trabajador que está en huelga.

style/estilo Manera distintiva, particular o característica de actuar o moverse.

suburb/suburbio Comunidad en las afueras de una ciudad, pero no muy alejada de esta.

suffrage/sufragio Derecho a votar.

suffragist/sufragista Persona que luchó por el sufragio de las mujeres.

T

target/blanco Lugar seleccionado como objetivo de un ataque.

tariff/arancel Impuesto a las importaciones.

technology/tecnología Uso del conocimiento científico con fines prácticos.

telegraph/telégrafo Sistema de comunicación inventado por Samuel Morse que usa corrientes codificadas de electricidad para enviar mensajes a larga distancia.

temperance/templanza Llamado a la gente para que reduzca o elimine el consumo de alcohol.

tenement/casa de vecindad Edificio que se ha dividido en departamentos pequeños.

tense/tenso Nervioso.

tepee/tipi Tipo de casa portátil usada por muchos indígenas americanos de las Grandes Llanuras, hecha de postes de madera cubiertos de corteza y pieles de animales.

terrorism/terrorismo Uso de la violencia y el miedo con fines políticos.

test/prueba Desafío que muestra cuán fuerte es alguien en una situación difícil.

Tet Offensive/ofensiva del Tet Ataque que organizaron los vietnamitas del norte durante el día festivo del Tet.

total war/guerra total Método de guerra que busca destruir objetivos civiles y militares por igual para obligar al enemigo a rendirse.

transcontinental railroad/ferrocarril transcontinental Ferrocarril que recorre todo un continente.

trust/*trust* Grupo de empresas grande y poderoso.

U

Underground Railroad/Tren Clandestino Organización secreta que ayudó a afroamericanos esclavizados a escapar y llegar al Norte o a Canadá.

unemployment/desempleo Condición de no tener empleo.

Union/Unión Otro nombre para los Estados Unidos, especialmente los estados norteños durante la Guerra Civil.

urbanization/urbanización Crecimiento o expansión de las ciudades.

V

V-E Day/Día V-E 8 de mayo de 1945, el día en que Alemania se rindió y la Segunda Guerra Mundial llegó a su fin en Europa.

veteran/veterano Persona que combatió en una guerra.

Vietnam War/Guerra de Vietnam Guerra por delegación librada en Vietnam.

W

war bond/bono de guerra Dinero que los ciudadanos estadounidenses invierten en el gobierno para ayudar a pagar una guerra y que, al final de la guerra, se devuelve con intereses.

weapons of mass destruction WMD/arma de destrucción masiva Arma diseñada para matar a muchas personas al mismo tiempo.

widespread/extendido Que se encuentra en un área grande.

Y

yellow journalism/periodismo amarillo Tipo de noticias falsas o exageradas de los medios de comunicación, en especial los periódicos de finales del siglo xix.

Index

This index lists the pages on which topics appear in this book. Page numbers followed by *m* refer to maps. Page numbers followed by *p* refer to photographs. Page numbers followed by *c* refer to charts or graphs. Page numbers followed by *t* refer to timelines. Bold page numbers indicate vocabulary definitions. The terms *See* and *See also* direct the reader to alternate entries.

O

P

Credits

Text Acknowledgments

Boeing Corporation
Quote by William E. Boeing, founder, The Boeing Company. Copyright © William Boeing.

Earhart, Amelia
Quote by Amelia Earhart. Copyright © Amelia Earhart.

Harold Ober Associates
Langston Hughes, "I, Too" from Collected Poems. Reprinted by permission of Harold Ober Associated Incorporated. Copyright © 1994 by The Estate of Langston Hughes.

Penguin Random House.
"I, Too" from THE COLLECTED POEMS OF LANGSTON HUGHES by Langston Hughes, edited by Arnold Rampersad with David Roessel, Associate Editor, copyright © 1994 by the Estate of Langston Hughes. Used by permission of Alfred A. Knopf, an imprint of the Knopf Doubleday Publishing Group, a division of Penguin Random House LLC. All rights reserved.

Harper Collins Publishers
House on the Prairie by Laura Ingalls Wilder. Copyright © by Harper Collins Publishers.

Harcourt, Inc.
The Encounter by Jane Yolen. Copyright © 1992 by Jane Yolen. Published by Harcourt Inc.

St. Martin's Press
Mankilller: A Chief and Her People by Wilma Mankiller. Published by St. Martin's Press.

Images

Cover
CVR: Scott Barrow/Getty Images

Front Matter
SSH1BL: Jjwithers/iStock Unreleased/Getty Images; SSH1BR: Jamie Pham/Alamy Stock Photo; SSH1TL: Li Hui Chen/Shutterstock; SSH1TR: Jenny E. Ross/Corbis Documentary/Getty Images; SSH11: Heritage Images/Hulton Fine Art Collection/Getty Images; SSH12: Lambert/Hulton Fine Art Collection/Getty Images; SSH14: Shalom Ormsby/Blend Images/Alamy Stock Photo; SSH15: National Museum of American History, Kenneth E. Behring Center; SSH16: Beeboys/Shutterstock; SSH17: Hulton Fine Art Collection/Fine Art Images/Heritage Images/Getty Images; SSH19: Erich Lessing/Art Resource, NY; copyright page: Rachid Dahnoun/Aurora Open RF/Alamy Stock Photo; i: Chris Putnam/Alamy Stock Photo; iii: Camarillo Dr. Albert M.; iii: Dr. James B. Kracht; iii: Dr. Kathy Swan; iii: Dr. Linda B. Bennett; iii: Elfrieda H. Hiebert;

iii: Jim Cummins; iii: Kathy Tuchman Glass; iii: Paul Apodaca; iii: Shirley A. James Hanshaw; iii: Warren J. Blumenfeld; iii: Xiaojian Zhao

Chapter 09
408: Juanmonino/E+/Getty Images; 406-407: Karen Bleier/AFP/Getty Images; 409TL: Stocktrek Images, Inc./Alamy Stock Photo; 409TR: Bettmann/Getty Images; 409BL: Pictorial Press Ltd/Alamy Stock Photo; 409BR: Stocktrek Images, Inc./Alamy Stock Photo; 412: North Wind Picture Archives/Alamy Stock Photo; 416T: PF-(bygone1)/Alamy Stock Photo; 416B: Sarin Images/Granger, NYC; 418: Granger, NYC; 419: Archive Pics/Alamy Stock Photo; 422: Niday Picture Library/Alamy Stock Photo; 424: North Wind Picture Archives/Alamy Stock Photo; 425: Granger, NYC; 426T: Library of Congress Prints and Photographs Division[LC-DIG-ppmsca-35446]; 426B: John Parrot/Stocktrek Images, Inc./Alamy Stock Photo; 430: Historical/Corbis Historical/Getty Images; 438: Historical Images Archive/Alamy Stock Photo; 432: Library of Congress Prints and Photographs Division[LC-DIG-ppmsca-34400]; 433: North Wind Picture Archives/Alamy Stock Photo; 434: Historical/Corbis Historical/Getty Images; 435: Bettmann/Getty Images; 436: Library of Congress Prints and Photographs Division[LC-DIG-ppmsca-33748]; 437: Pictorial Press Ltd/Alamy Stock Photo; 441: Historical/Corbis Historical/Getty Images; 442L: Everett Collection Historical/Alamy Stock Photo; 442R: Archive Photos/Getty Images; 443: Fototeca Storica Nazionale/Hulton Archive/Getty Images; 445: Granger, NYC; 446: North Wind Picture Archives/Alamy Stock Photo; 447: George Eastman House/Premium Archive/Getty Images; 448: MPI/Archive Photos/Getty Images; 450: Everett Collection Inc/Alamy Stock Photo; 412: Education Images/Universal Images Group/Getty Images; 451: New York Public Library/Science Source/Getty Images; 454: Sarin Images/Granger, NYC; 444: Everett Collection Inc/Alamy Stock Photo; 428: Blend Images/Brand X Pictures/Getty Images; 429: North Wind Picture Archives/Alamy Stock Photo; 420: Sergey Ryzhov/Shutterstock; 454: Paul Fearn/Alamy Stock Photo; 454bkgd: Debra Millet/Shutterstock;

Chapter 10
460-461: North Wind Picture Archives/Alamy Stock Photo; 463TL: Sarin Images/Granger, NYC; 463TR: Classic Image/Alamy Stock Photo; 463BL: JT Vintage/Glasshouse Images/Alamy Stock; 468: Photo Researchers/Science History Images/Alamy Stock Photo; 469: Granger, NYC; 470: Sarin Images/Granger, NYC; 474: Granger, NYC; 476: Pictorial Press Ltd/Alamy Stock Photo; 477: Surya Prakash Mullapudi/EyeEm/Alamy Stock Photo; 479: Granger, NYC; 483: Werner Forman Archive/Heritage Image Partnership Ltd/Alamy Stock Photo; 485: Granger, NYC; 486: Library of Congress/RGB Ventures/SuperStock/Alamy Stock Photo; 488: Granger, NYC; 489: Furlong Photography/Alamy Stock

Photo; 493: PJF Military Collection/Alamy Stock Photo;
494: Nawrocki/ClassicStock/Alamy Stock Photo; 484:
Granger, NYC; 463BR: Alpha Historica/Alamy Stock Photo;
498B: John Elk III/Alamy Stock Photo; 498T: World History
Archive/Alamy Stock Photo; 496: World History Archive/
Alamy Stock Photo; 490: Classic Image/Alamy Stock Photo;

Chapter 11
504-505: Monty Rakusen/Cultura/Getty Images; 506:
Victoria Lipov/Shutterstock; 507TL: Education Images/
Alamy Stock Photo; 507TR: Courtesy: CSU Archives /
Everett Collection/Alamy Stock Photo; 507BL: B
Christopher/Alamy Stock Photo; 507BC: JT Vintage/
Glasshouse Images/Alamy Stock Photo; 507BR: JT
Vintage/Glasshouse Images/Alamy Stock Photo; 511T:
Everett Collection Historical/Alamy Stock Photo; 511B:
North Wind Picture Archives/Alamy Stock Photo; 513:
GL Archive/Alamy Stock Photo; 514: ClassicStock/
Alamy Stock Photo; 515: SSPL/Getty Images; 516: Hulton
Archive/Getty Images; 518: atm2003/Shutterstock; 520:
Glasshouse Images/Alamy Stock Photo; 521: Steidle Art
Collection/Alamy Stock Photo; 522T: Everett Collection/
Alamy Stock Photo; 522B: Keystone-France/Gamma-
Keystone/Getty Images; 523: Bettmann/Getty Images;
524: Fotosearch/Archive Photos/Getty Images; 527:
Chronicle/Alamy Stock Photo; 528: The Print Collector/
Hulton Archive/Getty Images; 530: Bettmann/Getty
Images; 531: Lewis W. Hine/Buyenlarge/Archive Photos/
Getty Images; 533: Everett Collection Historical/Alamy
Stock Photo; 534: Diego G Diaz/Shutterstock; 535: World
History Archive/Alamy Stock Photo; 538T: Boddy, Elias
Manchester; 538B: Nednapa/Shutterstock; 539TL: Everett
Historical/Shutterstock; 539TC: Georgios Kollidas/123RF;
539TR: Photo Researchers/Getty Images; 539BL: Everett
Collection/Alamy Stock Photo; 539BC: Keystone-France/
Gamma-Keystone/Getty Images; 539BR: Chronicle/Alamy
Stock Photo;

Chapter 12
544-545: American Press Association/Library of Congress/
Corbis/Getty Images; 546: Jack Delano/PhotoQuest/Archive
Photos/Getty Images; 547TL: Bettmann/Getty Images;
547TR: Universal History Archive/UIG/Getty Images; 547BL:
Charles Phelps Cushing/ClassicStock/Archive Photos/
Getty Images; 547BR: GraphicaArtis/Archive Photos/Getty
Images; 550: Everett Collection/Alamy Stock Photo; 551:
PhotoQuest/Archive Photos/Getty Images; 552: Bettmann/
Getty Images; 554: The Museum of the City of New York/Art
Resource, NY; 556: For Alan/Alamy Stock Photo; 557: Kevin
Steele/Aurora/Getty Images; 559: VCG Wilson/Corbis/Getty
Images; 560: National Archive/Hulton Archive/Getty Images;
561: Bettmann/Getty Images; 563: PhotoQuest/Archive
Photos/Getty Images; 564: Bettmann/Getty Images; 566:
Bettmann/Getty Images; 568: Bettmann/Getty Images; 570:
Library of Congress Prints and Photographs Division[LC-
DIG-ppmsca-12512]; 572: Universal History Archive/UIG/
Getty Images; 573: Underwood Archives/Archive Photos/

Getty Images; 575: Bettmann/Getty Images; 576T: MPI/
Archive Photos/Getty Images; 576B: Nikreates/Alamy
Stock Photo; 577TL: Charles Phelps Cushing/ClassicStock/
Archive Photos/Getty Images; 577TC: Hulton-Deutsch
Collection/Corbis Historical/Getty Images; 577TR:
Universal History Archive/UIG/Getty Images; 577BR: Everett
Collection Inc/Alamy Stock Photo; 577BL: Bettmann/Getty
Images;

Chapter 13
582-583: Library of Congress Prints and Photographs
Division Washington[LC-USF34- 009098]; 584: Photo
Researchers/Alamy Stock Photo; 585TL: Ian Dagnall/
Alamy Stock Photo; 585TR: Photo Researchers/Alamy
Stock Photo; 585BL: Pictorial Press Ltd/Alamy Stock
Photo; 585BR: Everett Collection Inc/Alamy Stock Photo;
588: American Photo Archive/Alamy Stock Photo; 589:
Keystone-France/Gamma-Keystone/Getty Images; 591:
Roger Viollet/Getty Images; 592: US Army Signal Corps/The
LIFE Picture Collection/Getty Images; 593: Hi-Story/Alamy
Stock Photo; 595: U.S. General John J. Pershing Saluting
on Horseback while Leading World War I Veterans during
Parade, New York City, New York, USA, Bain News Service,
September 10, 1919 (b/w photo), Unknown photographer
(20th century) / Circa Images/BridgemanArt Library; 598:
Bettmann/Getty Images; 600: Bettmann/Getty Images; 602:
Photo Researchers/Alamy Stock Photo; 603: The Museum
of Modern Art/Licensed by SCALA/Art Resource, NY; 604:
Corbis Historical/Getty Images; 606: Corbis Historical/Getty
Images; 609: World History Archive/Alamy Stock Photo;
611: Bettmann/Getty Images; 612: Photo Researchers/
Alamy Stock Photo; 614T: Library of Congress Prints and
Photographs Division Washington[LC-USF34- 019203-E];
614B: Library of Congress Prints and Photographs Division
Washington[LC-USF34- 009095-C]; 616: Underwood
Archives/Getty Images; 618: MPI/Archive Photos/Getty
Images; 619: Buyenlarge/Getty Images;620: VCG Wilson/
Corbis//Getty Images; 624T: PJF Military Collection/Alamy
Stock Photo; 624B: US Army Signal Corps/American
Stock/Getty Images; 628: Library of Congress Prints and
Photographs Division Washington[LC-USF34- 018209-E];

Chapter 14
630-631: US Navy/Interim Archives/Getty Images; 632:
Central Press/Hulton Archive/Getty Images; 633TL: Stock
Montage/Archive Photos/Getty Images; 633TR: Bettmann/
Getty Images; 633BL: Afro American Newspapers/Gado/
Archive Photos/Getty Images; 633BR: ADN-Bildarchiv/
ullstein bild/Getty Images; 637: Keystone/Hulton Archive/
Getty Images; 640: Ullstein bild/ullstein bild/Getty
Images; 642L: Roger Viollet/Getty Images; 642CL: David
Waddington/Fox Photos/ Hulton Archive/Getty Images;
642CR: Swim ink 2/Corbis/Getty Images; 642R: Bettmann/
Getty Images; 644: George Strock/The LIFE Premium
Collection/Getty Images; 647: Library of Congress Prints
and Photographs Division Washington[LC-USW3- 042665-C];
648: Afro American Newspapers/Gado/Getty Images;

649: Margaret Bourke-White/The LIFE Picture Collection/Getty Images; 650: Corbis Historical/Getty Images; 652: Morris Engel/Premium Archive/Getty Images; 654: Popperfoto/Getty Images; 655: Corbis Historica/Getty Images; 656: Scherl/Süddeutsche Zeitung Photo/Alamy Stock Photo; 658: Popperfoto/Getty Images; 660: Corbis Historical/Getty Images; 661: Bettmann/Getty Images; 664: Galerie Bilderwelt/Hulton Archive/Getty Images; 665: Bettmann/Getty Images; 666: Frederic Lewis/Archive Photos/Getty Images; 667: ADN-Bildarchiv/ullstein bild/Getty Images; 668: Mondadori Portfolio/Getty Images; 670: Popperfoto/Getty Images; 672: Corbis Historical/Getty Images; 675: Smith Collection/Gado/Archive Photos/Getty Images; 677: Keystone/Hulton Archive/Getty Images; 678T: Tallandier/RDA/Hulton Archive/Getty Images; 678B: Dennis MacDonald/age fotostock/Alamy Stock Photo; 682: Ullstein bild/ullstein bild/Getty Images;

Chapter 15
684-685: Dick Swanson/The LIFE Images Collection/Getty Images; 686: Dick Swanson/The LIFE Images Collection/Getty Images; 687TL: Science History Images/Alamy Stock Photo; 687TR: Bettmann/Getty Images; 687BL: Nik wheeler/Alamy Stock Photo; 687BR: Wojtek Laski/Hulton Archive/Getty Images; 691: Popperfoto/Getty Images; 692: Bettmann/Getty Images; 693: Bettmann/Getty Images; 695T: Courtesy: CSU Archives / Everett Collection/Alamy Stock Photo; 695B: Keystone/Hulton Archive/Getty Images; 696: Popperfoto/Getty Images; 697: Heritage Image Partnership Ltd/Alamy Stock Photo; 698: Glasshouse Images/Alamy Stock Photo; 700: Gary Leonard/Corbis/Getty Images; 701: Everett Collection Historical/Alamy Stock Photo; 702: GraphicaArtis/Archive Photos/Getty Images; 705: Irisphoto1/Shutterstock; 706: Hank Walker/The LIFE Premium Collection/Getty Images; 708: FPG/Archive Photos/Getty Images; 710: Dick Swanson/The LIFE Images Collection/Getty Images; 711: Bettmann/Getty Images; 712: Bettmann/Getty Images; 714: Daily Mirror/Mirrorpix/Mirrorpix/Getty Images; 716: Popperfoto/Getty Images; 717: Henri Bureau/Getty Images; 718: Bettmann/Getty Images; 720: Everett Collection Inc/Alamy Stock Photo; 721: Patrick PIEL/Gamma-Rapho/Getty Images; 724T: NASA/Liaison/Handout/Hulton Archive/Getty Images; 724B: 3Dsculptor/Shutterstock; 728: Pictorial Parade/Archive Photos/Getty Images;

Chapter 16
730-731: Courtesy: CSU Archives/Everett Collection Inc/Alamy Stock Photo; 732: Bettmann/Getty Images; 733TL: RBM Vintage Images/Alamy Stock Photo; 733TR: Everett Collection Inc/Alamy Stock Photo; 733BL: Everett Collection Inc/Alamy Stock Photo; 733BR: Frank Hurley/

NY Daily News Archive/Getty Images; 736: Bettmann/Getty Images; 738: H. ARMSTRONG ROBERTS/ClassicStock/Alamy Stock Photo; 740: H. ARMSTRONG ROBERTS/ClassicStock/Alamy Stock Photo; 741: World History Archive/Alamy Stock Photo; 742: Michael Ochs Archives/Getty Images; 743: Granamour Weems Collection/Alamy Stock Photo; 746: Everett Collection Historical/Alamy Stock Photo; 749: Bettmann/Getty Images; 751: Bruce Roberts/Science Source/Getty Images; 752: Hulton Archive/Archive Photos/Getty Images; 753: NC Collections/Alamy Stock Photo; 756: White House Photo/Alamy Stock Photo; 757: Everett Collection Historical/Alamy Stock Photo; 758: Dennis Cook/ AP Images; 759: Robin Nelson/PhotoEdit; 760: CBS Photo Archive/Getty Images; 761: David Hume Kennerly/Hulton Archive/Getty Images; 763: Diana Walker//Time Life Pictures/Getty Images; 764: Bettmann/Getty Images; 766T: Courtesy: CSU Archives/Everett Collection Inc/Alamy Stock Photo; 766B: Bettmann/Getty Images; 767TL: CHARLES PHELPS CUSHING/ClassicStock/Alamy Stock Photo; 767TR: Everett Collection Historical/Alamy Stock Photo; 767BL: Everett Collection Historical/Alamy Stock Photo; 767BR: GL Archive/Alamy Stock Photo;

Chapter 17
772-773: US Marines Photo/Alamy Stock Photo; 775TL: ZUMA Press, Inc./Alamy Stock Photo; 775TR: Peter Jordan/Alamy Stock Photo; 775BL: Everett Collection Inc/Alamy Stock Photo; 775BR: GL Archive/Alamy Stock Photo; 778: David Hume Kennerly/Hulton Archive/Getty Images; 781T: Dominika Zarzycka/Alamy Stock Photo; 781C: Peter Jordan/Alamy Stock Photo; 781B: Richard Ellis/Alamy Stock Photo; 783: FEMA/Alamy Stock Photo; 786: dpa picture alliance/Alamy Stock Photo; 787: FEMA/Alamy Stock Photo; 788: Trinity Mirror/Mirrorpix/Alamy Stock Photo; 790: ZUMA Press, Inc./Alamy Stock Photo; 791: J. Conrad Williams Jr./Newsday/Tribune Content Agency LLC/Alamy Stock Photo; 794: Kristin Callahan/Everett Collection Inc/Alamy Stock Photo; 795: John Moore/Getty Images; 797: Monkey Business Images/Panther Media GmbH/Alamy Stock Photo; 799: fstop123/E+/Getty Images; 801: Rodrigo Abd/AP Images; 802: White House Photo/Alamy Stock Photo; 804: Elnur Amikishiyev/Alamy Stock Photo; 805: Pictorial Press Ltd/Alamy Stock Photo; 806: Ian Shaw/Alamy Stock Photo; 807: David Becker/Getty Images; 808: Robert Gilhooly/Alamy Stock Photo; 809: Dario Sabljak/Alamy Stock Photo; 810T: WDC Photos/Alamy Stock Photo; 810B: Ian Dagnall/Alamy Stock Photo; 811TL: David Hume Kennerly/Hulton Archive/Getty Images; 811TC: LUKE FRAZZA/AFP/Getty Images; 811TR: Keystone-France/Gamma-Keystone/Getty Images; 811BL: ZUMA Press, Inc./Alamy Stock Photo; 811BC: Danita Delimont / Alamy Stock Photo; 811BR: Mike Theiler/Xinhua/Alamy Stock Photo